Pathfinder®

Volume Two
Of Tooth And Claw

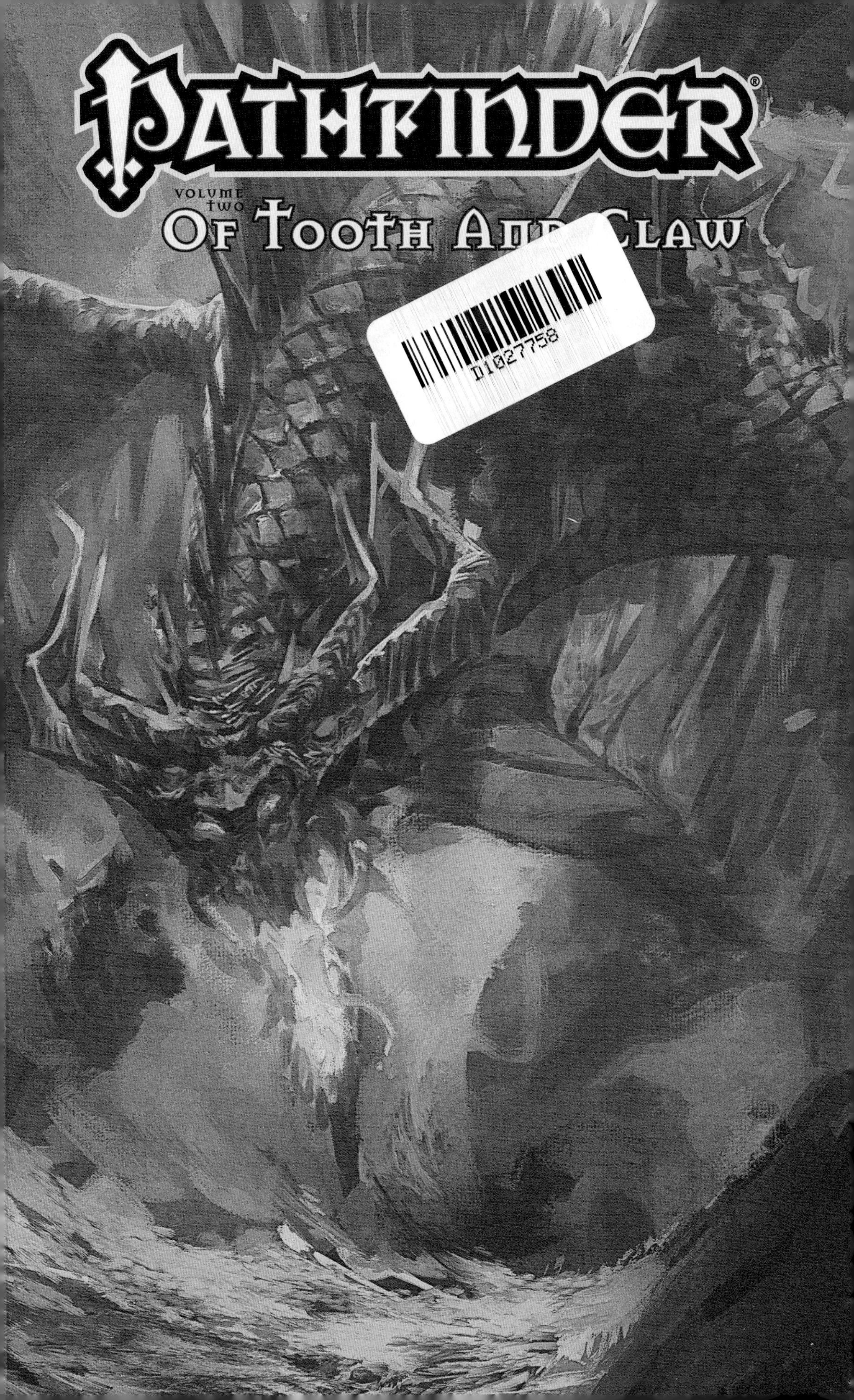

PATHFINDER

VOLUME TWO
OF TOOTH AND CLAW

Written by   **JIM ZUB**

Illustrated by   **JAKE BILBAO** (issues 7, 8, and first half of 9)
                  IVAN ANAYA (second halves of issues 9 and 12)
                  SEAN IZAAKSE (issues 10, 11 and first half of 12)
                  KEVIN STOKES (special 2013)

Colored by   **ROSS CAMPBELL** (issues 7 through 12)
                  MOHAN (special 2013)

Lettered by   **MARSHALL DILLON**

Collection cover by   **CARLOS LOPEZ** art
                  ROSS CAMPBELL colors

Editor   **RICH YOUNG**

Collection design by   **ALEXIS PERSSON**

Special thanks to ERIK MONA at Paizo Publishing

This volume collects Pathfinder issues #7-12 and the Pathfinder Special 2013 by Dynamite Entertainment.

Contents

Pathfinder: Of Tooth and Claw

Pathfinder: Night on the Town

Alternate Cover Gallery

Pathfinder Chronicles RPG Appendix

ISBN 13: 978-1-5241-0568-6

10 9 8 7 6 5 4 3 2 1

Online at www.DYNAMITE.com
On Instagram /Dynamitecomics
On Twitter @dynamitecomics

On Facebook /Dynamitecomics
On Tumblr dynamitecomics.tumblr.com
On YouTube /Dynamitecomics

PATHFINDER® VOLUME 2: OF TOOTH AND CLAW. First Printing. Contains materials originally published in Pathfinder #7-12 and 2013 special. Published by Dynamite Entertainment. 113 Gaither Dr., STE 205, Mt. Laurel, NJ 08054. PATHFINDER is a registered trademark of Paizo. © 2018 Paizo Publishing, LLC. Dynamite, Dynamite Entertainment and its logo are ® and © 2018 Dynamite. All Rights Reserved. All names, characters, events, and locales in this publication are entirely fictional. Any resemblance to actual persons (living or dead), events or places, without satiric intent, is coincidental. No portion of this book may be reproduced by any means (digital or print) without the written permission of Dynamite Entertainment except for review purposes. The scanning, uploading and distribution of this book via the Internet or via any other means without the permission of the publisher is illegal and punishable by law. Please purchase only authorized electronic editions, and do not participate in or encourage electronic piracy of copyrighted materials. **Printed in China.**

For media rights, foreign rights, promotions, licensing, and advertising:
marketing@dynamite.com

DYNAMITE®

Nick Barrucci, CEO / Publisher
Juan Collado, President / COO

Joe Rybandt, Executive Editor
Matt Idelson, Senior Editor
Anthony Marques, Associate Editor
Kevin Ketner, Assistant Editor

Jason Ullmeyer, Art Director
Geoff Harkins, Senior Graphic Designer
Cathleen Heard, Graphic Designer
Alexis Persson, Graphic Designer
Chris Caniano, Digital Associate
Rachel Kilbury, Digital Assistant

Brandon Dante Primavera, V.P. of IT and Operations
Rich Young, Director of Business Development

Alan Payne, V.P. of Sales and Marketing
Janie Mackenzie, Marketing Coordinator
Pat O'Connell, Sales Manager

Of Tooth And Claw
chapter I

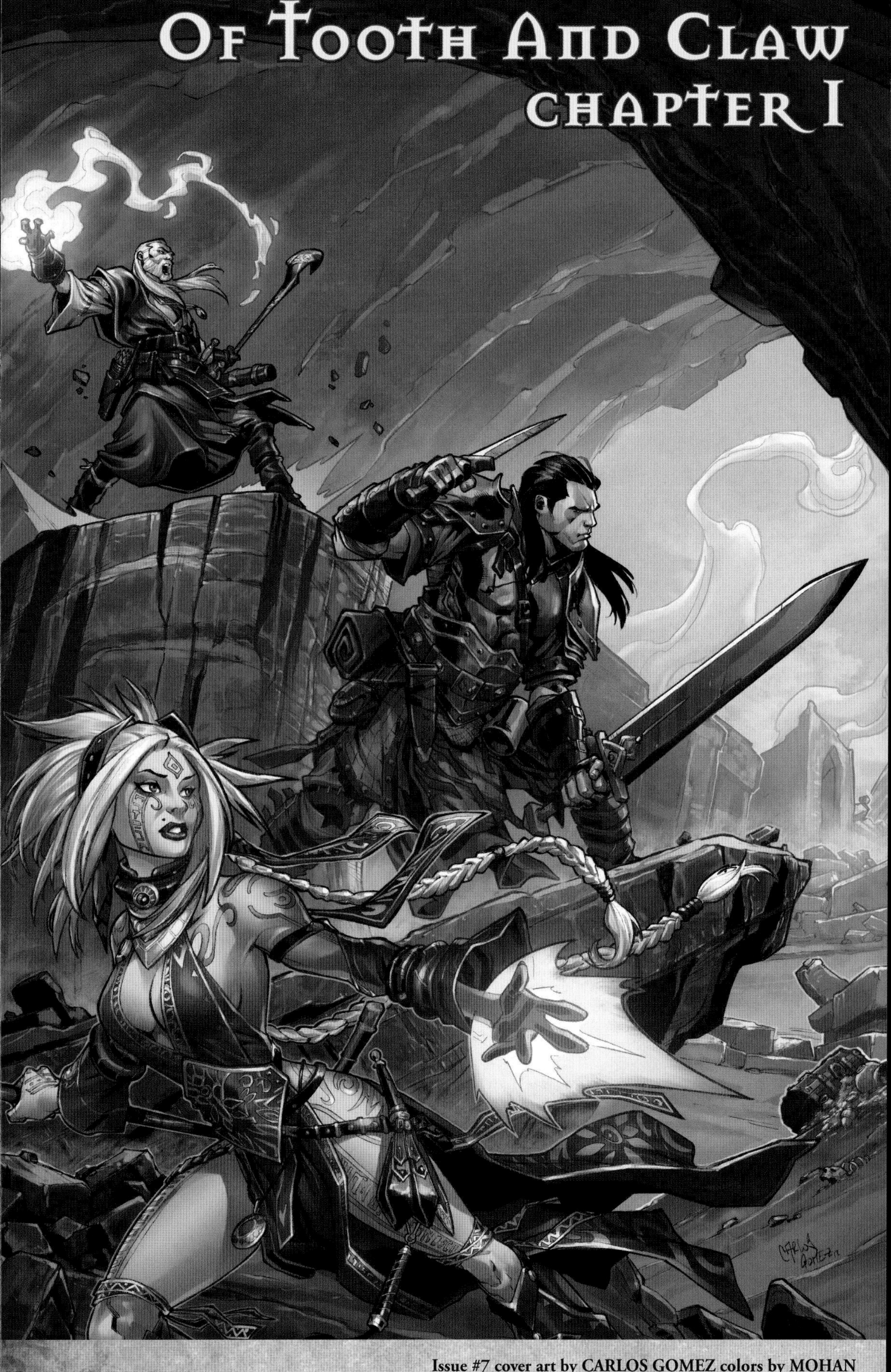

Issue #7 cover art by CARLOS GOMEZ colors by MOHAN

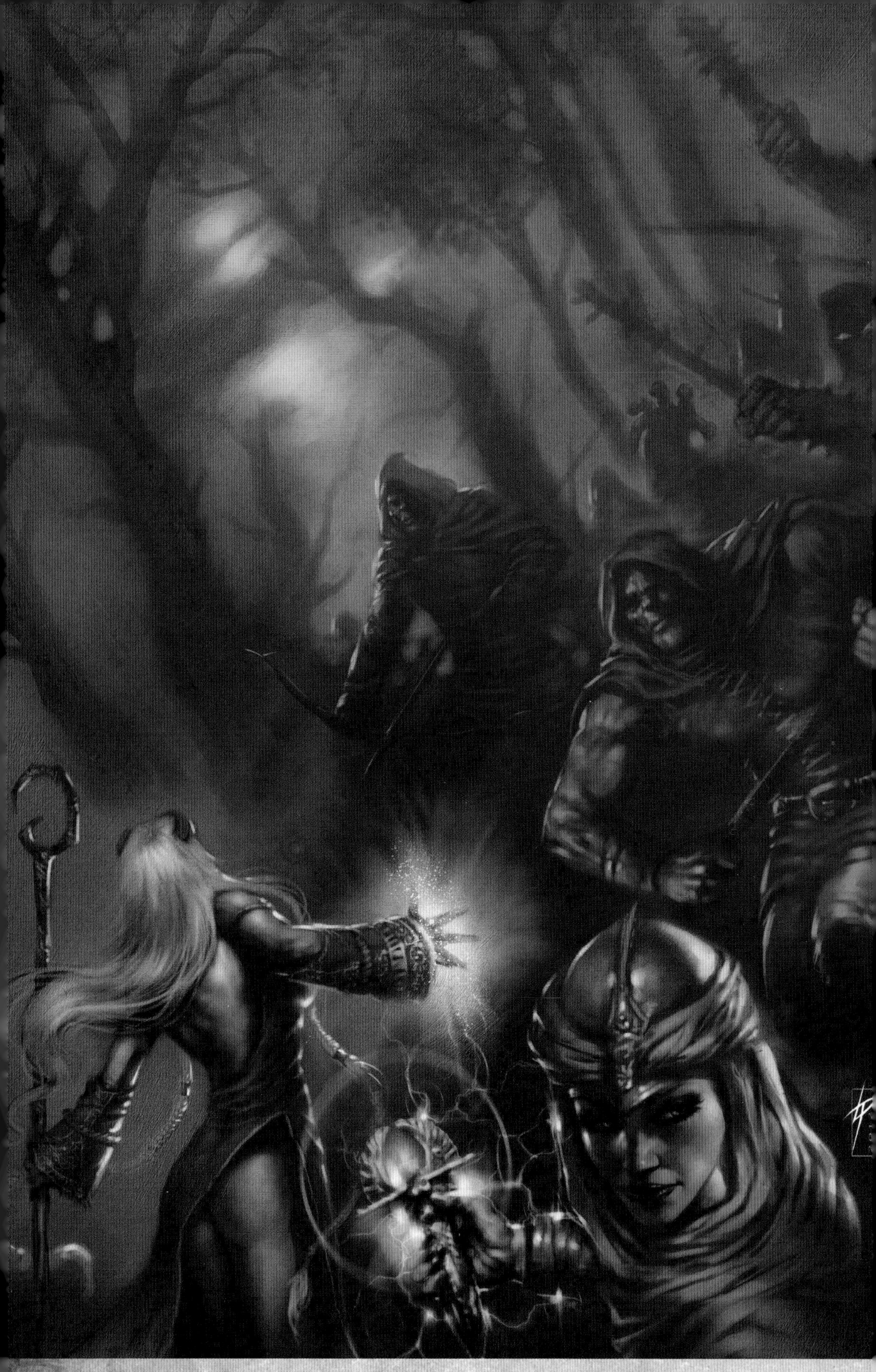

Issue #7 cover art by LUCIO PARRILLO

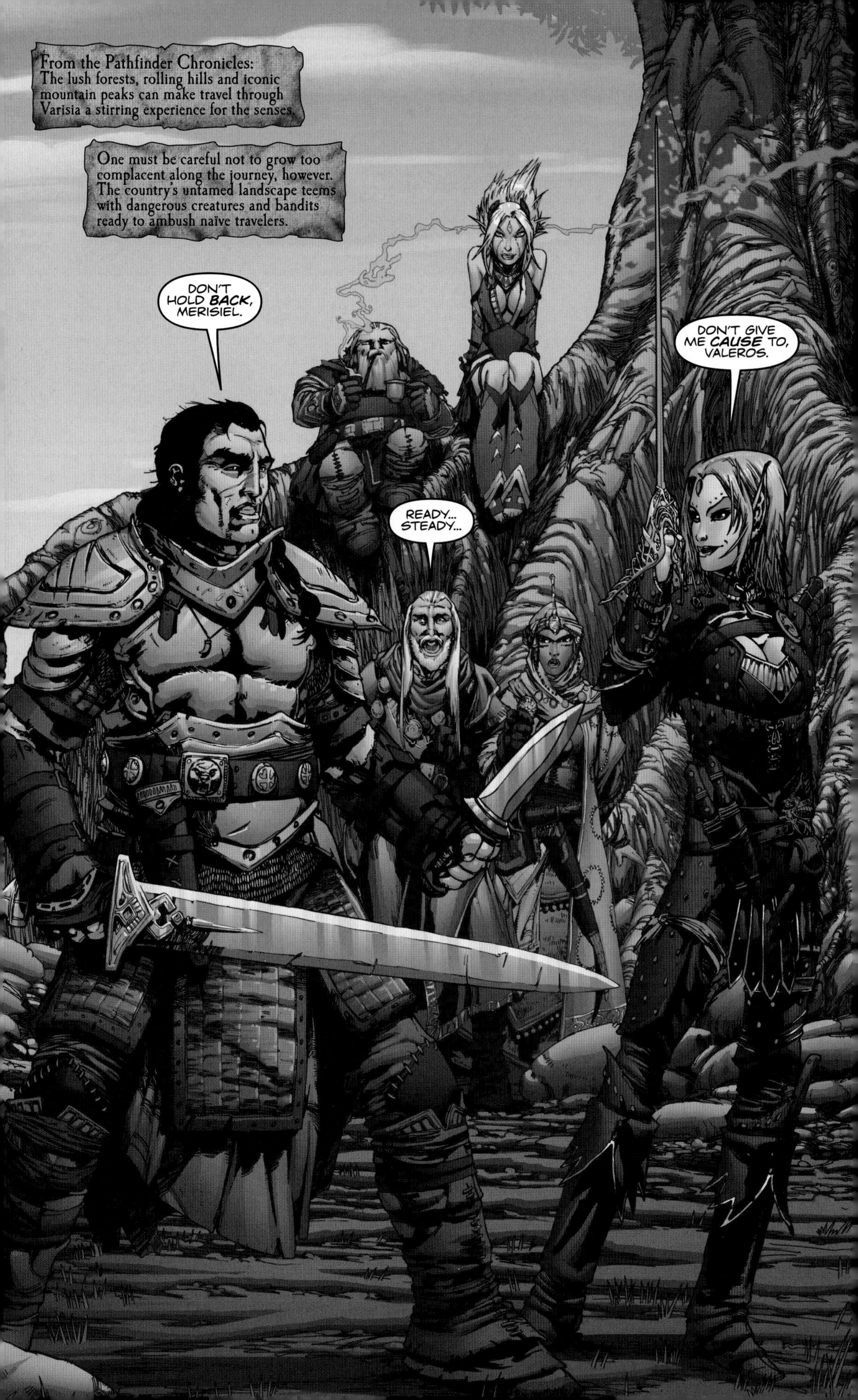
From the Pathfinder Chronicles:
The lush forests, rolling hills and iconic mountain peaks can make travel through Varisia a stirring experience for the senses.
One must be careful not to grow too complacent along the journey, however. The country's untamed landscape teems with dangerous creatures and bandits ready to ambush naive travelers.
DON'T HOLD BACK, MERISIEL.
DON'T GIVE ME CAUSE TO, VALEROS.
READY... STEADY...

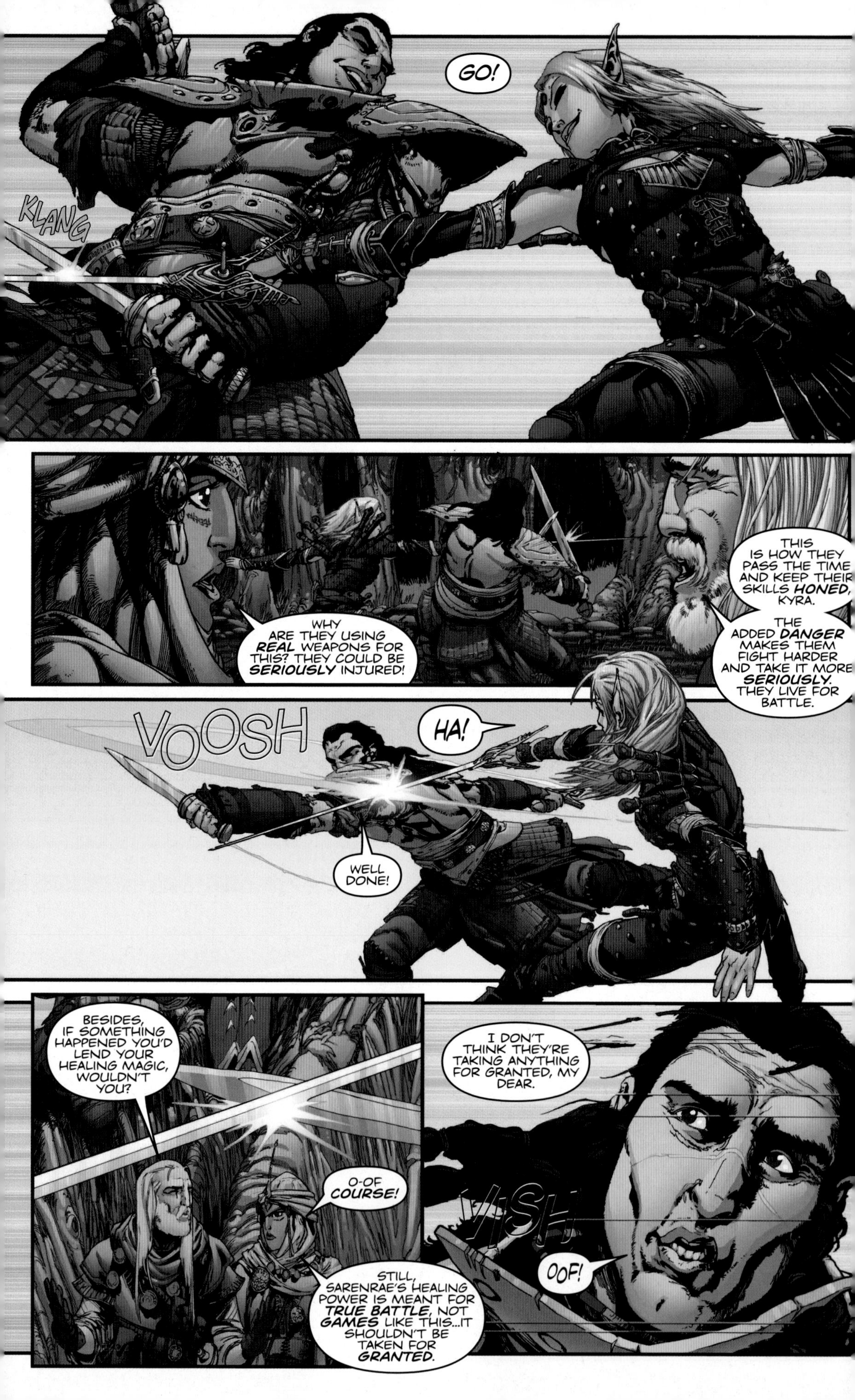
GO!
KLANG
WHY ARE THEY USING REAL WEAPONS FOR THIS? THEY COULD BE SERIOUSLY INJURED!
THIS IS HOW THEY PASS THE TIME AND KEEP THEIR SKILLS HONED, KYRA.
THE ADDED DANGER MAKES THEM FIGHT HARDER AND TAKE IT MORE SERIOUSLY. THEY LIVE FOR BATTLE.
VOOSH
HA!
WELL DONE!
BESIDES, IF SOMETHING HAPPENED YOU'D LEND YOUR HEALING MAGIC, WOULDN'T YOU?
O-OF COURSE!
STILL, SARENRAE'S HEALING POWER IS MEANT FOR TRUE BATTLE, NOT GAMES LIKE THIS...IT SHOULDN'T BE TAKEN FOR GRANTED.
I DON'T THINK THEY'RE TAKING ANYTHING FOR GRANTED, MY DEAR.
WISH
OOF!

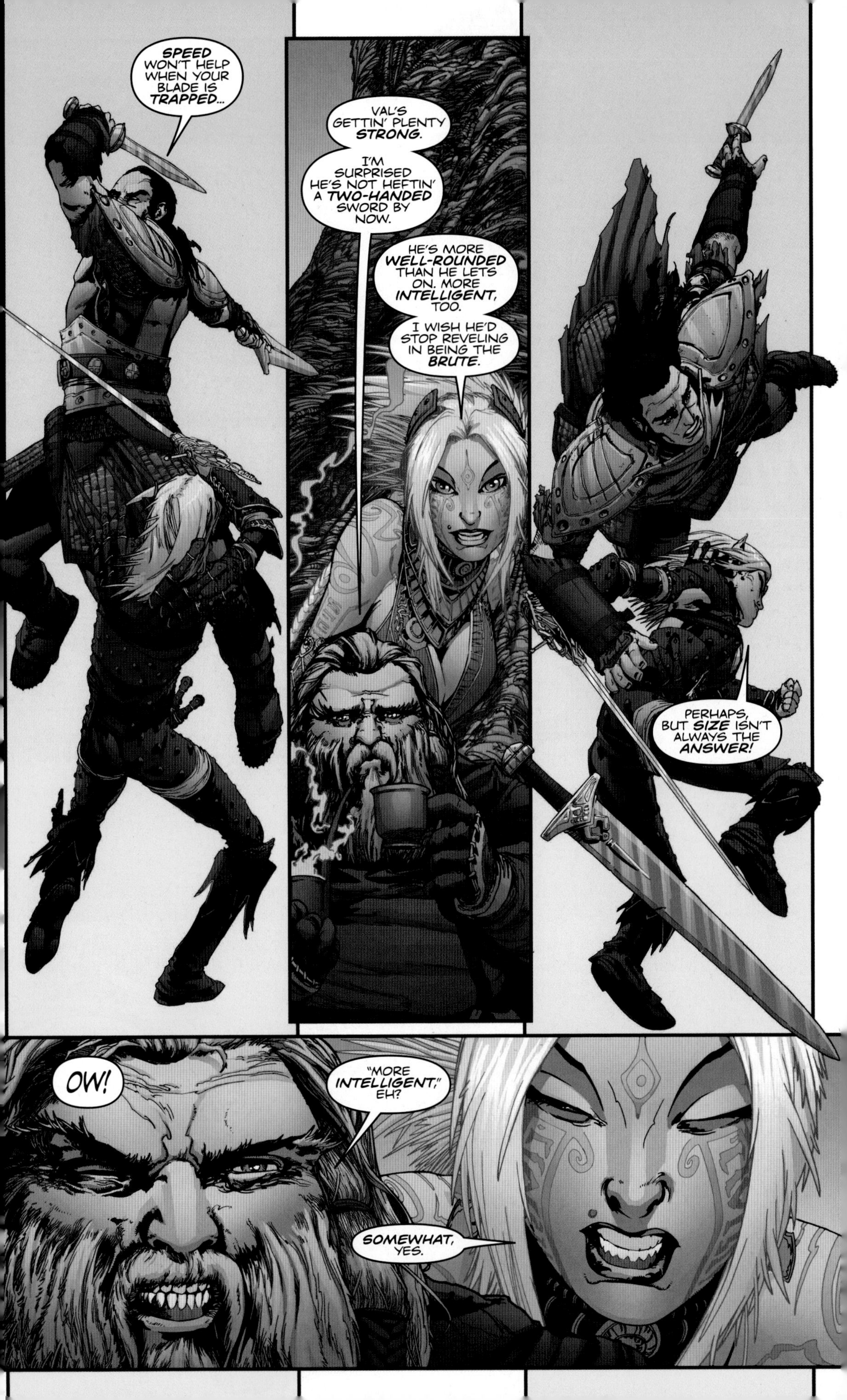
SPEED WON'T HELP WHEN YOUR BLADE IS TRAPPED...
VAL'S GETTIN' PLENTY STRONG.
I'M SURPRISED HE'S NOT HEFTIN' A TWO-HANDED SWORD BY NOW.
HE'S MORE WELL-ROUNDED THAN HE LETS ON. MORE INTELLIGENT, TOO.
I WISH HE'D STOP REVELING IN BEING THE BRUTE.
PERHAPS, BUT SIZE ISN'T ALWAYS THE ANSWER!
OW!
"MORE INTELLIGENT," EH?
SOMEWHAT, YES.

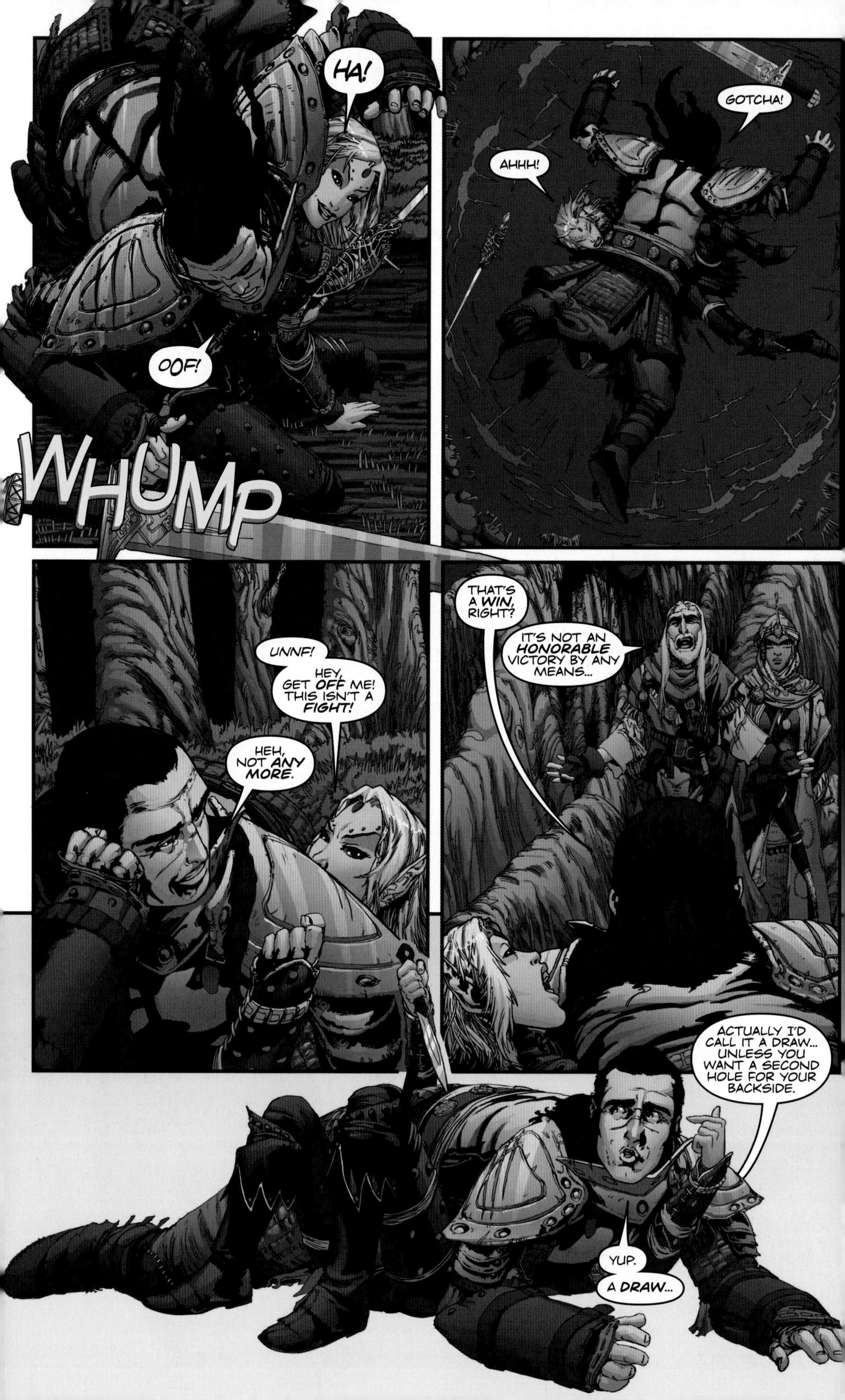
HA!
OOF!
WHUMP
GOTCHA!
AHHH!
UNNF!
HEY, GET OFF ME! THIS ISN'T A FIGHT!
HEH, NOT ANY MORE.
THAT'S A WIN, RIGHT?
IT'S NOT AN HONORABLE VICTORY BY ANY MEANS...
ACTUALLY I'D CALL IT A DRAW... UNLESS YOU WANT A SECOND HOLE FOR YOUR BACKSIDE.
YUP.
A DRAW...

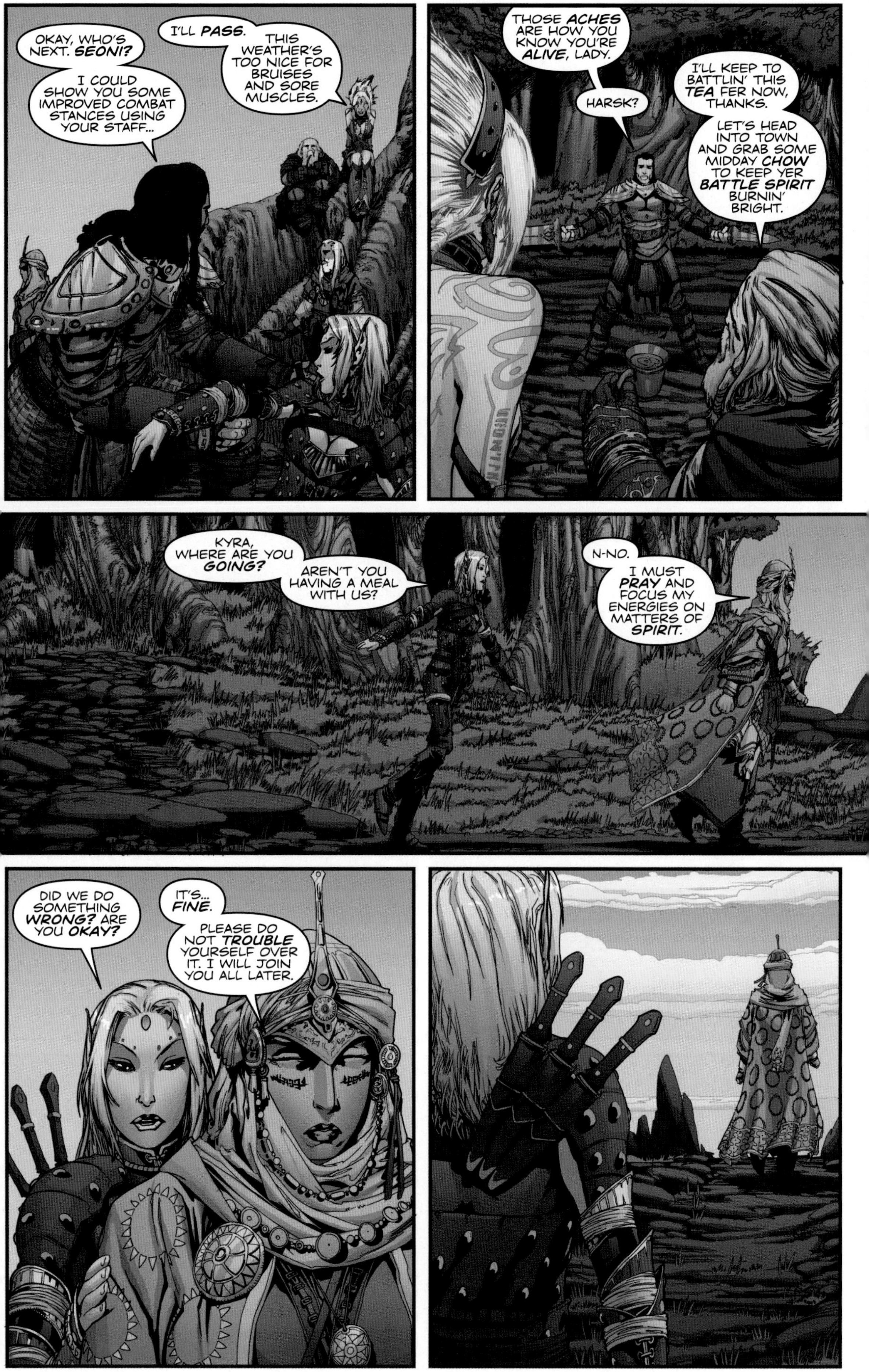
OKAY, WHO'S NEXT. SEONI?
I COULD SHOW YOU SOME IMPROVED COMBAT STANCES USING YOUR STAFF...
I'LL PASS.
THIS WEATHER'S TOO NICE FOR BRUISES AND SORE MUSCLES.
THOSE ACHES ARE HOW YOU KNOW YOU'RE ALIVE, LADY.
HARSK?
I'LL KEEP TO BATTLIN' THIS TEA FER NOW, THANKS.
LET'S HEAD INTO TOWN AND GRAB SOME MIDDAY CHOW TO KEEP YER BATTLE SPIRIT BURNIN' BRIGHT.
KYRA, WHERE ARE YOU GOING?
AREN'T YOU HAVING A MEAL WITH US?
N-NO.
I MUST PRAY AND FOCUS MY ENERGIES ON MATTERS OF SPIRIT.
DID WE DO SOMETHING WRONG? ARE YOU OKAY?
IT'S... FINE.
PLEASE DO NOT TROUBLE YOURSELF OVER IT. I WILL JOIN YOU ALL LATER.

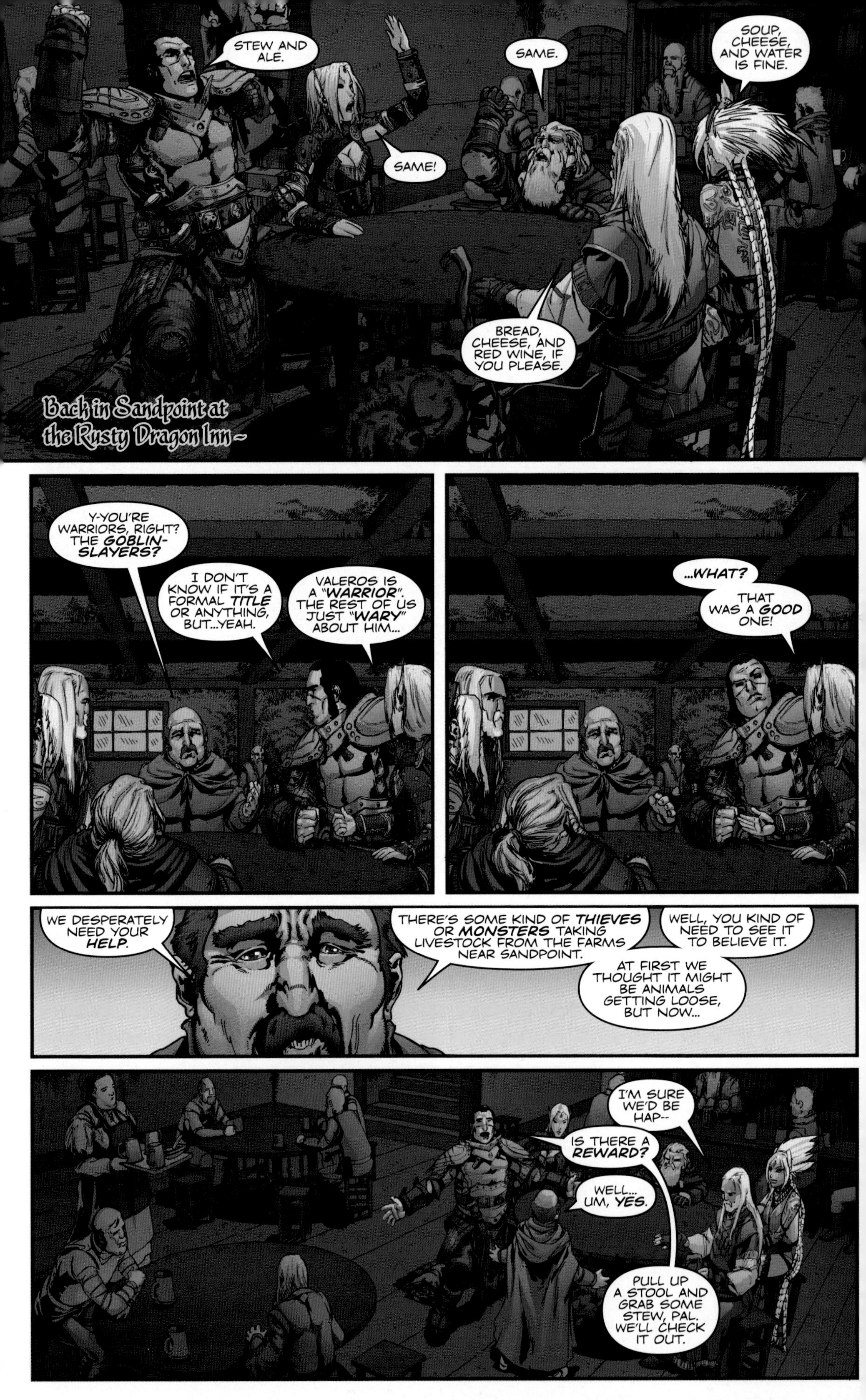
STEW AND ALE.
SAME!
SAME.
SOUP, CHEESE, AND WATER IS FINE.
BREAD, CHEESE, AND RED WINE, IF YOU PLEASE.
Back in Sandpoint at the Rusty Dragon Inn ~
Y-YOU'RE WARRIORS, RIGHT? THE GOBLIN-SLAYERS?
I DON'T KNOW IF IT'S A FORMAL TITLE OR ANYTHING, BUT...YEAH.
VALEROS IS A "WARRIOR". THE REST OF US JUST "WARY" ABOUT HIM...
...WHAT?
THAT WAS A GOOD ONE!
WE DESPERATELY NEED YOUR HELP.
THERE'S SOME KIND OF THIEVES OR MONSTERS TAKING LIVESTOCK FROM THE FARMS NEAR SANDPOINT.
WELL, YOU KIND OF NEED TO SEE IT TO BELIEVE IT.
AT FIRST WE THOUGHT IT MIGHT BE ANIMALS GETTING LOOSE, BUT NOW...
I'M SURE WE'D BE HAP--
IS THERE A REWARD?
WELL... UM, YES.
PULL UP A STOOL AND GRAB SOME STEW, PAL. WE'LL CHECK IT OUT.

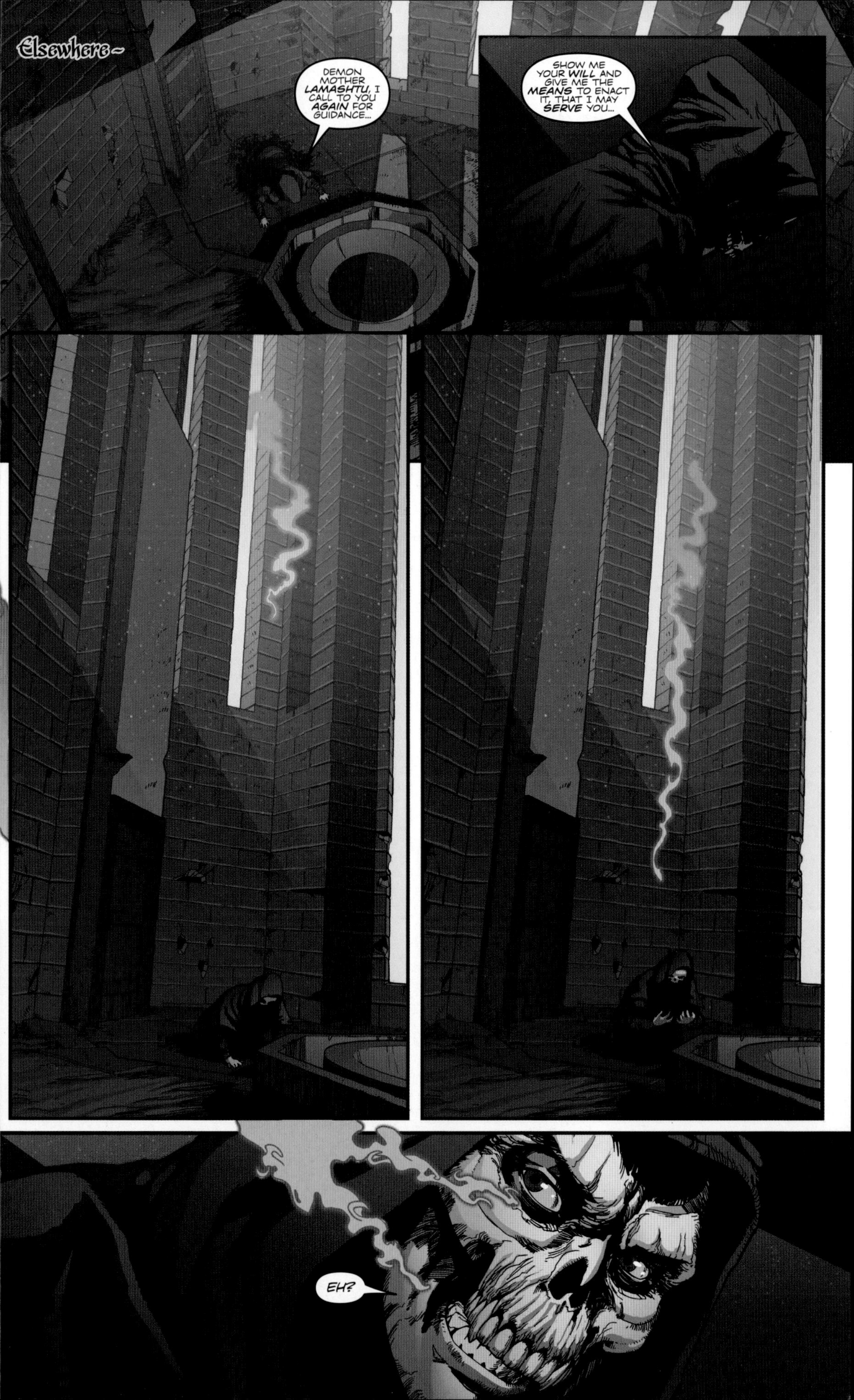
Elsewhere~
DEMON MOTHER LAMASHTU, I CALL TO YOU AGAIN FOR GUIDANCE...
SHOW ME YOUR WILL AND GIVE ME THE MEANS TO ENACT IT, THAT I MAY SERVE YOU...
EH?

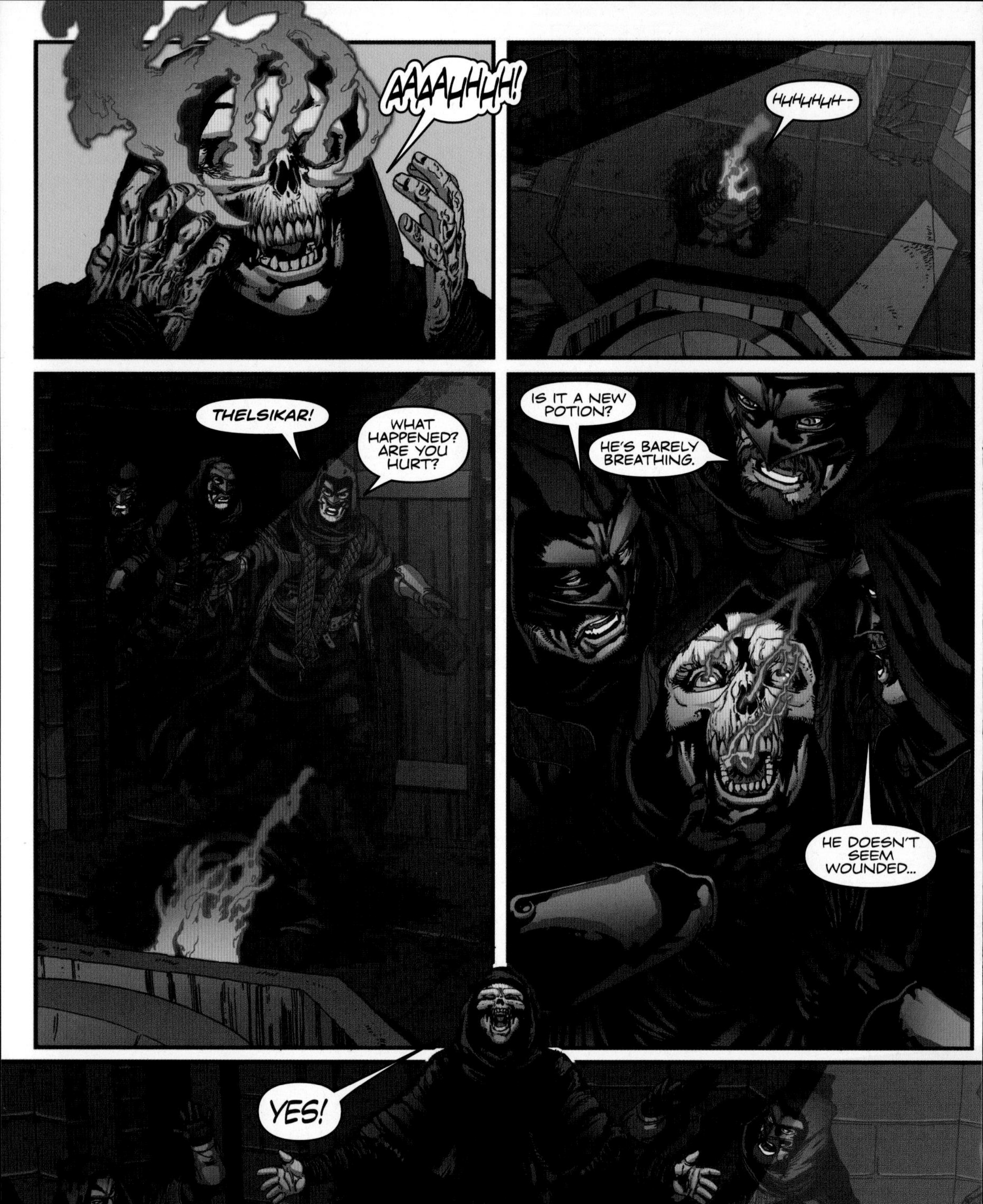
AAAAHHHH!
HHHHHHH--
THELSIKAR!
WHAT HAPPENED? ARE YOU HURT?
IS IT A NEW POTION?
HE'S BARELY BREATHING.
HE DOESN'T SEEM WOUNDED...
YES!

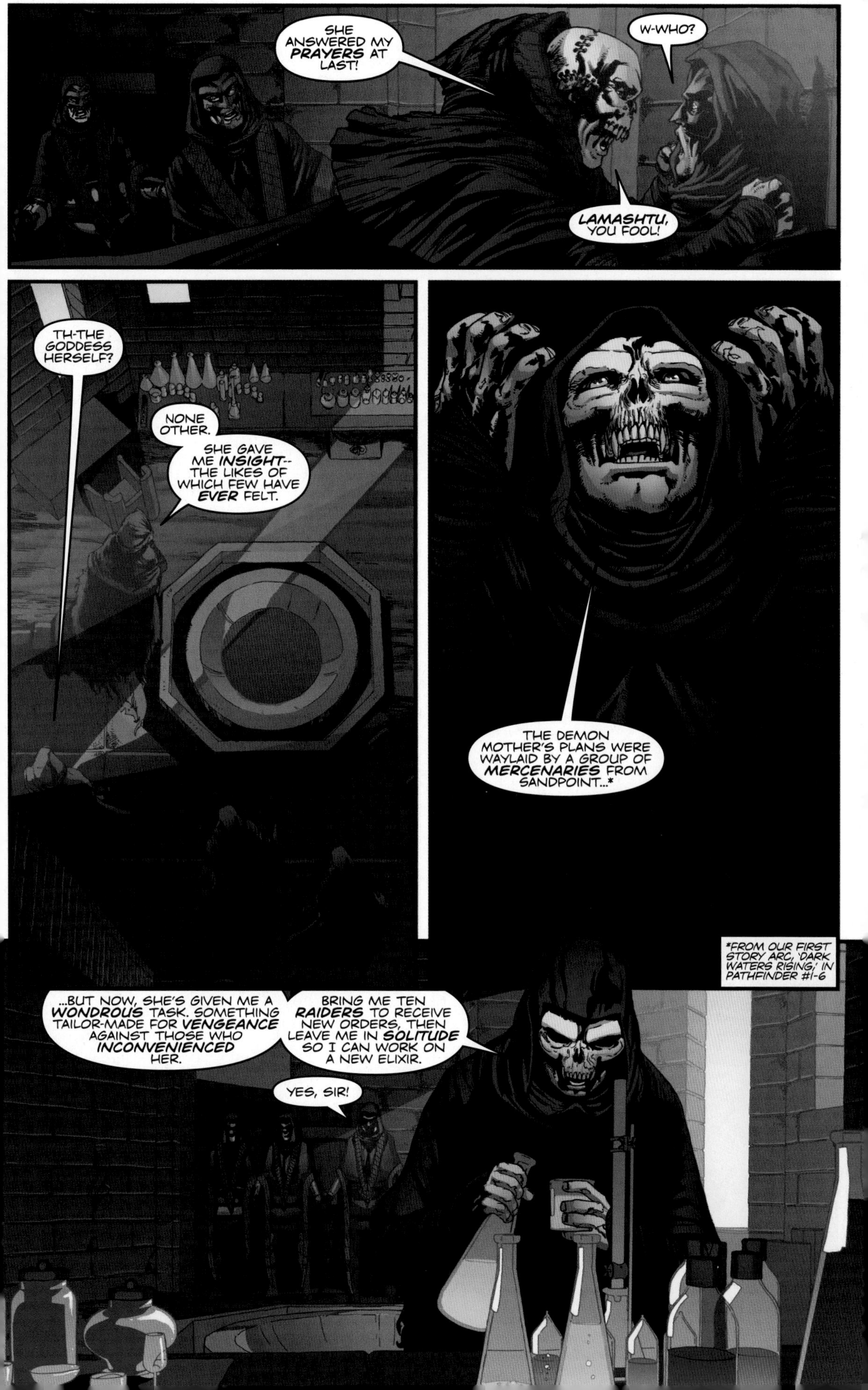
SHE ANSWERED MY PRAYERS AT LAST!
W-WHO?
LAMASHTU, YOU FOOL!
TH-THE GODDESS HERSELF?
NONE OTHER.
SHE GAVE ME INSIGHT-- THE LIKES OF WHICH FEW HAVE EVER FELT.
THE DEMON MOTHER'S PLANS WERE WAYLAID BY A GROUP OF MERCENARIES FROM SANDPOINT...*
*FROM OUR FIRST STORY ARC, 'DARK WATERS RISING,' IN PATHFINDER #1-6
...BUT NOW, SHE'S GIVEN ME A WONDROUS TASK. SOMETHING TAILOR-MADE FOR VENGEANCE AGAINST THOSE WHO INCONVENIENCED HER.
BRING ME TEN RAIDERS TO RECEIVE NEW ORDERS, THEN LEAVE ME IN SOLITUDE SO I CAN WORK ON A NEW ELIXIR.
YES, SIR!

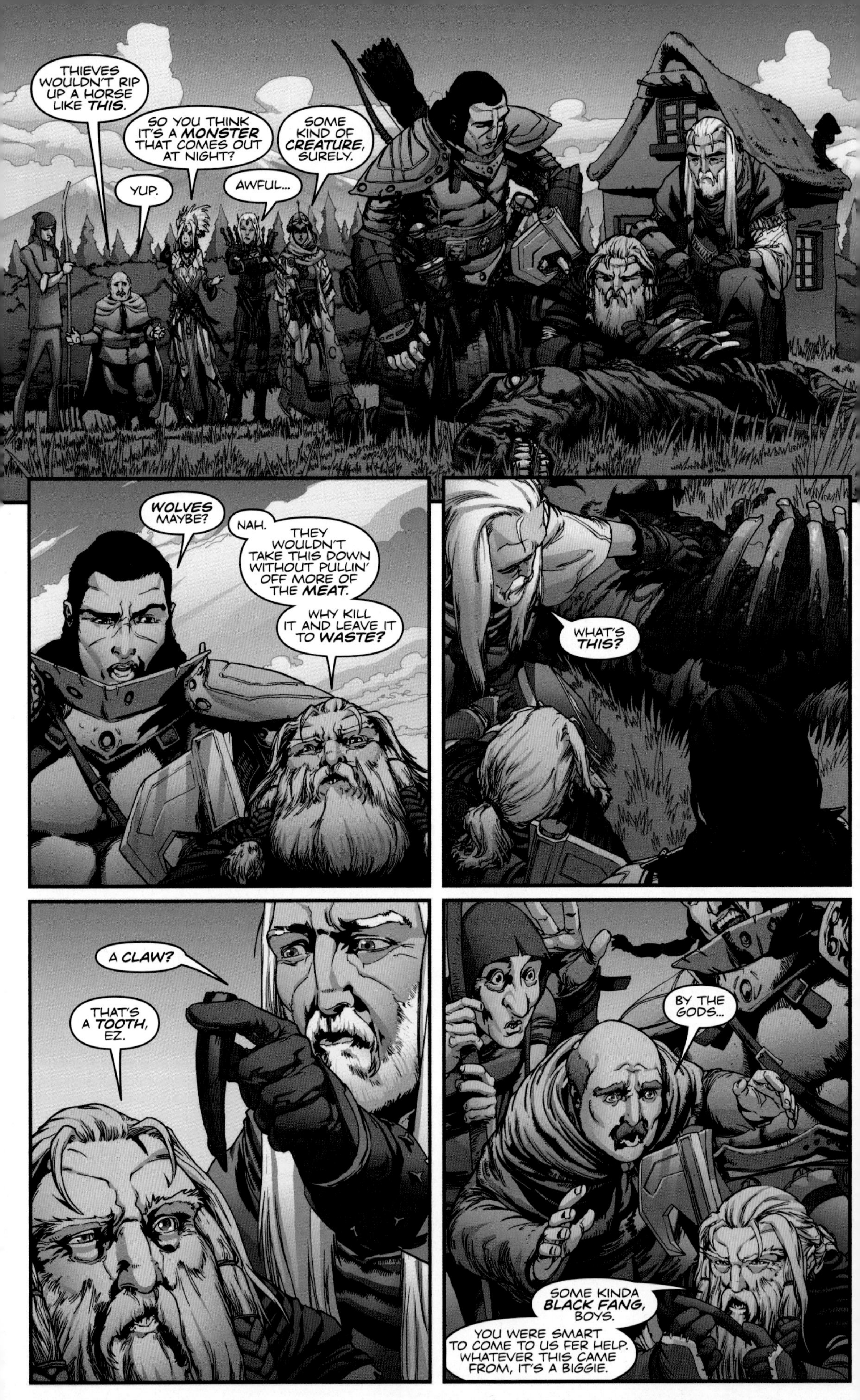
THIEVES WOULDN'T RIP UP A HORSE LIKE THIS.
SO YOU THINK IT'S A MONSTER THAT COMES OUT AT NIGHT?
YUP.
SOME KIND OF CREATURE, SURELY.
AWFUL...
WOLVES MAYBE?
NAH.
THEY WOULDN'T TAKE THIS DOWN WITHOUT PULLIN' OFF MORE OF THE MEAT.
WHY KILL IT AND LEAVE IT TO WASTE?
WHAT'S THIS?
A CLAW?
THAT'S A TOOTH, EZ.
BY THE GODS...
SOME KINDA BLACK FANG, BOYS.
YOU WERE SMART TO COME TO US FER HELP. WHATEVER THIS CAME FROM, IT'S A BIGGIE.

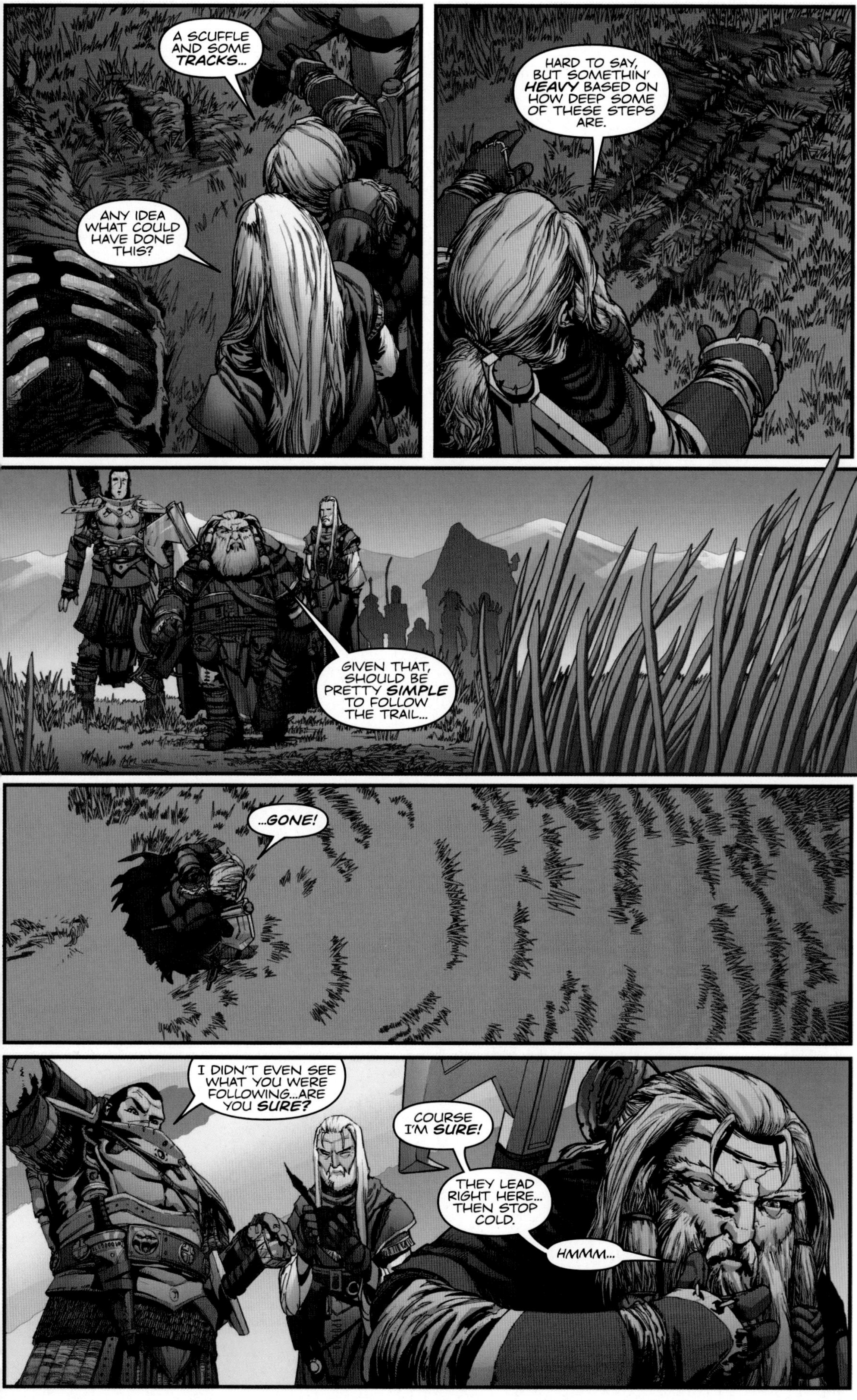
A SCUFFLE AND SOME TRACKS...
ANY IDEA WHAT COULD HAVE DONE THIS?
HARD TO SAY, BUT SOMETHIN' HEAVY BASED ON HOW DEEP SOME OF THESE STEPS ARE.
GIVEN THAT, SHOULD BE PRETTY SIMPLE TO FOLLOW THE TRAIL...
...GONE!
I DIDN'T EVEN SEE WHAT YOU WERE FOLLOWING...ARE YOU SURE?
COURSE I'M SURE!
THEY LEAD RIGHT HERE... THEN STOP COLD.
HMMM...

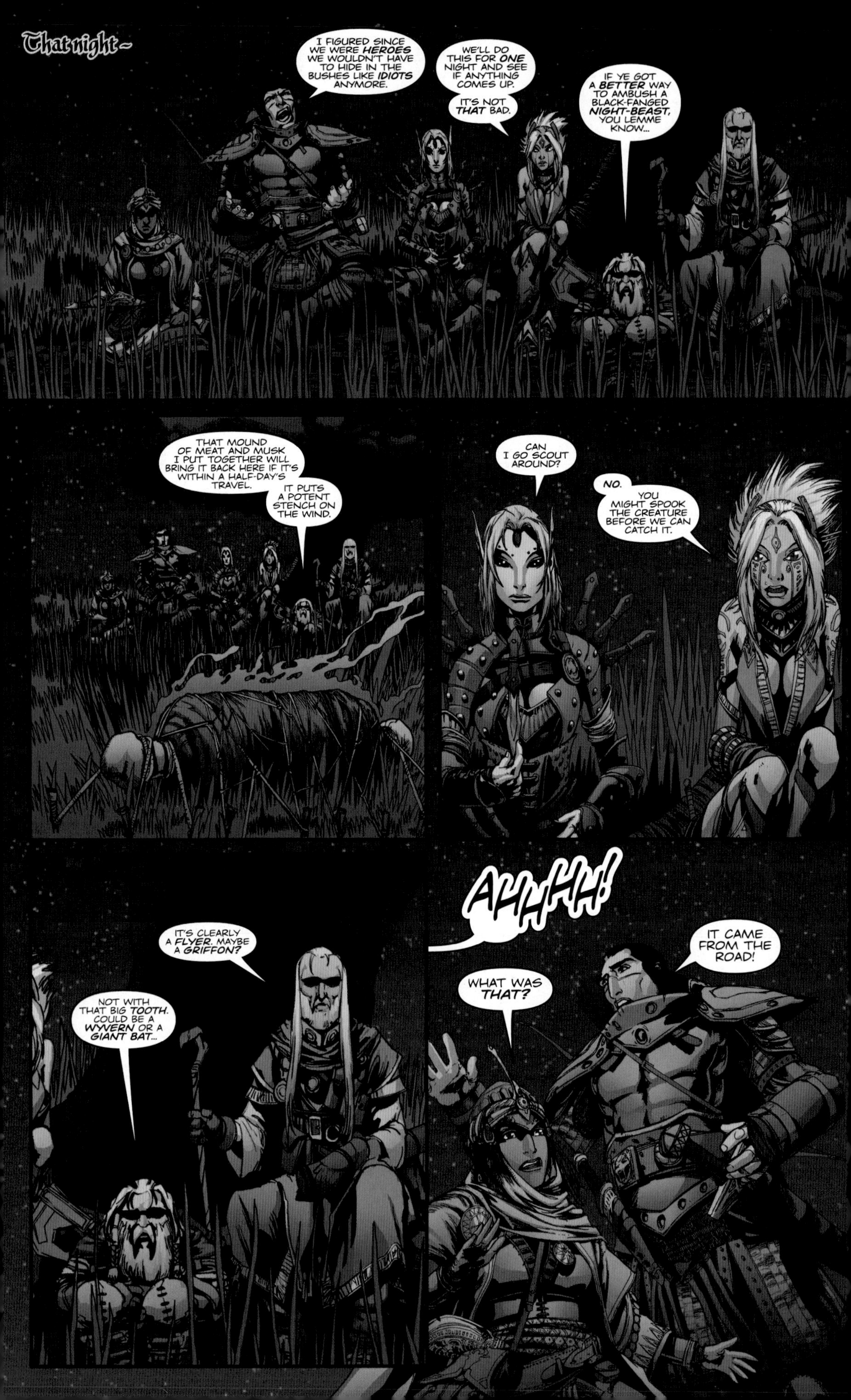
That night ~
I FIGURED SINCE WE WERE HEROES WE WOULDN'T HAVE TO HIDE IN THE BUSHES LIKE IDIOTS ANYMORE.
WE'LL DO THIS FOR ONE NIGHT AND SEE IF ANYTHING COMES UP.
IT'S NOT THAT BAD.
IF YE GOT A BETTER WAY TO AMBUSH A BLACK-FANGED NIGHT-BEAST, YOU LEMME KNOW...
THAT MOUND OF MEAT AND MUSK I PUT TOGETHER WILL BRING IT BACK HERE IF IT'S WITHIN A HALF-DAY'S TRAVEL.
IT PUTS A POTENT STENCH ON THE WIND.
CAN I GO SCOUT AROUND?
NO.
YOU MIGHT SPOOK THE CREATURE BEFORE WE CAN CATCH IT.
IT'S CLEARLY A FLYER. MAYBE A GRIFFON?
NOT WITH THAT BIG TOOTH. COULD BE A WYVERN OR A GIANT BAT...
AHHHH!
WHAT WAS THAT?
IT CAME FROM THE ROAD!

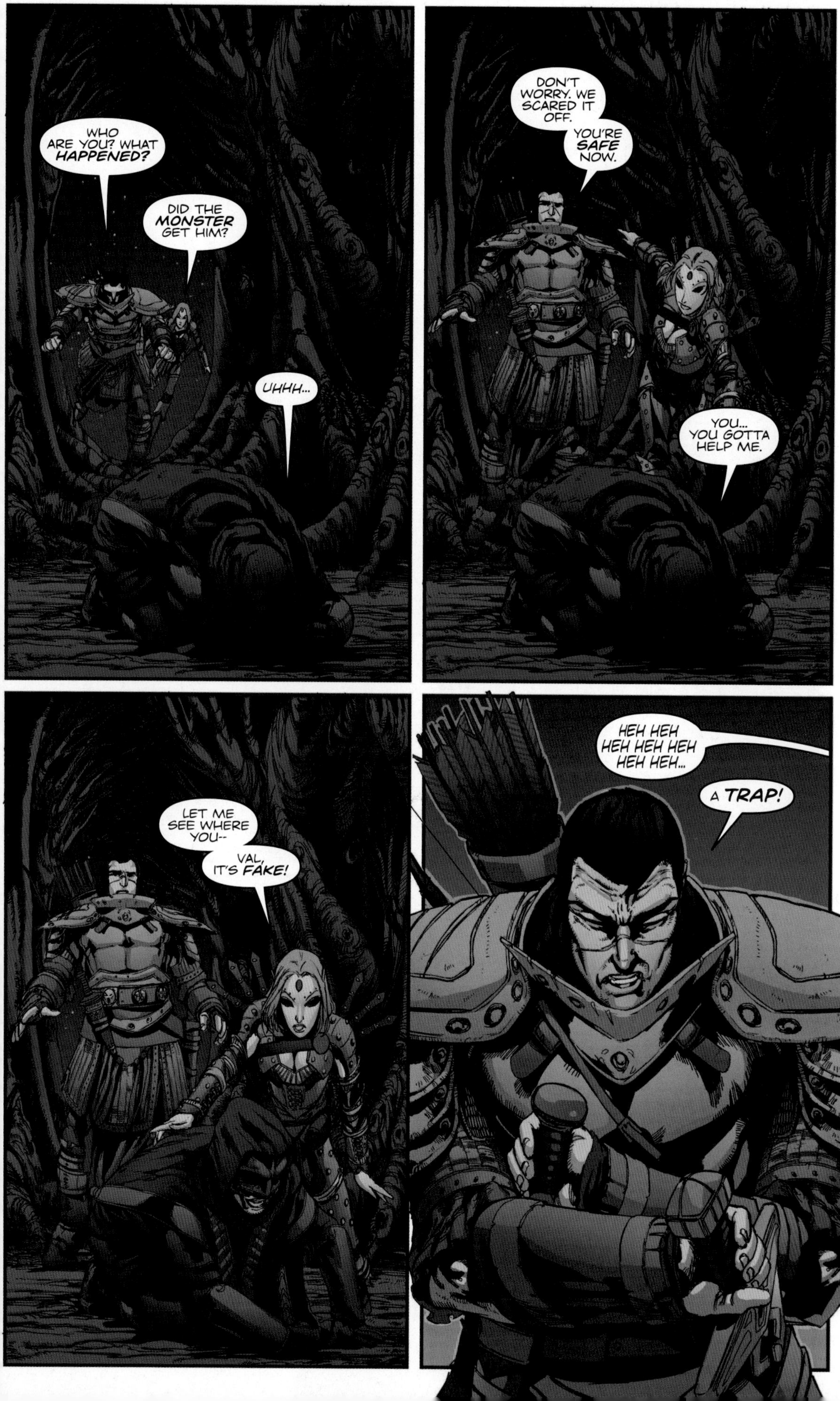
WHO ARE YOU? WHAT HAPPENED?
DID THE MONSTER GET HIM?
UHHH...
DON'T WORRY. WE SCARED IT OFF.
YOU'RE SAFE NOW.
YOU... YOU GOTTA HELP ME.
LET ME SEE WHERE YOU--
VAL, IT'S FAKE!
HEH HEH HEH HEH HEH HEH HEH...
A TRAP!

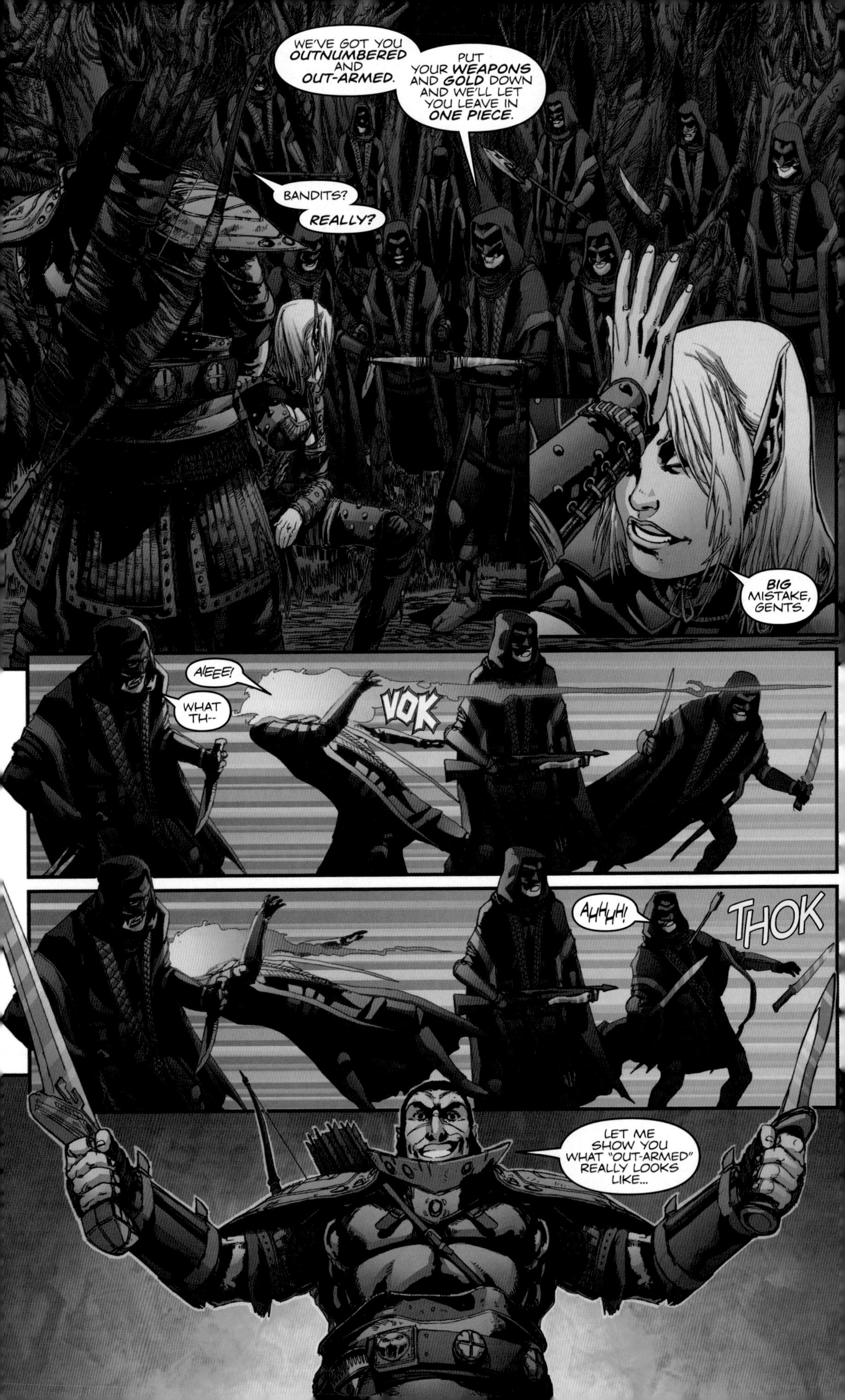
WE'VE GOT YOU OUTNUMBERED AND OUT-ARMED.
PUT YOUR WEAPONS AND GOLD DOWN AND WE'LL LET YOU LEAVE IN ONE PIECE.
BANDITS?
REALLY?
BIG MISTAKE, GENTS.
AIEEE!
WHAT TH--
VOK
AHHHH!
THOK
LET ME SHOW YOU WHAT "OUT-ARMED" REALLY LOOKS LIKE...

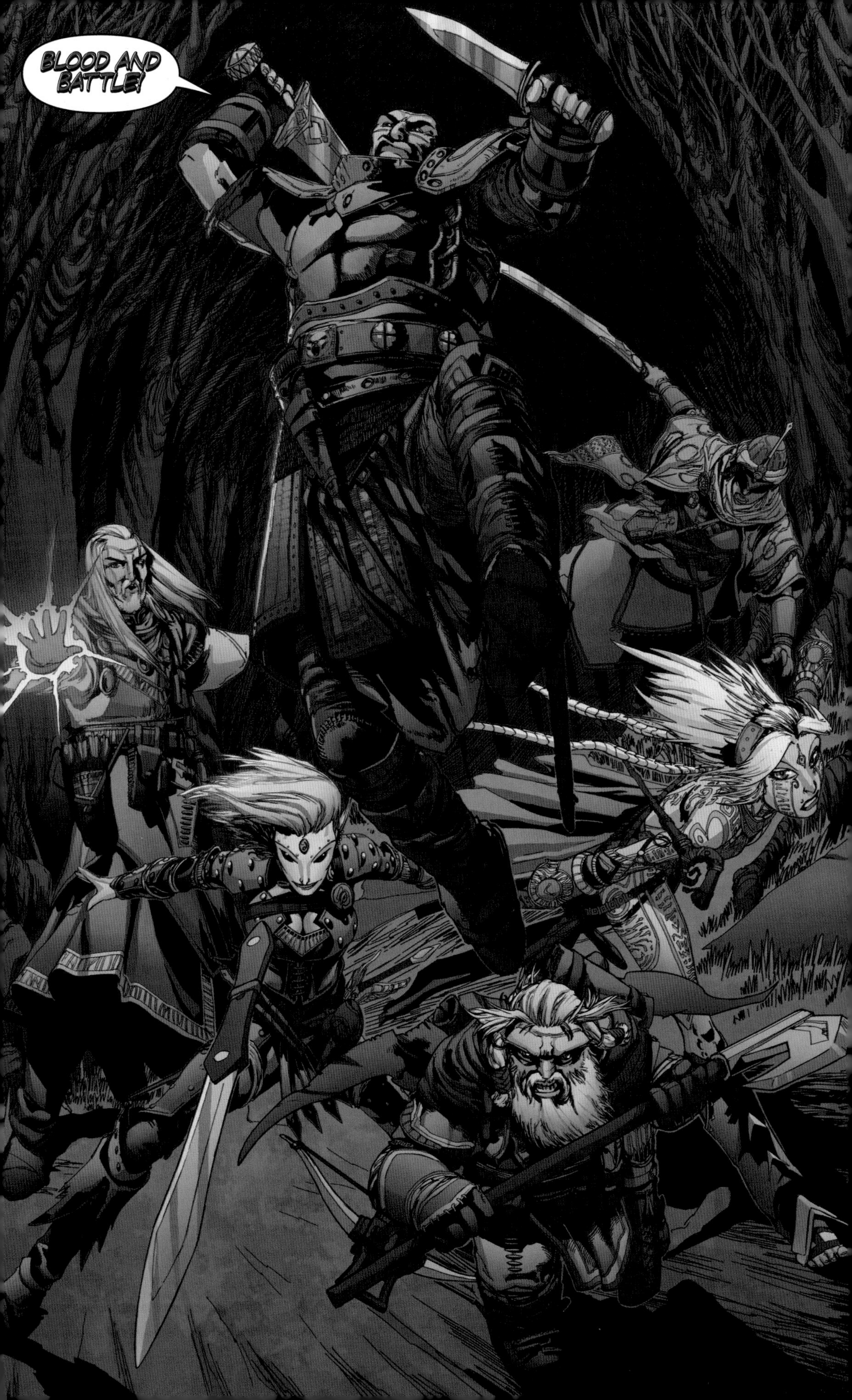
BLOOD AND BATTLE!

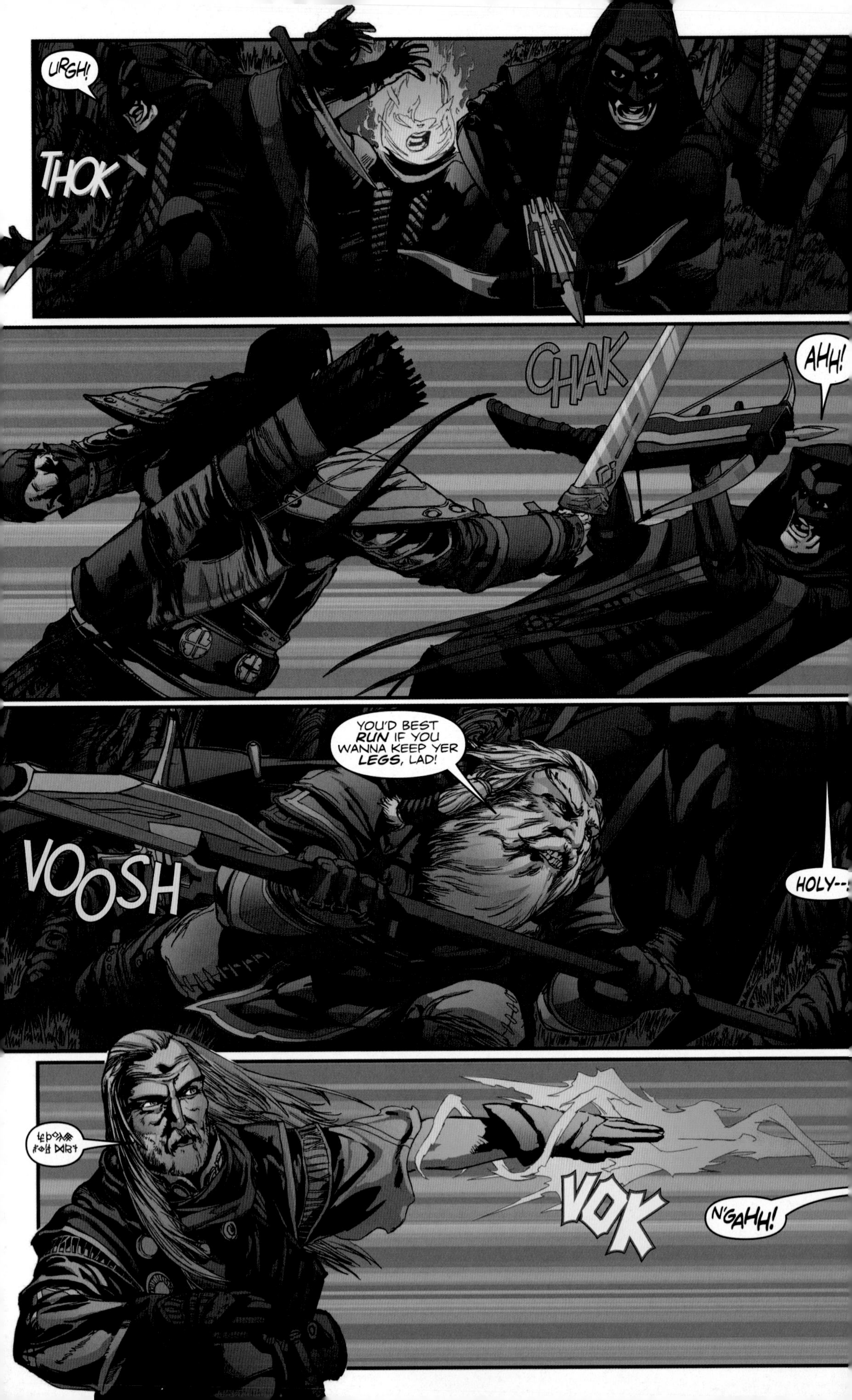
URGH!
THOK
CHAK
AHH!
YOU'D BEST RUN IF YOU WANNA KEEP YER LEGS, LAD!
VOOSH
HOLY--!
VOK
N'GAHH!

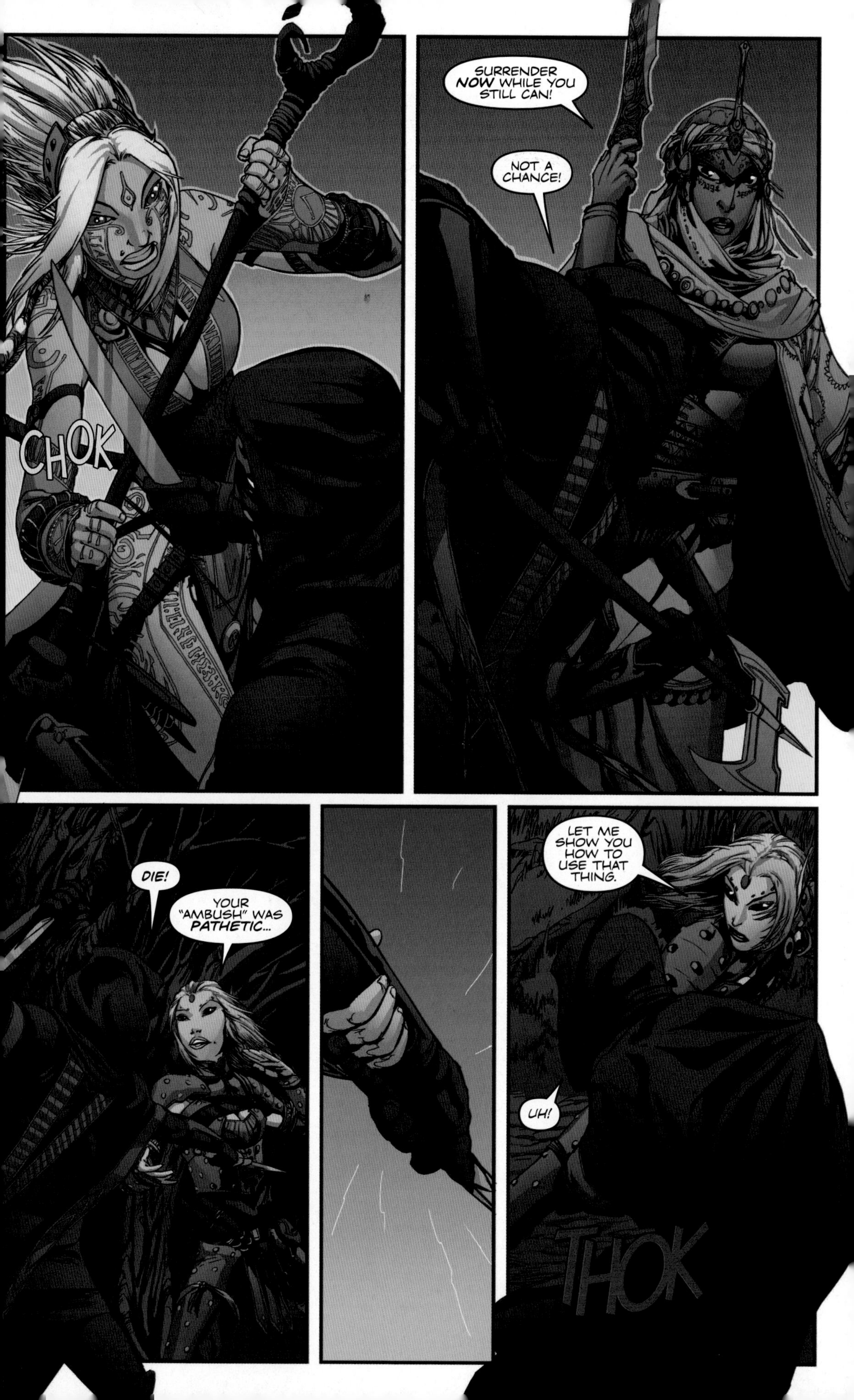
CHOK
SURRENDER NOW WHILE YOU STILL CAN!
NOT A CHANCE!
DIE!
YOUR "AMBUSH" WAS PATHETIC...
LET ME SHOW YOU HOW TO USE THAT THING.
UH!
THOK

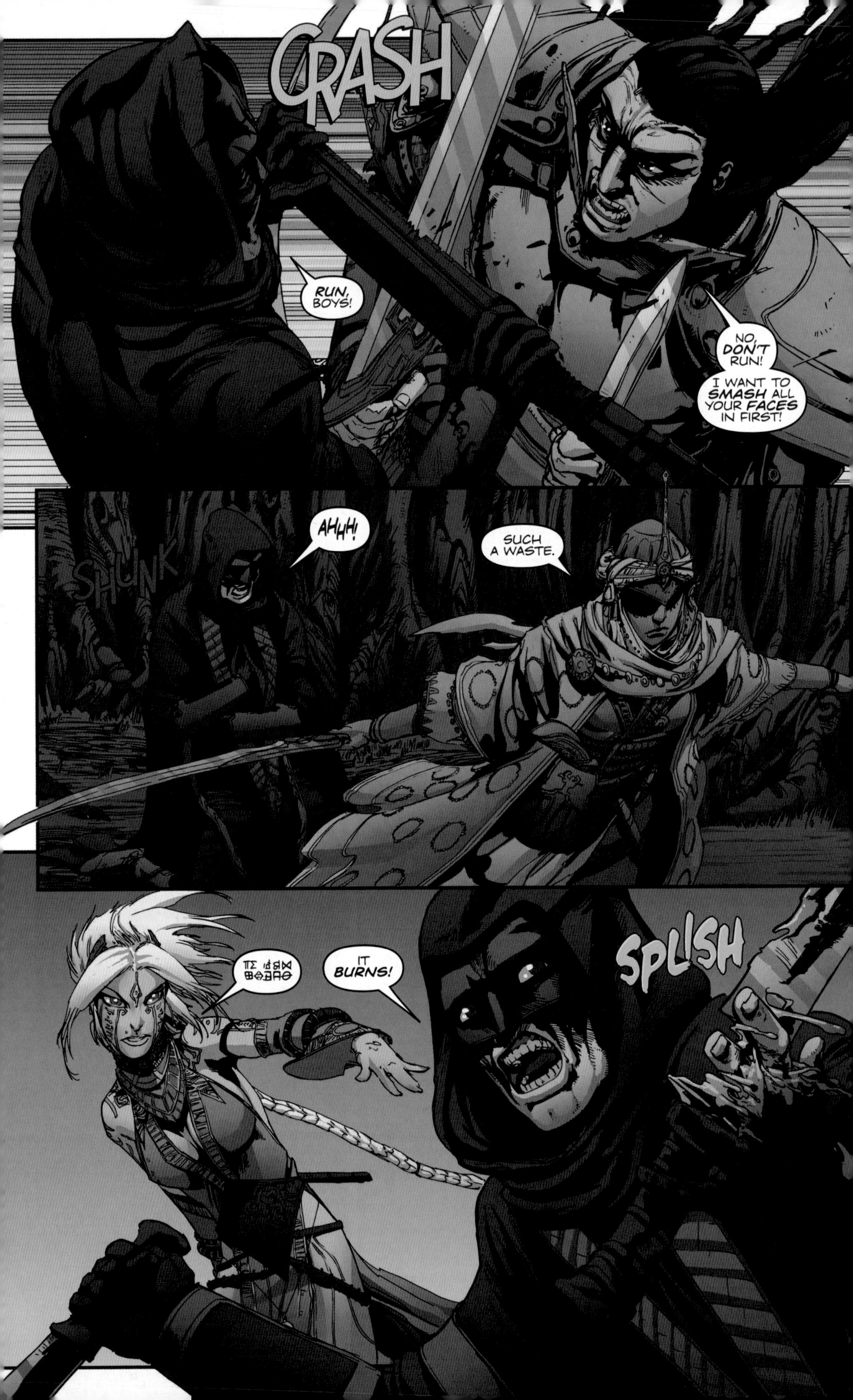
CRASH
RUN, BOYS!
NO, DON'T RUN!
I WANT TO SMASH ALL YOUR FACES IN FIRST!
SHUNK
AHHH!
SUCH A WASTE.
IT BURNS!
SPLISH

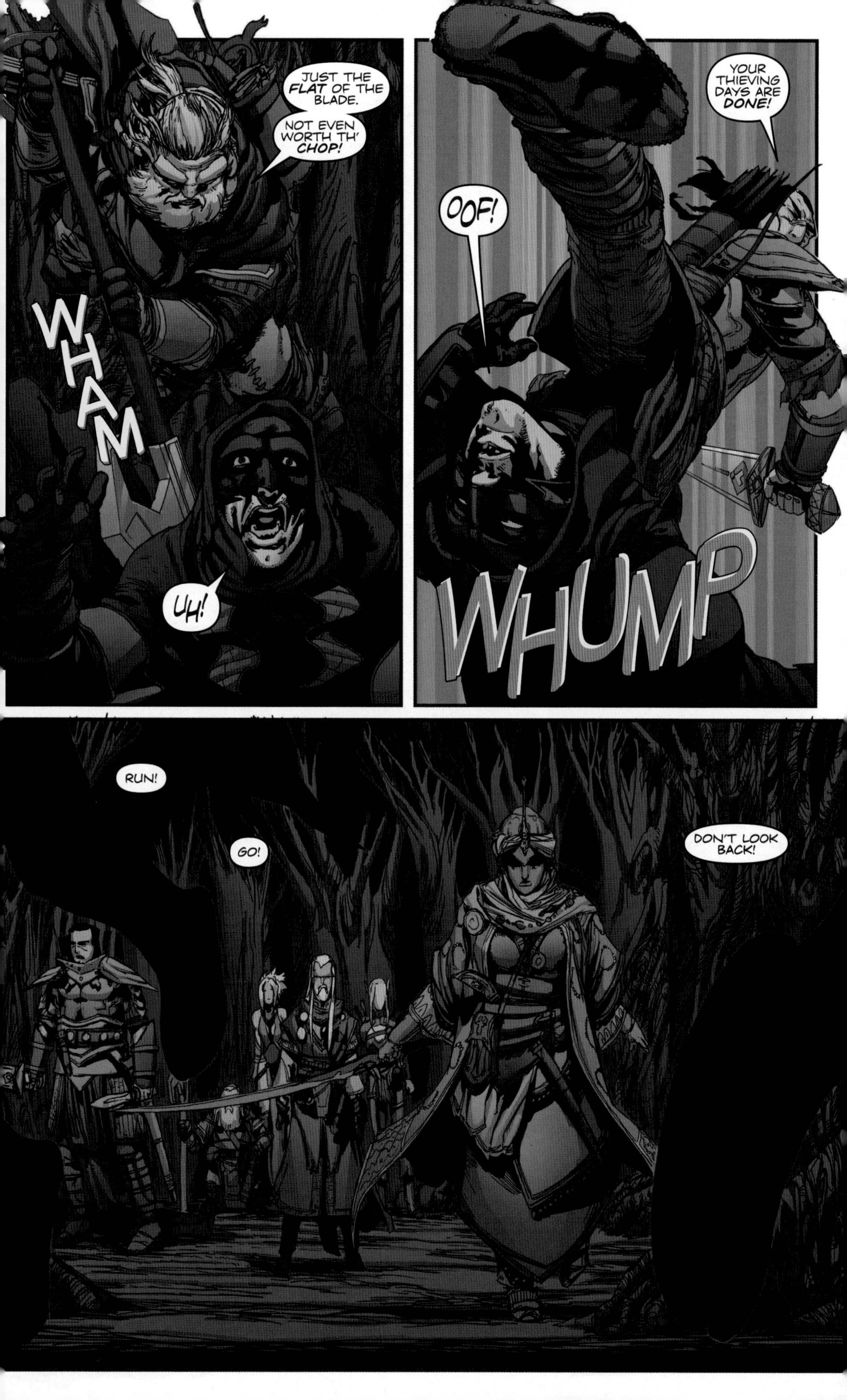
JUST THE FLAT OF THE BLADE.
NOT EVEN WORTH TH' CHOP!
WHAM
UH!
YOUR THIEVING DAYS ARE DONE!
OOF!
WHUMP
RUN!
GO!
DON'T LOOK BACK!

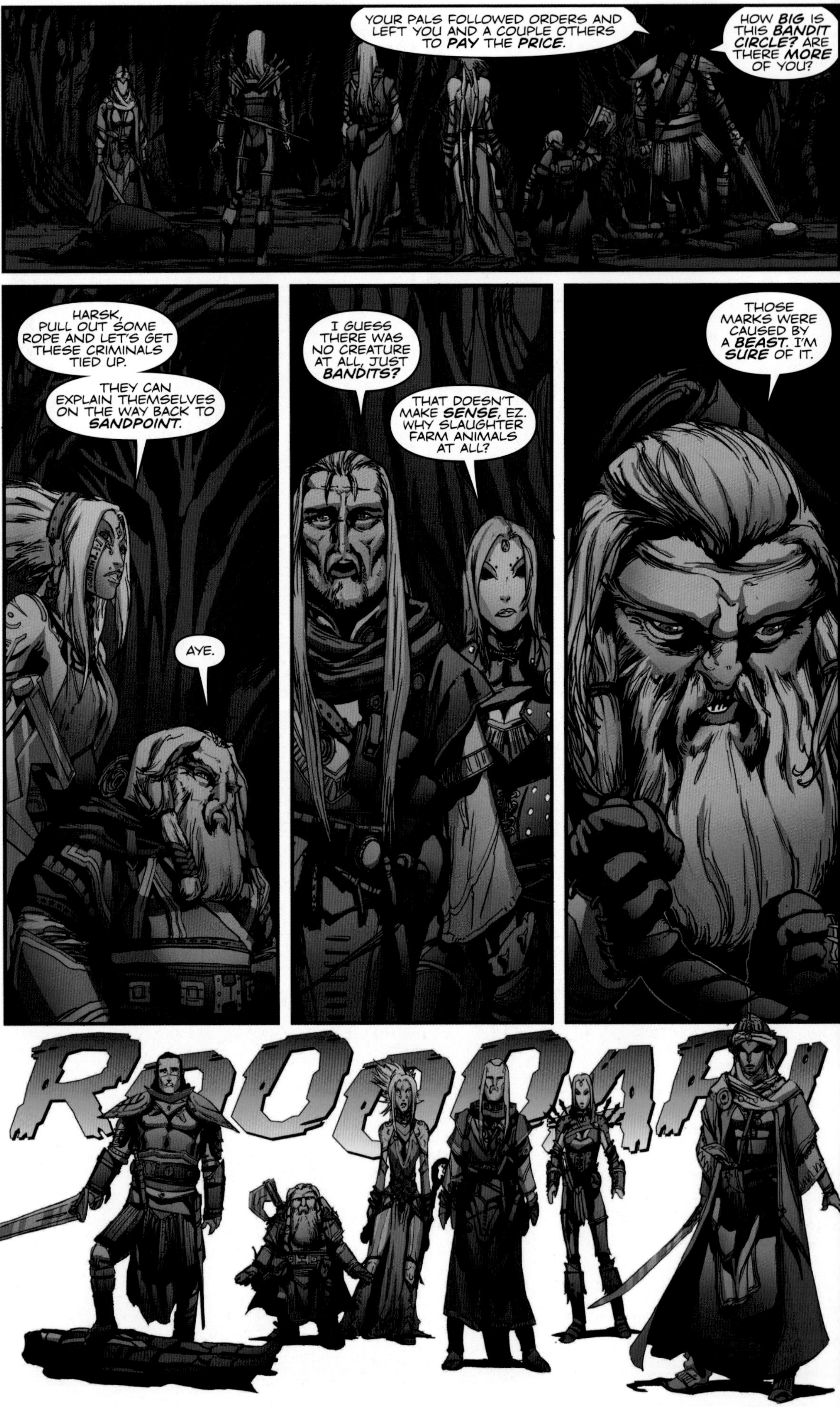
YOUR PALS FOLLOWED ORDERS AND LEFT YOU AND A COUPLE OTHERS TO PAY THE PRICE.
HOW BIG IS THIS BANDIT CIRCLE? ARE THERE MORE OF YOU?
HARSK, PULL OUT SOME ROPE AND LET'S GET THESE CRIMINALS TIED UP.
THEY CAN EXPLAIN THEMSELVES ON THE WAY BACK TO SANDPOINT.
AYE.
I GUESS THERE WAS NO CREATURE AT ALL, JUST BANDITS?
THAT DOESN'T MAKE SENSE, EZ. WHY SLAUGHTER FARM ANIMALS AT ALL?
THOSE MARKS WERE CAUSED BY A BEAST. I'M SURE OF IT.

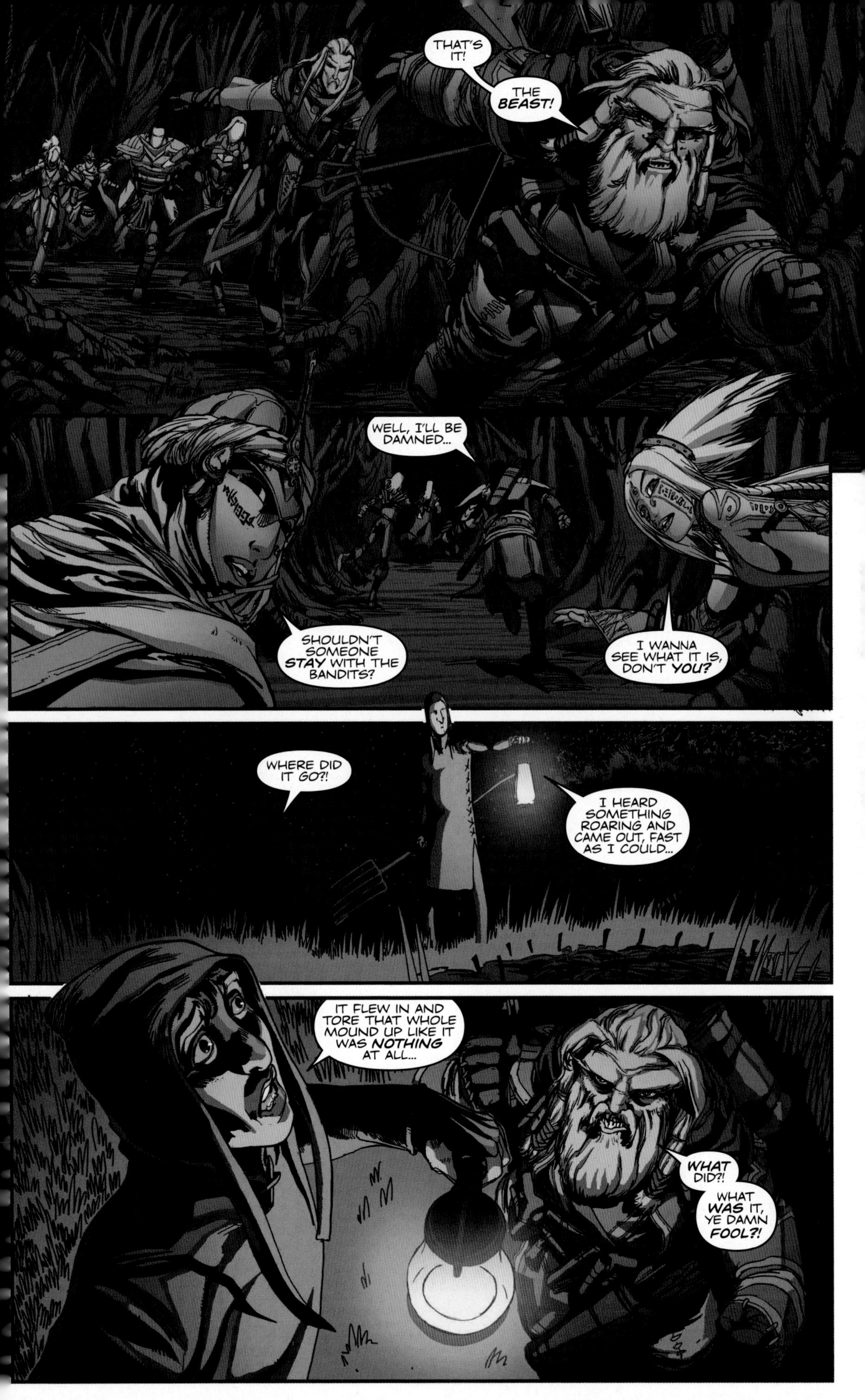
THAT'S IT!
THE BEAST!
WELL, I'LL BE DAMNED...
SHOULDN'T SOMEONE STAY WITH THE BANDITS?
I WANNA SEE WHAT IT IS, DON'T YOU?
WHERE DID IT GO?!
I HEARD SOMETHING ROARING AND CAME OUT, FAST AS I COULD...
IT FLEW IN AND TORE THAT WHOLE MOUND UP LIKE IT WAS NOTHING AT ALL...
WHAT DID?!
WHAT WAS IT, YE DAMN FOOL?!

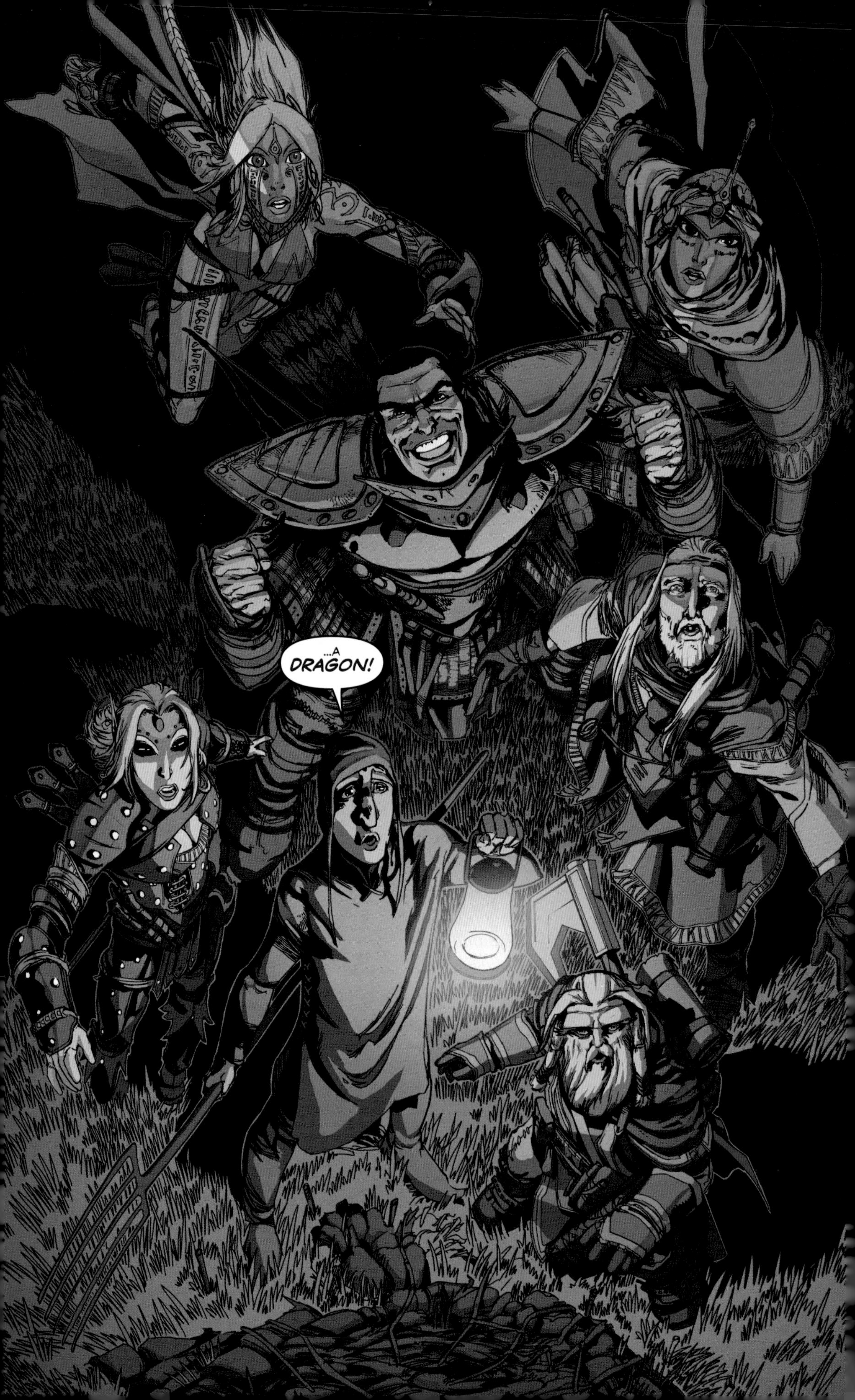
...A DRAGON!

CHAPTER 2

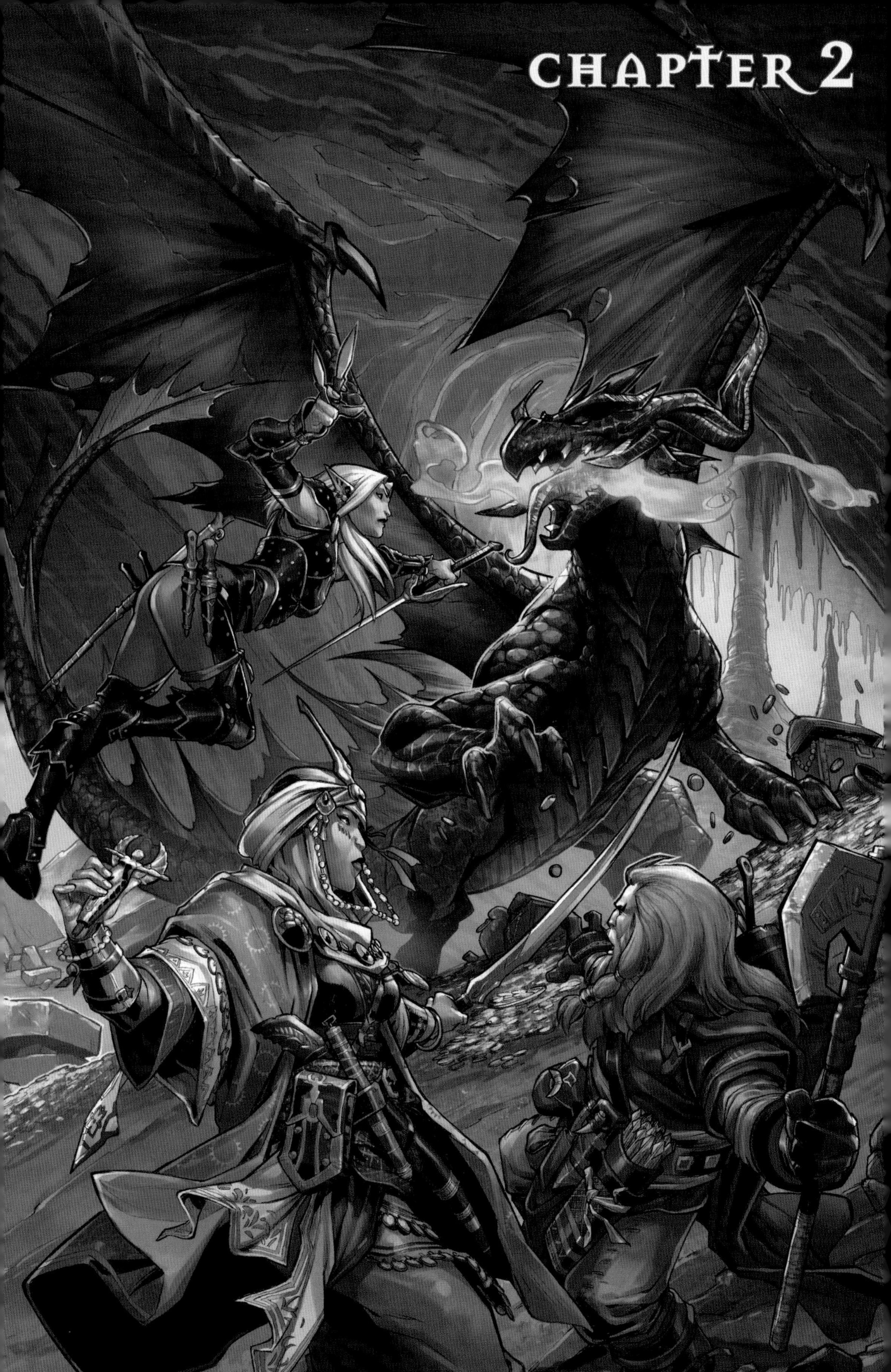

Issue #8 cover art by CARLOS GOMEZ colors by MOHAN

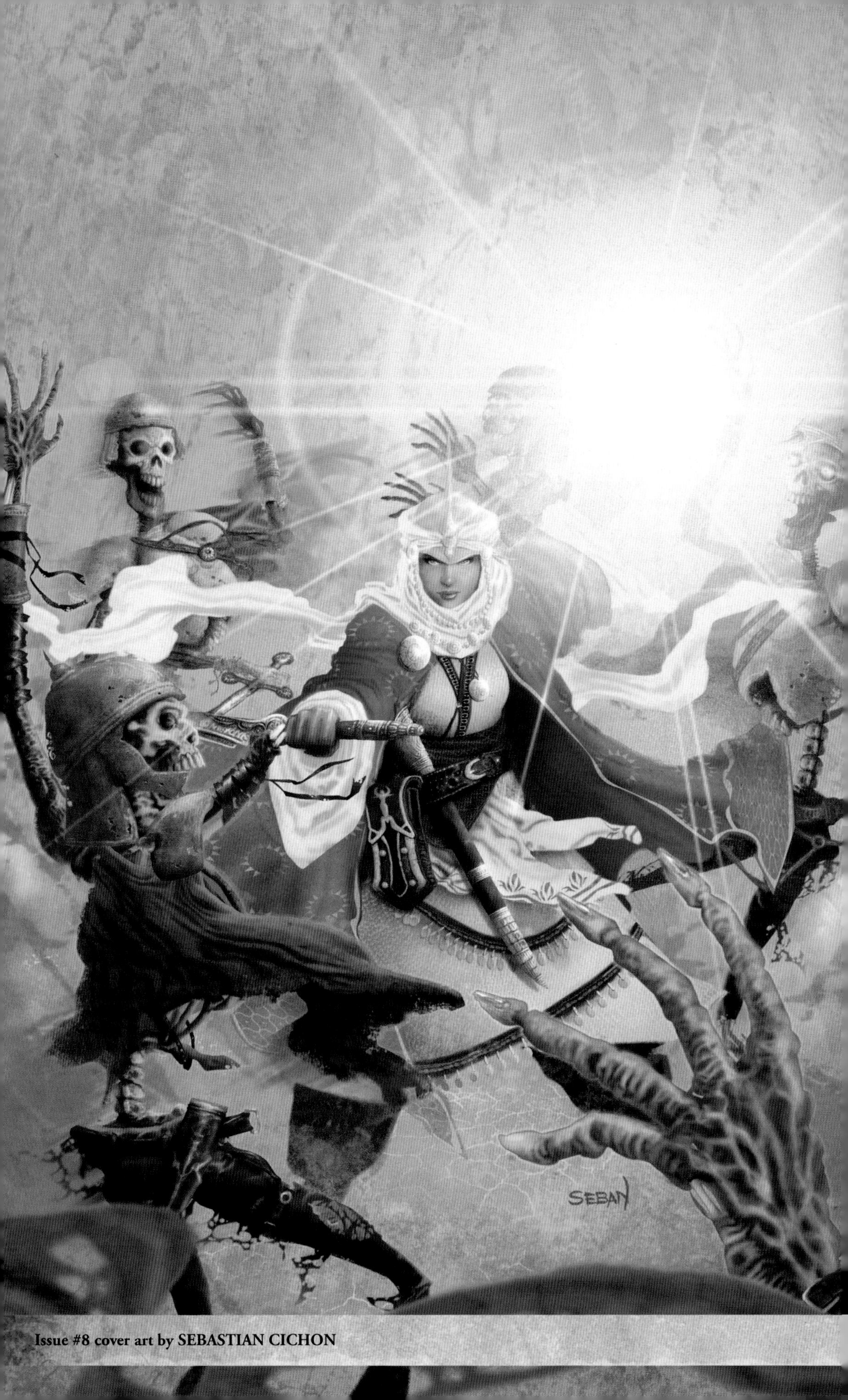
SEBAN

Issue #8 cover art by SEBASTIAN CICHON

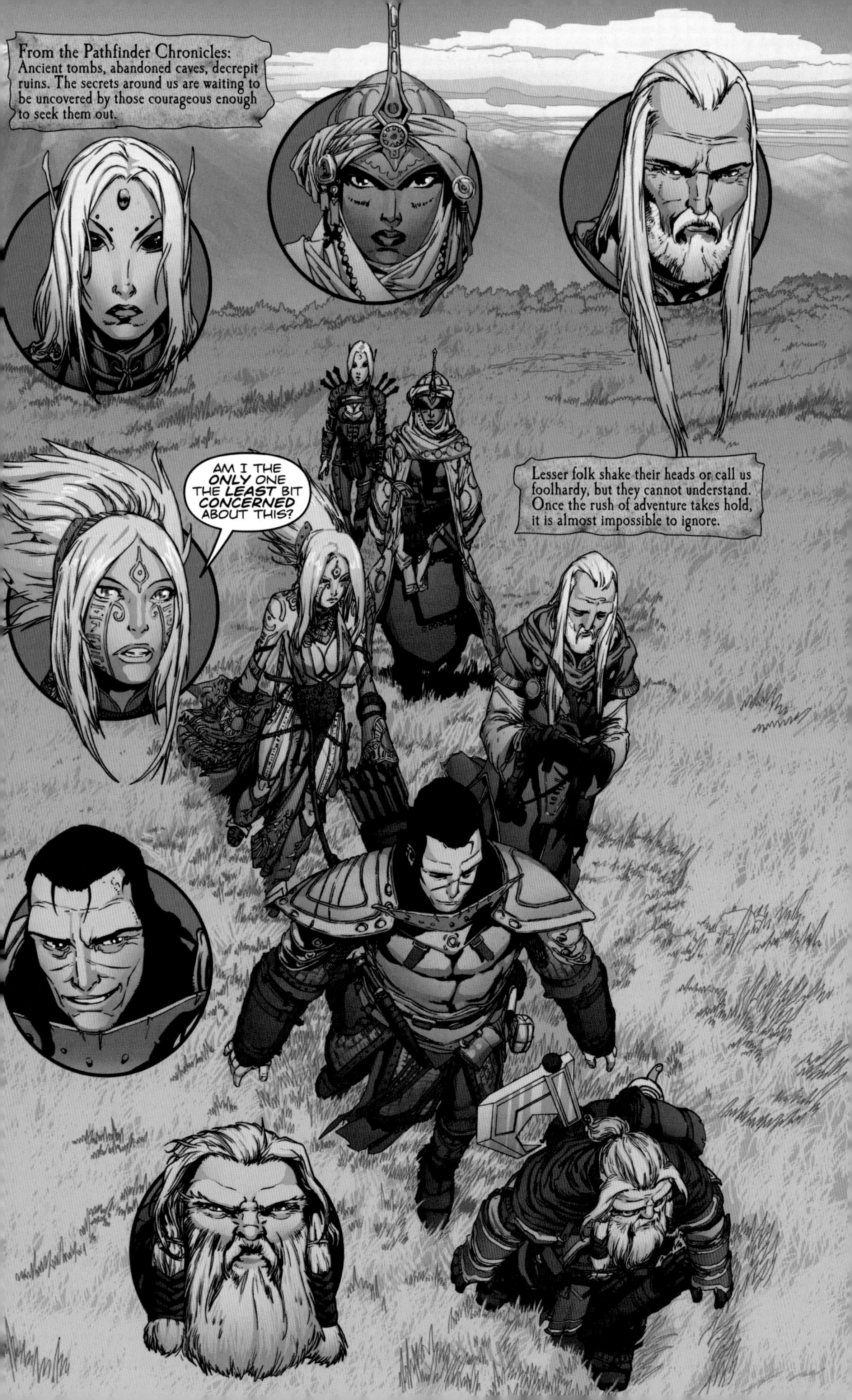
From the Pathfinder Chronicles:
Ancient tombs, abandoned caves, decrepit ruins. The secrets around us are waiting to be uncovered by those courageous enough to seek them out.
AM I THE ONLY ONE THE LEAST BIT CONCERNED ABOUT THIS?
Lesser folk shake their heads or call us foolhardy, but they cannot understand. Once the rush of adventure takes hold, it is almost impossible to ignore.

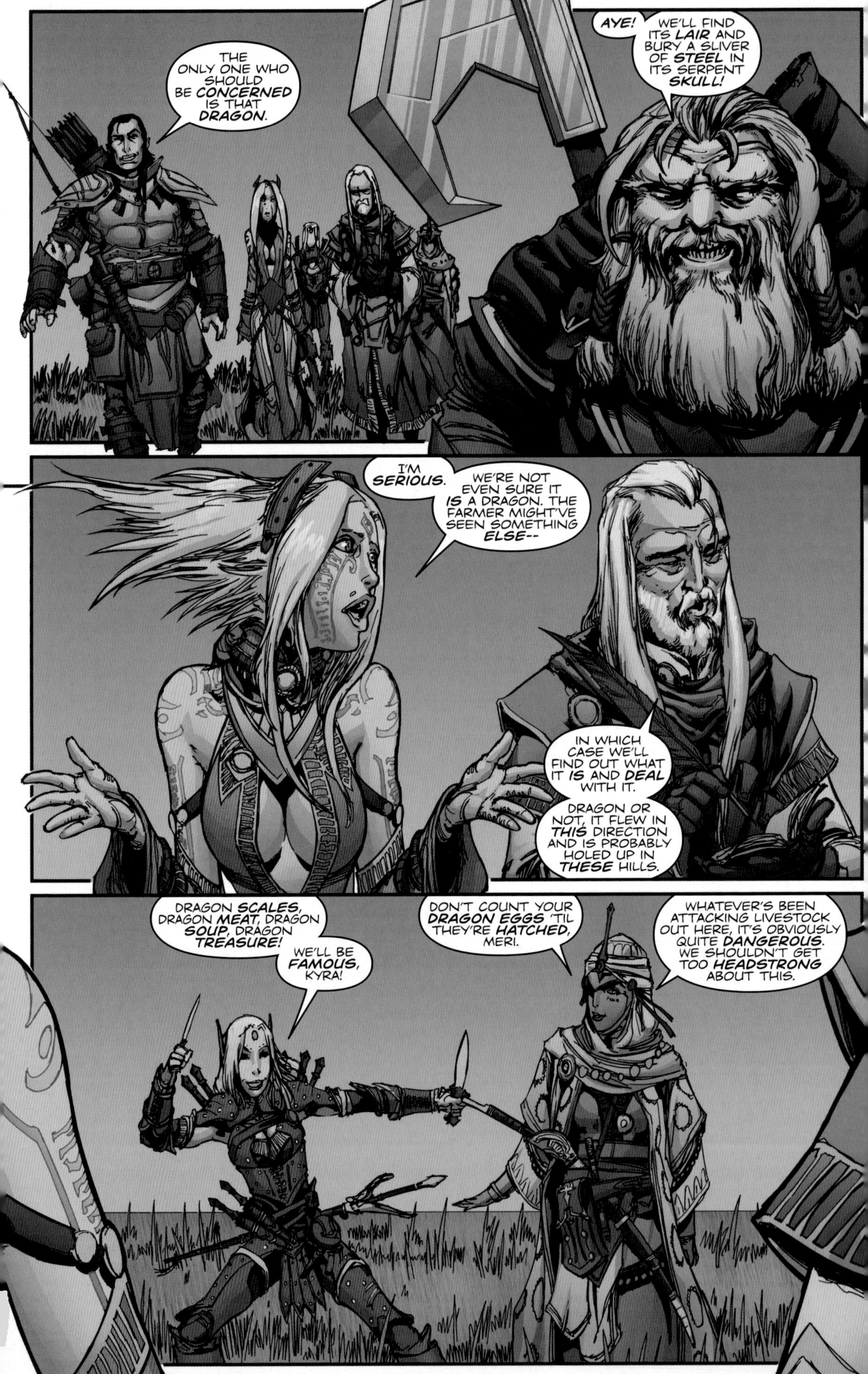
THE ONLY ONE WHO SHOULD BE CONCERNED IS THAT DRAGON.
AYE!
WE'LL FIND ITS LAIR AND BURY A SLIVER OF STEEL IN ITS SERPENT SKULL!
I'M SERIOUS.
WE'RE NOT EVEN SURE IT IS A DRAGON. THE FARMER MIGHT'VE SEEN SOMETHING ELSE--
IN WHICH CASE WE'LL FIND OUT WHAT IT IS AND DEAL WITH IT.
DRAGON OR NOT, IT FLEW IN THIS DIRECTION AND IS PROBABLY HOLED UP IN THESE HILLS.
DRAGON SCALES, DRAGON MEAT, DRAGON SOUP, DRAGON TREASURE!
WE'LL BE FAMOUS, KYRA!
DON'T COUNT YOUR DRAGON EGGS 'TIL THEY'RE HATCHED, MERI.
WHATEVER'S BEEN ATTACKING LIVESTOCK OUT HERE, IT'S OBVIOUSLY QUITE DANGEROUS. WE SHOULDN'T GET TOO HEADSTRONG ABOUT THIS.

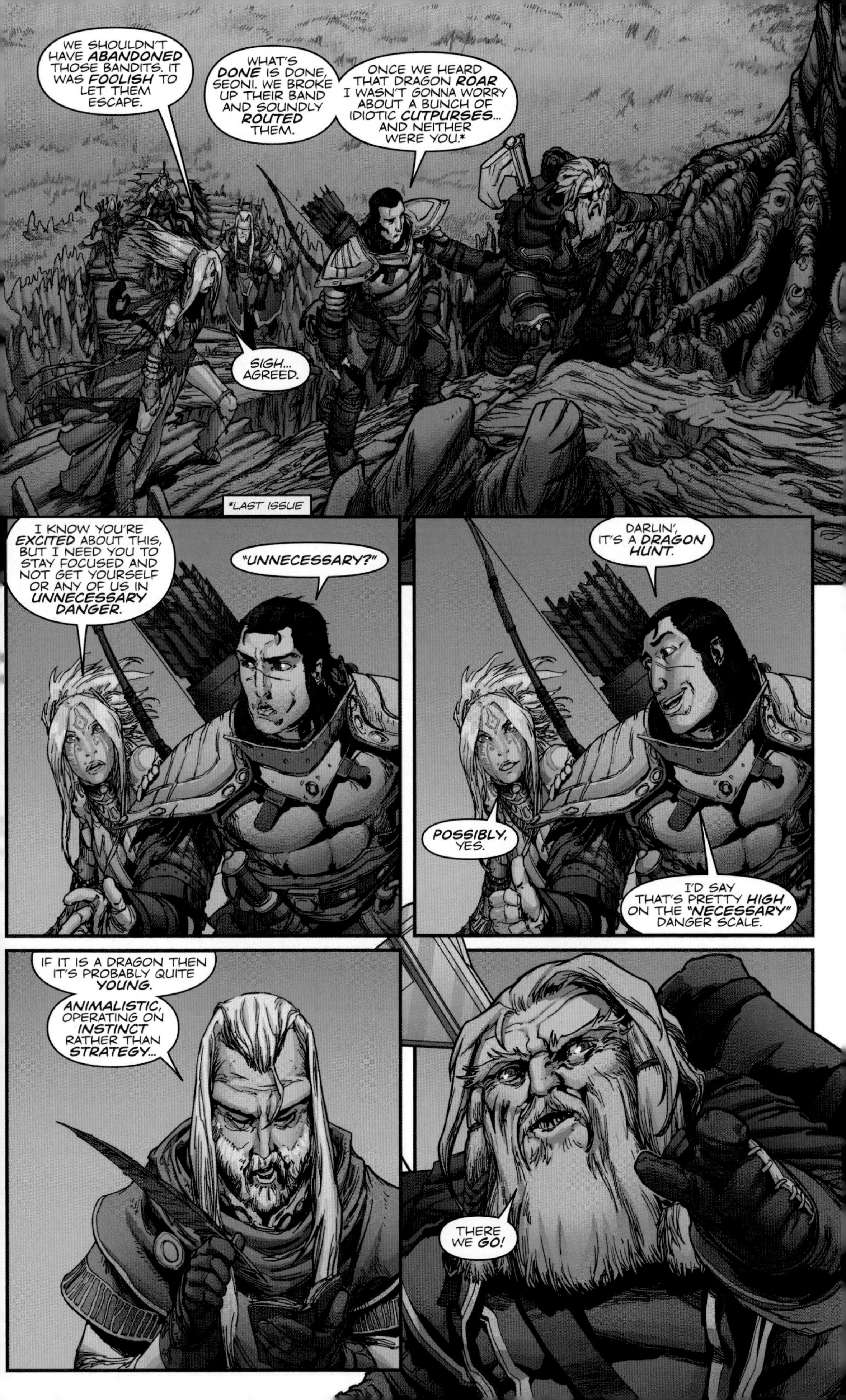
WE SHOULDN'T HAVE ABANDONED THOSE BANDITS. IT WAS FOOLISH TO LET THEM ESCAPE.
WHAT'S DONE IS DONE, SEONI. WE BROKE UP THEIR BAND AND SOUNDLY ROUTED THEM.
ONCE WE HEARD THAT DRAGON ROAR I WASN'T GONNA WORRY ABOUT A BUNCH OF IDIOTIC CUTPURSES... AND NEITHER WERE YOU.*
SIGH... AGREED.
*LAST ISSUE
I KNOW YOU'RE EXCITED ABOUT THIS, BUT I NEED YOU TO STAY FOCUSED AND NOT GET YOURSELF OR ANY OF US IN UNNECESSARY DANGER.
"UNNECESSARY?"
DARLIN', IT'S A DRAGON HUNT.
POSSIBLY, YES.
I'D SAY THAT'S PRETTY HIGH ON THE "NECESSARY" DANGER SCALE.
IF IT IS A DRAGON THEN IT'S PROBABLY QUITE YOUNG.
ANIMALISTIC, OPERATING ON INSTINCT RATHER THAN STRATEGY...
THERE WE GO!

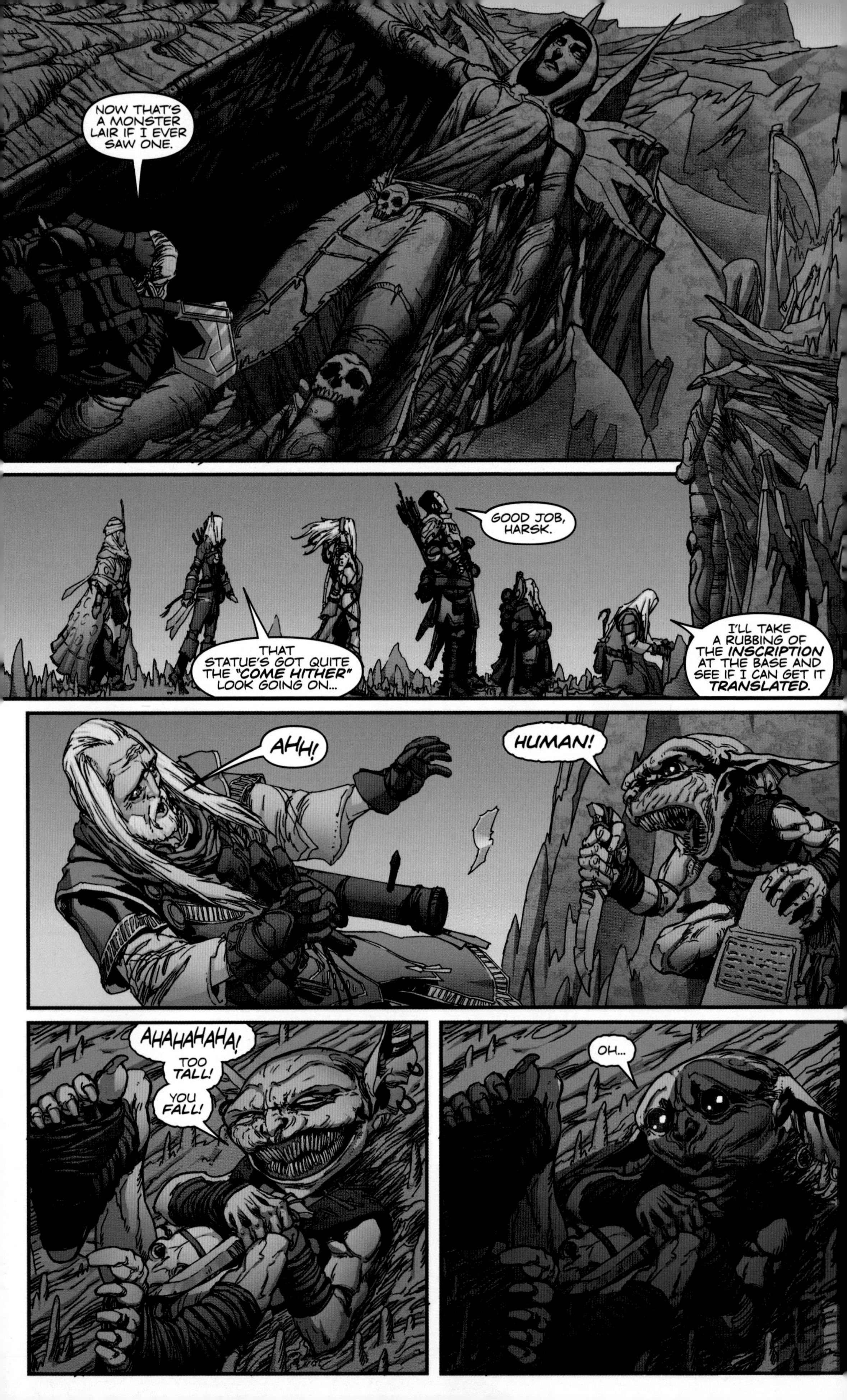
NOW THAT'S A MONSTER LAIR IF I EVER SAW ONE.
GOOD JOB, HARSK.
THAT STATUE'S GOT QUITE THE "COME HITHER" LOOK GOING ON...
I'LL TAKE A RUBBING OF THE INSCRIPTION AT THE BASE AND SEE IF I CAN GET IT TRANSLATED.
AHH!
HUMAN!
AHAHAHAHA!
TOO TALL!
YOU FALL!
OH...

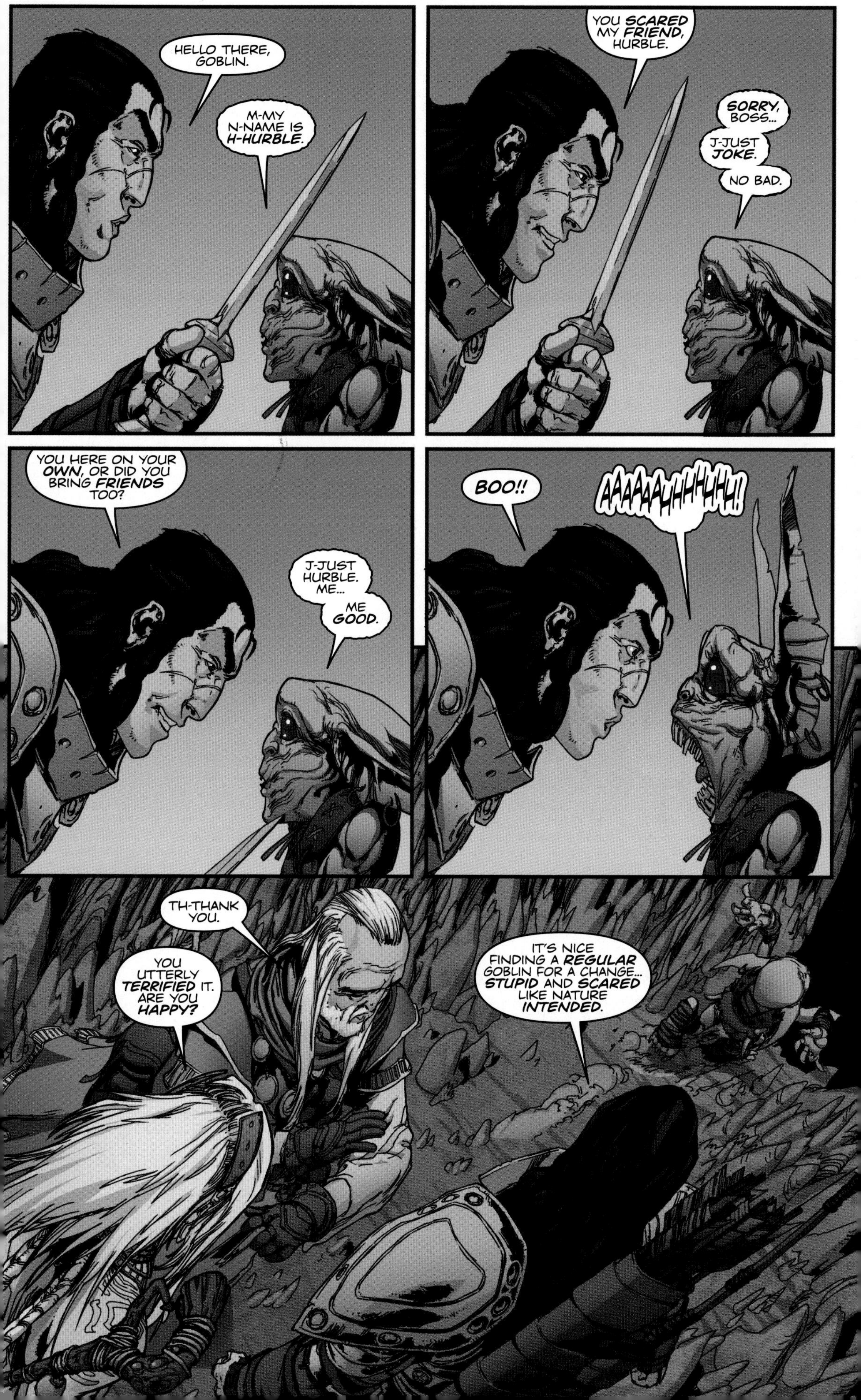

HELLO THERE, GOBLIN.
M-MY N-NAME IS H-HURBLE.
YOU SCARED MY FRIEND, HURBLE.
SORRY, BOSS...
J-JUST JOKE.
NO BAD.
YOU HERE ON YOUR OWN, OR DID YOU BRING FRIENDS TOO?
J-JUST HURBLE. ME...
ME GOOD.
BOO!!
AAAAAAHHHHHH!
TH-THANK YOU.
YOU UTTERLY TERRIFIED IT. ARE YOU HAPPY?
IT'S NICE FINDING A REGULAR GOBLIN FOR A CHANGE... STUPID AND SCARED LIKE NATURE INTENDED.

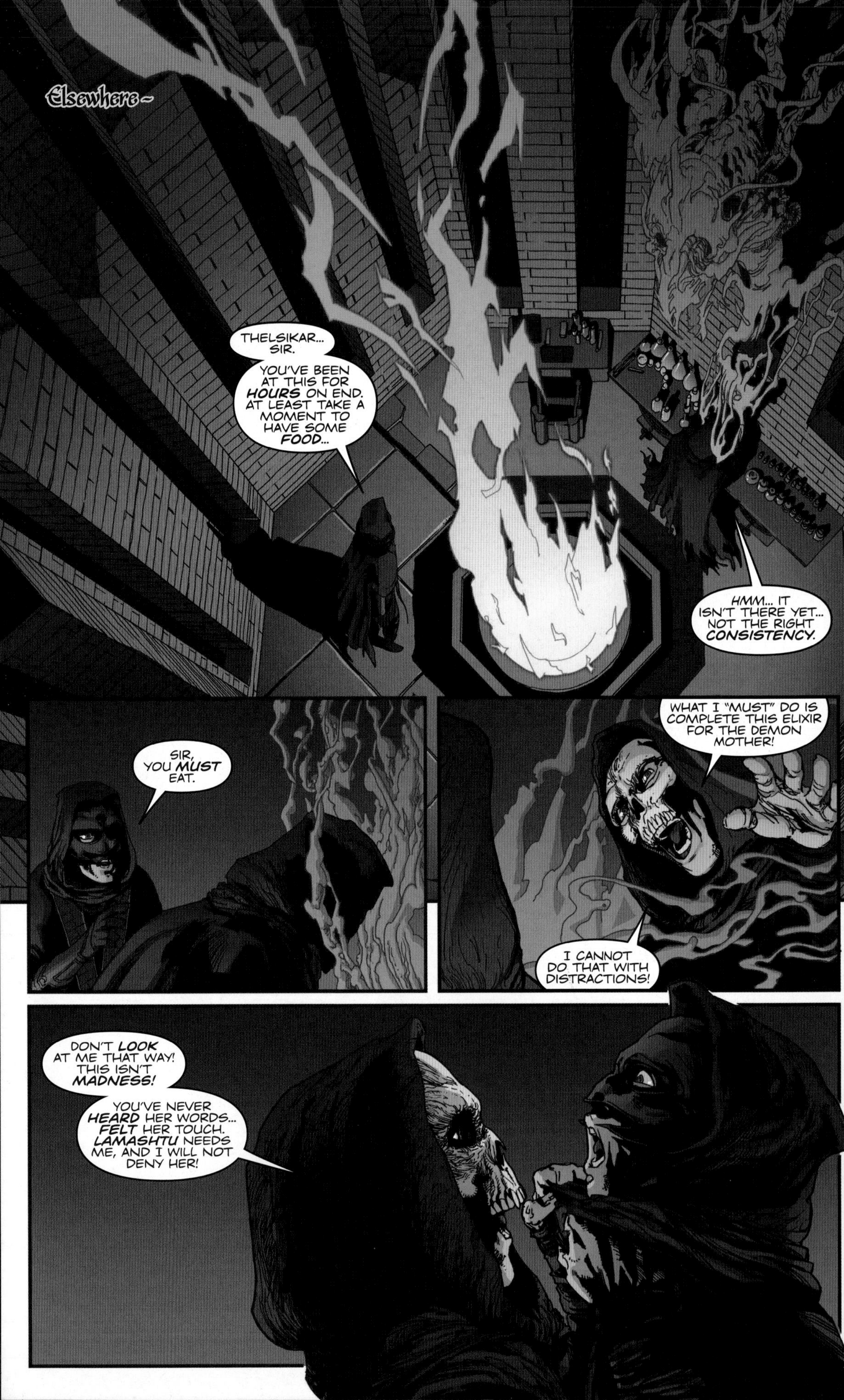
Elsewhere ~
THELSIKAR... SIR.
YOU'VE BEEN AT THIS FOR HOURS ON END. AT LEAST TAKE A MOMENT TO HAVE SOME FOOD...
HMM... IT ISN'T THERE YET... NOT THE RIGHT CONSISTENCY.
SIR, YOU MUST EAT.
WHAT I "MUST" DO IS COMPLETE THIS ELIXIR FOR THE DEMON MOTHER!
I CANNOT DO THAT WITH DISTRACTIONS!
DON'T LOOK AT ME THAT WAY! THIS ISN'T MADNESS!
YOU'VE NEVER HEARD HER WORDS... FELT HER TOUCH. LAMASHTU NEEDS ME, AND I WILL NOT DENY HER!

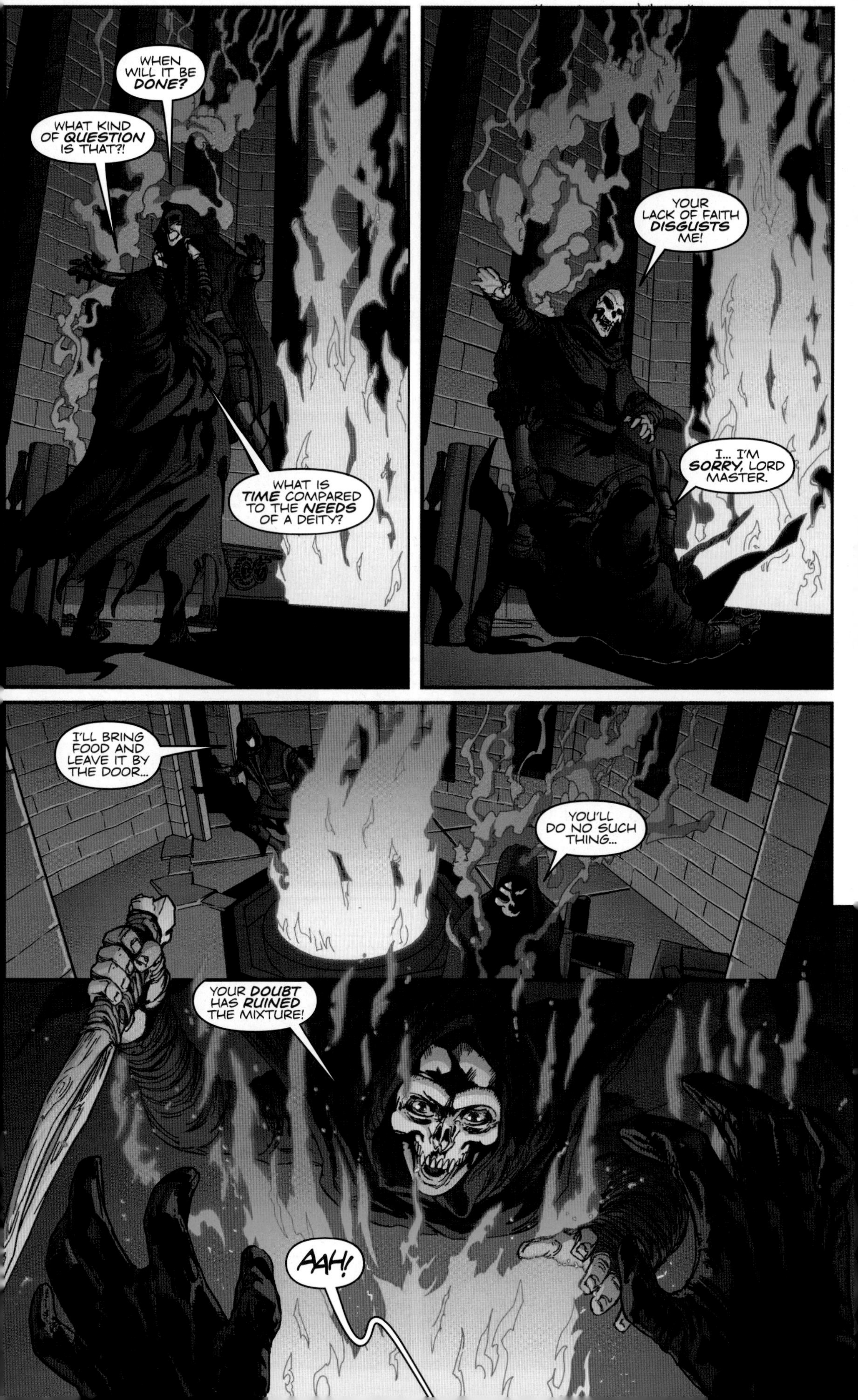
WHEN WILL IT BE DONE?
WHAT KIND OF QUESTION IS THAT?!
WHAT IS TIME COMPARED TO THE NEEDS OF A DEITY?
YOUR LACK OF FAITH DISGUSTS ME!
I... I'M SORRY, LORD MASTER.
I'LL BRING FOOD AND LEAVE IT BY THE DOOR...
YOU'LL DO NO SUCH THING...
YOUR DOUBT HAS RUINED THE MIXTURE!
AAH!

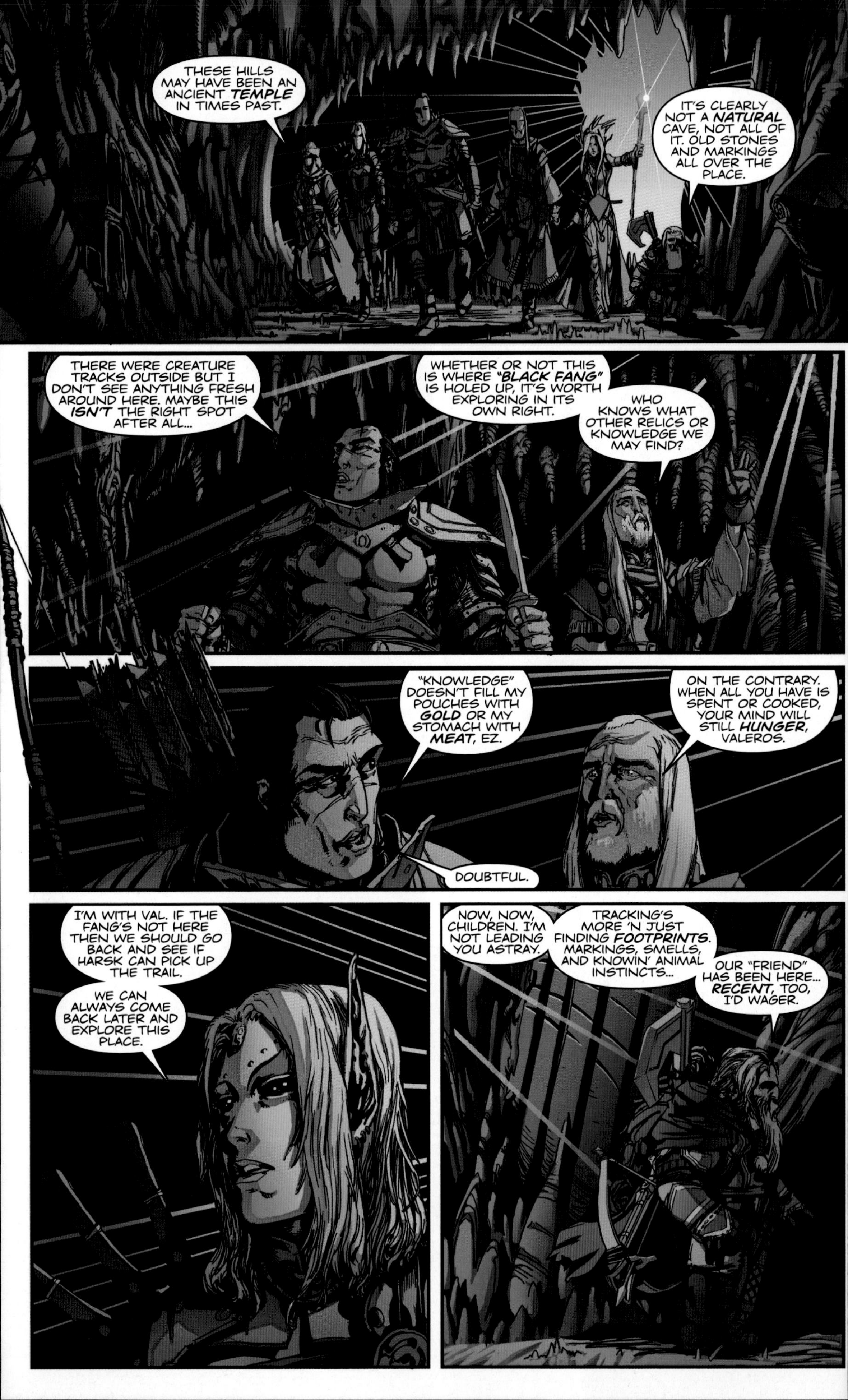
THESE HILLS MAY HAVE BEEN AN ANCIENT TEMPLE IN TIMES PAST.
IT'S CLEARLY NOT A NATURAL CAVE, NOT ALL OF IT. OLD STONES AND MARKINGS ALL OVER THE PLACE.
THERE WERE CREATURE TRACKS OUTSIDE BUT I DON'T SEE ANYTHING FRESH AROUND HERE. MAYBE THIS ISN'T THE RIGHT SPOT AFTER ALL...
WHETHER OR NOT THIS IS WHERE "BLACK FANG" IS HOLED UP, IT'S WORTH EXPLORING IN ITS OWN RIGHT.
WHO KNOWS WHAT OTHER RELICS OR KNOWLEDGE WE MAY FIND?
"KNOWLEDGE" DOESN'T FILL MY POUCHES WITH GOLD OR MY STOMACH WITH MEAT, EZ.
ON THE CONTRARY. WHEN ALL YOU HAVE IS SPENT OR COOKED, YOUR MIND WILL STILL HUNGER, VALEROS.
DOUBTFUL.
I'M WITH VAL. IF THE FANG'S NOT HERE THEN WE SHOULD GO BACK AND SEE IF HARSK CAN PICK UP THE TRAIL.
WE CAN ALWAYS COME BACK LATER AND EXPLORE THIS PLACE.
NOW, NOW, CHILDREN. I'M NOT LEADING YOU ASTRAY.
TRACKING'S MORE 'N JUST FINDING FOOTPRINTS. MARKINGS, SMELLS, AND KNOWIN' ANIMAL INSTINCTS...
OUR "FRIEND" HAS BEEN HERE... RECENT, TOO, I'D WAGER.

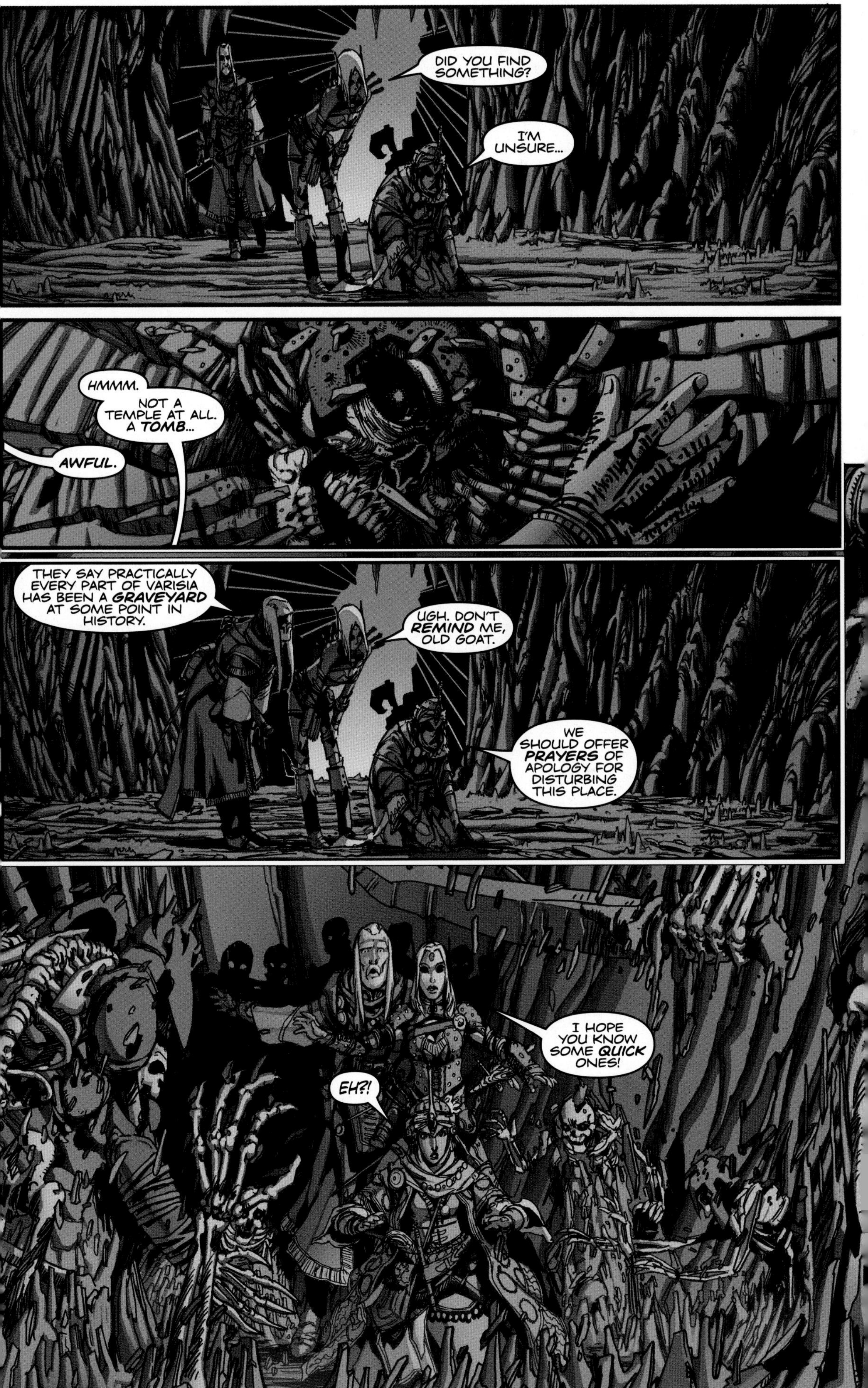
DID YOU FIND SOMETHING?
I'M UNSURE...
HMMM. NOT A TEMPLE AT ALL. A TOMB...
AWFUL.
THEY SAY PRACTICALLY EVERY PART OF VARISIA HAS BEEN A GRAVEYARD AT SOME POINT IN HISTORY.
UGH. DON'T REMIND ME, OLD GOAT.
WE SHOULD OFFER PRAYERS OF APOLOGY FOR DISTURBING THIS PLACE.
I HOPE YOU KNOW SOME QUICK ONES!
EH?!

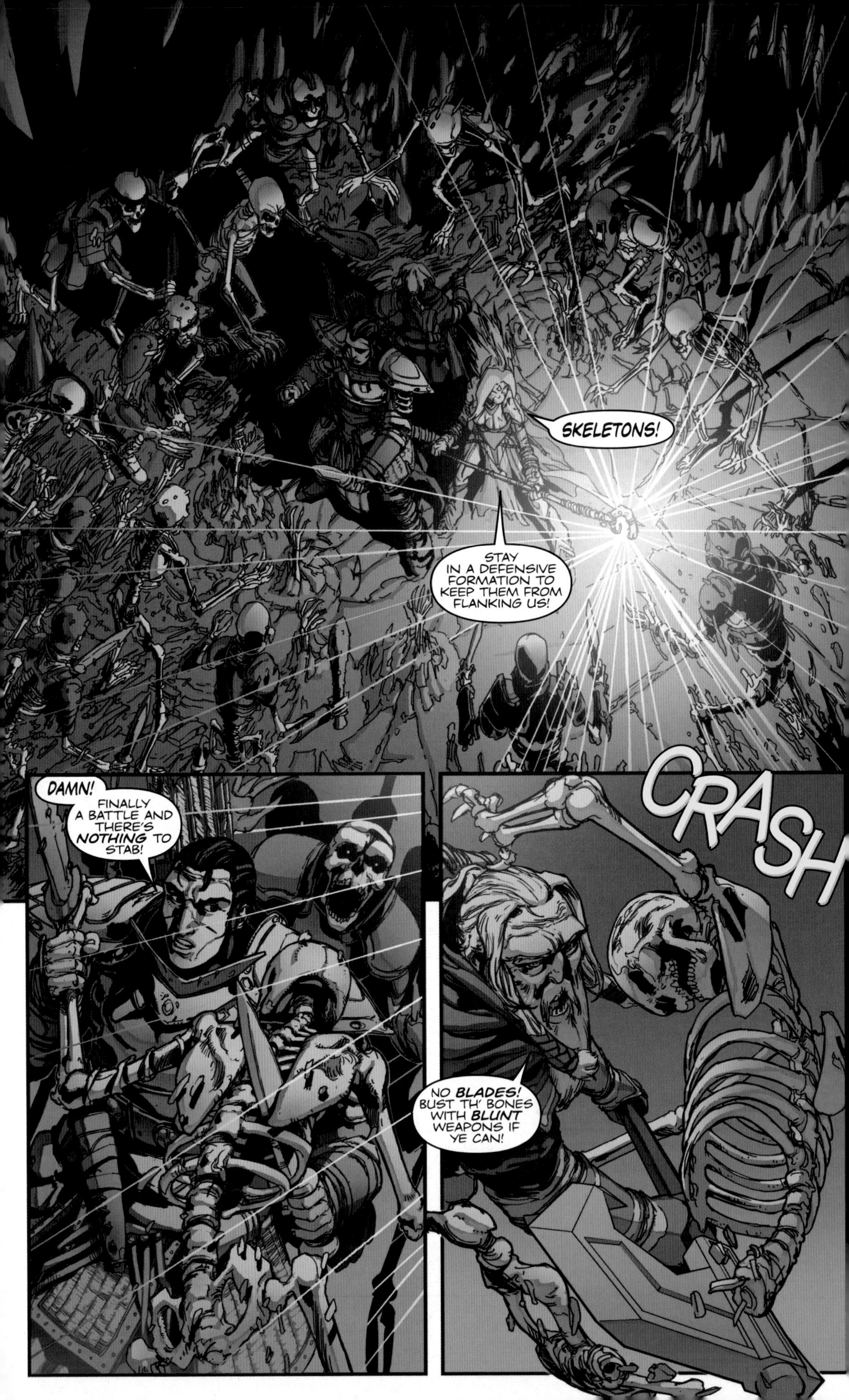
SKELETONS!
STAY IN A DEFENSIVE FORMATION TO KEEP THEM FROM FLANKING US!
DAMN!
FINALLY A BATTLE AND THERE'S **NOTHING** TO STAB!
CRASH
NO **BLADES!** BUST TH' BONES WITH **BLUNT** WEAPONS IF YE CAN!

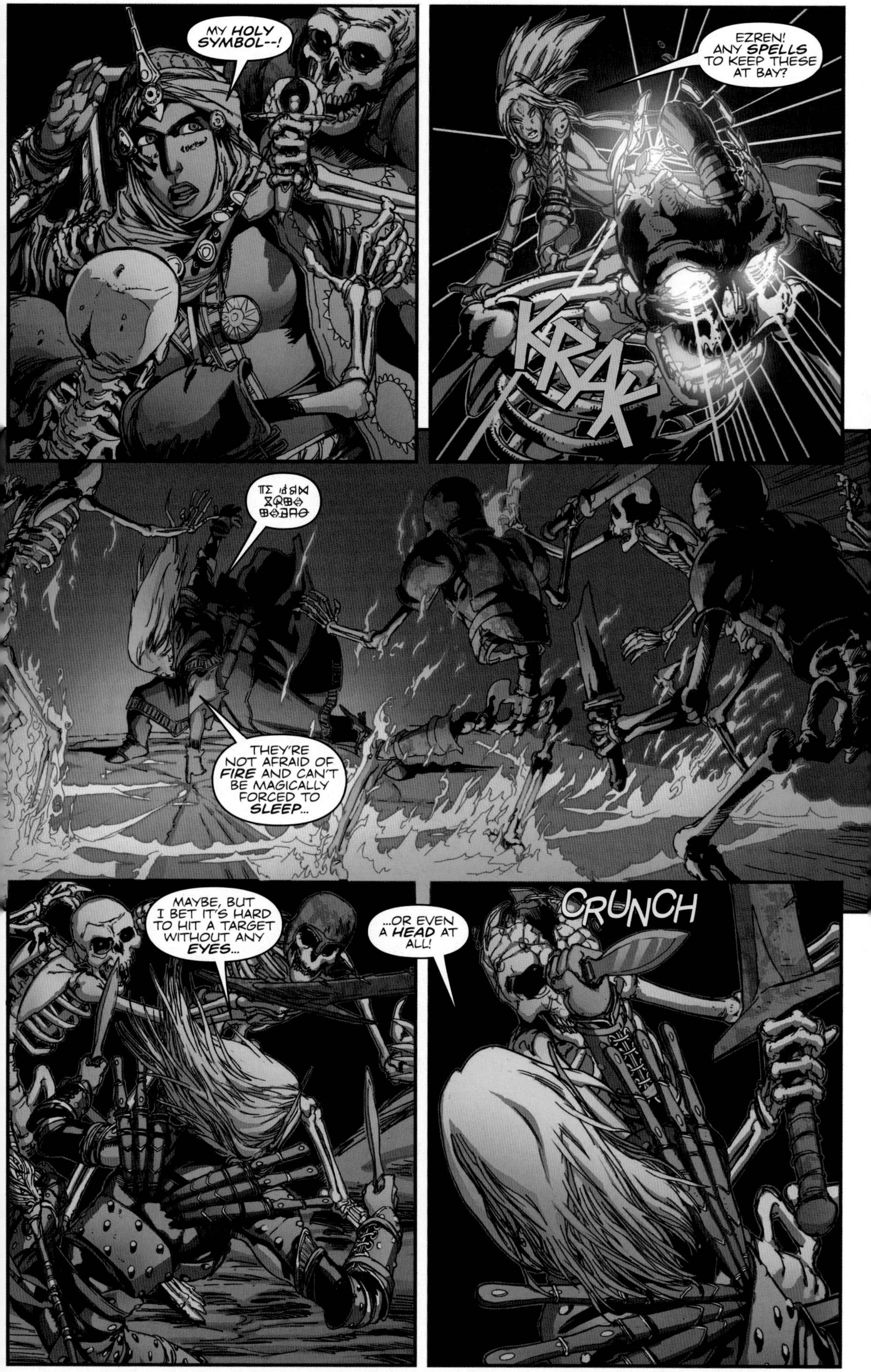
MY HOLY SYMBOL--!
EZREN! ANY SPELLS TO KEEP THESE AT BAY?
KRAK
THEY'RE NOT AFRAID OF FIRE AND CAN'T BE MAGICALLY FORCED TO SLEEP...
MAYBE, BUT I BET IT'S HARD TO HIT A TARGET WITHOUT ANY EYES...
...OR EVEN A HEAD AT ALL!
CRUNCH

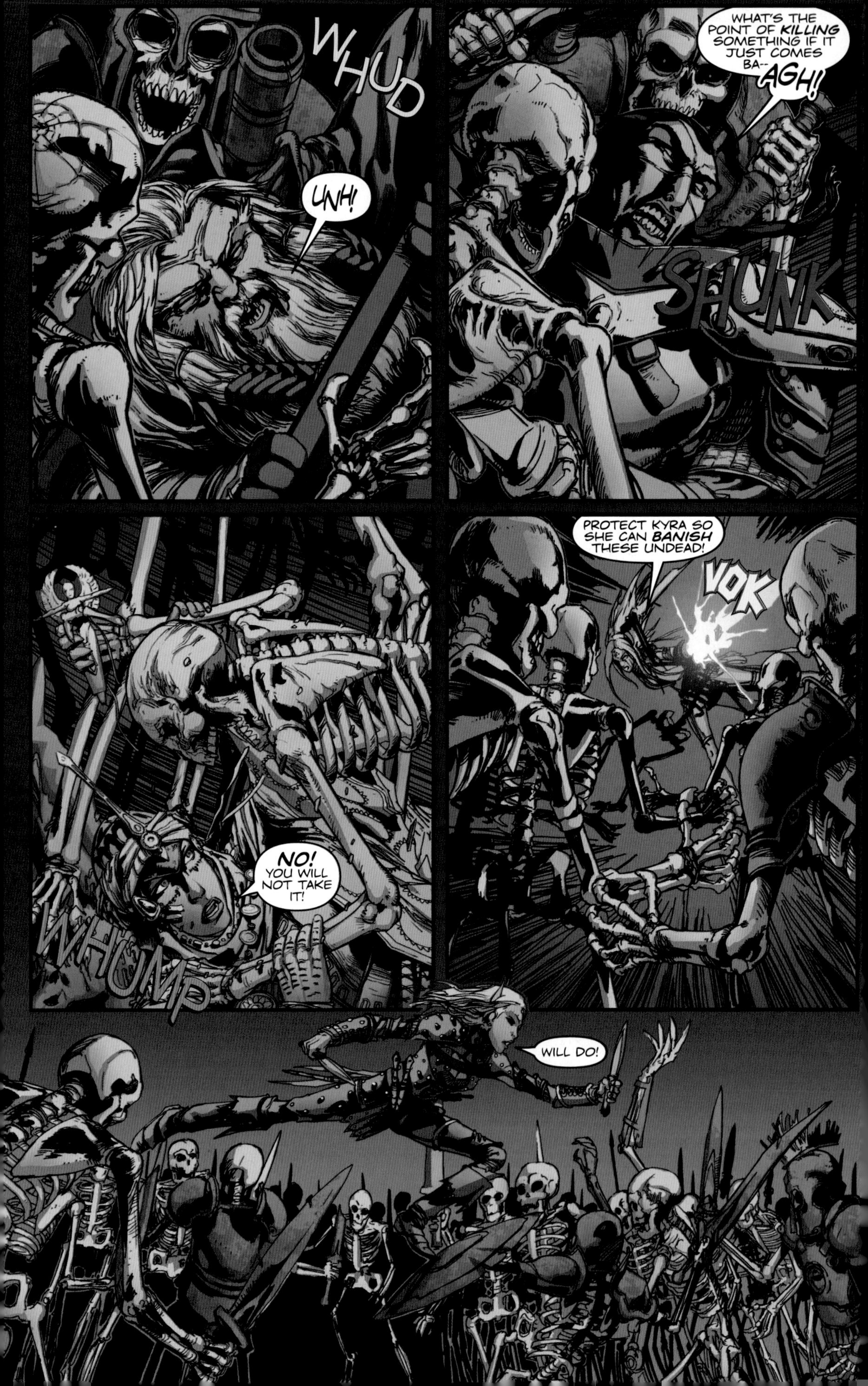
WHUD
UNH!
WHAT'S THE POINT OF KILLING SOMETHING IF IT JUST COMES BA-- AGH!
SHUNK
NO! YOU WILL NOT TAKE IT!
WHUMP
PROTECT KYRA SO SHE CAN BANISH THESE UNDEAD!
VOK
WILL DO!

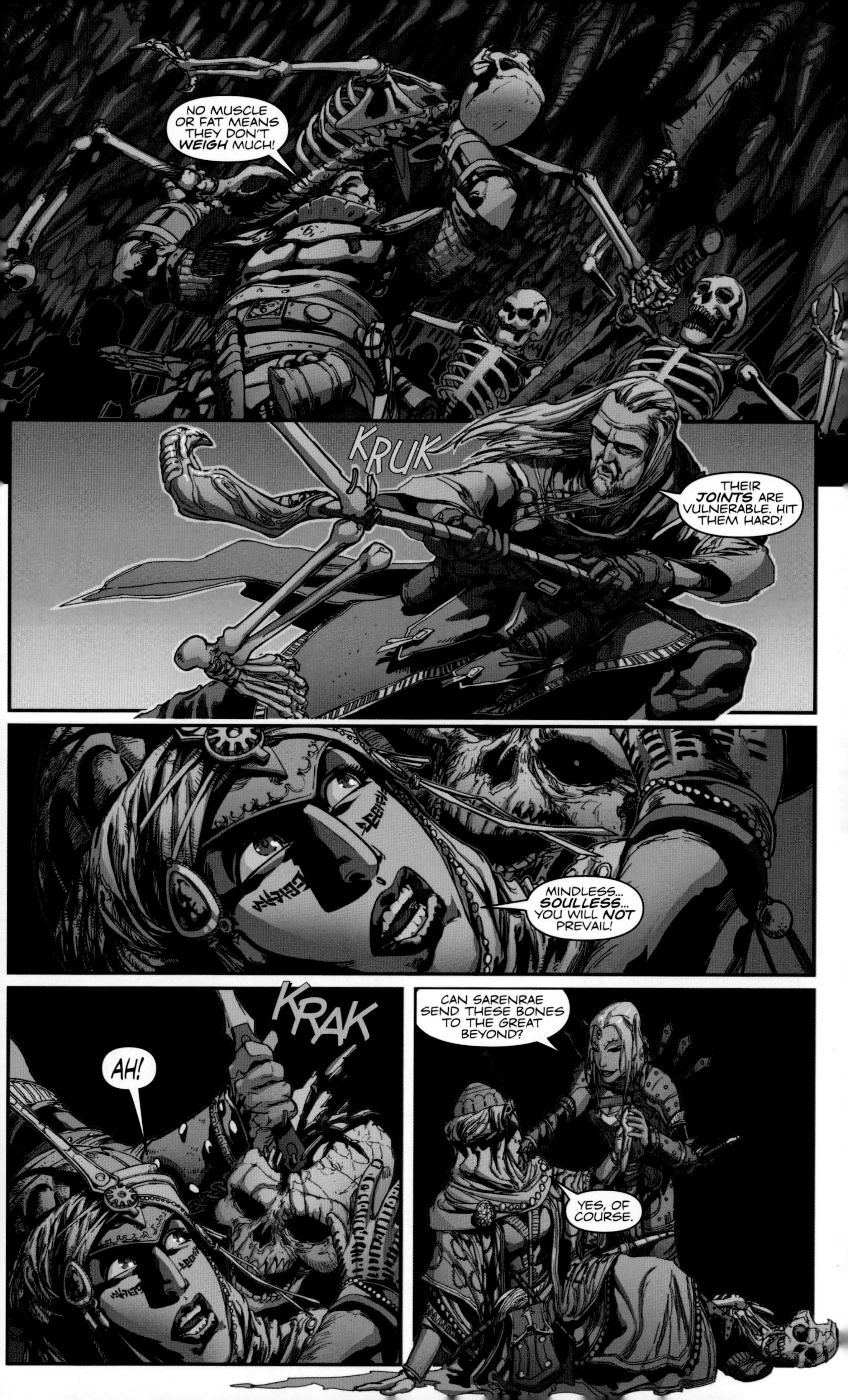
NO MUSCLE OR FAT MEANS THEY DON'T WEIGH MUCH!
KRUK
THEIR JOINTS ARE VULNERABLE. HIT THEM HARD!
MINDLESS... SOULLESS... YOU WILL NOT PREVAIL!
KRAK
AH!
CAN SARENRAE SEND THESE BONES TO THE GREAT BEYOND?
YES, OF COURSE.

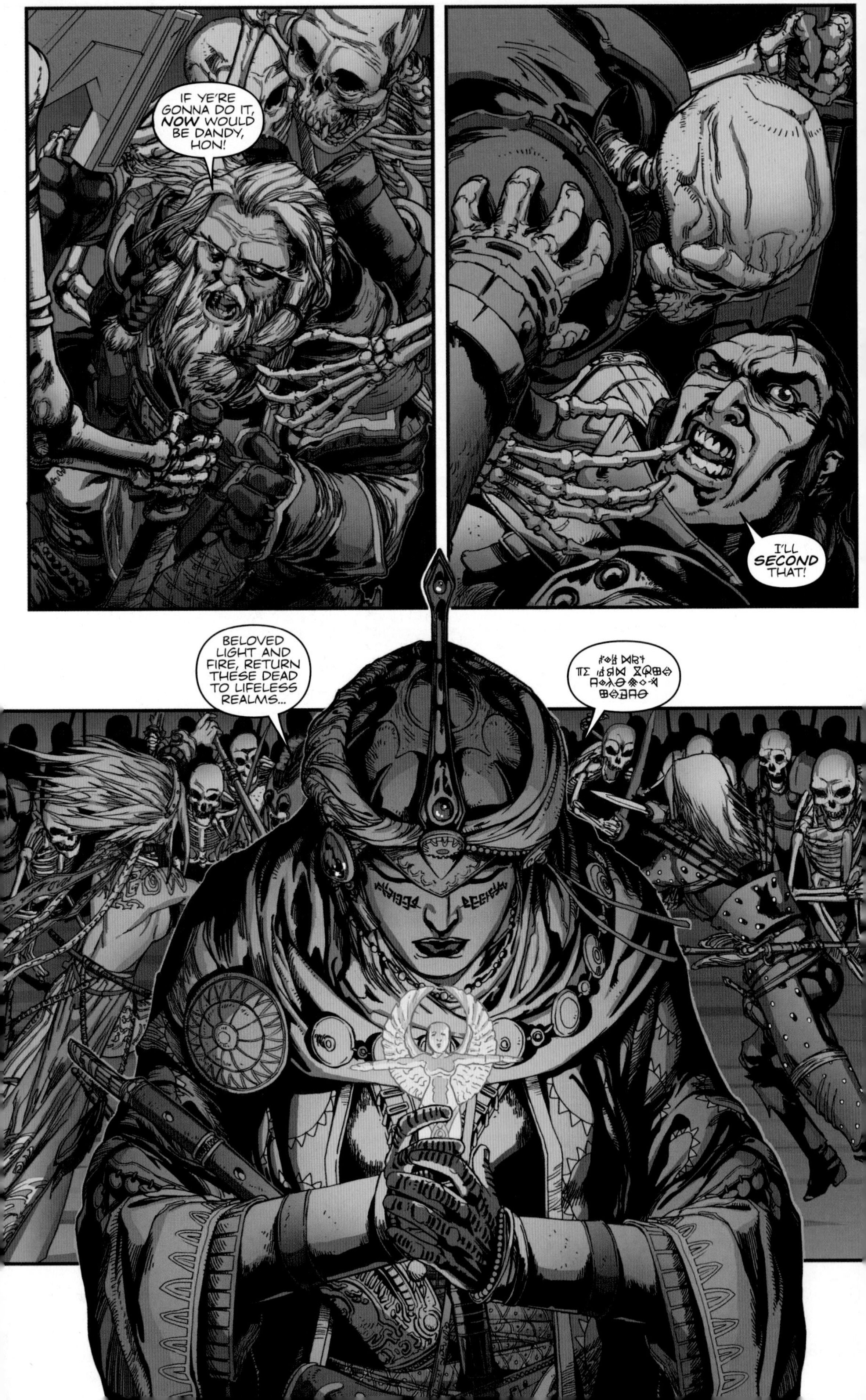
IF YE'RE GONNA DO IT, NOW WOULD BE DANDY, HON!
I'LL SECOND THAT!
BELOVED LIGHT AND FIRE, RETURN THESE DEAD TO LIFELESS REALMS...

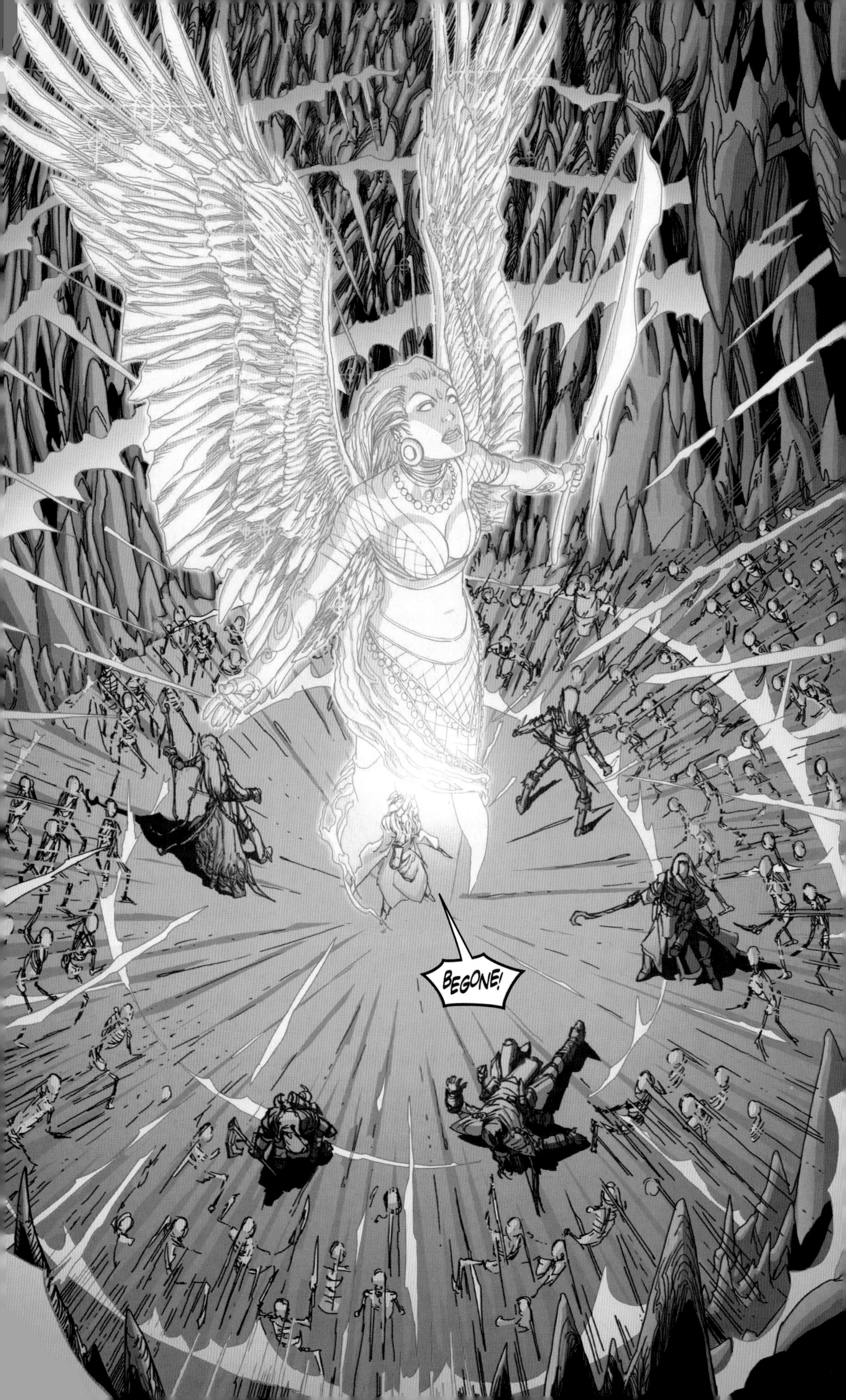
BEGONE!

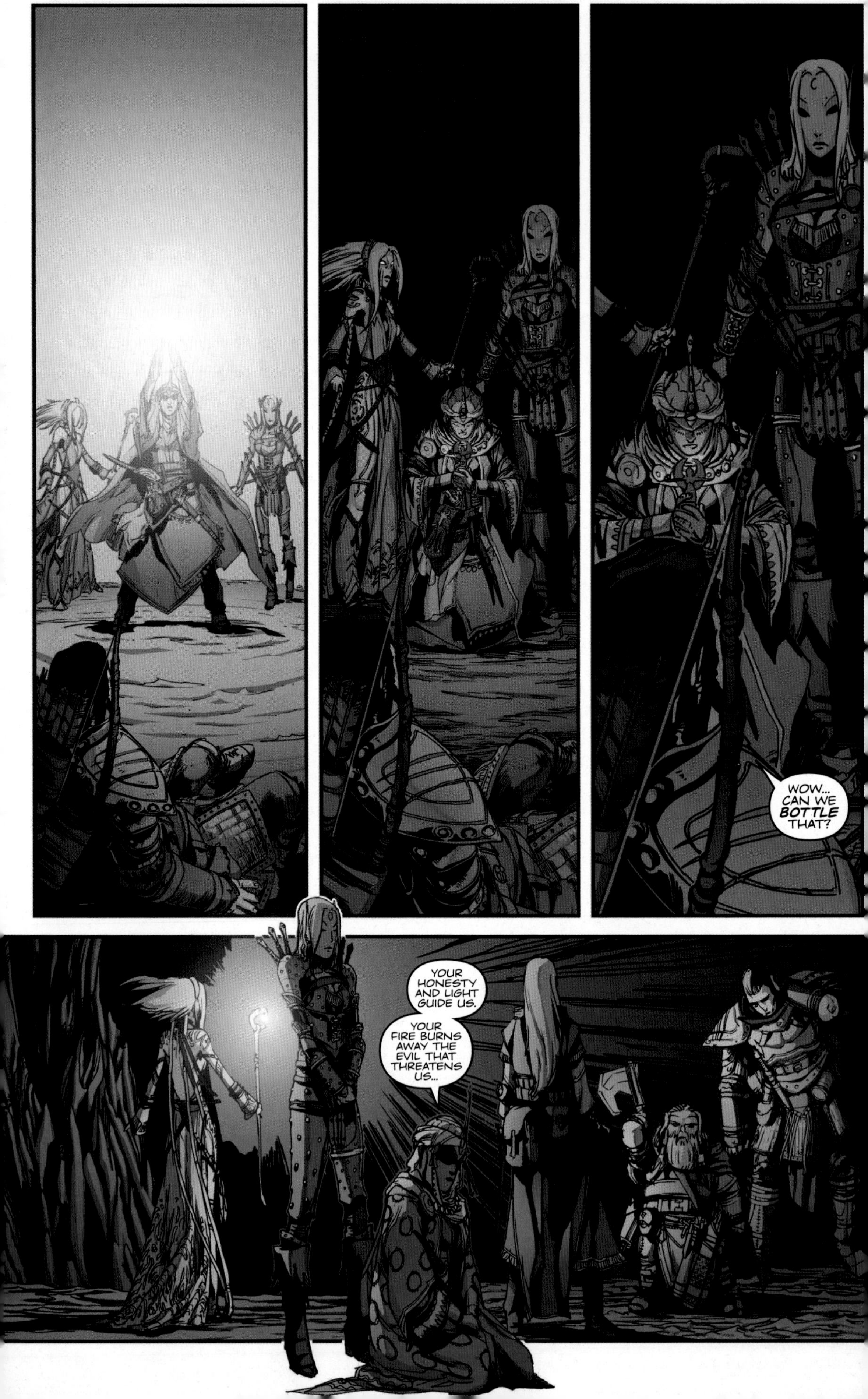
WOW... CAN WE BOTTLE THAT?
YOUR HONESTY AND LIGHT GUIDE US.
YOUR FIRE BURNS AWAY THE EVIL THAT THREATENS US...

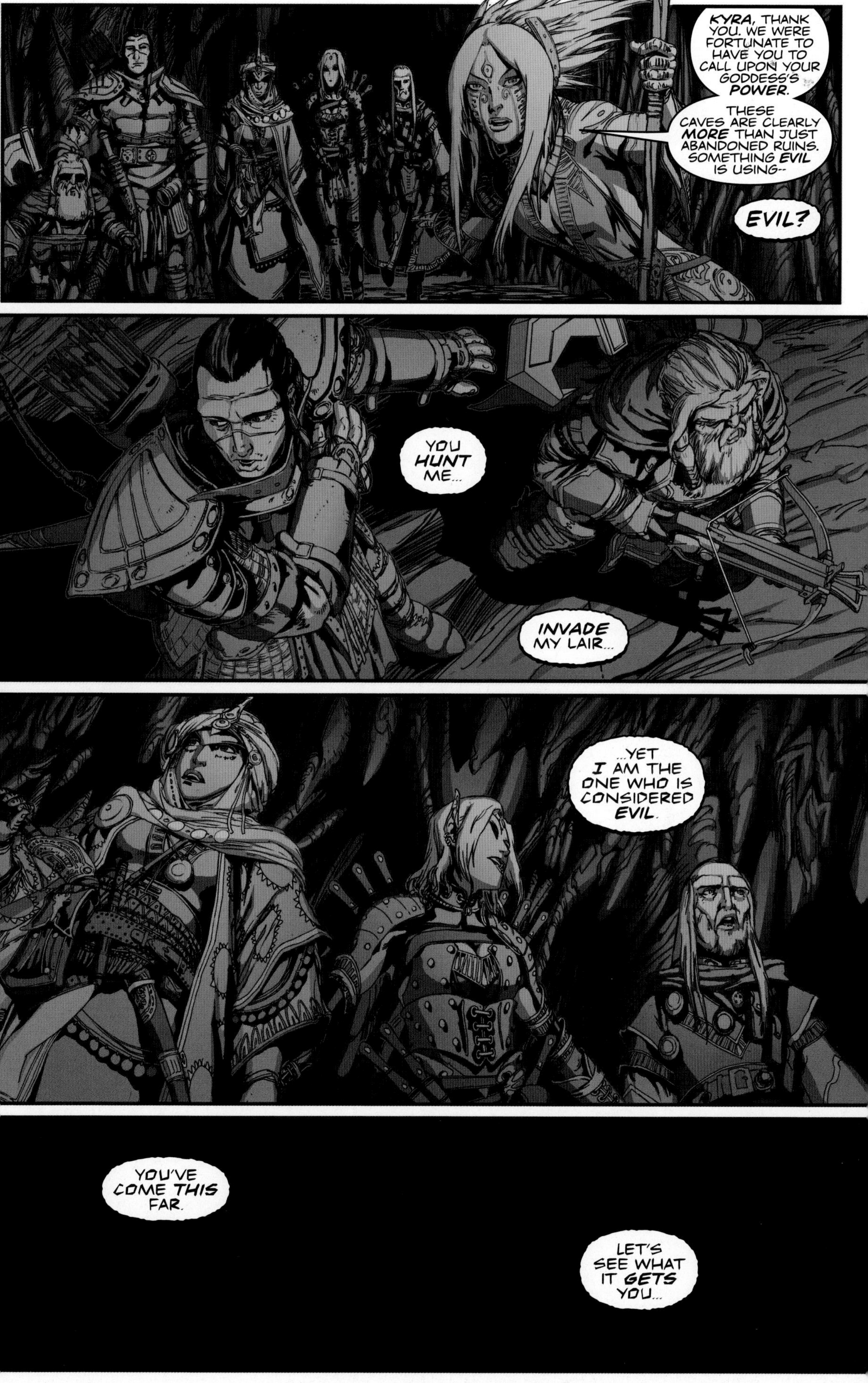
KYRA, THANK YOU. WE WERE FORTUNATE TO HAVE YOU TO CALL UPON YOUR GODDESS'S POWER.
THESE CAVES ARE CLEARLY MORE THAN JUST ABANDONED RUINS. SOMETHING EVIL IS USING--
EVIL?
YOU HUNT ME...
INVADE MY LAIR...
...YET I AM THE ONE WHO IS CONSIDERED EVIL.
YOU'VE COME THIS FAR.
LET'S SEE WHAT IT GETS YOU...

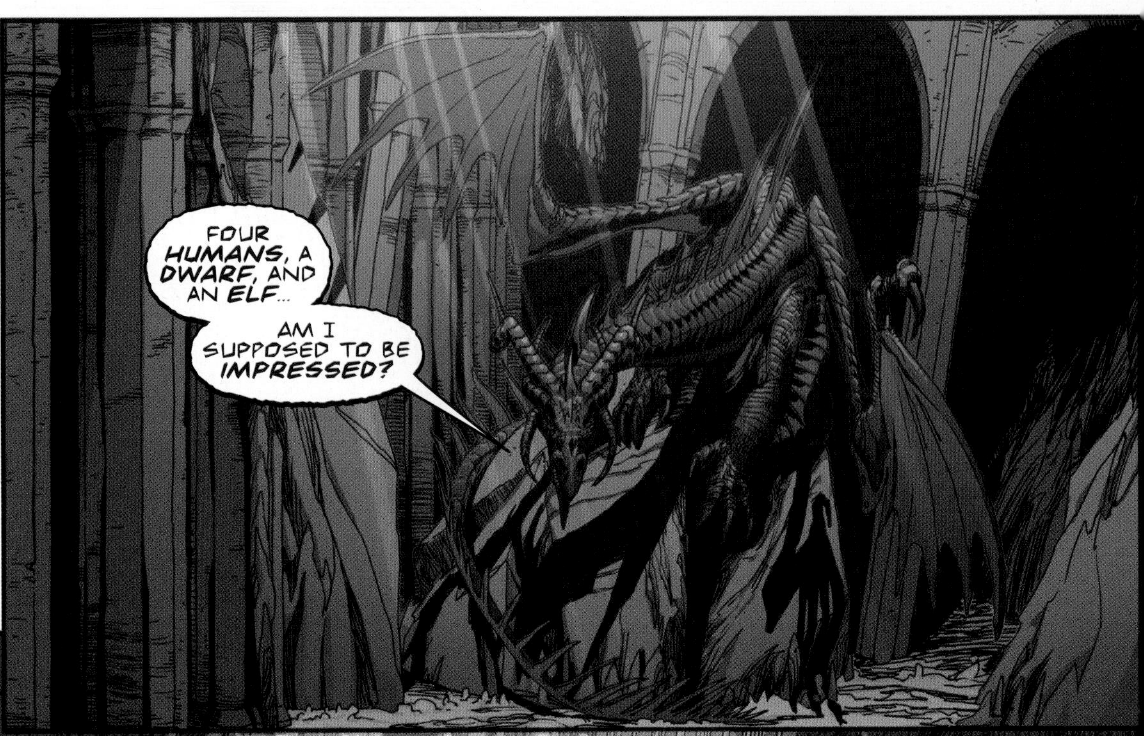
FOUR **HUMANS**, A **DWARF**, AND AN **ELF**...
AM I SUPPOSED TO BE ***IMPRESSED?***

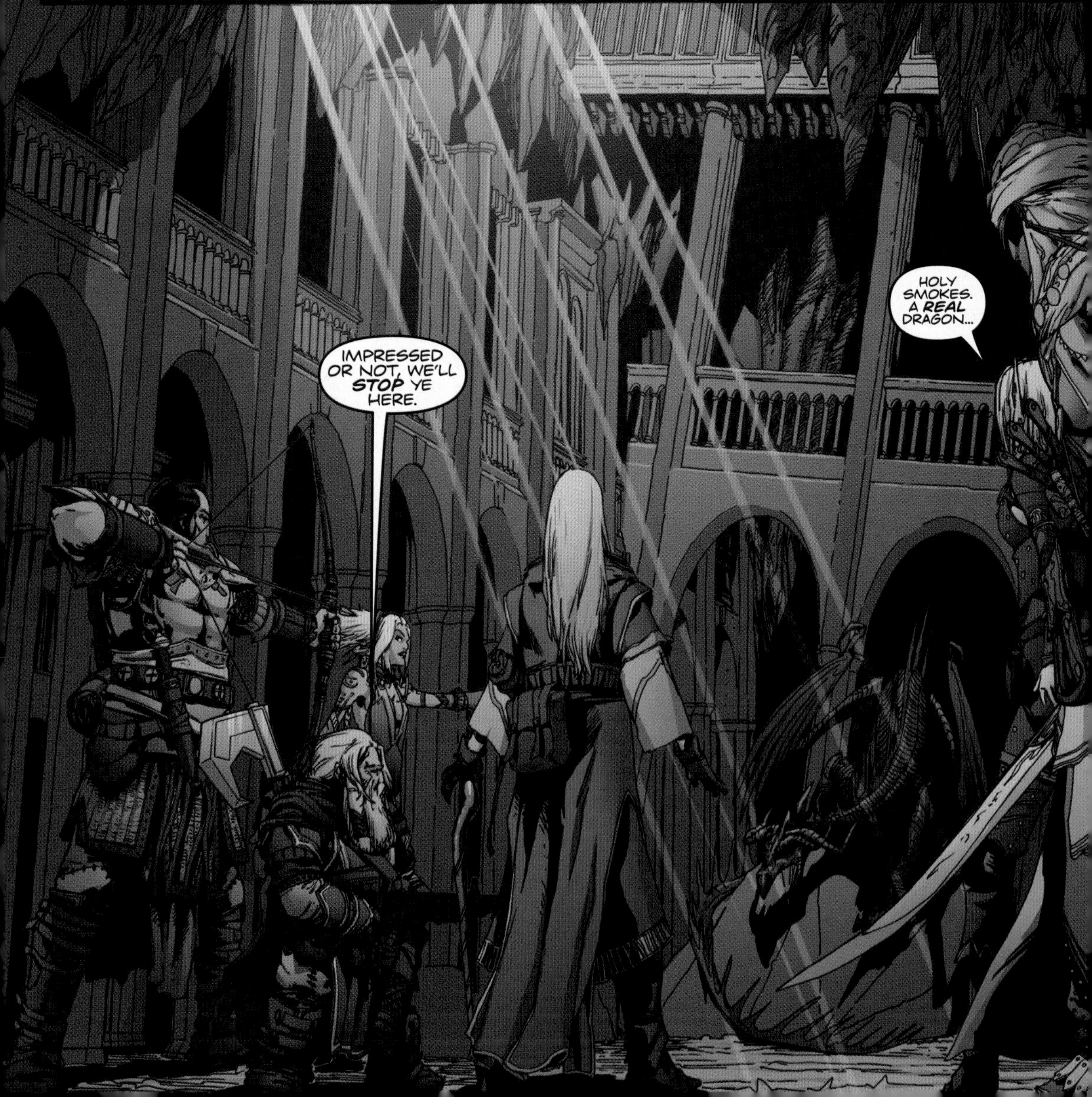
HOLY SMOKES. A ***REAL*** DRAGON...
IMPRESSED OR NOT, WE'LL ***STOP*** YE HERE.

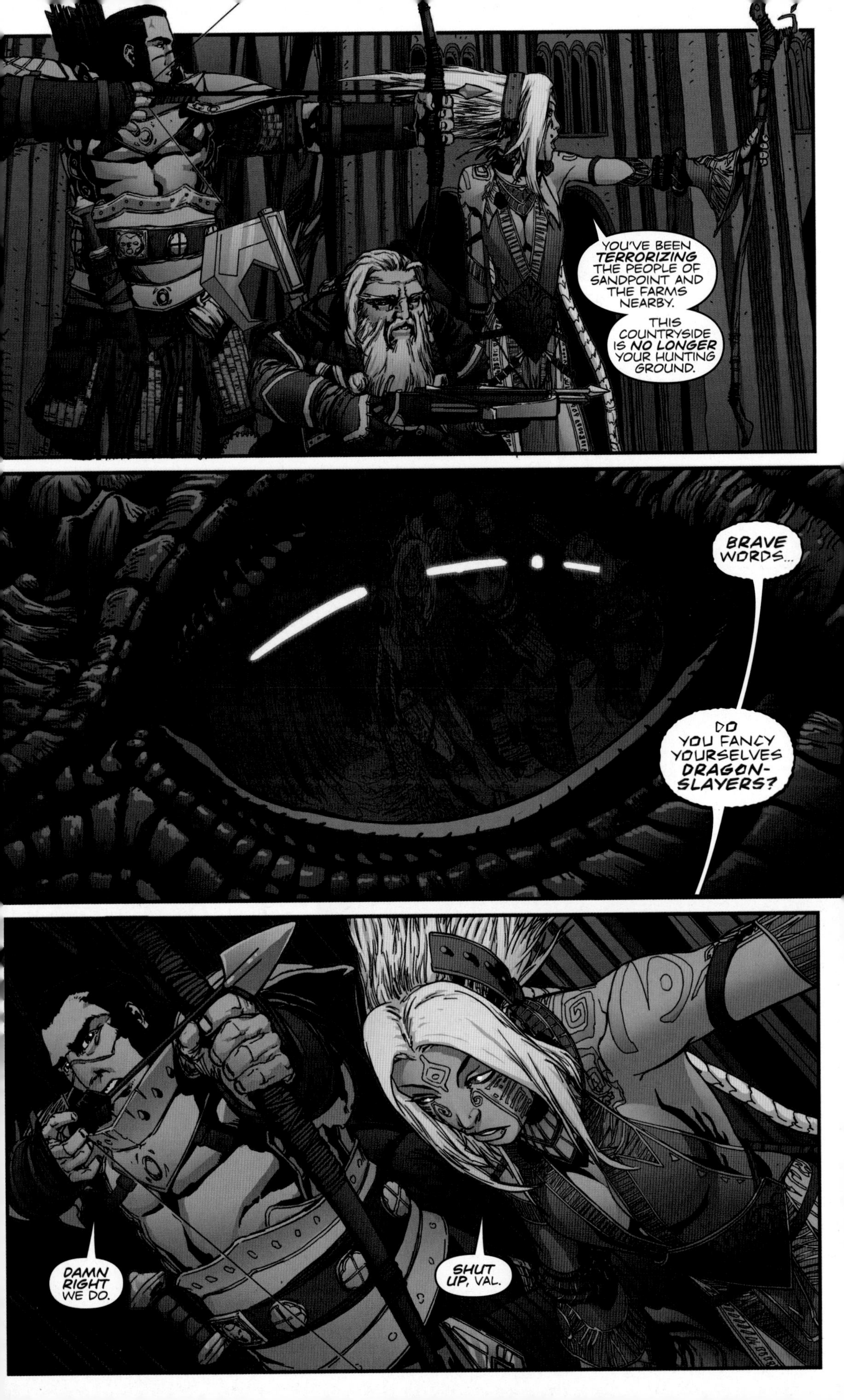
YOU'VE BEEN TERRORIZING THE PEOPLE OF SANDPOINT AND THE FARMS NEARBY.
THIS COUNTRYSIDE IS NO LONGER YOUR HUNTING GROUND.
BRAVE WORDS...
DO YOU FANCY YOURSELVES DRAGON-SLAYERS?
DAMN RIGHT WE DO.
SHUT UP, VAL.

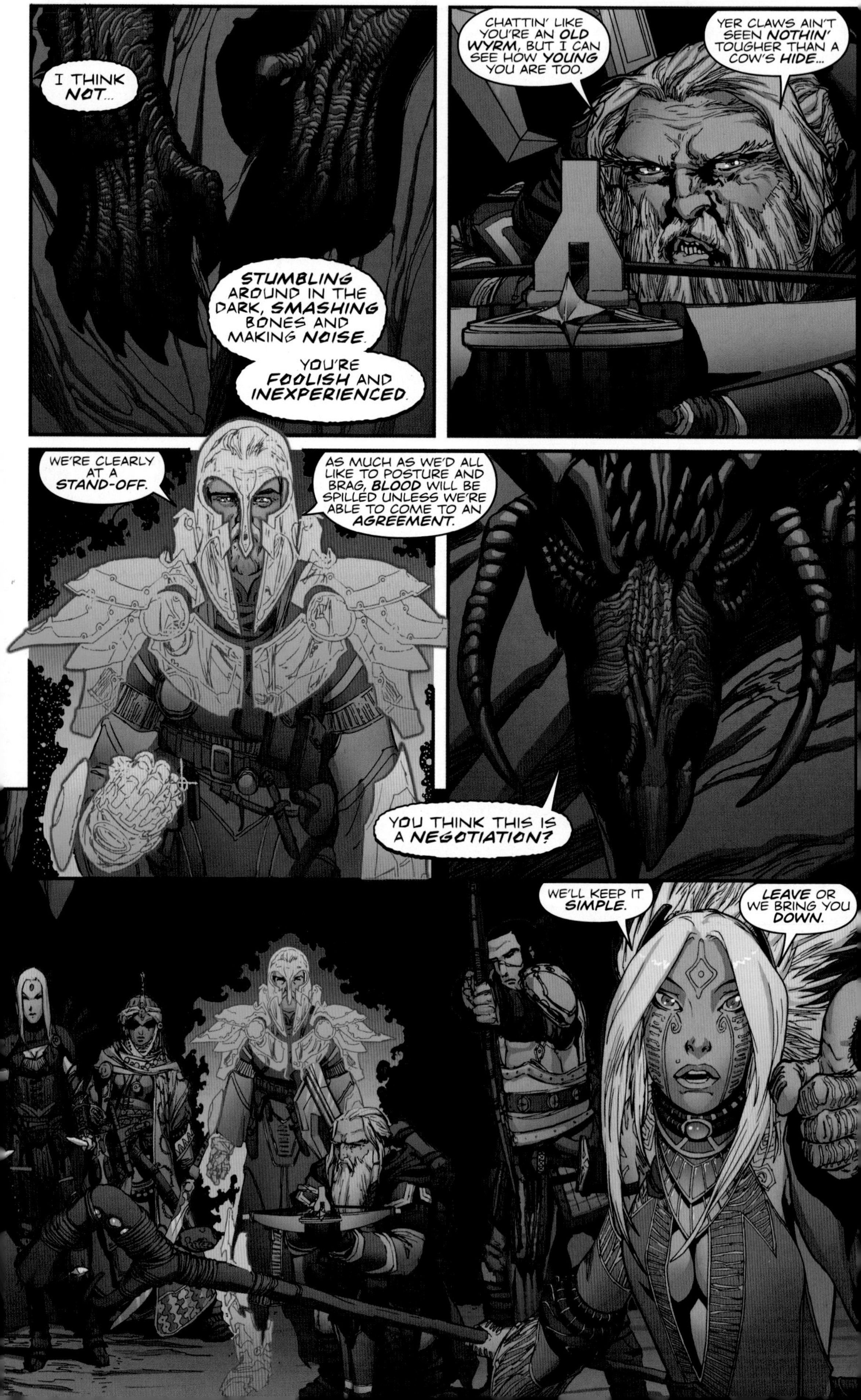
I THINK NOT...
STUMBLING AROUND IN THE DARK, SMASHING BONES AND MAKING NOISE.
YOU'RE FOOLISH AND INEXPERIENCED.
CHATTIN' LIKE YOU'RE AN OLD WYRM, BUT I CAN SEE HOW YOUNG YOU ARE TOO.
YER CLAWS AIN'T SEEN NOTHIN' TOUGHER THAN A COW'S HIDE...
WE'RE CLEARLY AT A STAND-OFF.
AS MUCH AS WE'D ALL LIKE TO POSTURE AND BRAG, BLOOD WILL BE SPILLED UNLESS WE'RE ABLE TO COME TO AN AGREEMENT.
YOU THINK THIS IS A NEGOTIATION?
WE'LL KEEP IT SIMPLE.
LEAVE OR WE BRING YOU DOWN.

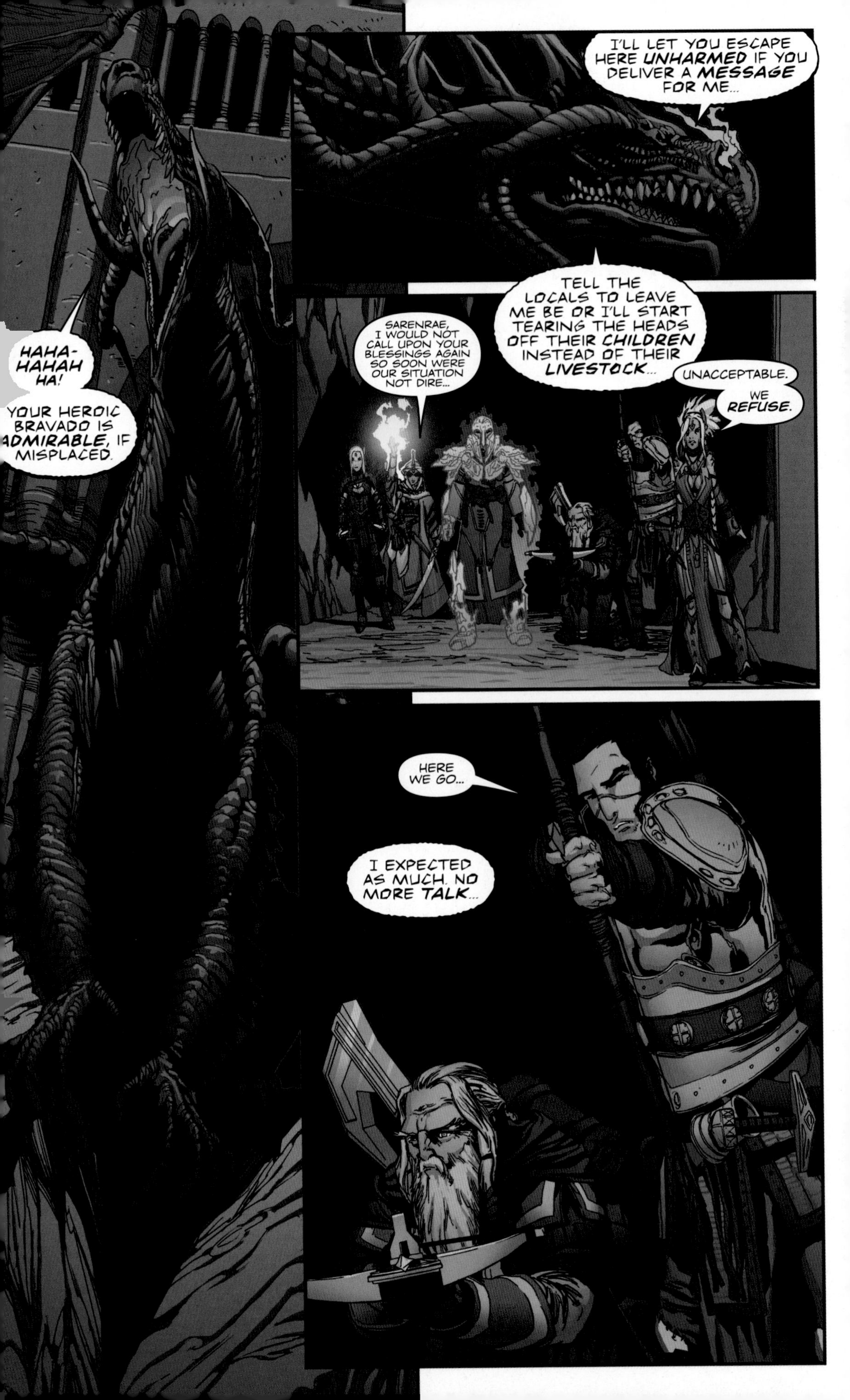
HAHA-HAHAH HA!
YOUR HEROIC BRAVADO IS ADMIRABLE, IF MISPLACED.
I'LL LET YOU ESCAPE HERE UNHARMED IF YOU DELIVER A MESSAGE FOR ME...
TELL THE LOCALS TO LEAVE ME BE OR I'LL START TEARING THE HEADS OFF THEIR CHILDREN INSTEAD OF THEIR LIVESTOCK...
SARENRAE, I WOULD NOT CALL UPON YOUR BLESSINGS AGAIN SO SOON WERE OUR SITUATION NOT DIRE...
UNACCEPTABLE.
WE REFUSE.
HERE WE GO...
I EXPECTED AS MUCH. NO MORE TALK...

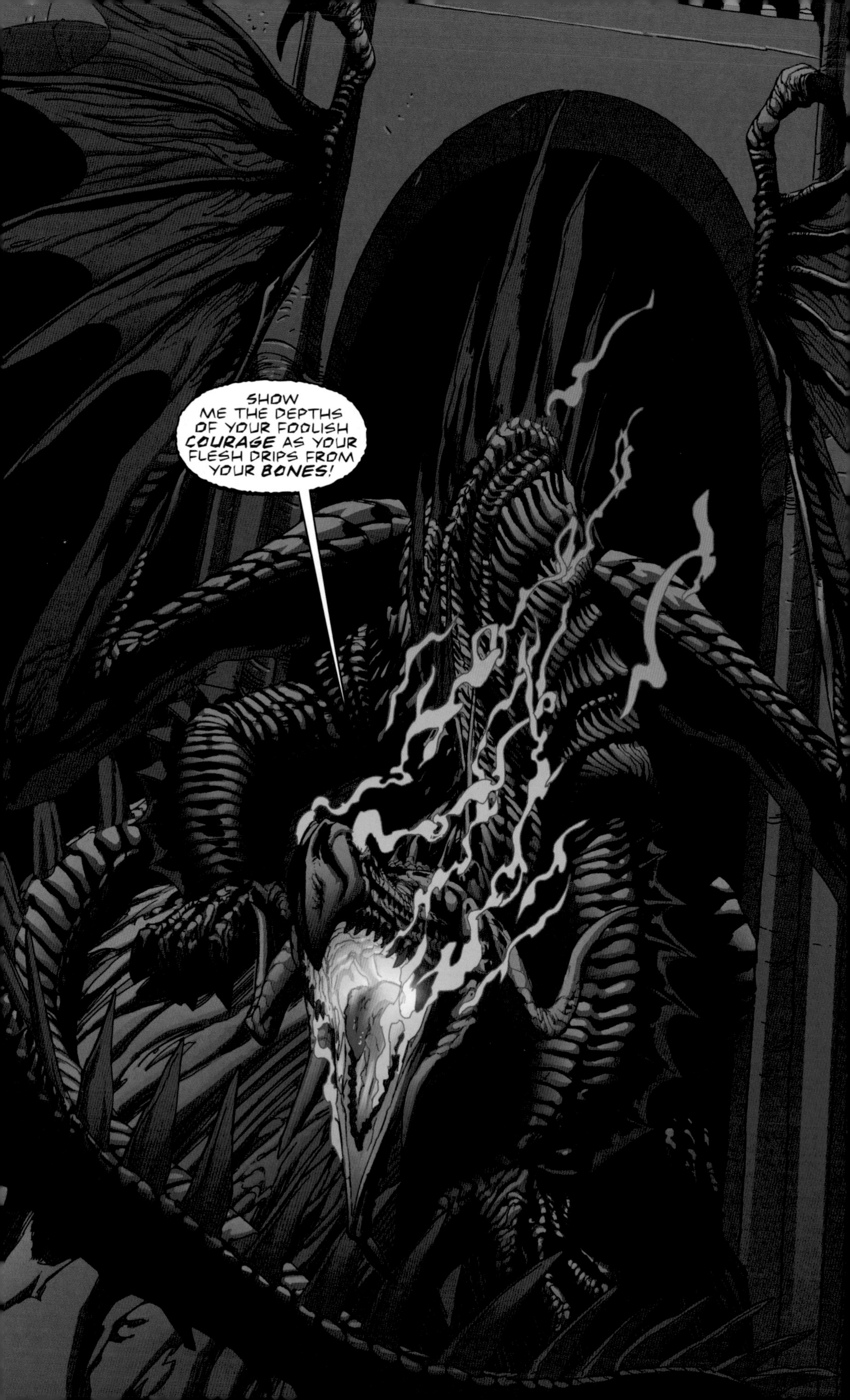
SHOW ME THE DEPTHS OF YOUR FOOLISH COURAGE AS YOUR FLESH DRIPS FROM YOUR BONES!

CHAPTER 3

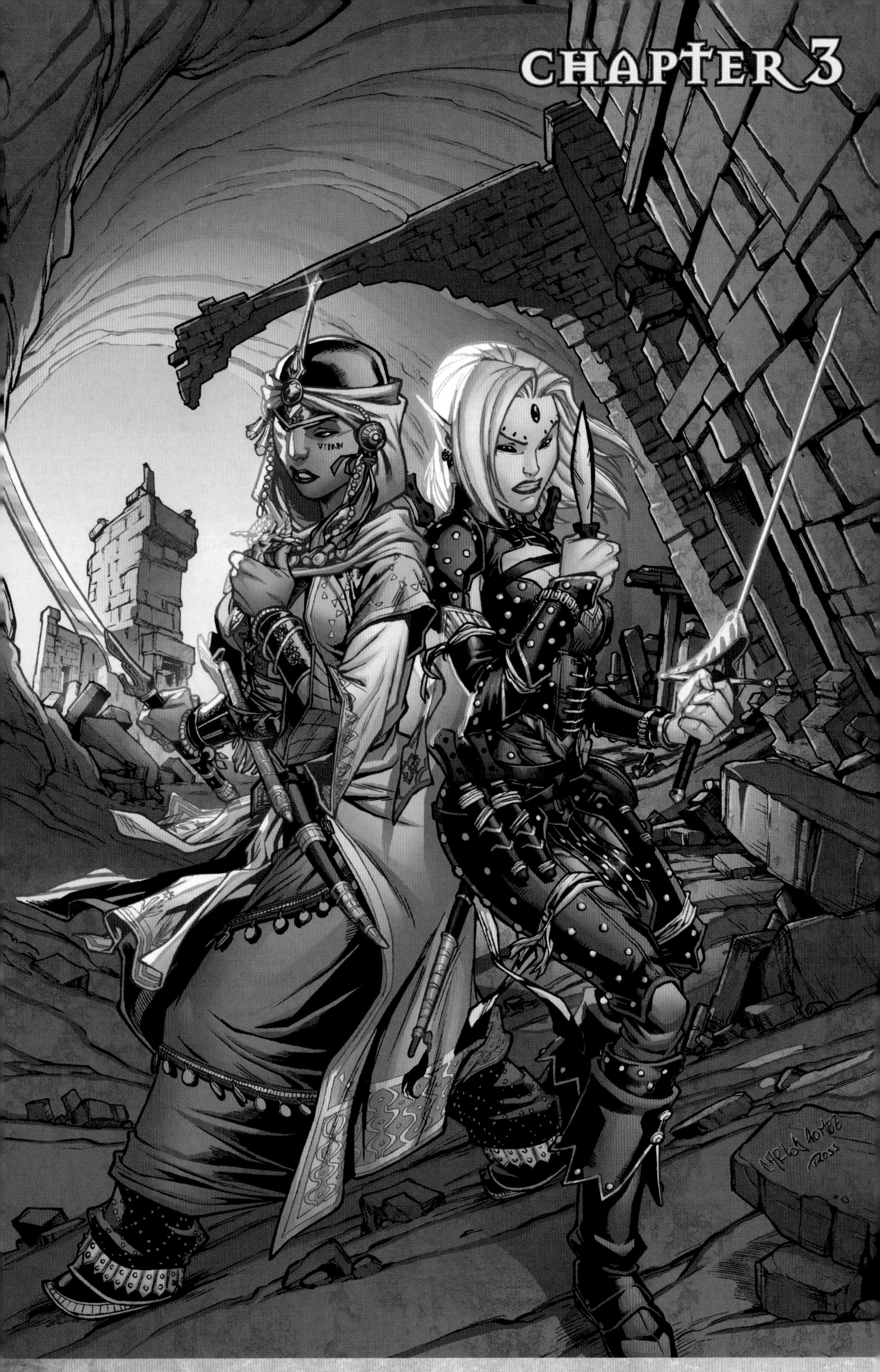

Issue #9 cover art by CARLOS GOMEZ colors by MOHAN

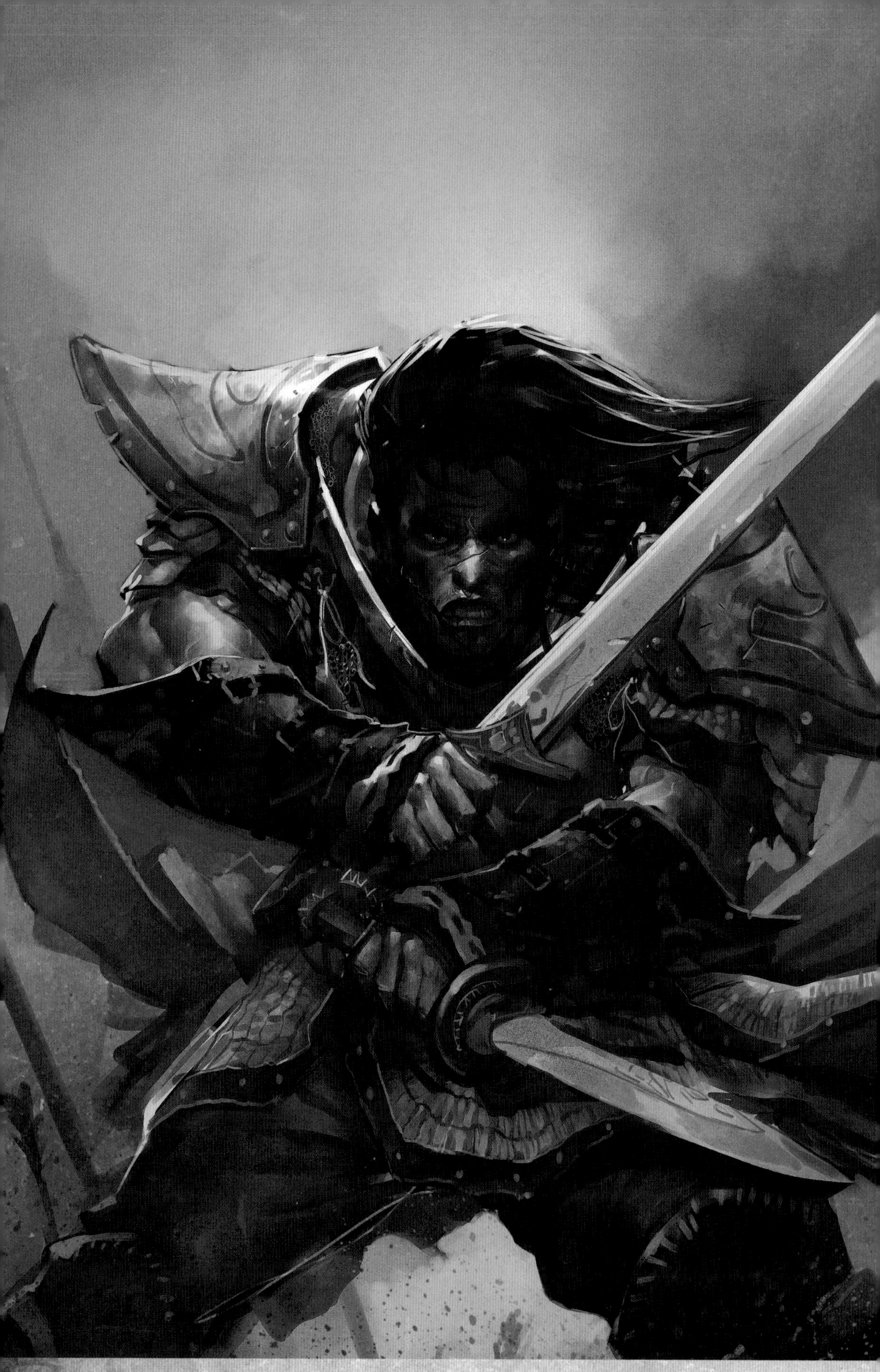

Issue #9 cover art by JORGE FARAS

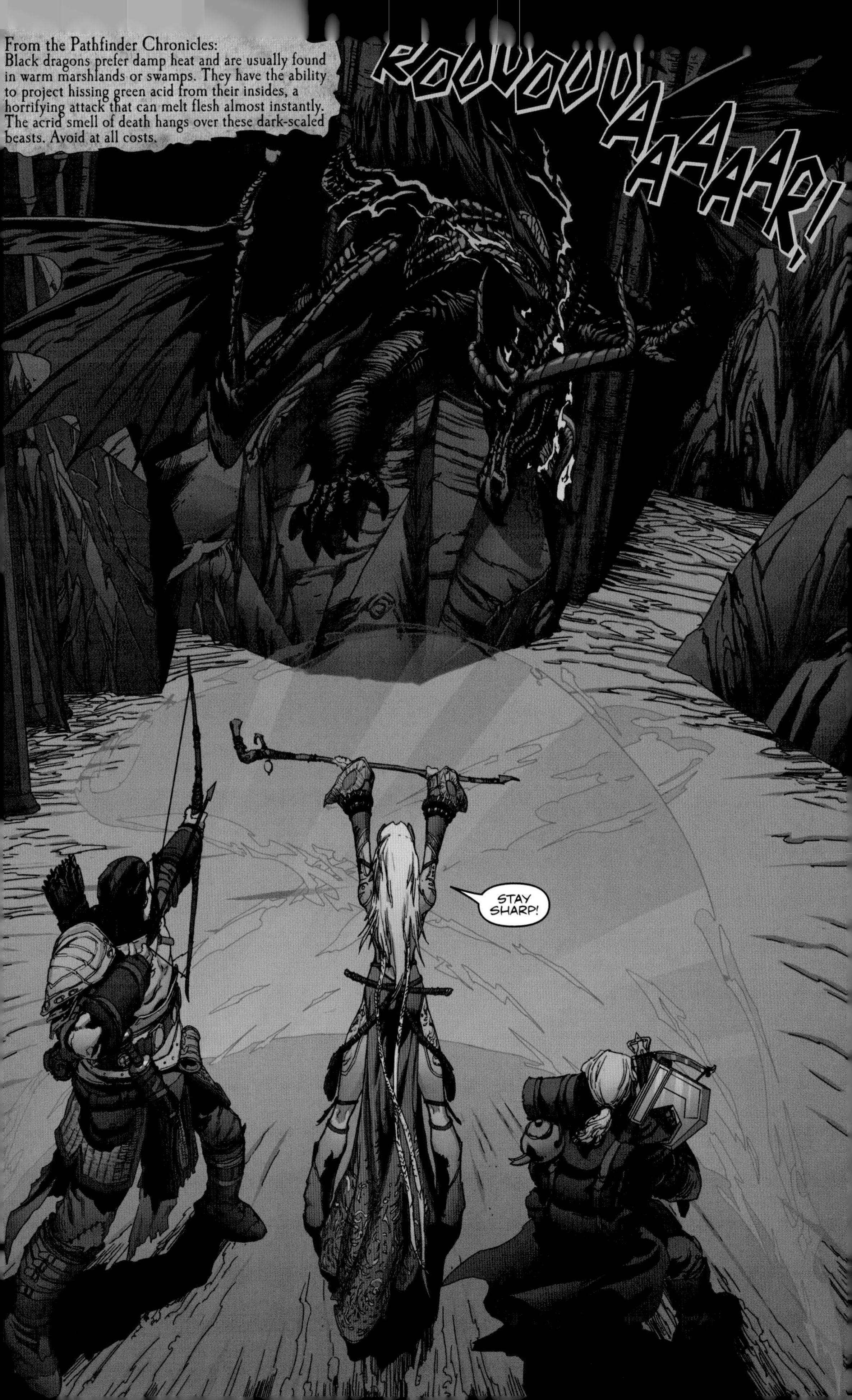
From the Pathfinder Chronicles:
Black dragons prefer damp heat and are usually found in warm marshlands or swamps. They have the ability to project hissing green acid from their insides, a horrifying attack that can melt flesh almost instantly. The acrid smell of death hangs over these dark-scaled beasts. Avoid at all costs.
ROOOOOAAAAAR!
STAY SHARP!

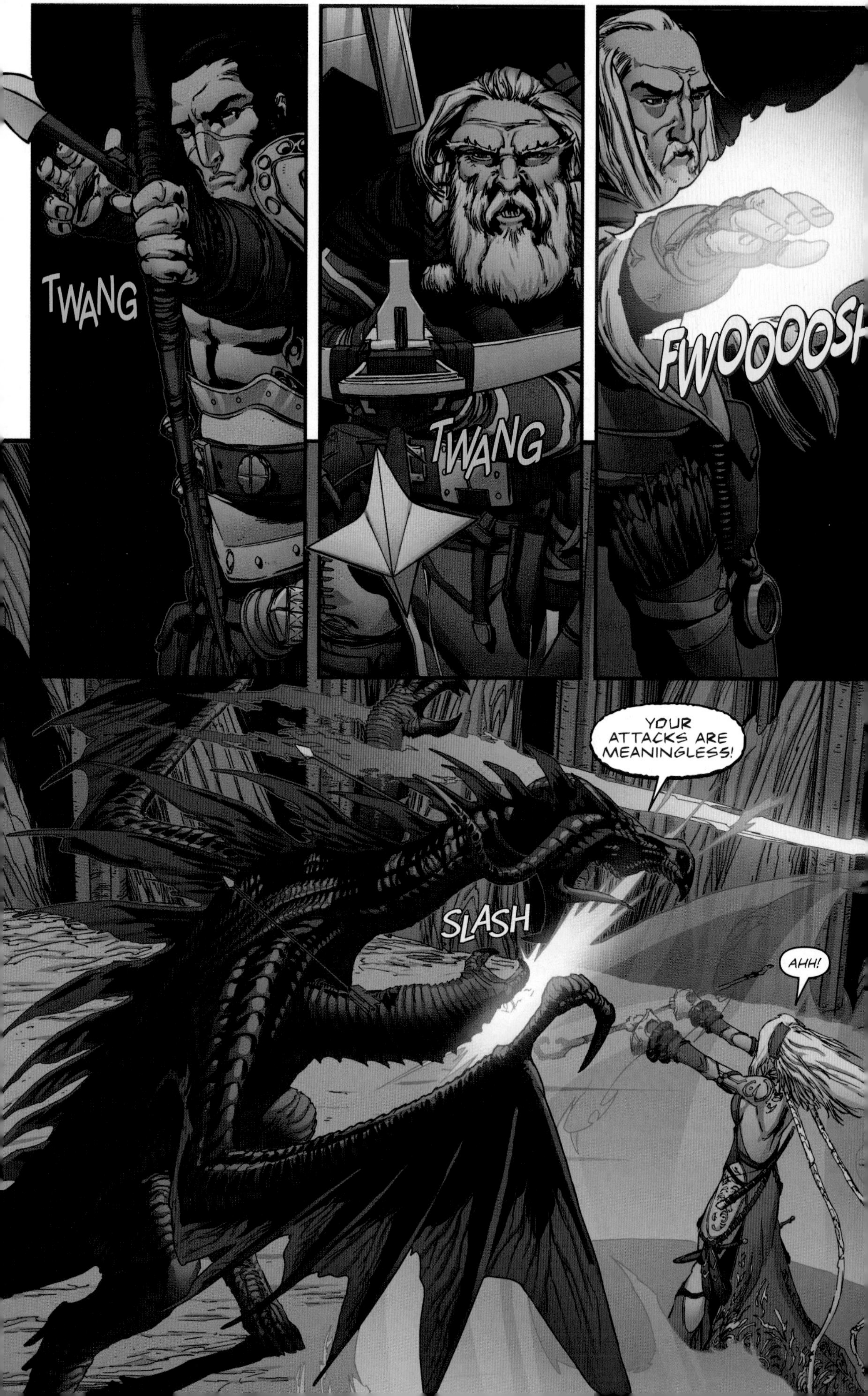
TWANG
TWANG
FWOOOOSH
YOUR ATTACKS ARE MEANINGLESS!
SLASH
AHH!

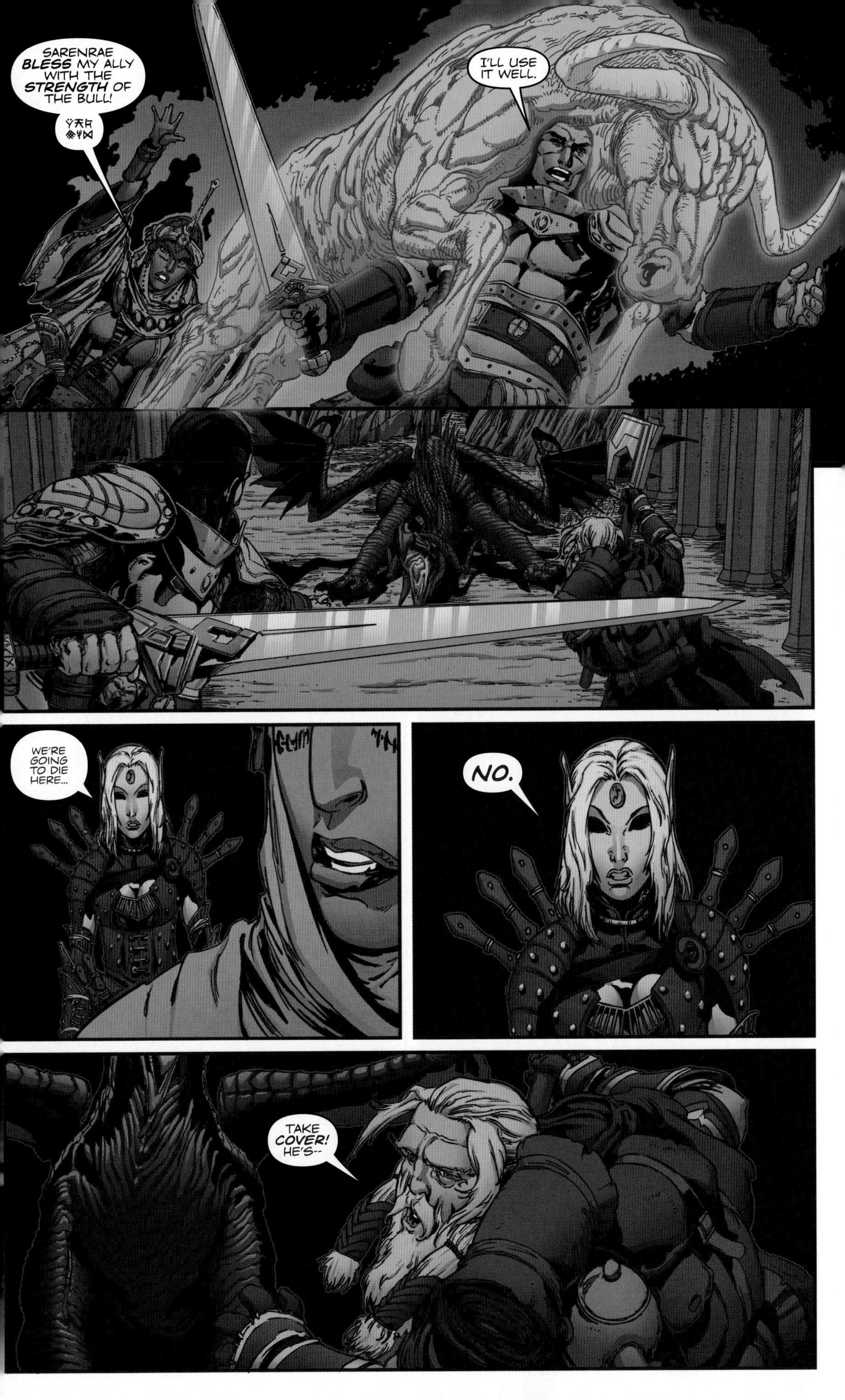

SARENRAE BLESS MY ALLY WITH THE STRENGTH OF THE BULL!
I'LL USE IT WELL.
WE'RE GOING TO DIE HERE...
NO.
TAKE COVER! HE'S--

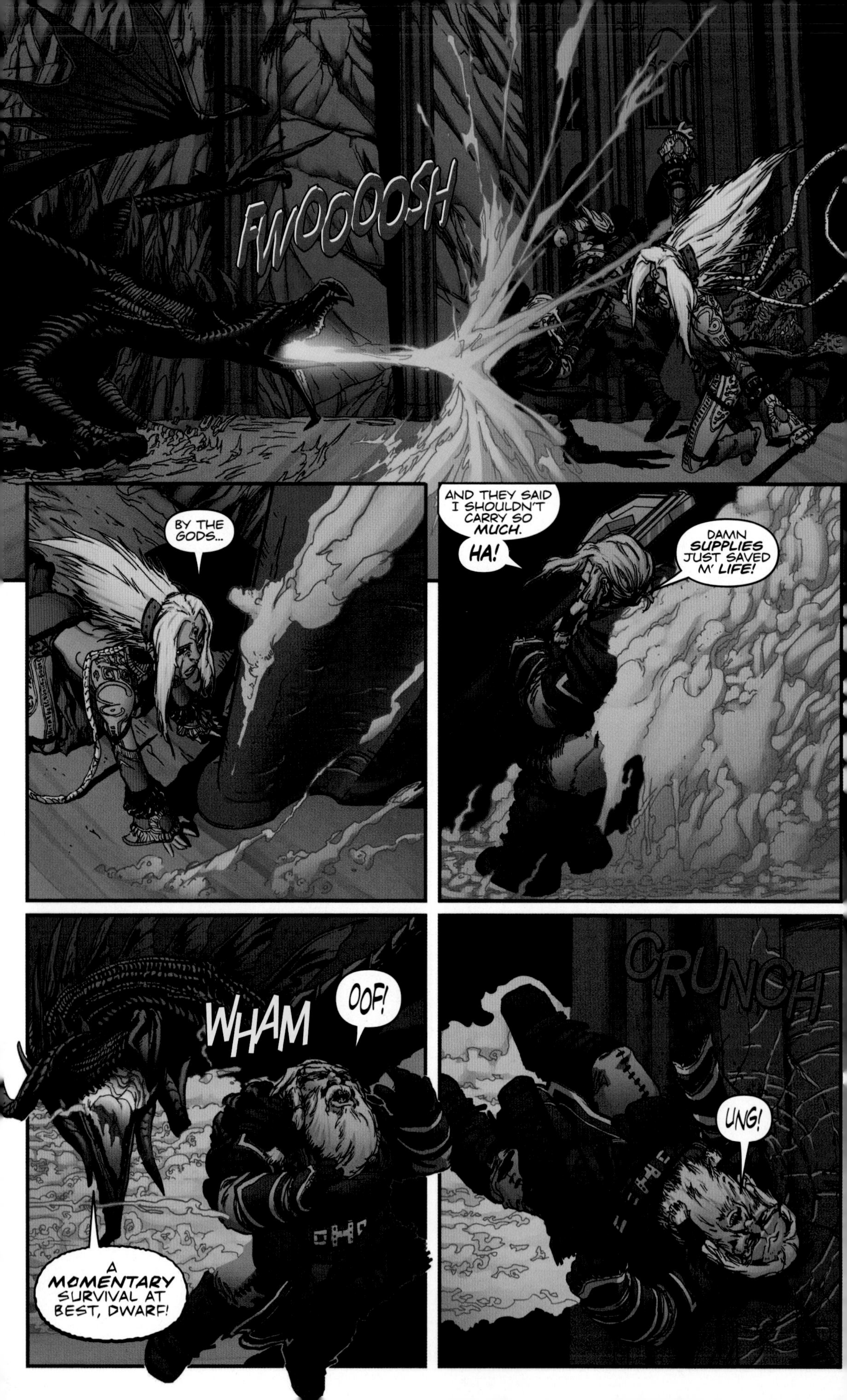
FWOOOOSH
BY THE GODS...
AND THEY SAID I SHOULDN'T CARRY SO **MUCH**.
HA!
DAMN **SUPPLIES** JUST SAVED M' **LIFE!**
WHAM
OOF!
A **MOMENTARY** SURVIVAL AT BEST, DWARF!
CRUNCH
UNG!

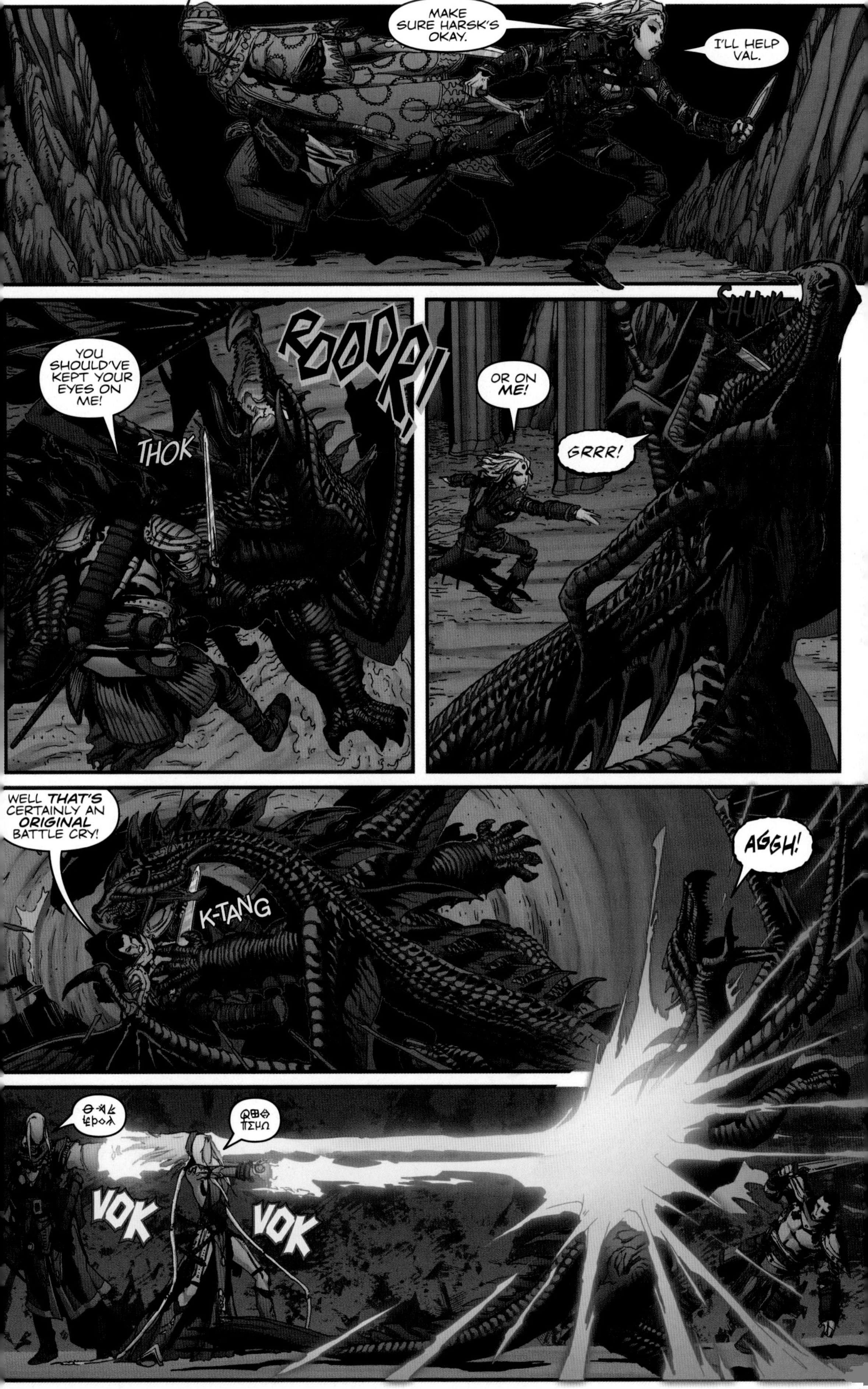
MAKE SURE HARSK'S OKAY.
I'LL HELP VAL.
YOU SHOULD'VE KEPT YOUR EYES ON ME!
ROOOR!
THOK
SHUNK
OR ON ME!
GRRR!
WELL THAT'S CERTAINLY AN ORIGINAL BATTLE CRY!
K-TANG
AGGH!
VOK
VOK

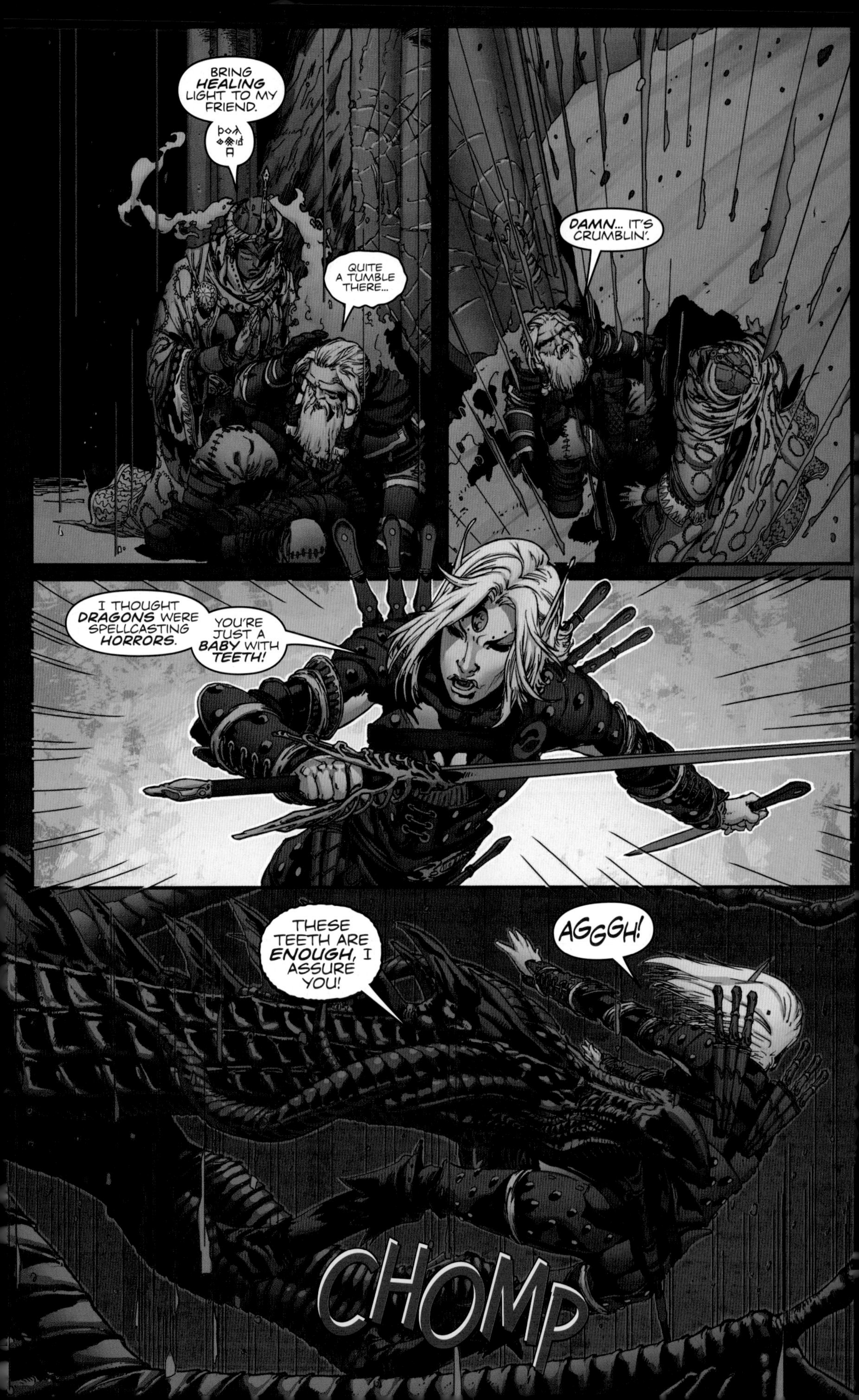
BRING HEALING LIGHT TO MY FRIEND.
QUITE A TUMBLE THERE...
DAMN... IT'S CRUMBLIN'.
I THOUGHT DRAGONS WERE SPELLCASTING HORRORS.
YOU'RE JUST A BABY WITH TEETH!
THESE TEETH ARE ENOUGH, I ASSURE YOU!
AGGGH!
CHOMP

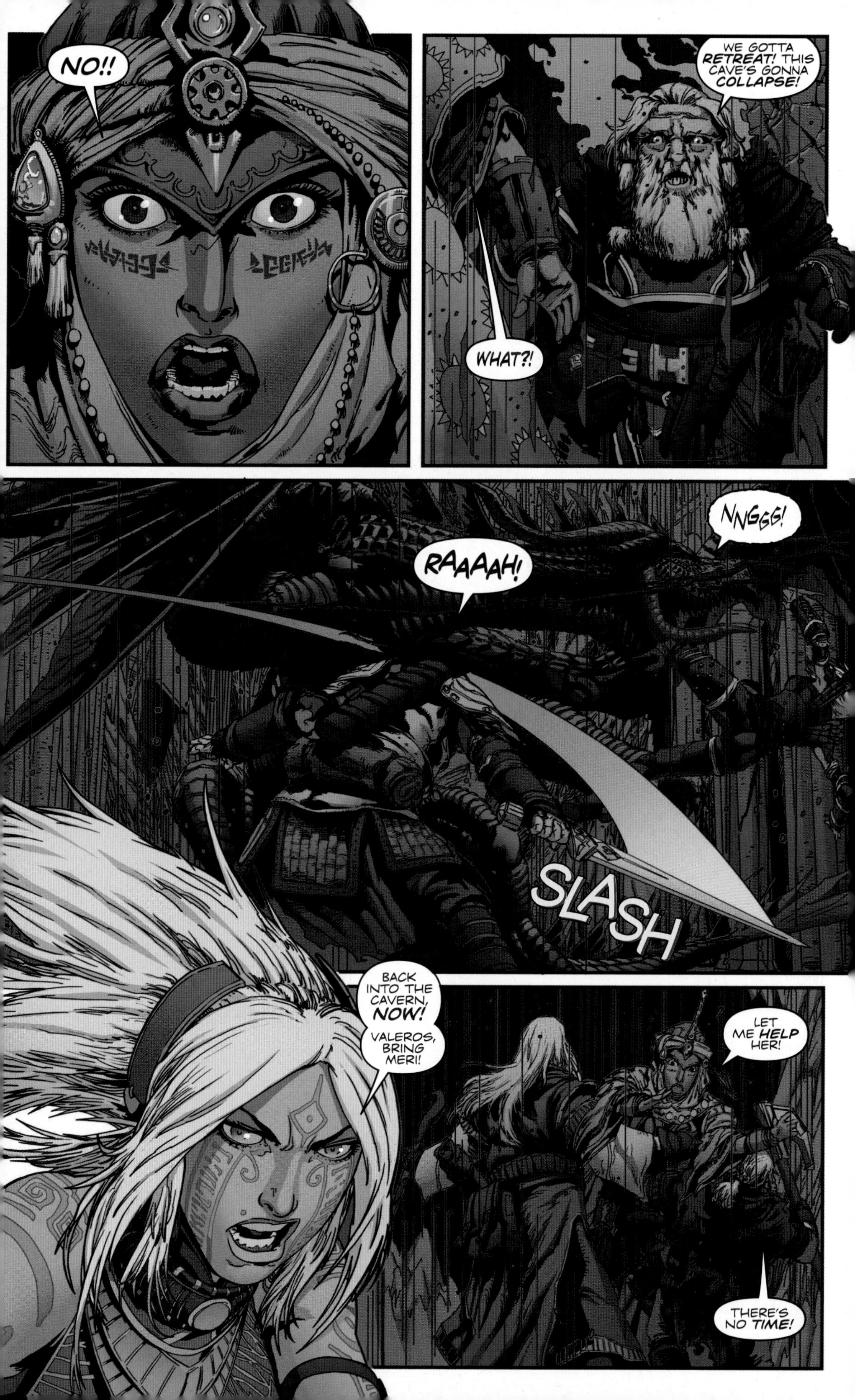
NO!!
WE GOTTA RETREAT! THIS CAVE'S GONNA COLLAPSE!
WHAT?!
NNGGG!
RAAAAH!
SLASH
BACK INTO THE CAVERN, NOW!
VALEROS, BRING MERI!
LET ME HELP HER!
THERE'S NO TIME!

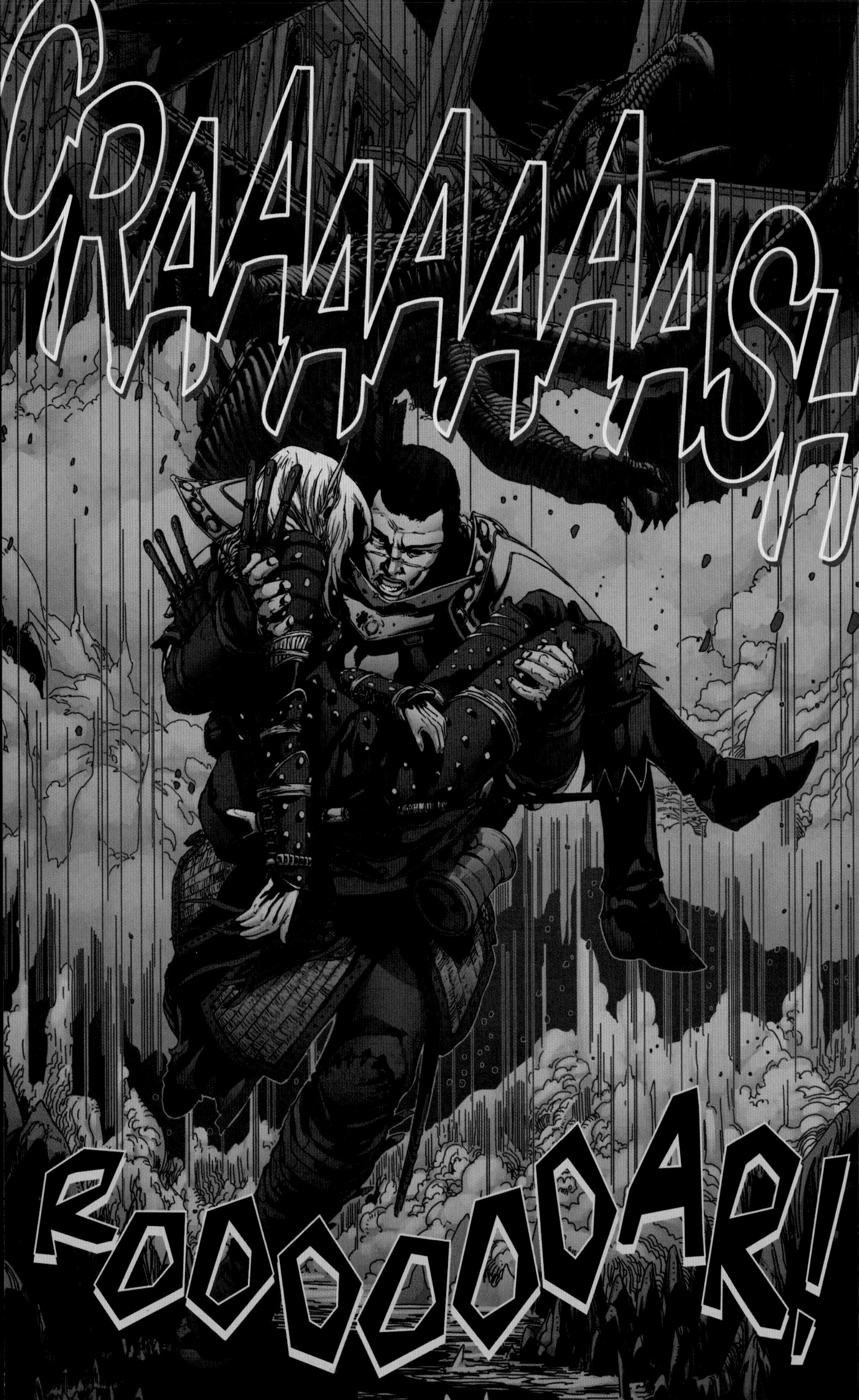
CRAAAAAAASH!
ROOOOOOAR!

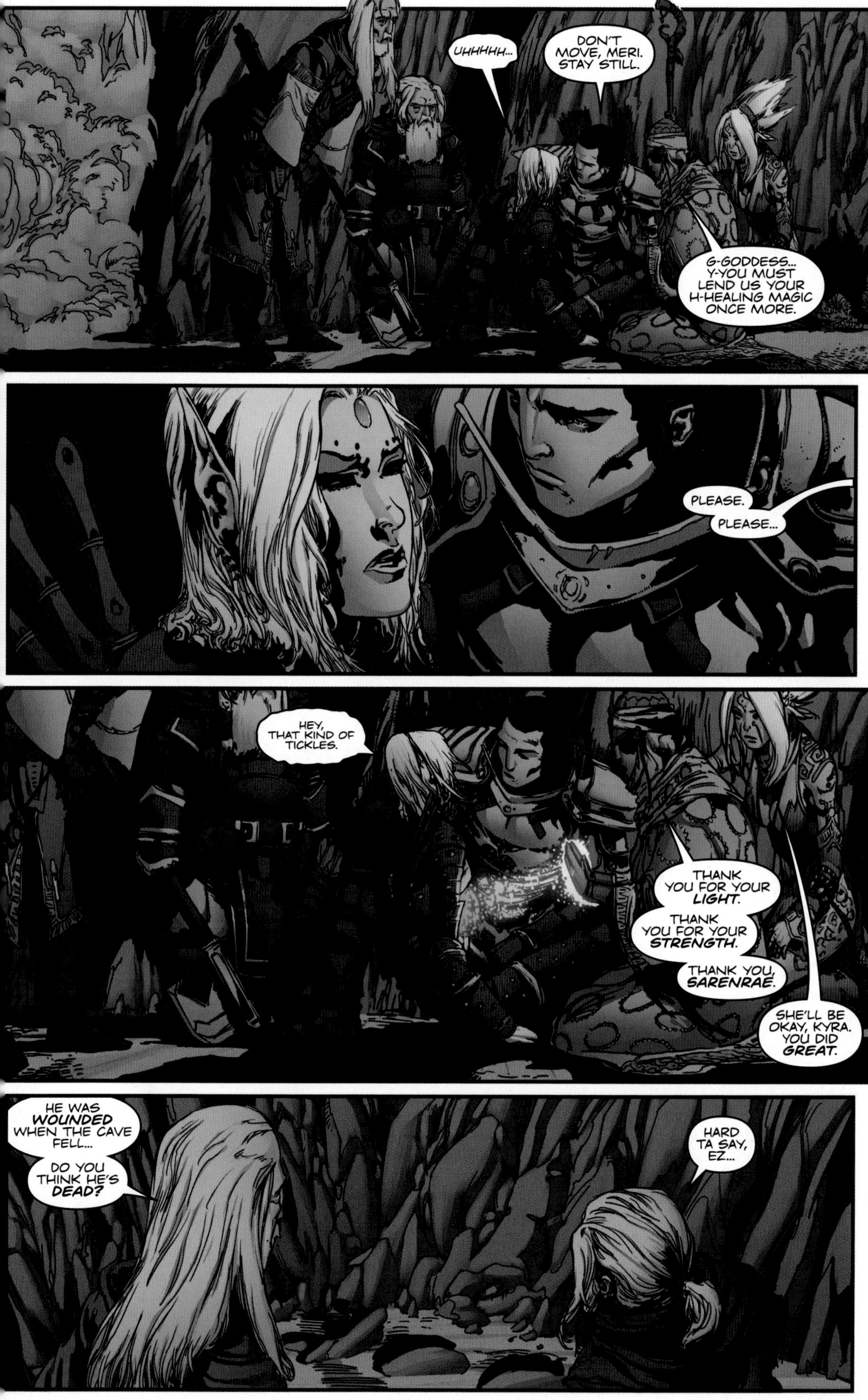
UHHHHH...
DON'T MOVE, MERI. STAY STILL.
G-GODDESS... Y-YOU MUST LEND US YOUR H-HEALING MAGIC ONCE MORE.
PLEASE.
PLEASE...
HEY, THAT KIND OF TICKLES.
THANK YOU FOR YOUR LIGHT.
THANK YOU FOR YOUR STRENGTH.
THANK YOU, SARENRAE.
SHE'LL BE OKAY, KYRA. YOU DID GREAT.
HE WAS WOUNDED WHEN THE CAVE FELL...
DO YOU THINK HE'S DEAD?
HARD TA SAY, EZ...

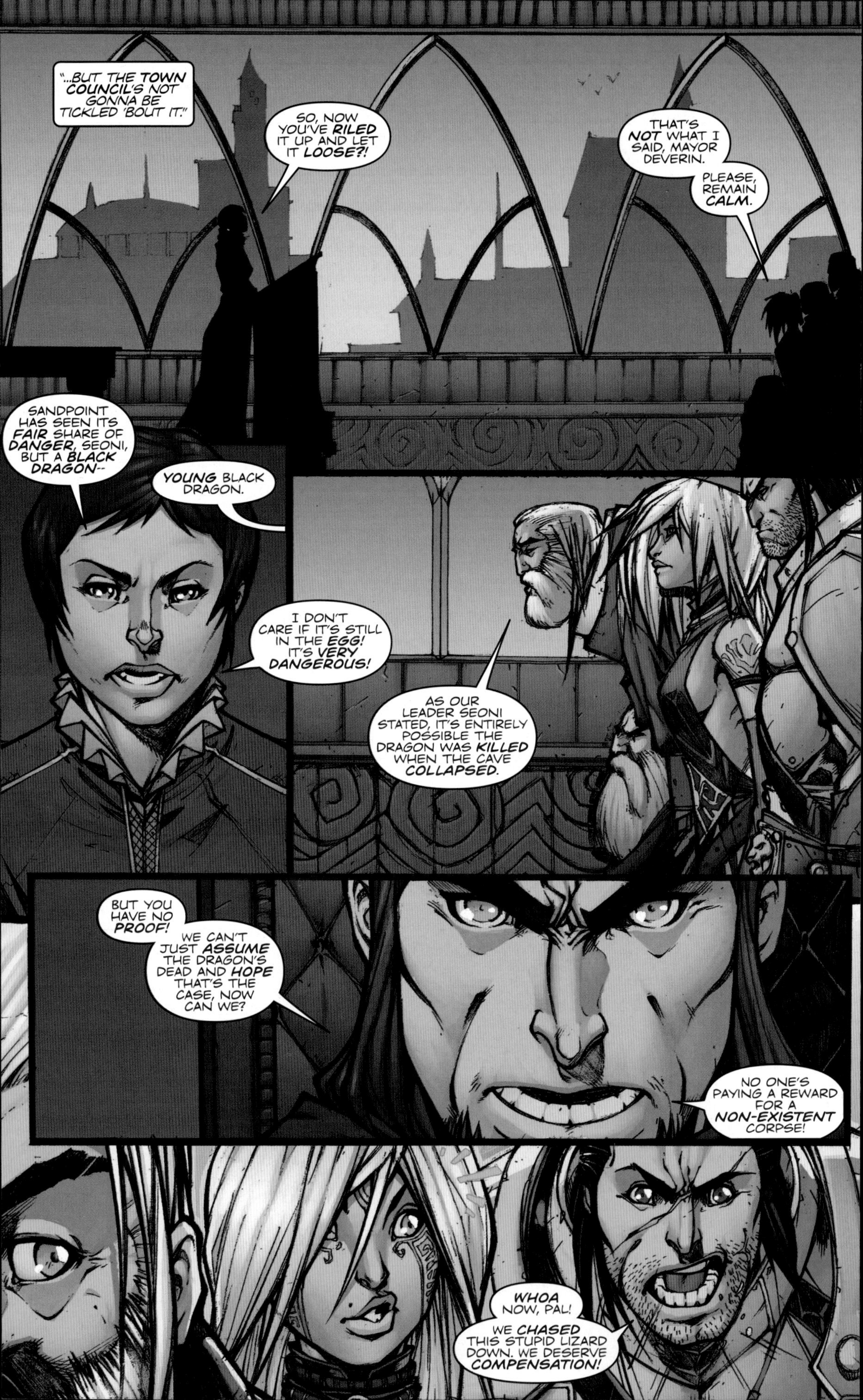
"...BUT THE TOWN COUNCIL'S NOT GONNA BE TICKLED 'BOUT IT."
SO, NOW YOU'VE RILED IT UP AND LET IT LOOSE?!
THAT'S NOT WHAT I SAID, MAYOR DEVERIN.
PLEASE, REMAIN CALM.
SANDPOINT HAS SEEN ITS FAIR SHARE OF DANGER, SEONI, BUT A BLACK DRAGON--
YOUNG BLACK DRAGON.
I DON'T CARE IF IT'S STILL IN THE EGG! IT'S VERY DANGEROUS!
AS OUR LEADER SEONI STATED, IT'S ENTIRELY POSSIBLE THE DRAGON WAS KILLED WHEN THE CAVE COLLAPSED.
BUT YOU HAVE NO PROOF!
WE CAN'T JUST ASSUME THE DRAGON'S DEAD AND HOPE THAT'S THE CASE, NOW CAN WE?
NO ONE'S PAYING A REWARD FOR A NON-EXISTENT CORPSE!
WHOA NOW, PAL!
WE CHASED THIS STUPID LIZARD DOWN. WE DESERVE COMPENSATION!

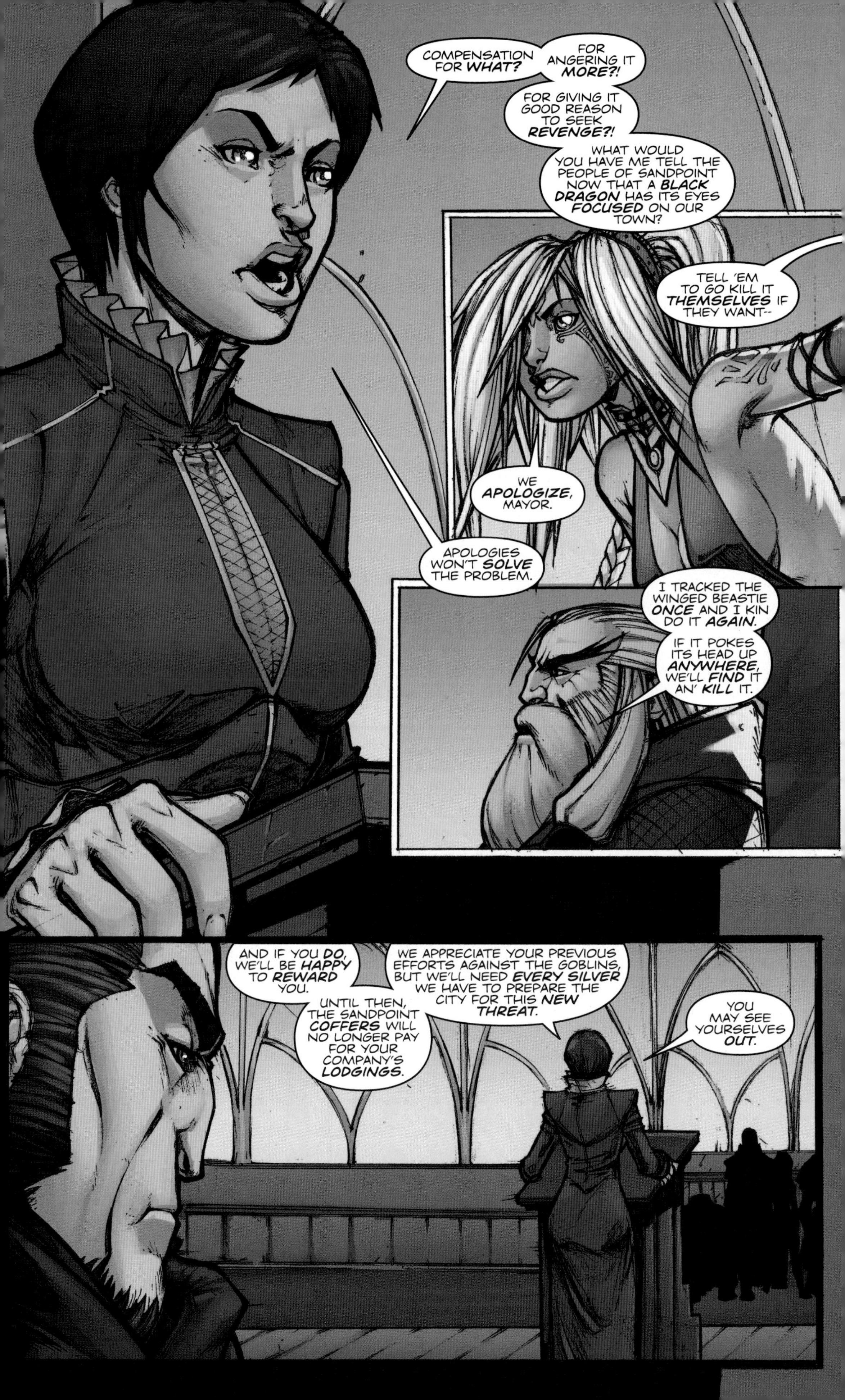
COMPENSATION FOR WHAT?
FOR ANGERING IT MORE?!
FOR GIVING IT GOOD REASON TO SEEK REVENGE?!
WHAT WOULD YOU HAVE ME TELL THE PEOPLE OF SANDPOINT NOW THAT A BLACK DRAGON HAS ITS EYES FOCUSED ON OUR TOWN?
TELL 'EM TO GO KILL IT THEMSELVES IF THEY WANT--
WE APOLOGIZE, MAYOR.
APOLOGIES WON'T SOLVE THE PROBLEM.
I TRACKED THE WINGED BEASTIE ONCE AND I KIN DO IT AGAIN.
IF IT POKES ITS HEAD UP ANYWHERE, WE'LL FIND IT AN' KILL IT.
AND IF YOU DO, WE'LL BE HAPPY TO REWARD YOU.
UNTIL THEN, THE SANDPOINT COFFERS WILL NO LONGER PAY FOR YOUR COMPANY'S LODGINGS.
WE APPRECIATE YOUR PREVIOUS EFFORTS AGAINST THE GOBLINS, BUT WE'LL NEED EVERY SILVER WE HAVE TO PREPARE THE CITY FOR THIS NEW THREAT.
YOU MAY SEE YOURSELVES OUT.

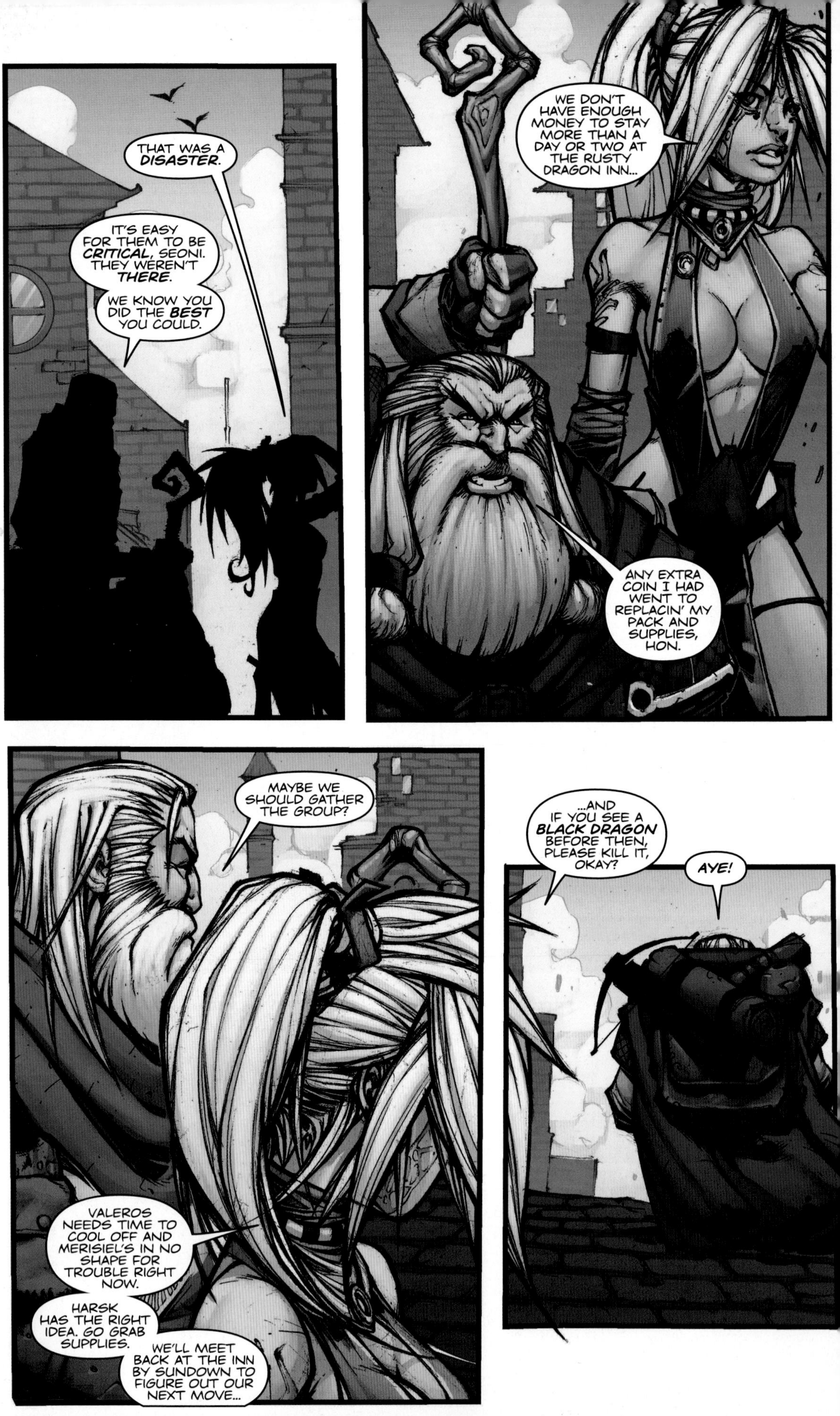
THAT WAS A *DISASTER*.
IT'S EASY FOR THEM TO BE *CRITICAL*, SEONI. THEY WEREN'T *THERE*.
WE KNOW YOU DID THE *BEST* YOU COULD.
WE DON'T HAVE ENOUGH MONEY TO STAY MORE THAN A DAY OR TWO AT THE RUSTY DRAGON INN...
ANY EXTRA COIN I HAD WENT TO REPLACIN' MY PACK AND SUPPLIES, HON.
MAYBE WE SHOULD GATHER THE GROUP?
VALEROS NEEDS TIME TO COOL OFF AND MERISIEL'S IN NO SHAPE FOR TROUBLE RIGHT NOW.
HARSK HAS THE RIGHT IDEA. GO GRAB SUPPLIES.
WE'LL MEET BACK AT THE INN BY SUNDOWN TO FIGURE OUT OUR NEXT MOVE...
...AND IF YOU SEE A *BLACK DRAGON* BEFORE THEN, PLEASE KILL IT, OKAY?
AYE!

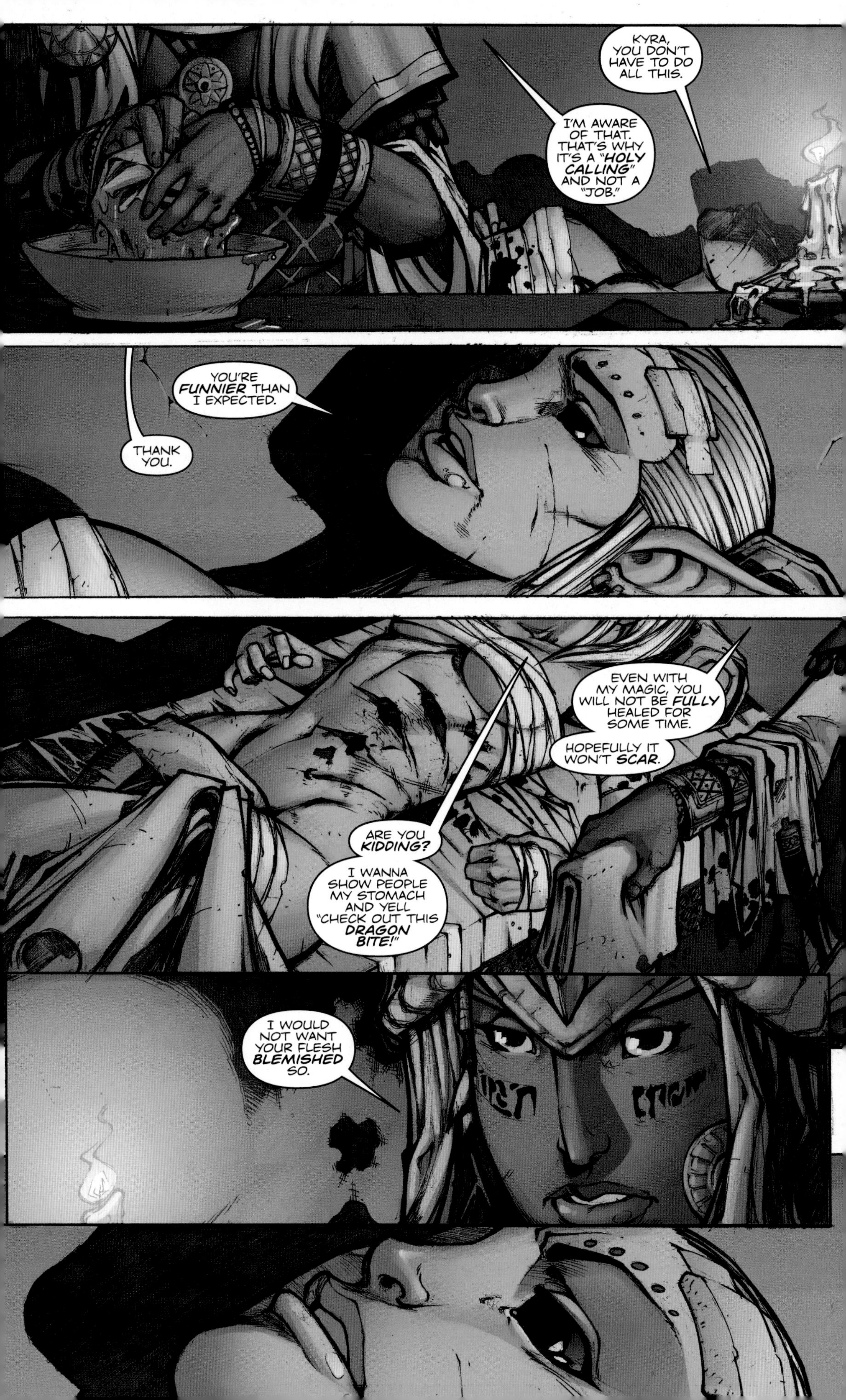
KYRA, YOU DON'T HAVE TO DO ALL THIS.
I'M AWARE OF THAT. THAT'S WHY IT'S A "HOLY CALLING" AND NOT A "JOB."
YOU'RE FUNNIER THAN I EXPECTED.
THANK YOU.
EVEN WITH MY MAGIC, YOU WILL NOT BE FULLY HEALED FOR SOME TIME.
HOPEFULLY IT WON'T SCAR.
ARE YOU KIDDING?
I WANNA SHOW PEOPLE MY STOMACH AND YELL "CHECK OUT THIS DRAGON BITE!"
I WOULD NOT WANT YOUR FLESH BLEMISHED SO.

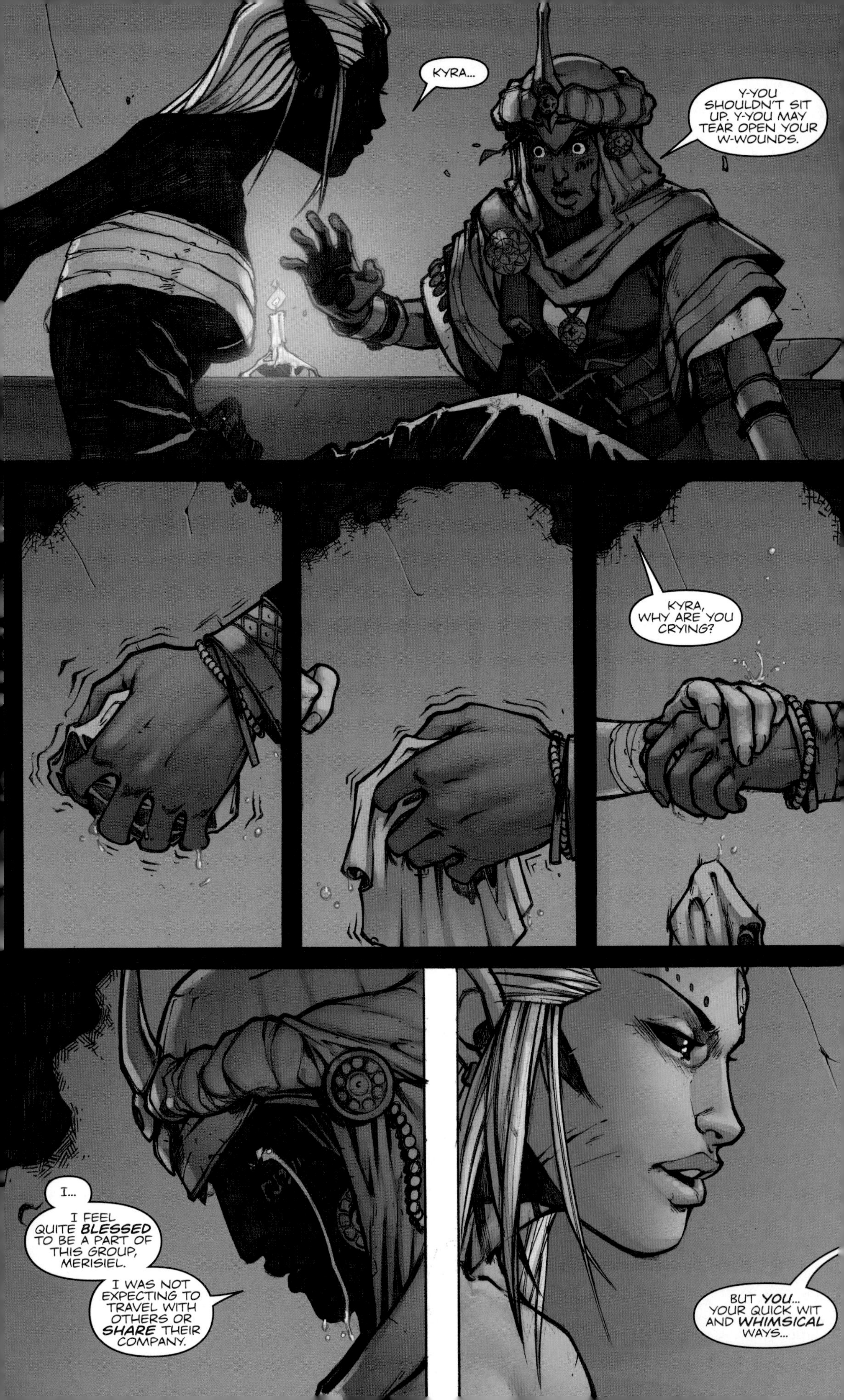
KYRA...
Y-YOU SHOULDN'T SIT UP. Y-YOU MAY TEAR OPEN YOUR W-WOUNDS.
KYRA, WHY ARE YOU CRYING?
I...
I FEEL QUITE **BLESSED** TO BE A PART OF THIS GROUP, MERISIEL.
I WAS NOT EXPECTING TO TRAVEL WITH OTHERS OR **SHARE** THEIR COMPANY.
BUT **YOU**... YOUR QUICK WIT AND **WHIMSICAL** WAYS...

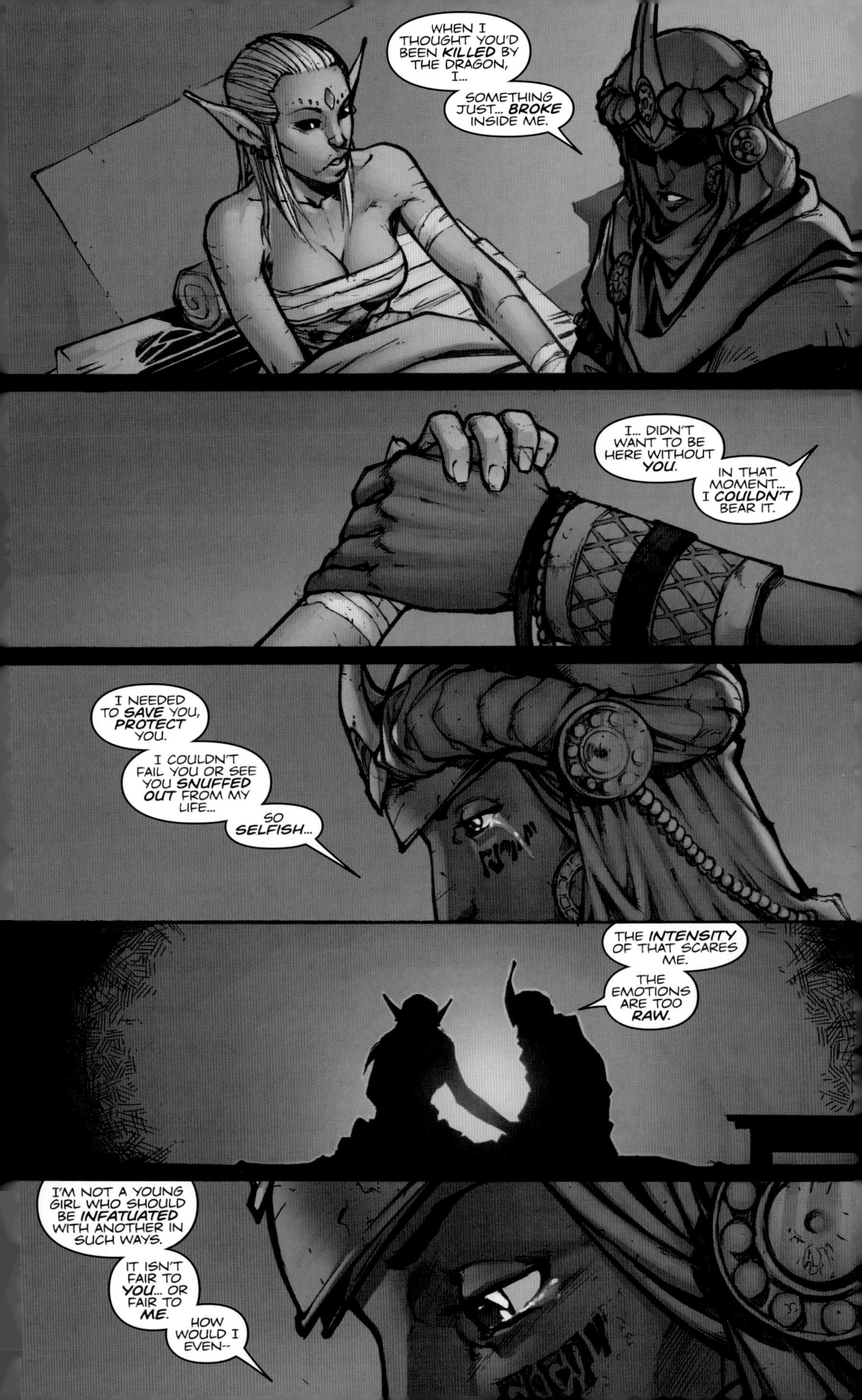
WHEN I THOUGHT YOU'D BEEN KILLED BY THE DRAGON, I...
SOMETHING JUST... BROKE INSIDE ME.
I... DIDN'T WANT TO BE HERE WITHOUT YOU.
IN THAT MOMENT... I COULDN'T BEAR IT.
I NEEDED TO SAVE YOU, PROTECT YOU.
I COULDN'T FAIL YOU OR SEE YOU SNUFFED OUT FROM MY LIFE...
SO SELFISH...
THE INTENSITY OF THAT SCARES ME.
THE EMOTIONS ARE TOO RAW.
I'M NOT A YOUNG GIRL WHO SHOULD BE INFATUATED WITH ANOTHER IN SUCH WAYS.
IT ISN'T FAIR TO YOU... OR FAIR TO ME.
HOW WOULD I EVEN--

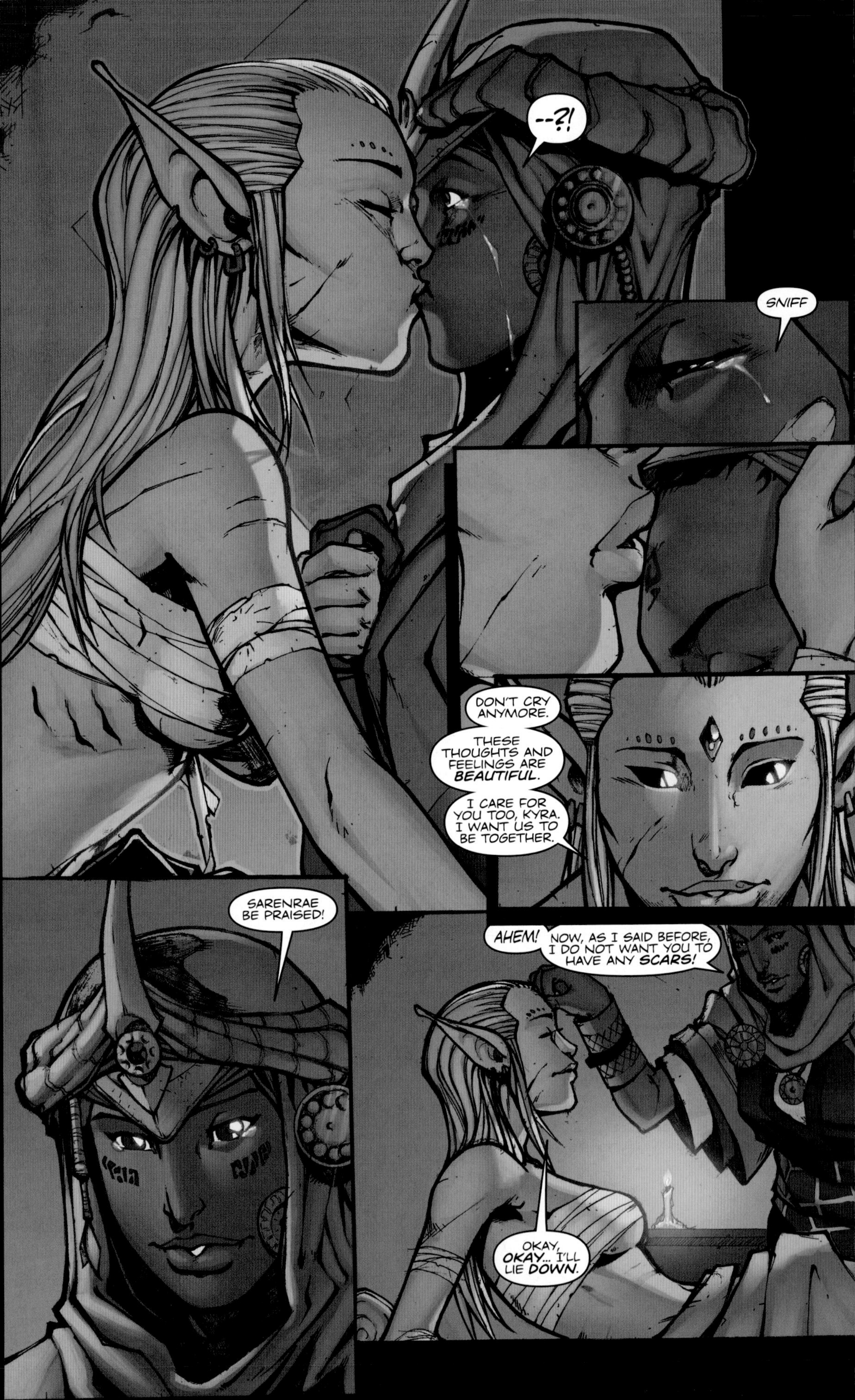
--?!
SNIFF
DON'T CRY ANYMORE.
THESE THOUGHTS AND FEELINGS ARE BEAUTIFUL.
I CARE FOR YOU TOO, KYRA. I WANT US TO BE TOGETHER.
SARENRAE BE PRAISED!
AHEM!
NOW, AS I SAID BEFORE, I DO NOT WANT YOU TO HAVE ANY SCARS!
OKAY, OKAY... I'LL LIE DOWN.

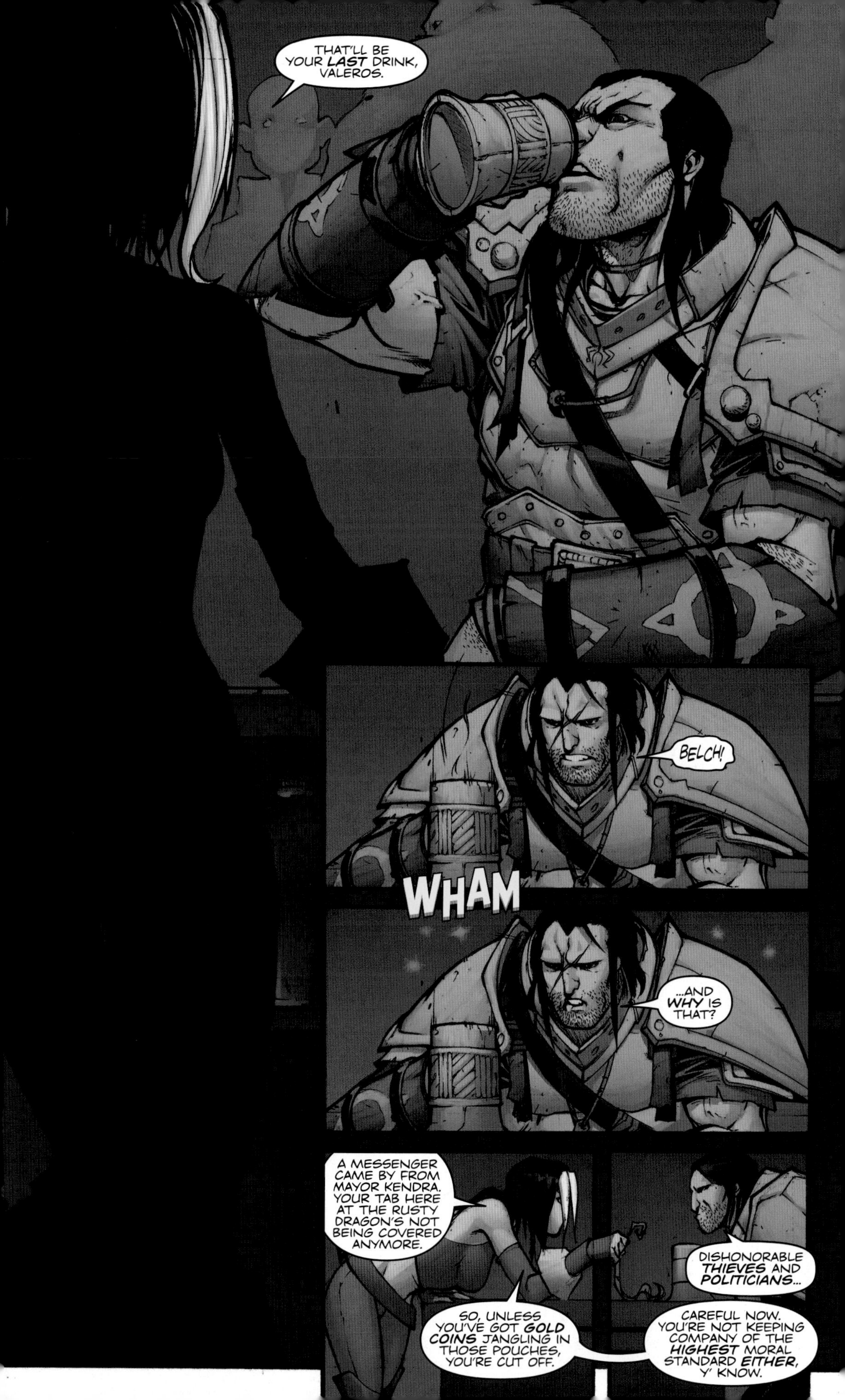
THAT'LL BE YOUR LAST DRINK, VALEROS.
BELCH!
WHAM
...AND WHY IS THAT?
A MESSENGER CAME BY FROM MAYOR KENDRA. YOUR TAB HERE AT THE RUSTY DRAGON'S NOT BEING COVERED ANYMORE.
SO, UNLESS YOU'VE GOT GOLD COINS JANGLING IN THOSE POUCHES, YOU'RE CUT OFF.
DISHONORABLE THIEVES AND POLITICIANS...
CAREFUL NOW. YOU'RE NOT KEEPING COMPANY OF THE HIGHEST MORAL STANDARD EITHER, Y' KNOW.

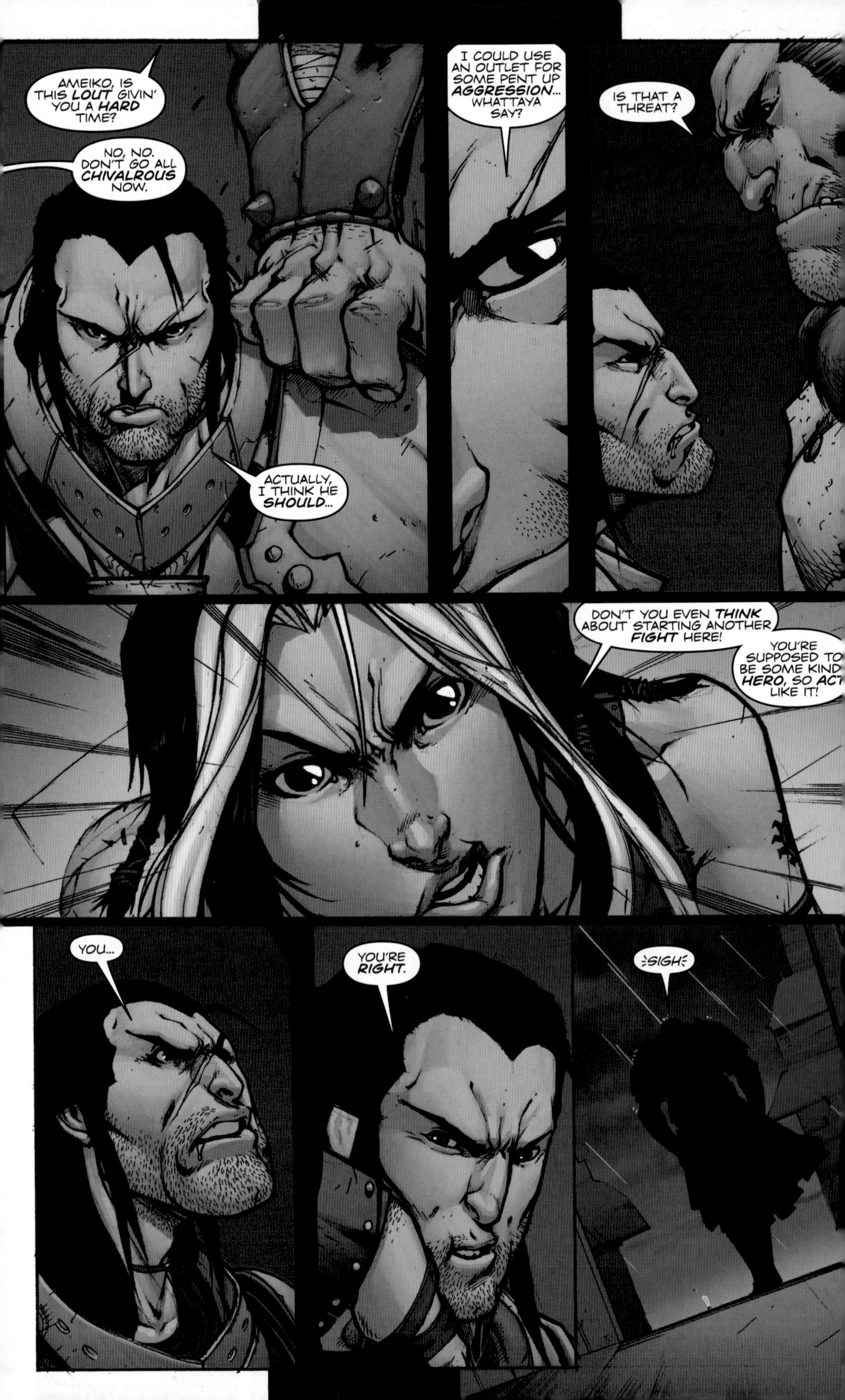
AMEIKO, IS THIS **LOUT** GIVIN' YOU A **HARD** TIME?
NO, NO. DON'T GO ALL **CHIVALROUS** NOW.
ACTUALLY, I THINK HE **SHOULD**...
I COULD USE AN OUTLET FOR SOME PENT UP **AGGRESSION**... WHATTAYA SAY?
IS THAT A THREAT?
DON'T YOU EVEN **THINK** ABOUT STARTING ANOTHER **FIGHT** HERE!
YOU'RE SUPPOSED TO BE SOME KIND **HERO**, SO **ACT** LIKE IT!
YOU...
YOU'RE **RIGHT**.
SIGH

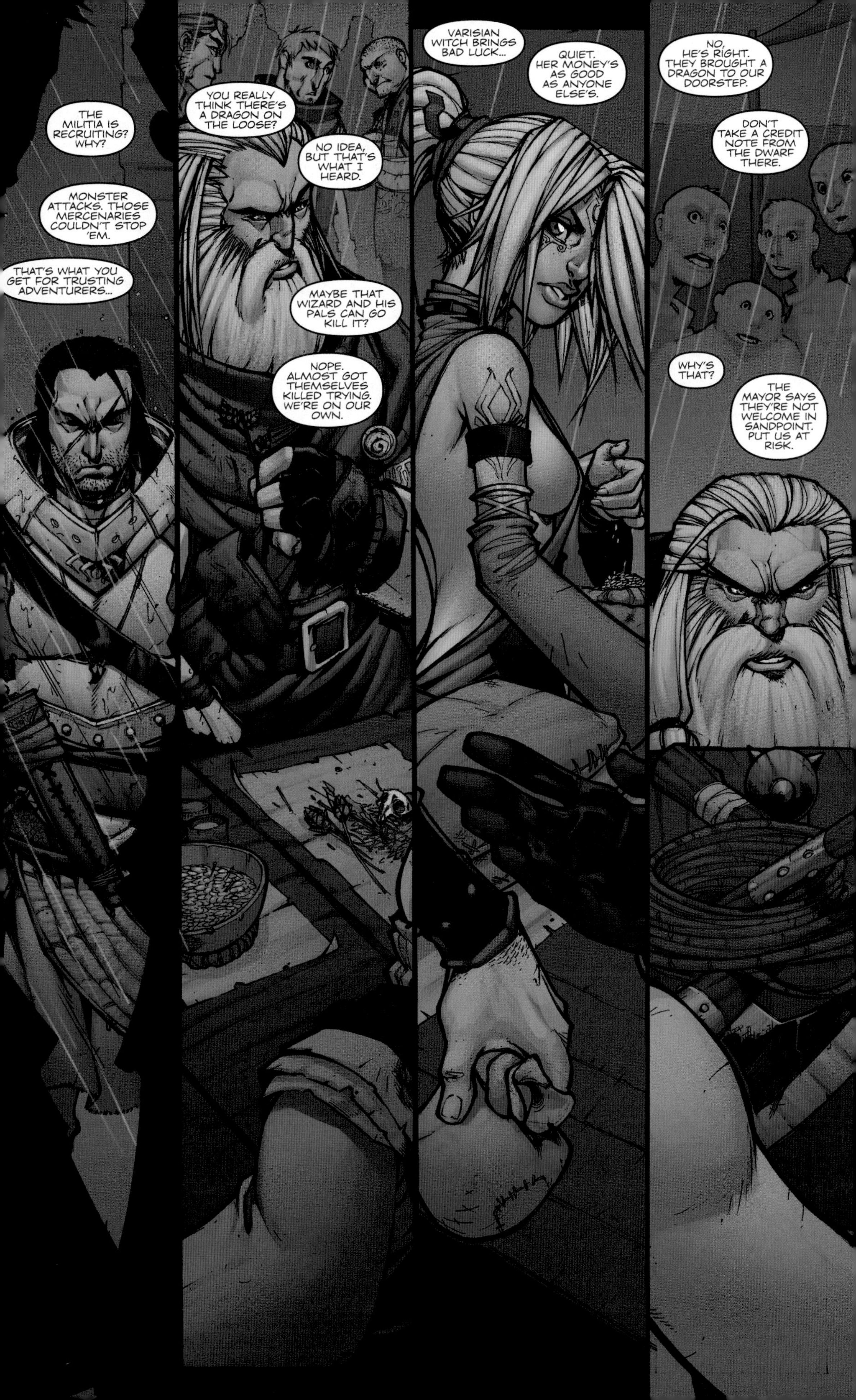
THE MILITIA IS RECRUITING? WHY?
MONSTER ATTACKS. THOSE MERCENARIES COULDN'T STOP 'EM.
THAT'S WHAT YOU GET FOR TRUSTING ADVENTURERS...
YOU REALLY THINK THERE'S A DRAGON ON THE LOOSE?
NO IDEA, BUT THAT'S WHAT I HEARD.
MAYBE THAT WIZARD AND HIS PALS CAN GO KILL IT?
NOPE. ALMOST GOT THEMSELVES KILLED TRYING. WE'RE ON OUR OWN.
VARISIAN WITCH BRINGS BAD LUCK...
QUIET. HER MONEY'S AS GOOD AS ANYONE ELSE'S.
NO, HE'S RIGHT. THEY BROUGHT A DRAGON TO OUR DOORSTEP.
DON'T TAKE A CREDIT NOTE FROM THE DWARF THERE.
WHY'S THAT?
THE MAYOR SAYS THEY'RE NOT WELCOME IN SANDPOINT. PUT US AT RISK.

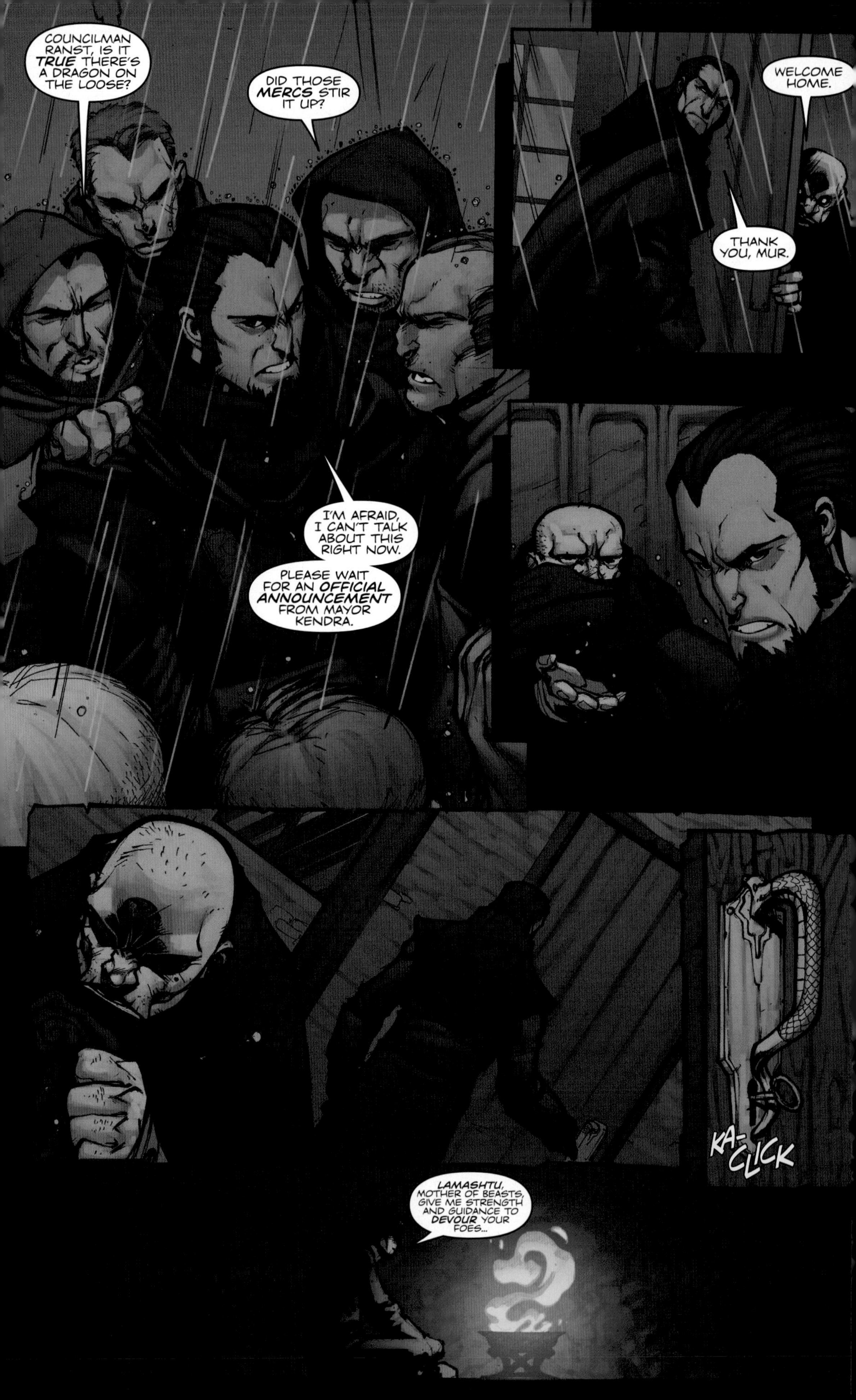
COUNCILMAN RANST, IS IT TRUE THERE'S A DRAGON ON THE LOOSE?
DID THOSE MERCS STIR IT UP?
I'M AFRAID, I CAN'T TALK ABOUT THIS RIGHT NOW.
PLEASE WAIT FOR AN OFFICIAL ANNOUNCEMENT FROM MAYOR KENDRA.
WELCOME HOME.
THANK YOU, MUR.
KA-CLICK
LAMASHTU, MOTHER OF BEASTS, GIVE ME STRENGTH AND GUIDANCE TO DEVOUR YOUR FOES...

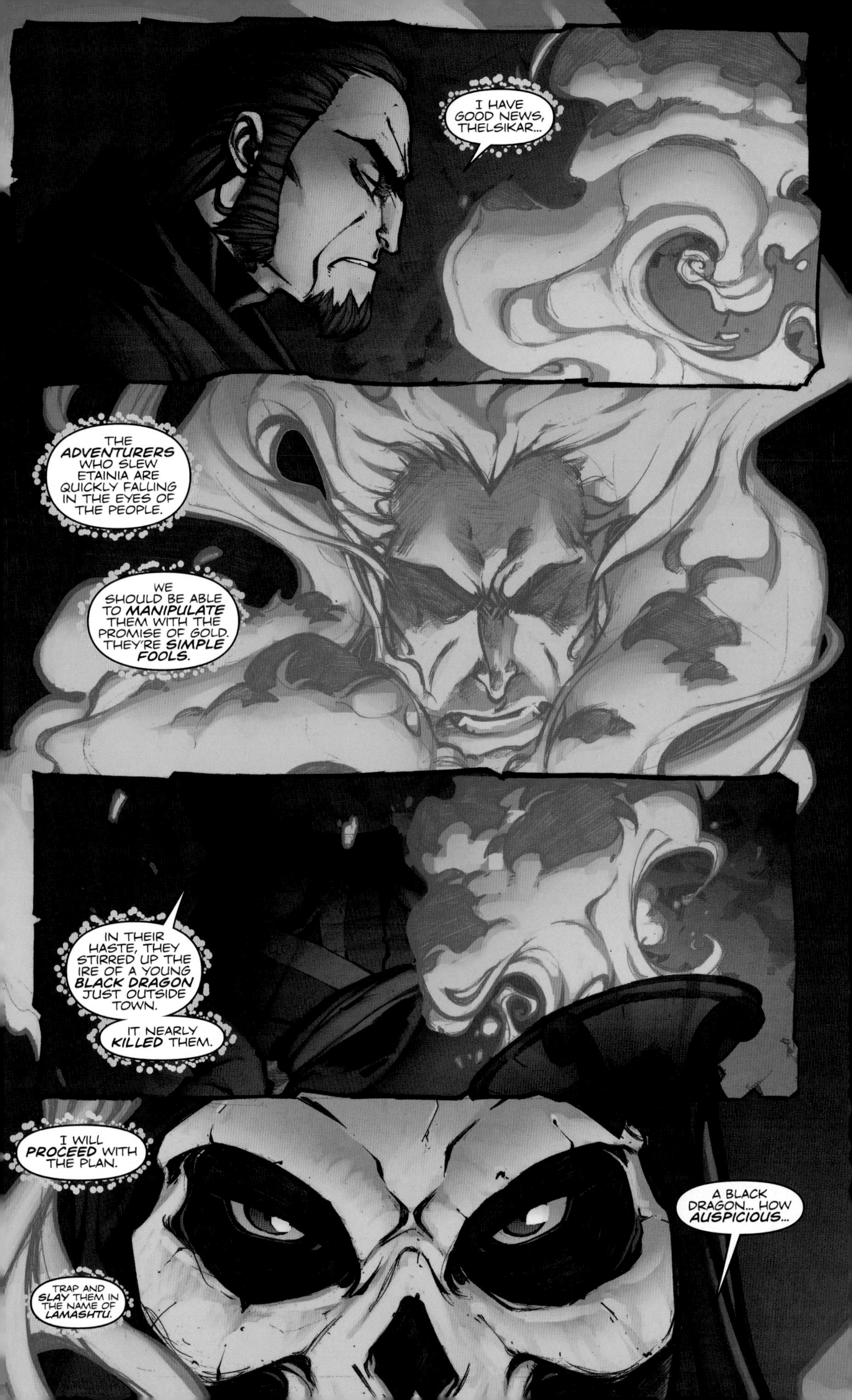
I HAVE GOOD NEWS, THELSIKAR...
THE ADVENTURERS WHO SLEW ETAINIA ARE QUICKLY FALLING IN THE EYES OF THE PEOPLE.
WE SHOULD BE ABLE TO MANIPULATE THEM WITH THE PROMISE OF GOLD. THEY'RE SIMPLE FOOLS.
IN THEIR HASTE, THEY STIRRED UP THE IRE OF A YOUNG BLACK DRAGON JUST OUTSIDE TOWN.
IT NEARLY KILLED THEM.
I WILL PROCEED WITH THE PLAN.
A BLACK DRAGON... HOW AUSPICIOUS...
TRAP AND SLAY THEM IN THE NAME OF LAMASHTU.

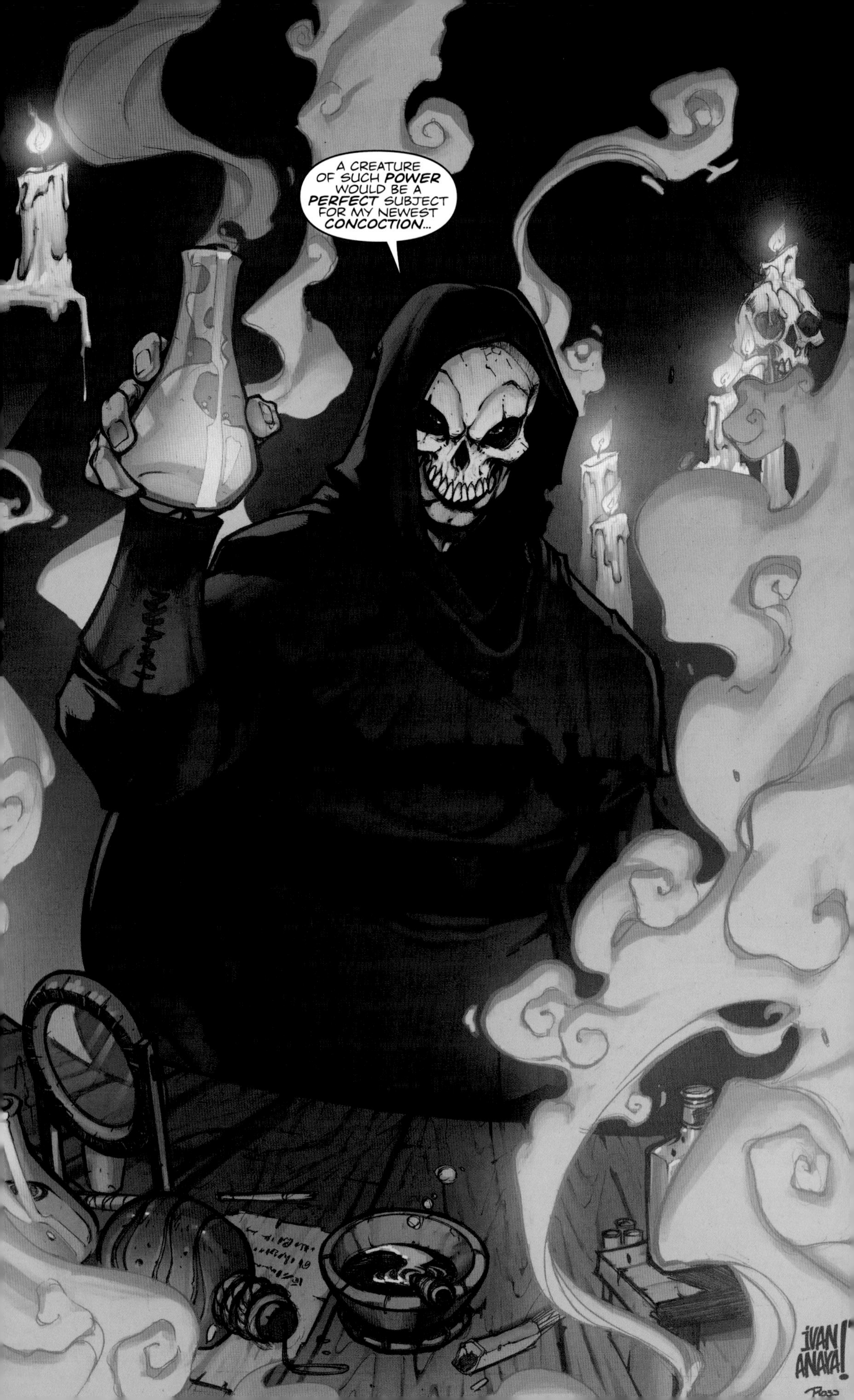
A CREATURE OF SUCH POWER WOULD BE A PERFECT SUBJECT FOR MY NEWEST CONCOCTION...
IVAN ANAYA!

CHAPTER 4

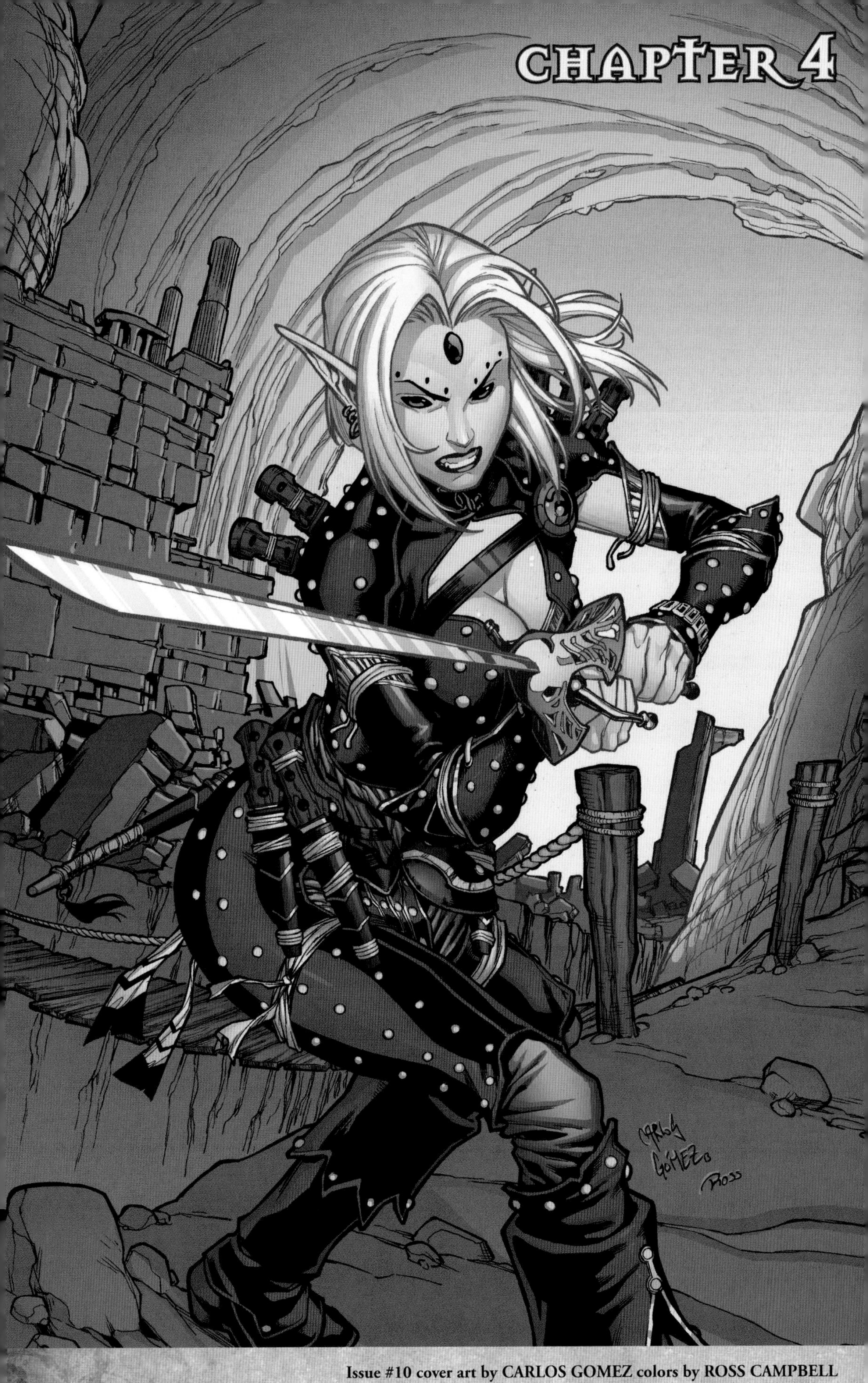

Issue #10 cover art by CARLOS GOMEZ colors by ROSS CAMPBELL

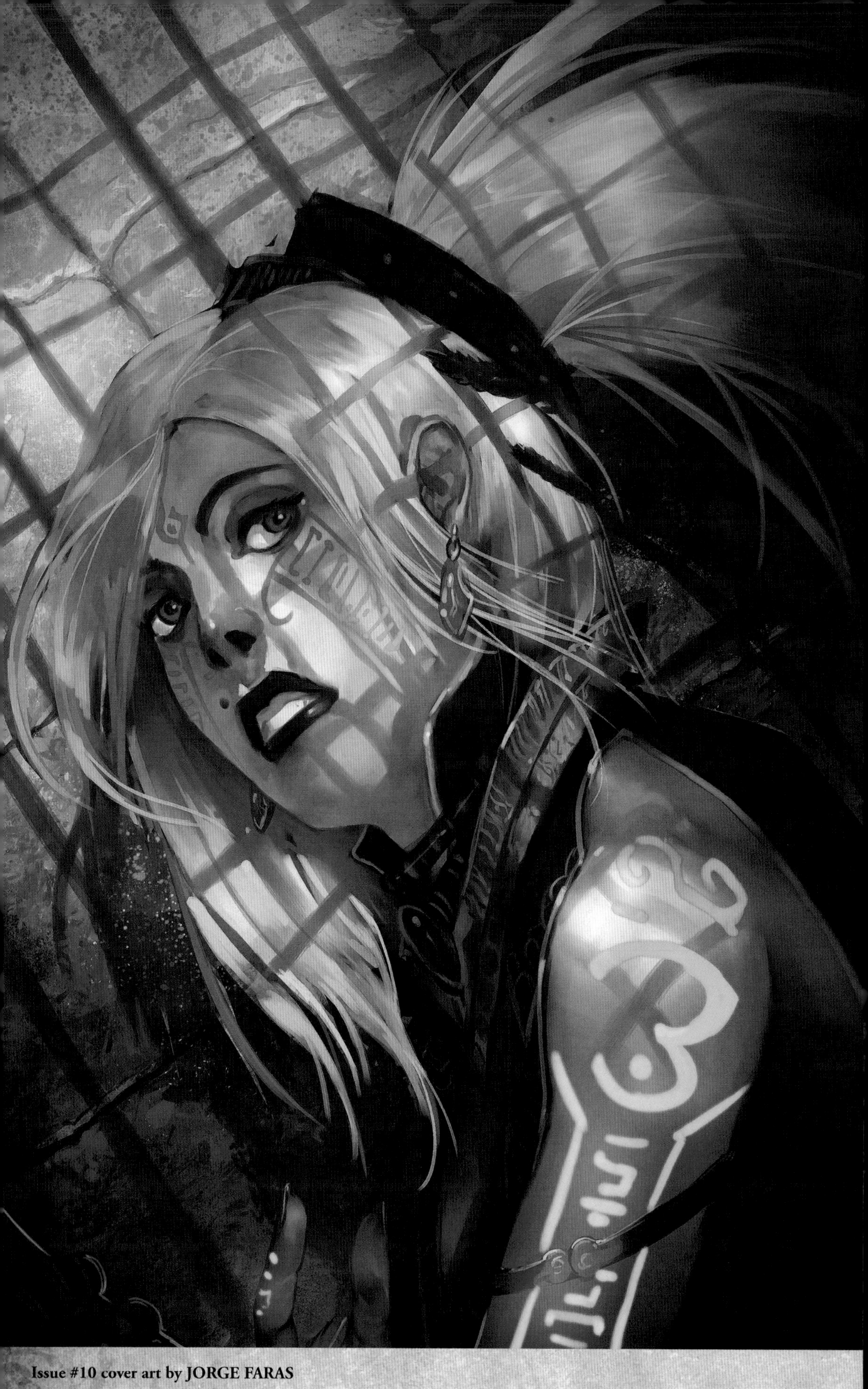

Issue #10 cover art by JORGE FARAS

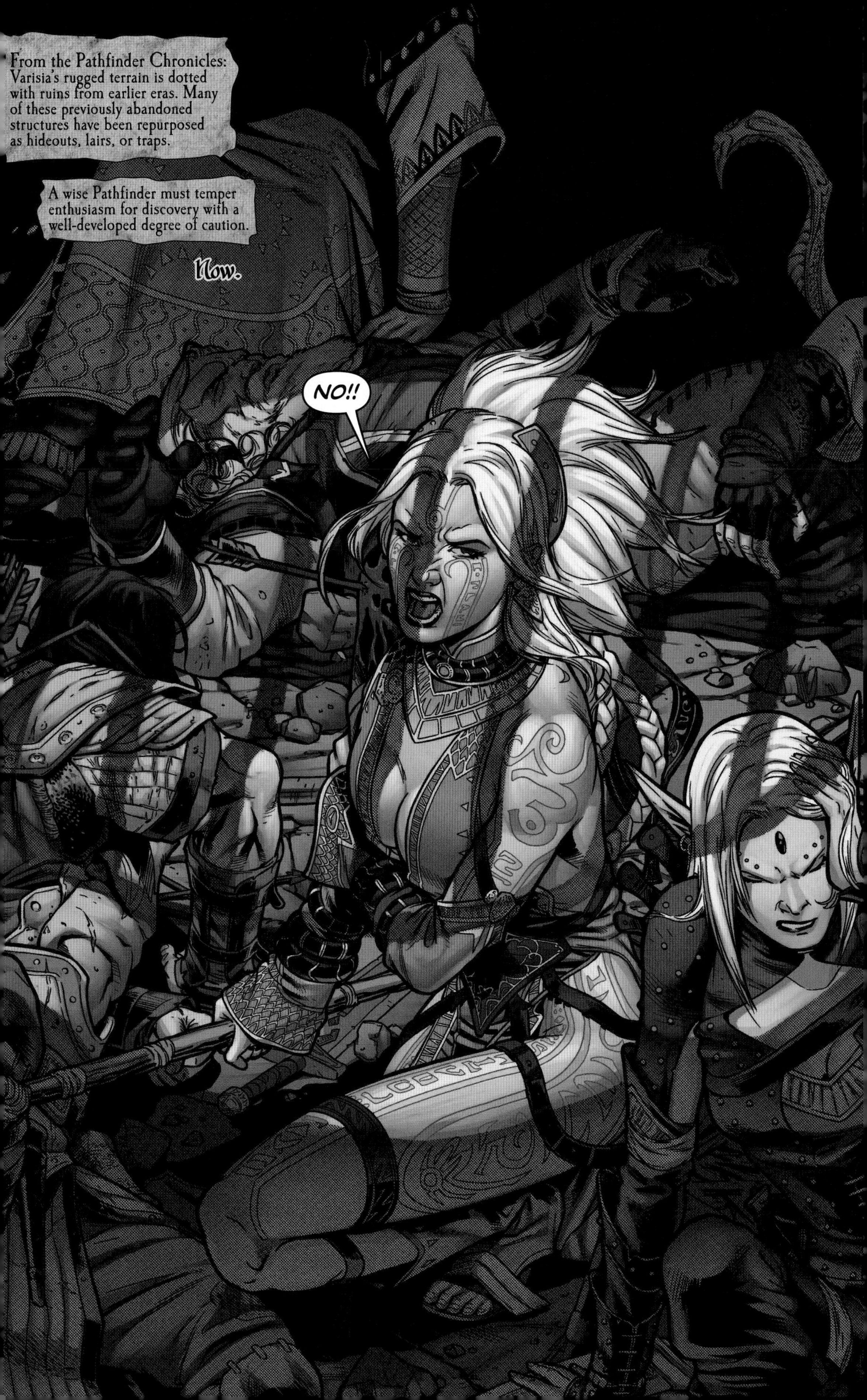
From the Pathfinder Chronicles:
Varisia's rugged terrain is dotted with ruins from earlier eras. Many of these previously abandoned structures have been repurposed as hideouts, lairs, or traps.
A wise Pathfinder must temper enthusiasm for discovery with a well-developed degree of caution.
Now.
NO!!

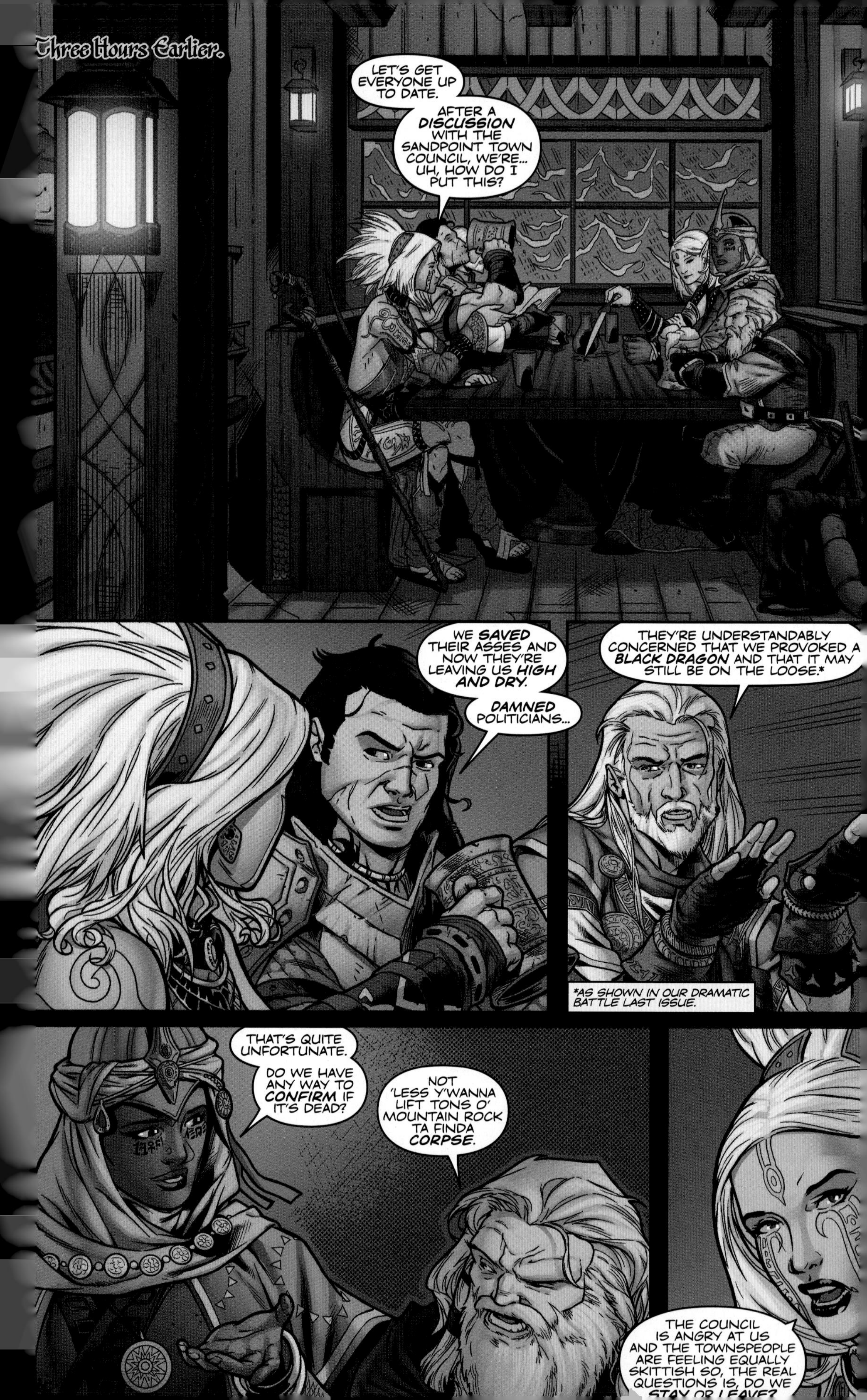
Three Hours Earlier.
LET'S GET EVERYONE UP TO DATE.
AFTER A DISCUSSION WITH THE SANDPOINT TOWN COUNCIL, WE'RE... UH, HOW DO I PUT THIS?
WE SAVED THEIR ASSES AND NOW THEY'RE LEAVING US HIGH AND DRY.
DAMNED POLITICIANS...
THEY'RE UNDERSTANDABLY CONCERNED THAT WE PROVOKED A BLACK DRAGON AND THAT IT MAY STILL BE ON THE LOOSE.*
*AS SHOWN IN OUR DRAMATIC BATTLE LAST ISSUE.
THAT'S QUITE UNFORTUNATE.
DO WE HAVE ANY WAY TO CONFIRM IF IT'S DEAD?
NOT 'LESS Y'WANNA LIFT TONS O' MOUNTAIN ROCK TA FINDA CORPSE.
THE COUNCIL IS ANGRY AT US AND THE TOWNSPEOPLE ARE FEELING EQUALLY SKITTISH SO, THE REAL QUESTIONS IS, DO WE STAY OR LEAVE?

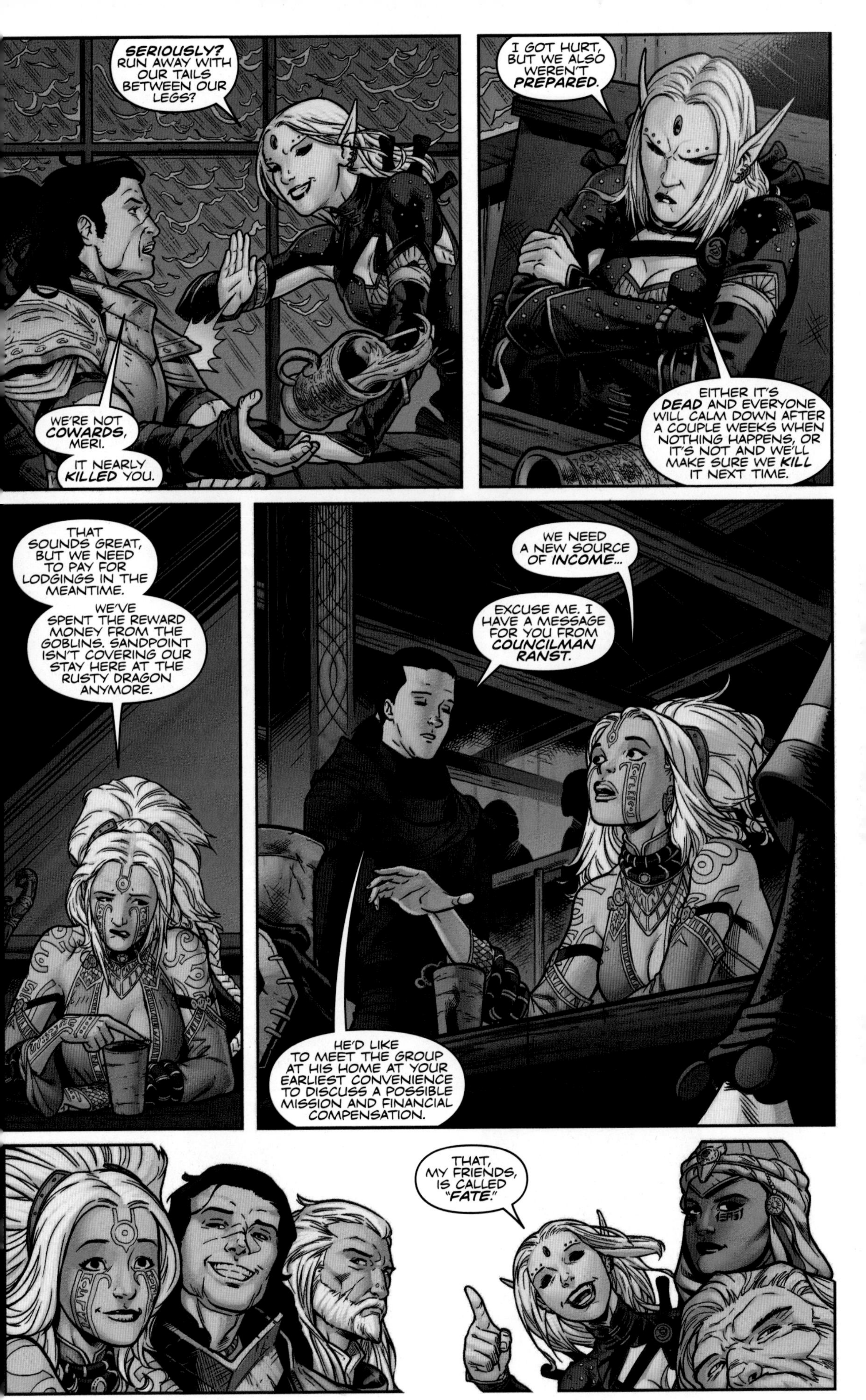
SERIOUSLY? RUN AWAY WITH OUR TAILS BETWEEN OUR LEGS?
WE'RE NOT COWARDS, MERI.
IT NEARLY KILLED YOU.
I GOT HURT, BUT WE ALSO WEREN'T PREPARED.
EITHER IT'S DEAD AND EVERYONE WILL CALM DOWN AFTER A COUPLE WEEKS WHEN NOTHING HAPPENS, OR IT'S NOT AND WE'LL MAKE SURE WE KILL IT NEXT TIME.
THAT SOUNDS GREAT, BUT WE NEED TO PAY FOR LODGINGS IN THE MEANTIME.
WE'VE SPENT THE REWARD MONEY FROM THE GOBLINS. SANDPOINT ISN'T COVERING OUR STAY HERE AT THE RUSTY DRAGON ANYMORE.
WE NEED A NEW SOURCE OF INCOME...
EXCUSE ME. I HAVE A MESSAGE FOR YOU FROM COUNCILMAN RANST.
HE'D LIKE TO MEET THE GROUP AT HIS HOME AT YOUR EARLIEST CONVENIENCE TO DISCUSS A POSSIBLE MISSION AND FINANCIAL COMPENSATION.
THAT, MY FRIENDS, IS CALLED "FATE."

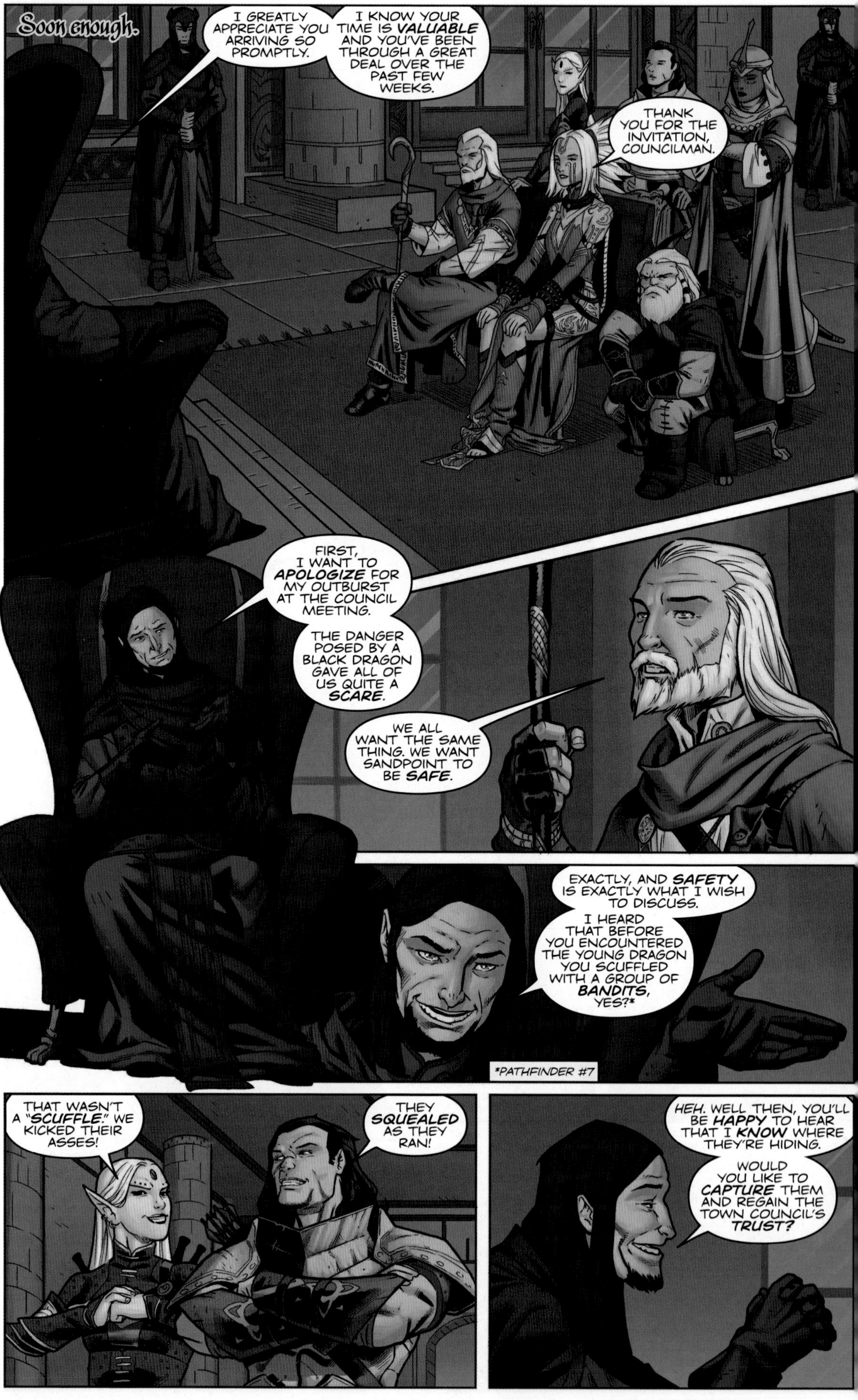
Soon enough.
I GREATLY APPRECIATE YOU ARRIVING SO PROMPTLY.
I KNOW YOUR TIME IS VALUABLE AND YOU'VE BEEN THROUGH A GREAT DEAL OVER THE PAST FEW WEEKS.
THANK YOU FOR THE INVITATION, COUNCILMAN.
FIRST, I WANT TO APOLOGIZE FOR MY OUTBURST AT THE COUNCIL MEETING.
THE DANGER POSED BY A BLACK DRAGON GAVE ALL OF US QUITE A SCARE.
WE ALL WANT THE SAME THING. WE WANT SANDPOINT TO BE SAFE.
EXACTLY, AND SAFETY IS EXACTLY WHAT I WISH TO DISCUSS.
I HEARD THAT BEFORE YOU ENCOUNTERED THE YOUNG DRAGON YOU SCUFFLED WITH A GROUP OF BANDITS, YES?*
*PATHFINDER #7
THAT WASN'T A "SCUFFLE." WE KICKED THEIR ASSES!
THEY SQUEALED AS THEY RAN!
HEH. WELL THEN, YOU'LL BE HAPPY TO HEAR THAT I KNOW WHERE THEY'RE HIDING.
WOULD YOU LIKE TO CAPTURE THEM AND REGAIN THE TOWN COUNCIL'S TRUST?

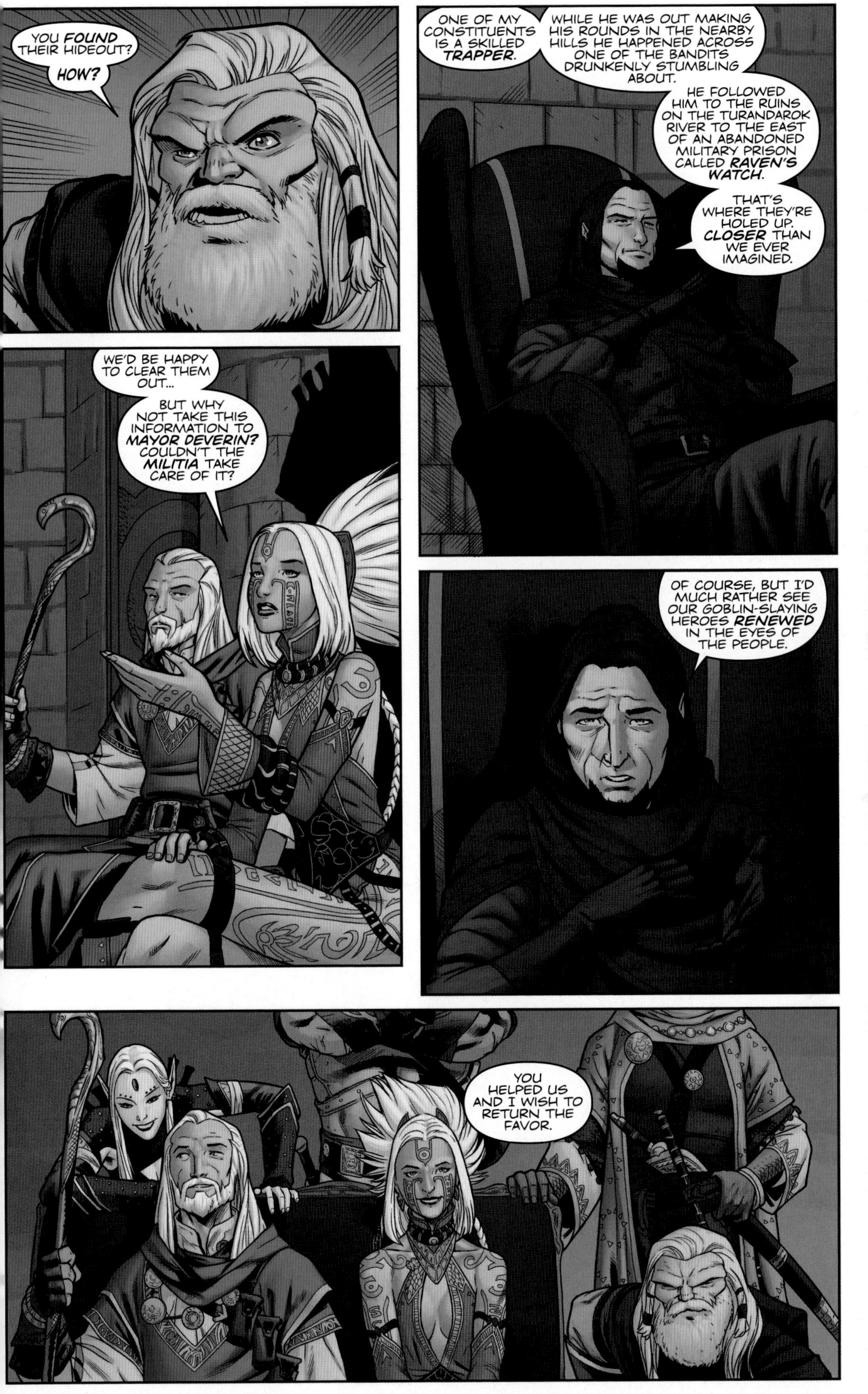
YOU FOUND THEIR HIDEOUT? HOW?
ONE OF MY CONSTITUENTS IS A SKILLED TRAPPER.
WHILE HE WAS OUT MAKING HIS ROUNDS IN THE NEARBY HILLS HE HAPPENED ACROSS ONE OF THE BANDITS DRUNKENLY STUMBLING ABOUT.
HE FOLLOWED HIM TO THE RUINS ON THE TURANDAROK RIVER TO THE EAST OF AN ABANDONED MILITARY PRISON CALLED RAVEN'S WATCH.
THAT'S WHERE THEY'RE HOLED UP. CLOSER THAN WE EVER IMAGINED.
WE'D BE HAPPY TO CLEAR THEM OUT...
BUT WHY NOT TAKE THIS INFORMATION TO MAYOR DEVERIN? COULDN'T THE MILITIA TAKE CARE OF IT?
OF COURSE, BUT I'D MUCH RATHER SEE OUR GOBLIN-SLAYING HEROES RENEWED IN THE EYES OF THE PEOPLE.
YOU HELPED US AND I WISH TO RETURN THE FAVOR.

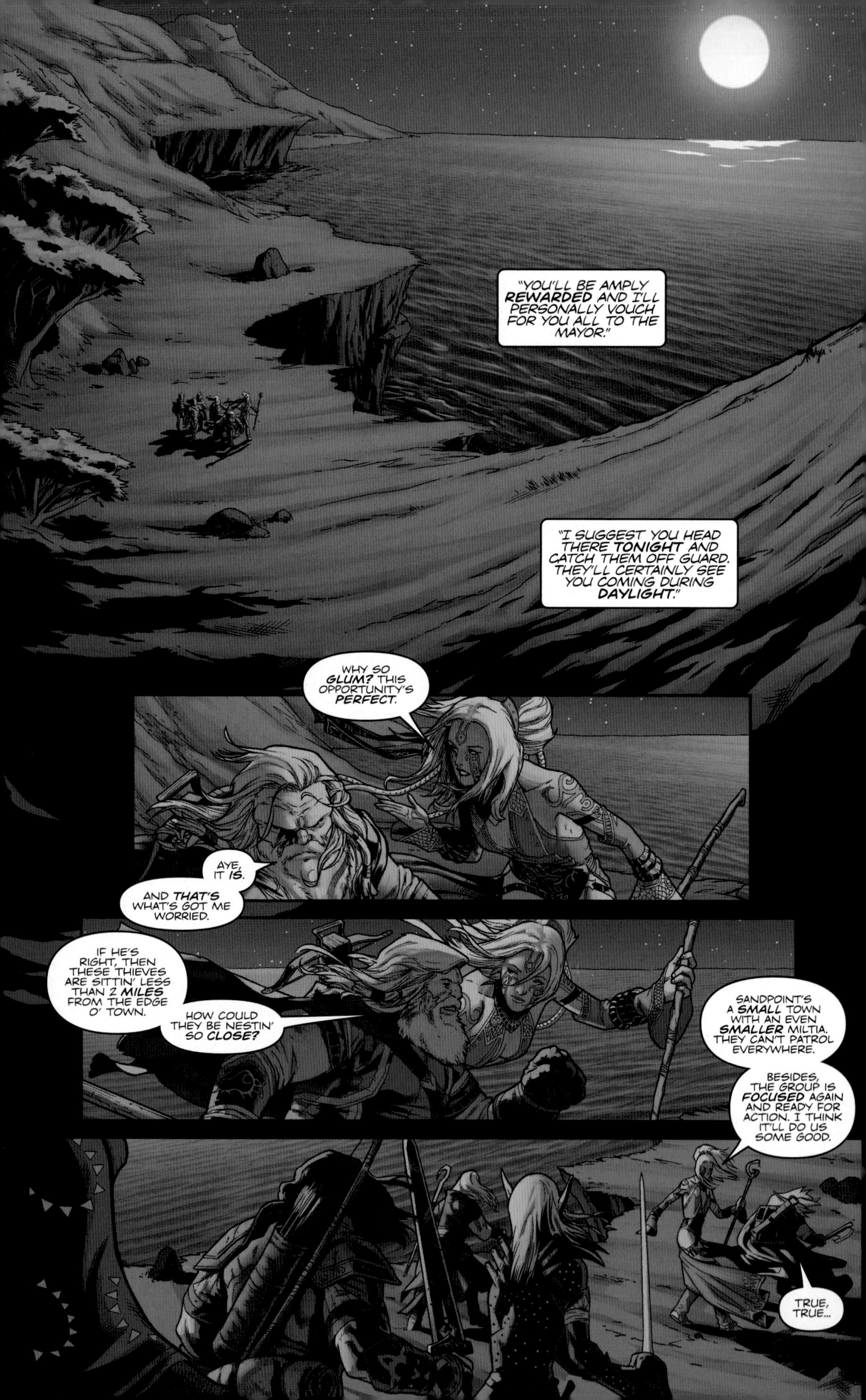
"YOU'LL BE AMPLY REWARDED AND I'LL PERSONALLY VOUCH FOR YOU ALL TO THE MAYOR."
"I SUGGEST YOU HEAD THERE TONIGHT AND CATCH THEM OFF GUARD. THEY'LL CERTAINLY SEE YOU COMING DURING DAYLIGHT."
WHY SO GLUM? THIS OPPORTUNITY'S PERFECT.
AYE, IT IS.
AND THAT'S WHAT'S GOT ME WORRIED.
IF HE'S RIGHT, THEN THESE THIEVES ARE SITTIN' LESS THAN 2 MILES FROM THE EDGE O' TOWN.
HOW COULD THEY BE NESTIN' SO CLOSE?
SANDPOINT'S A SMALL TOWN WITH AN EVEN SMALLER MILTIA. THEY CAN'T PATROL EVERYWHERE.
BESIDES, THE GROUP IS FOCUSED AGAIN AND READY FOR ACTION. I THINK IT'LL DO US SOME GOOD.
TRUE, TRUE...

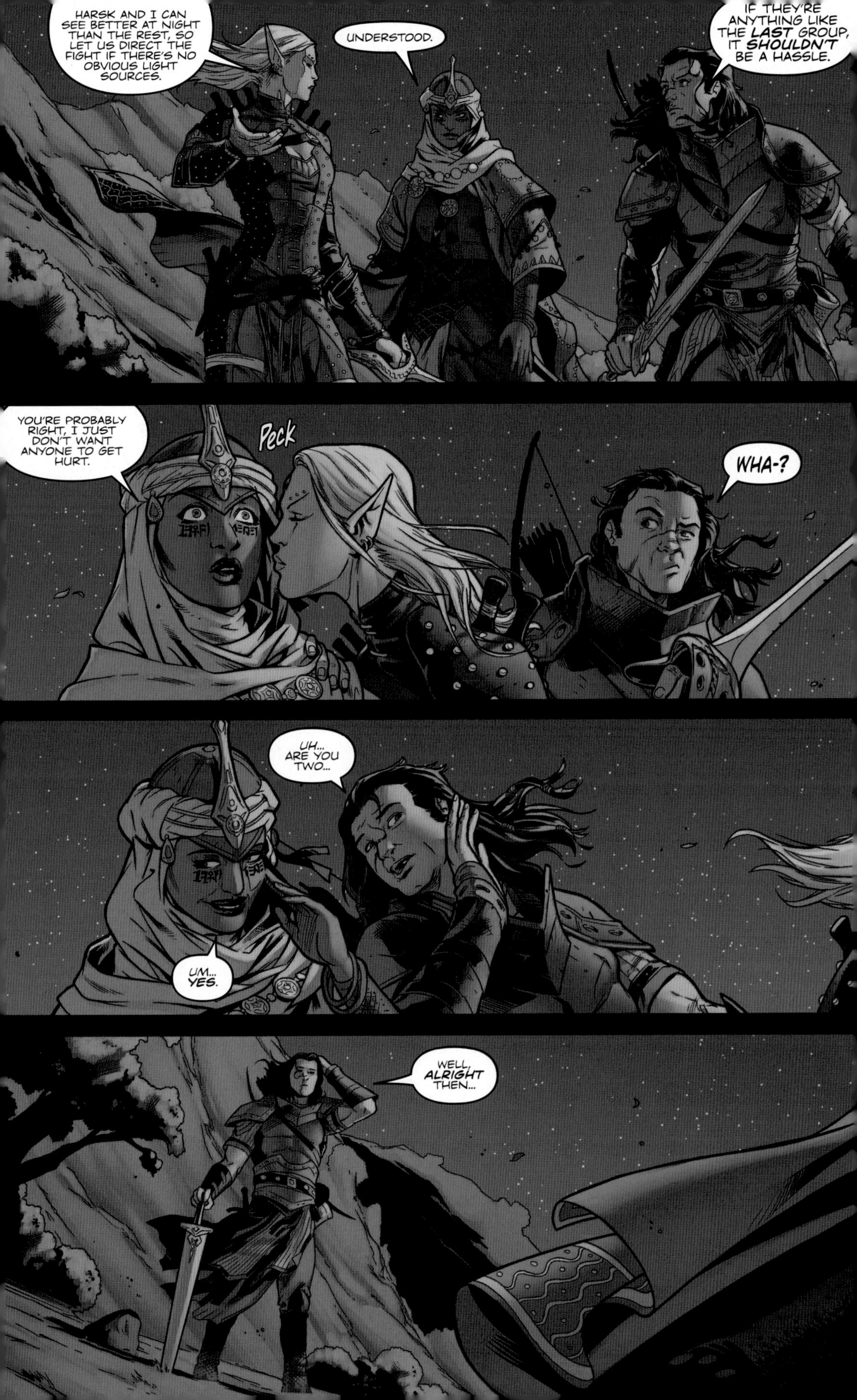
HARSK AND I CAN SEE BETTER AT NIGHT THAN THE REST, SO LET US DIRECT THE FIGHT IF THERE'S NO OBVIOUS LIGHT SOURCES.
UNDERSTOOD.
IF THEY'RE ANYTHING LIKE THE **LAST** GROUP, IT **SHOULDN'T** BE A HASSLE.
YOU'RE PROBABLY RIGHT, I JUST DON'T WANT ANYONE TO GET HURT.
Peck
WHA-?
UH... ARE YOU TWO...
UM... **YES.**
WELL, **ALRIGHT** THEN...

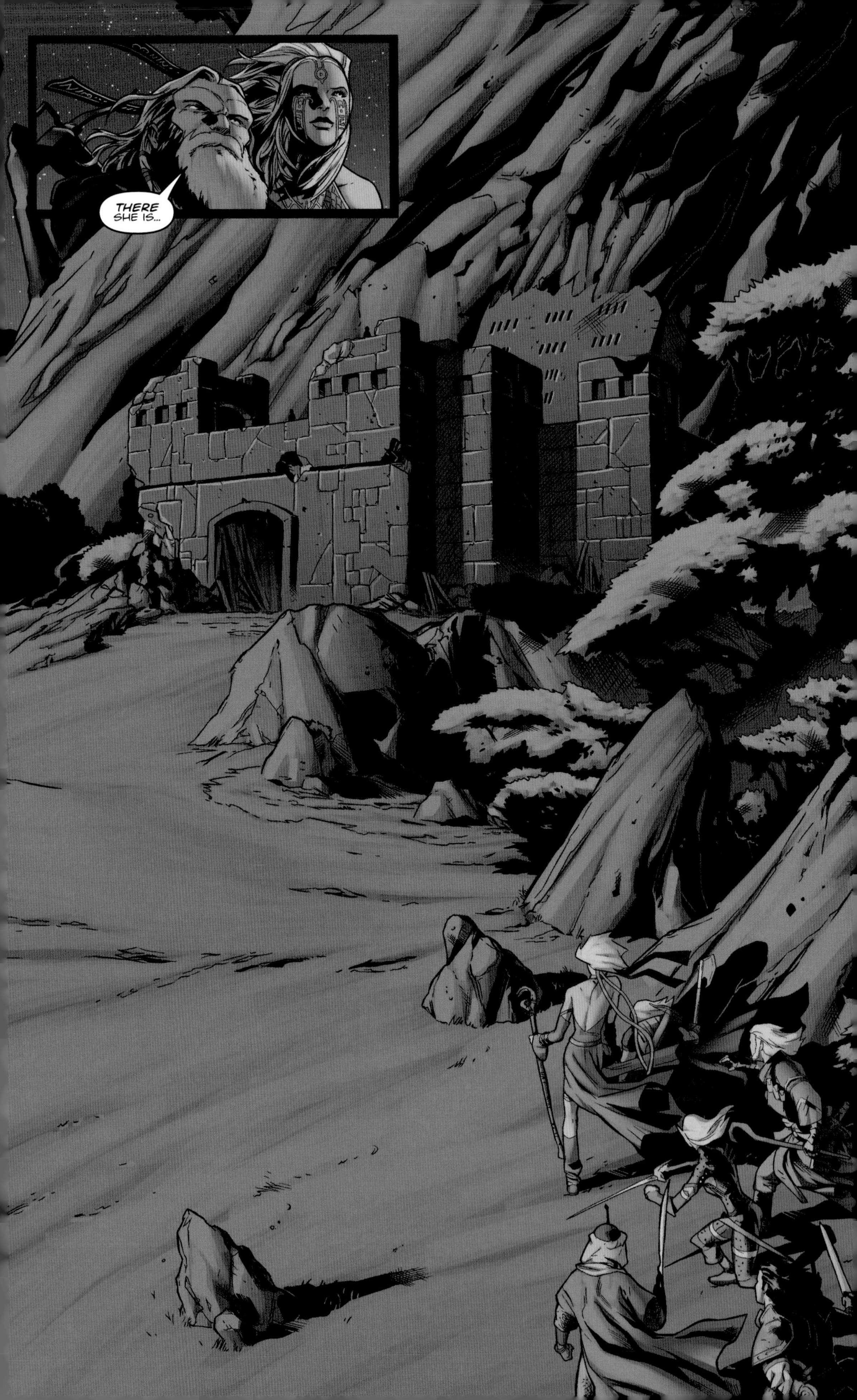
THERE SHE IS...

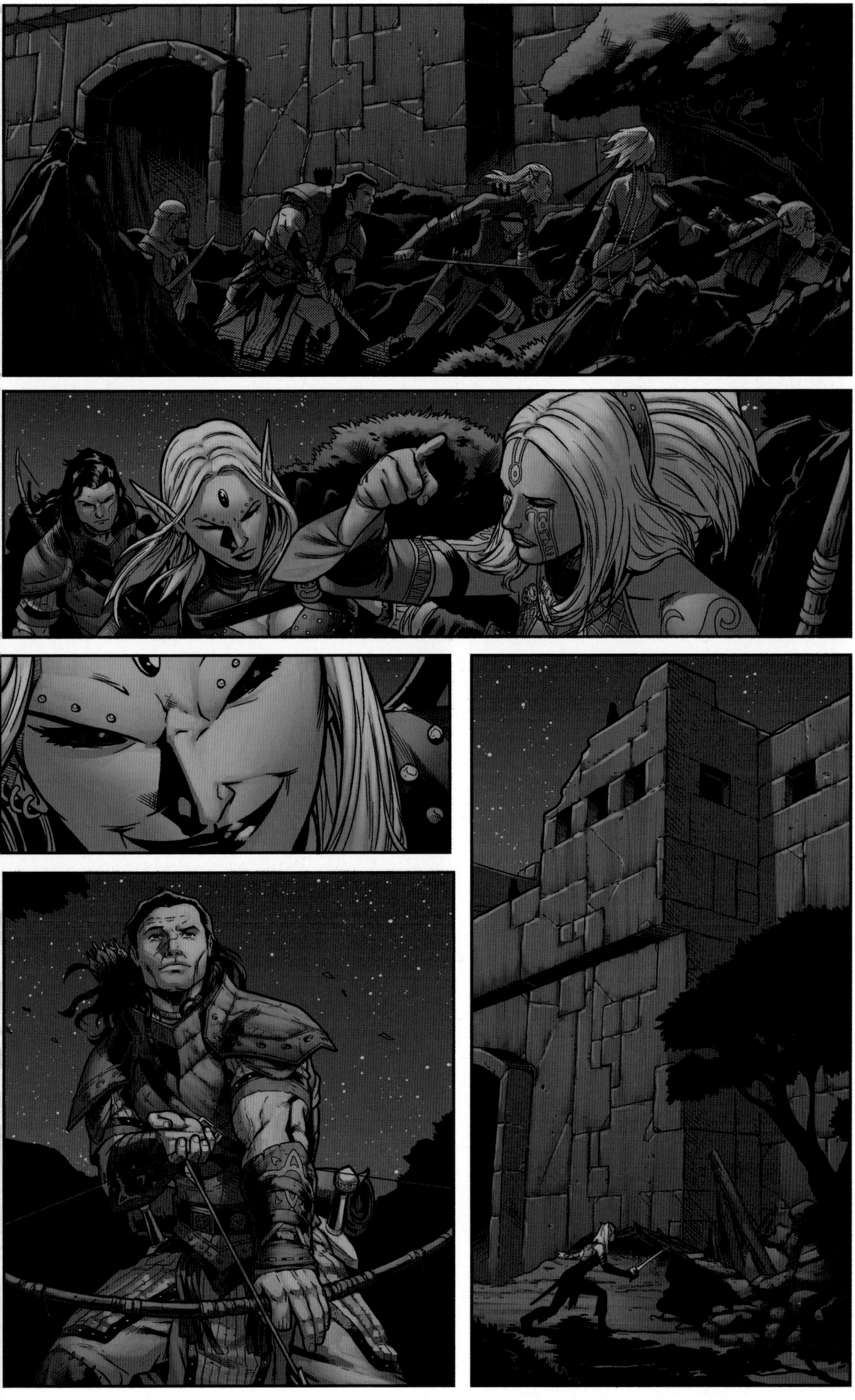

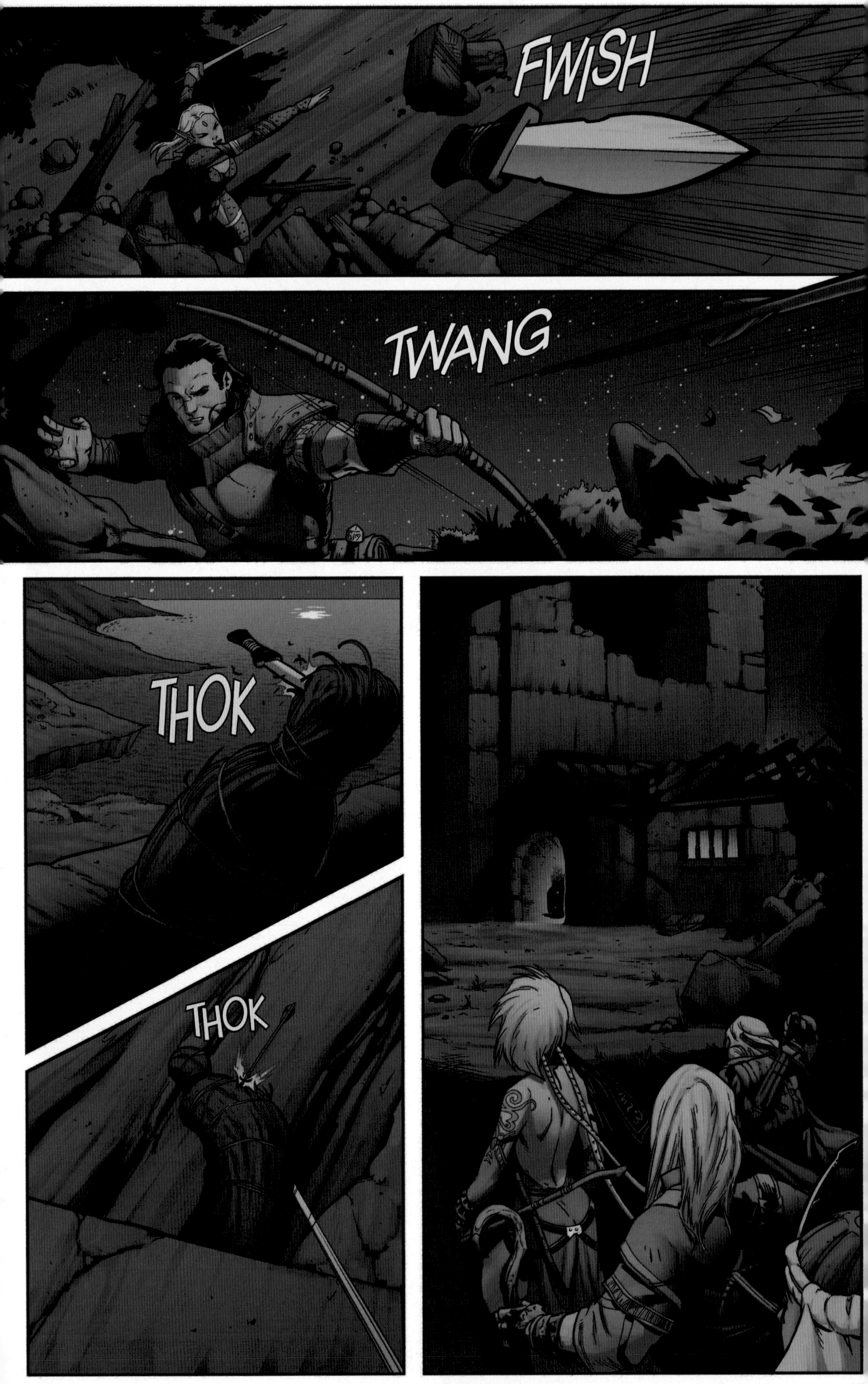
FWISH
TWANG
THOK
THOK

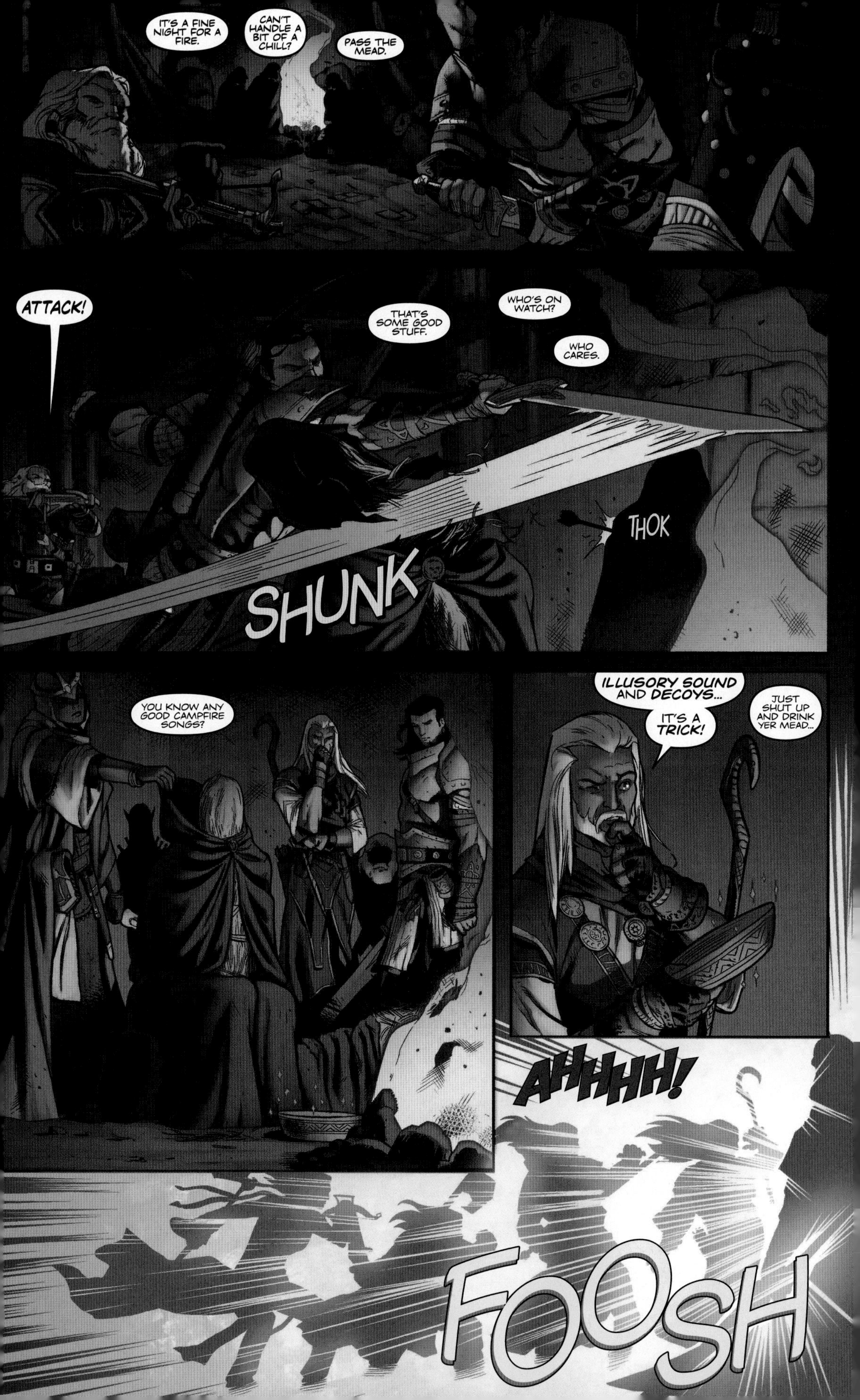
IT'S A FINE NIGHT FOR A FIRE.
CAN'T HANDLE A BIT OF A CHILL?
PASS THE MEAD.
ATTACK!
THAT'S SOME GOOD STUFF.
WHO'S ON WATCH?
WHO CARES.
THOK
SHUNK
YOU KNOW ANY GOOD CAMPFIRE SONGS?
ILLUSORY SOUND AND DECOYS...
IT'S A TRICK!
JUST SHUT UP AND DRINK YER MEAD...
AHHHH!
FOOSH

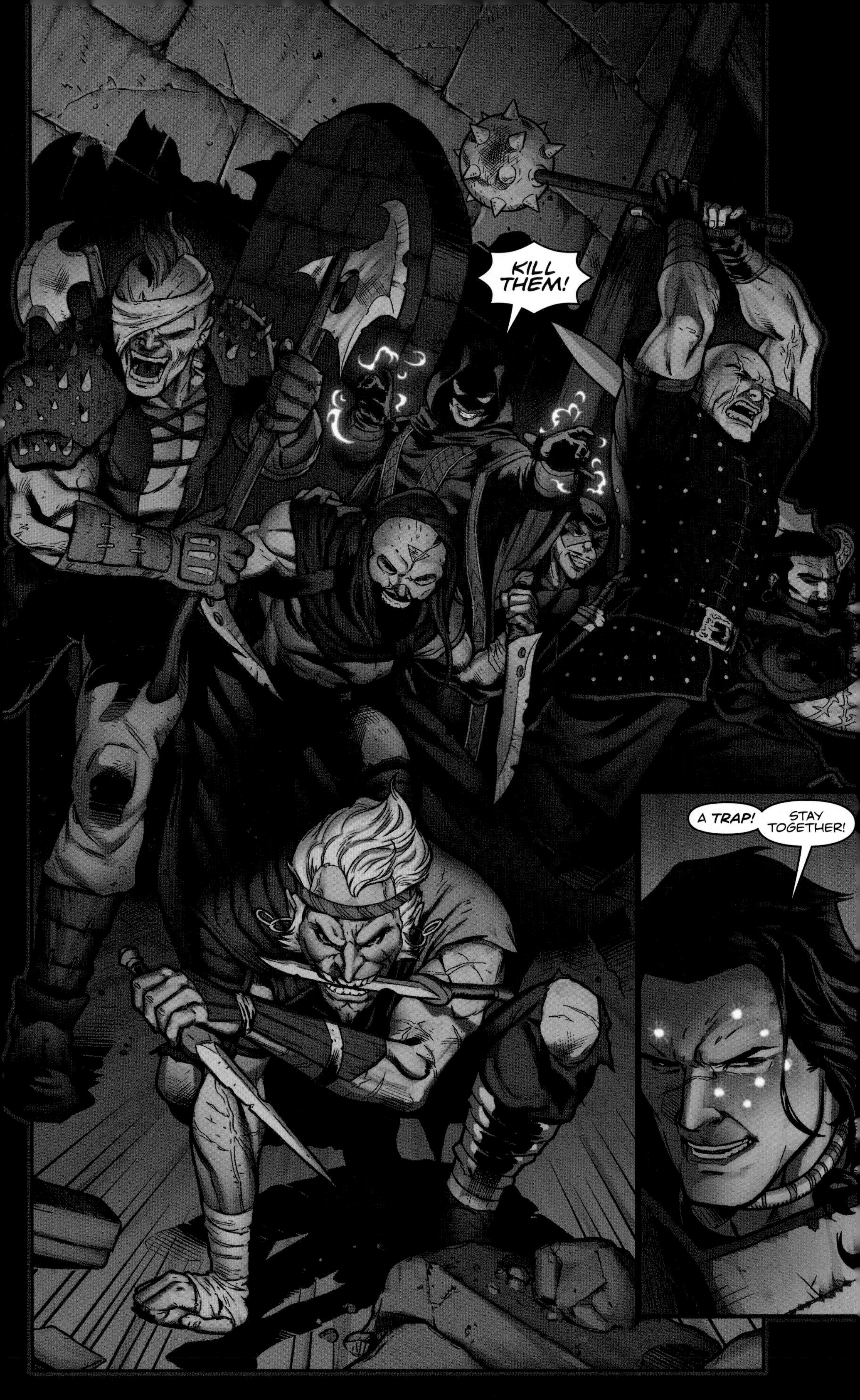
KILL THEM!
A TRAP!
STAY TOGETHER!

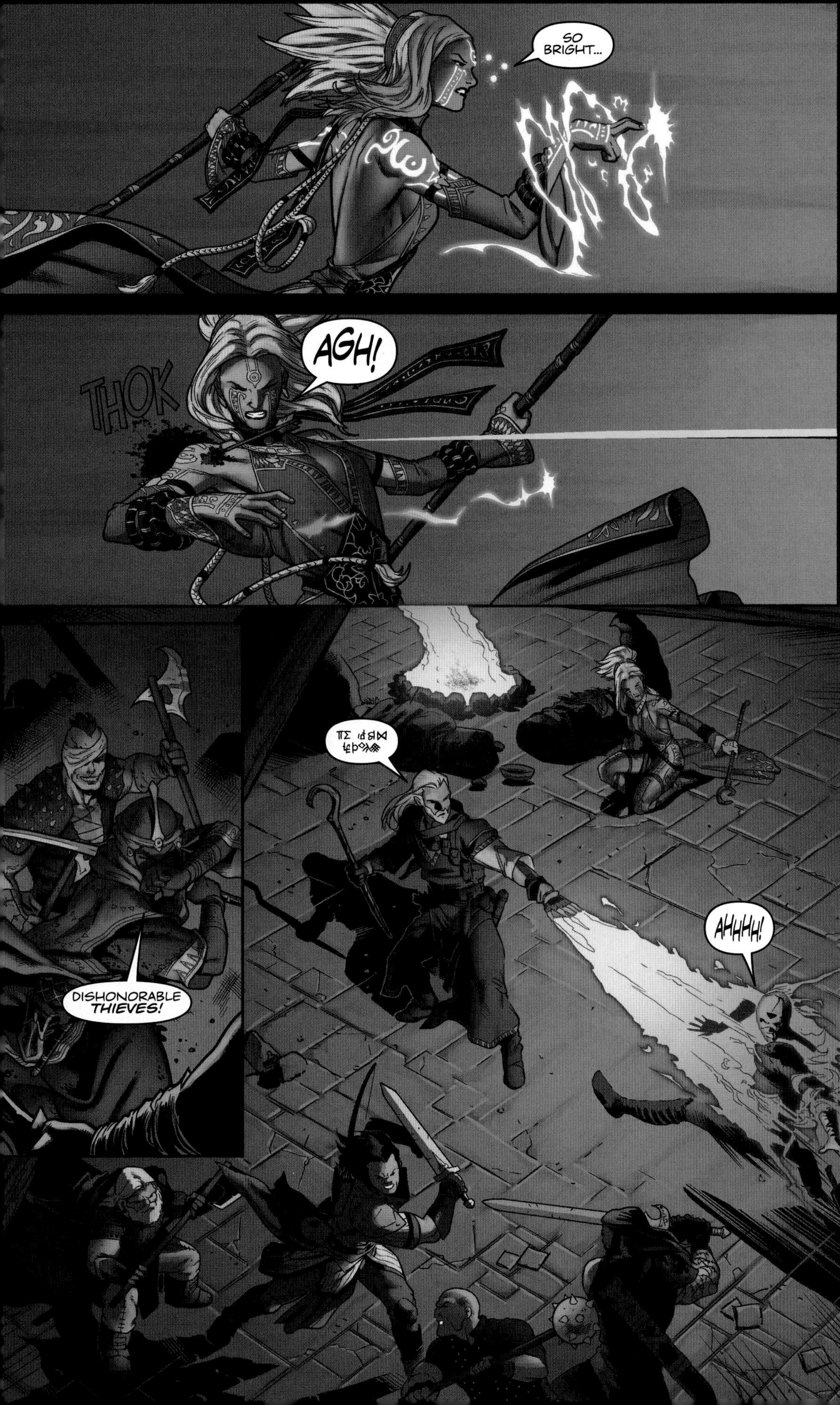
SO BRIGHT...
THOK
AGH!
DISHONORABLE THIEVES!
AHHHH!

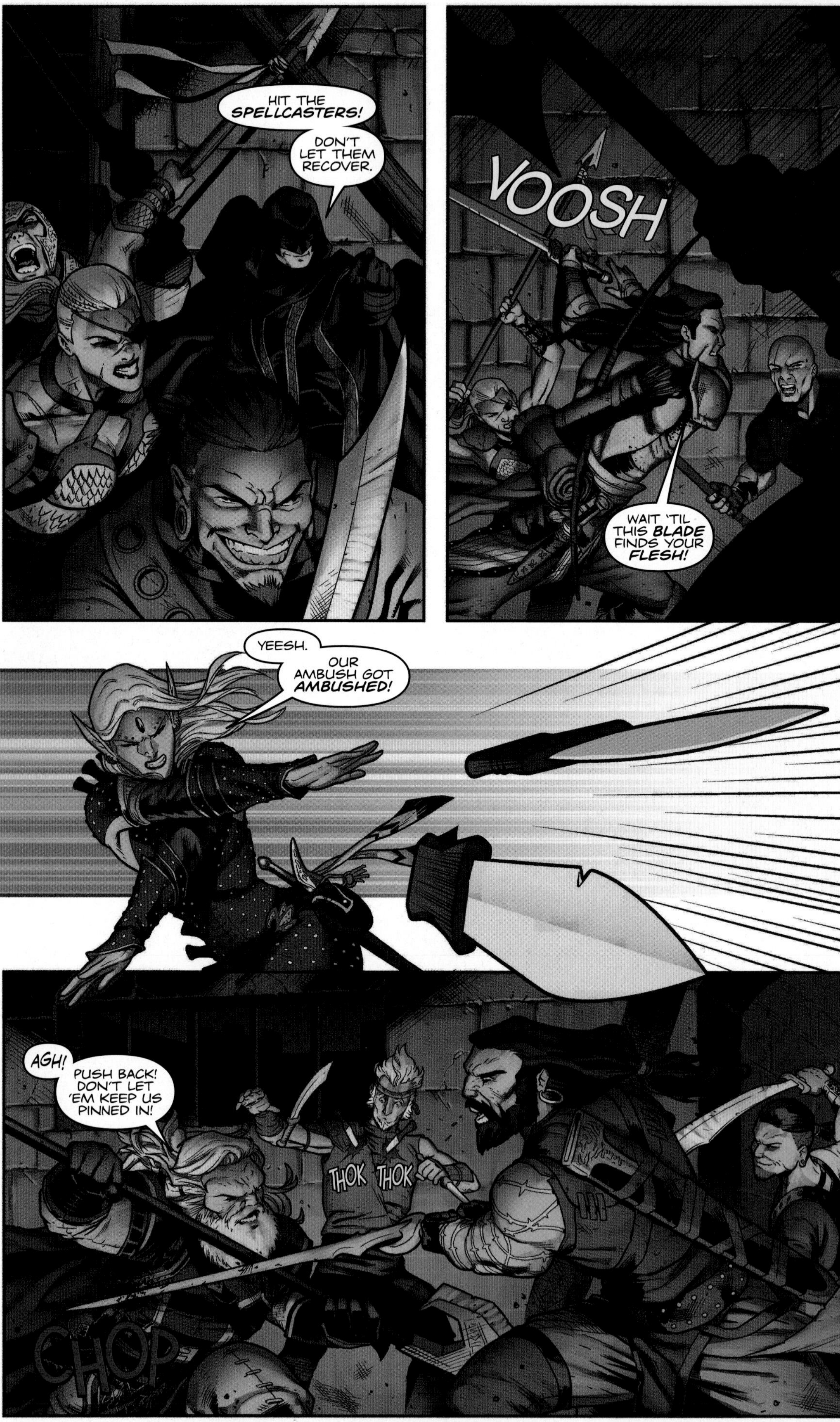
HIT THE SPELLCASTERS!
DON'T LET THEM RECOVER.
VOOSH
WAIT 'TIL THIS BLADE FINDS YOUR FLESH!
YEESH.
OUR AMBUSH GOT AMBUSHED!
AGH!
PUSH BACK! DON'T LET 'EM KEEP US PINNED IN!
THOK THOK
CHOP

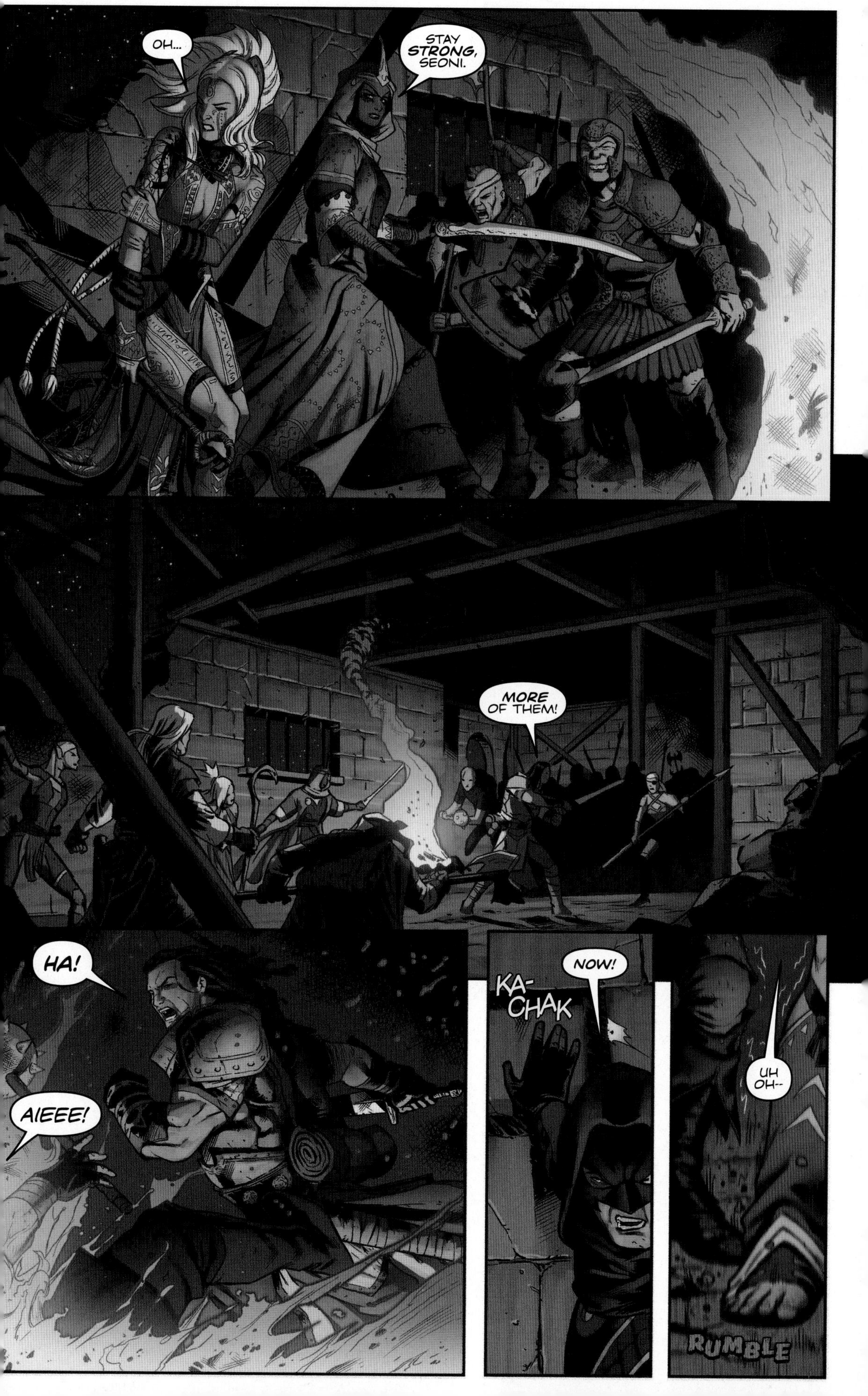
OH...
STAY STRONG, SEONI.
MORE OF THEM!
HA!
AIEEE!
KA-CHAK
NOW!
UH OH--
RUMBLE

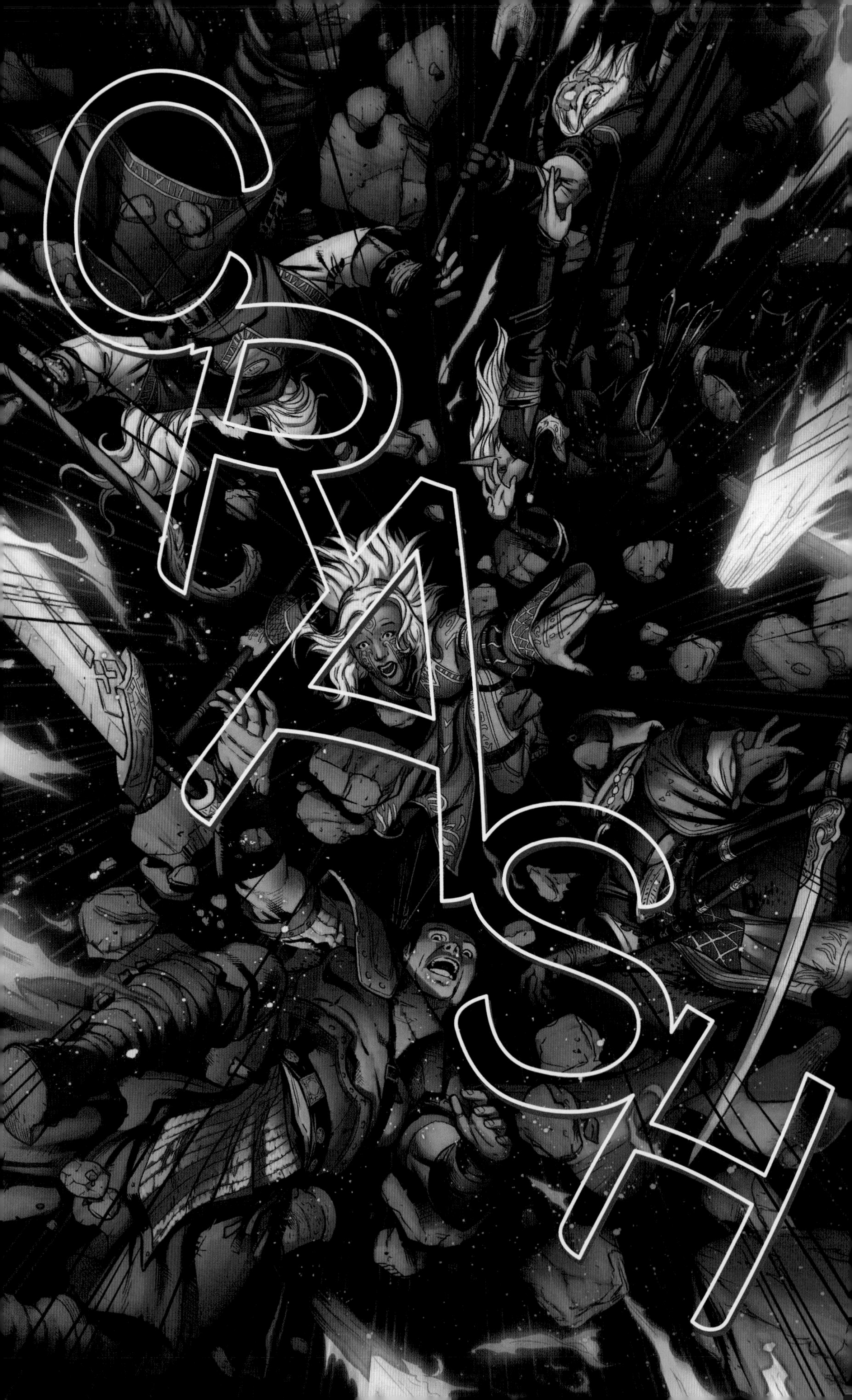
CRASH

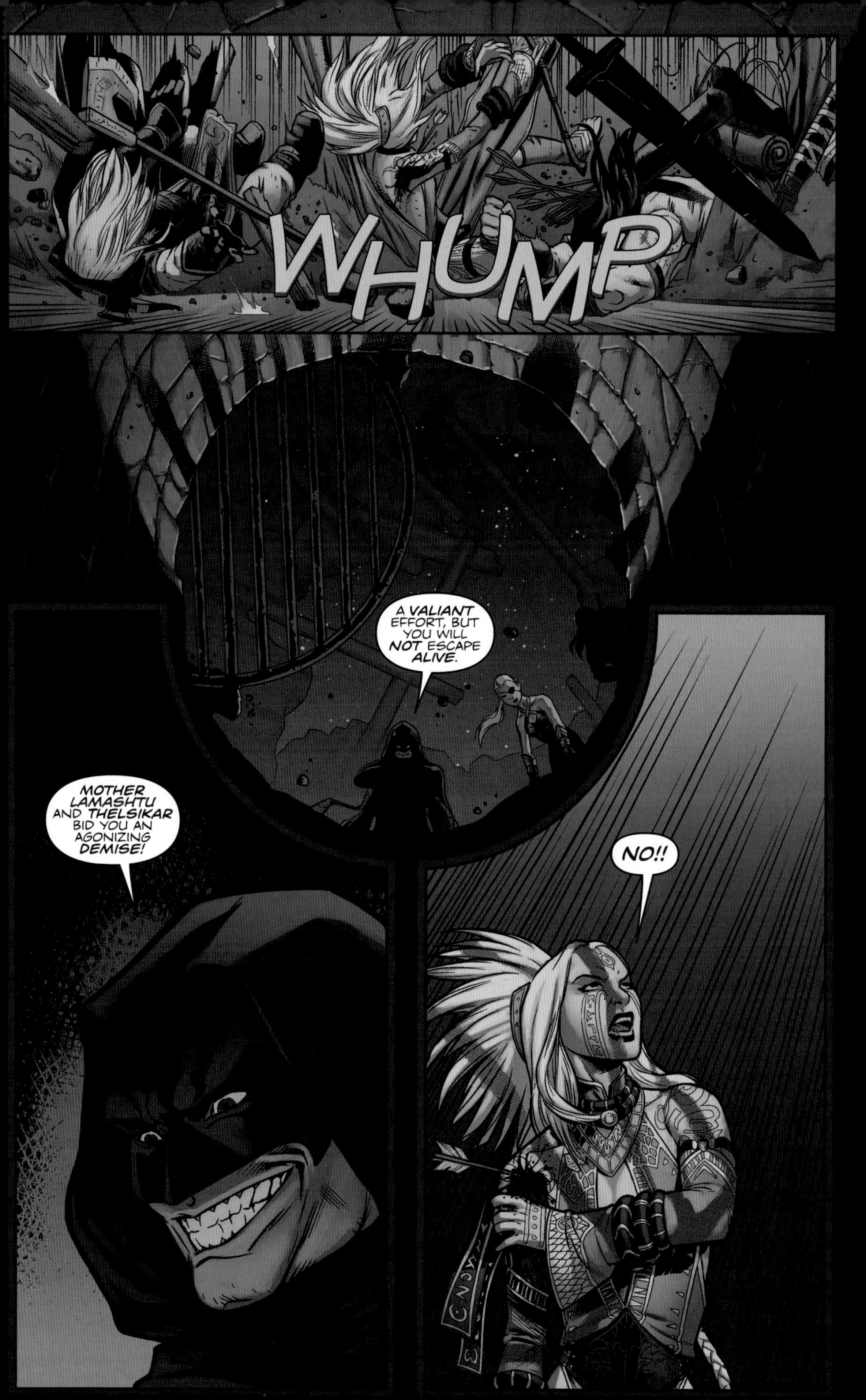
WHUMP
A VALIANT EFFORT, BUT YOU WILL NOT ESCAPE ALIVE.
MOTHER LAMASHTU AND THELSIKAR BID YOU AN AGONIZING DEMISE!
NO!!

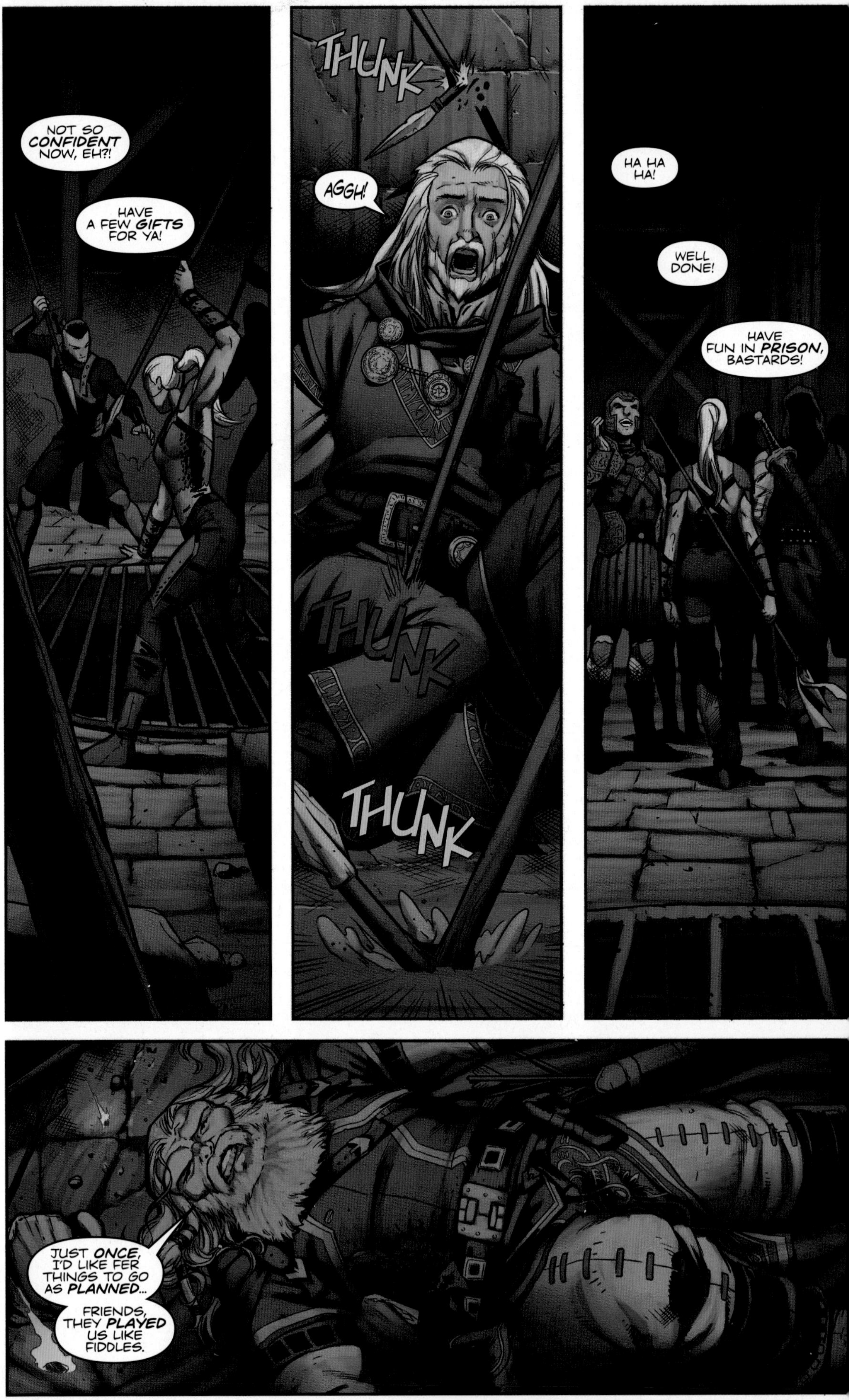
NOT SO CONFIDENT NOW, EH?!
HAVE A FEW GIFTS FOR YA!
THUNK
AGGH!
THUNK
THUNK
HA HA HA!
WELL DONE!
HAVE FUN IN PRISON, BASTARDS!
JUST ONCE, I'D LIKE FER THINGS TO GO AS PLANNED...
FRIENDS, THEY PLAYED US LIKE FIDDLES.

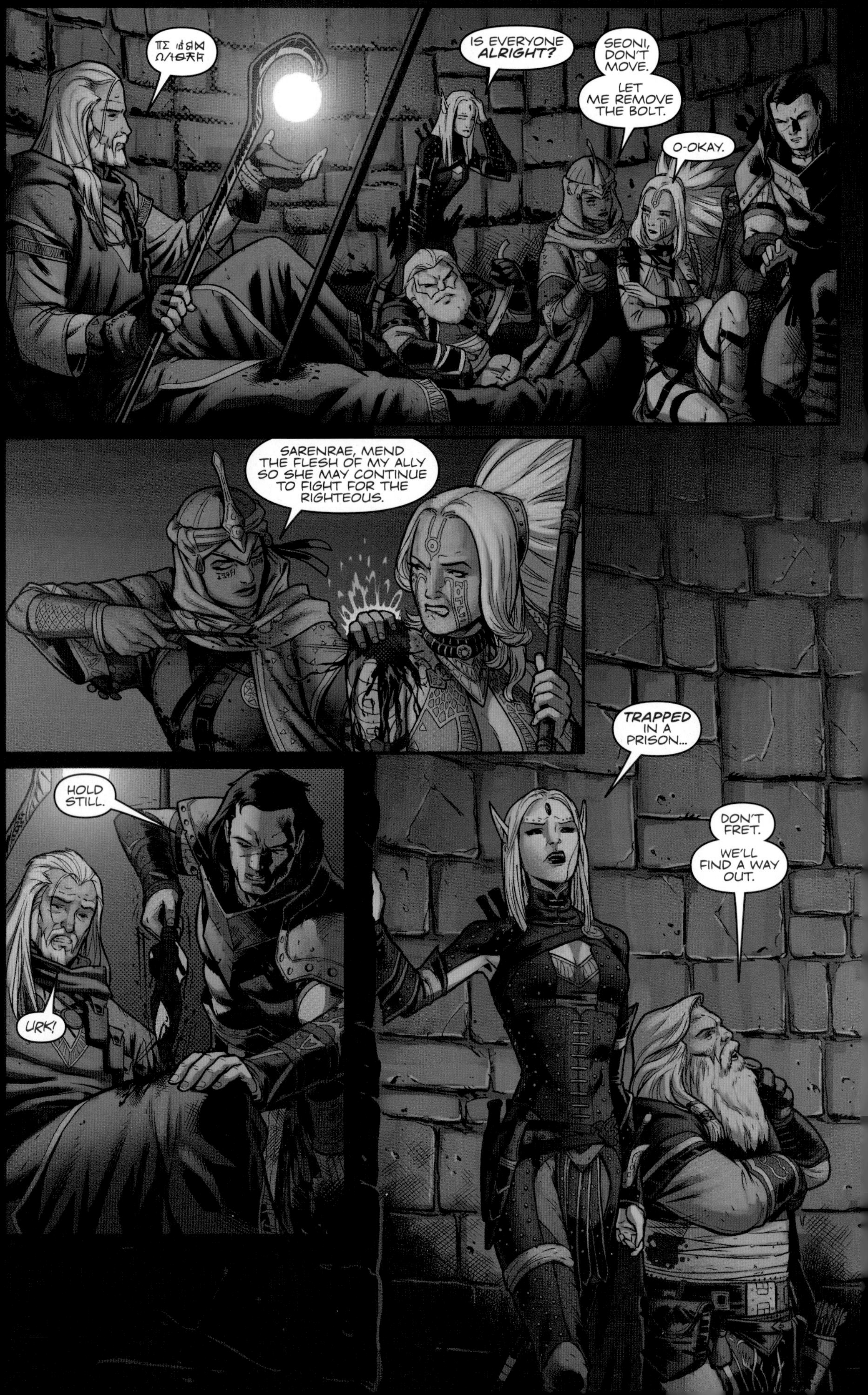

IS EVERYONE ALRIGHT?
SEONI, DON'T MOVE.
LET ME REMOVE THE BOLT.
O-OKAY.
SARENRAE, MEND THE FLESH OF MY ALLY SO SHE MAY CONTINUE TO FIGHT FOR THE RIGHTEOUS.
TRAPPED IN A PRISON...
DON'T FRET.
WE'LL FIND A WAY OUT.
HOLD STILL.
URK!

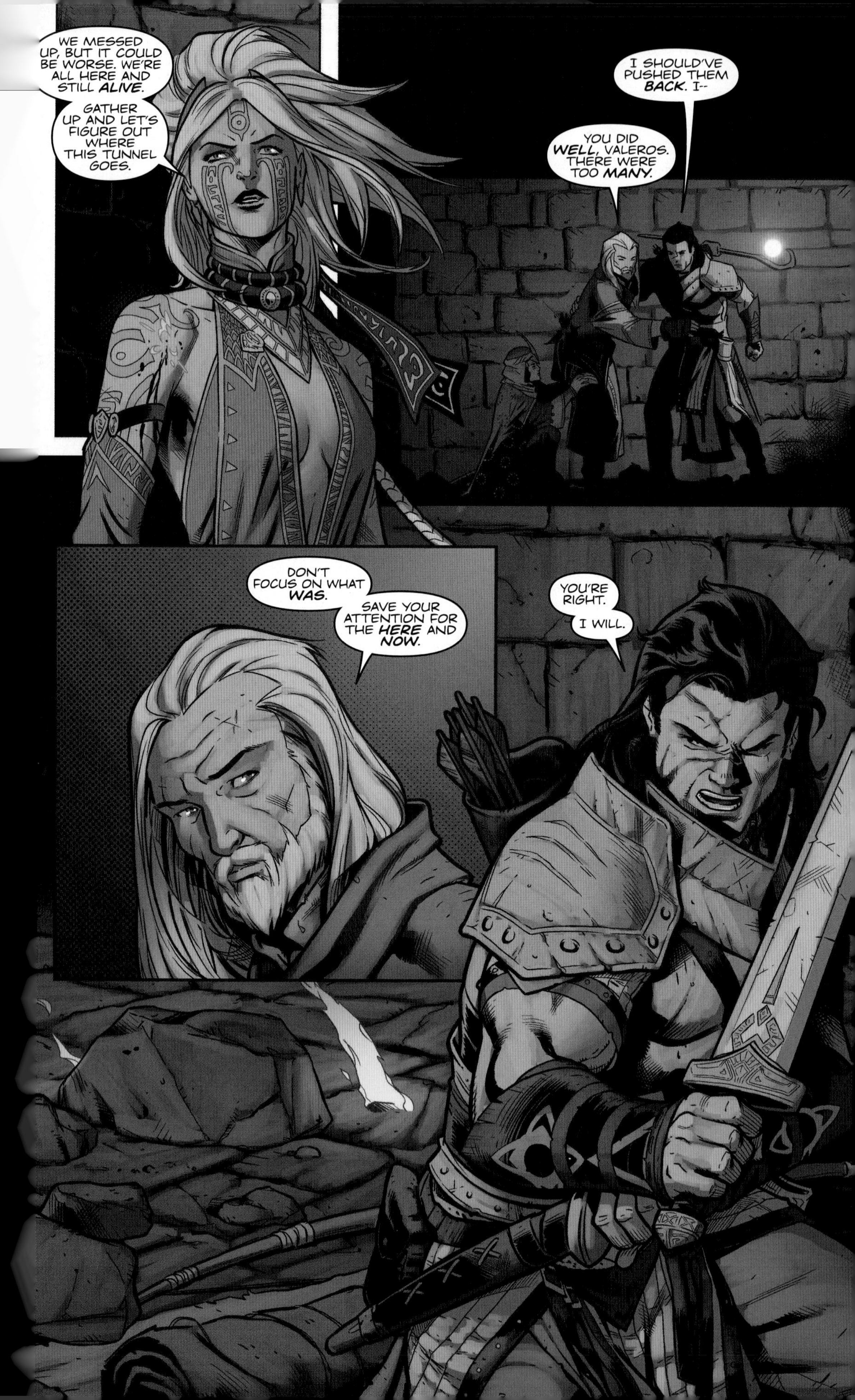
WE MESSED UP, BUT IT COULD BE WORSE. WE'RE ALL HERE AND STILL ALIVE.
GATHER UP AND LET'S FIGURE OUT WHERE THIS TUNNEL GOES.
I SHOULD'VE PUSHED THEM BACK. I--
YOU DID WELL, VALEROS. THERE WERE TOO MANY.
DON'T FOCUS ON WHAT WAS.
SAVE YOUR ATTENTION FOR THE HERE AND NOW.
YOU'RE RIGHT.
I WILL.

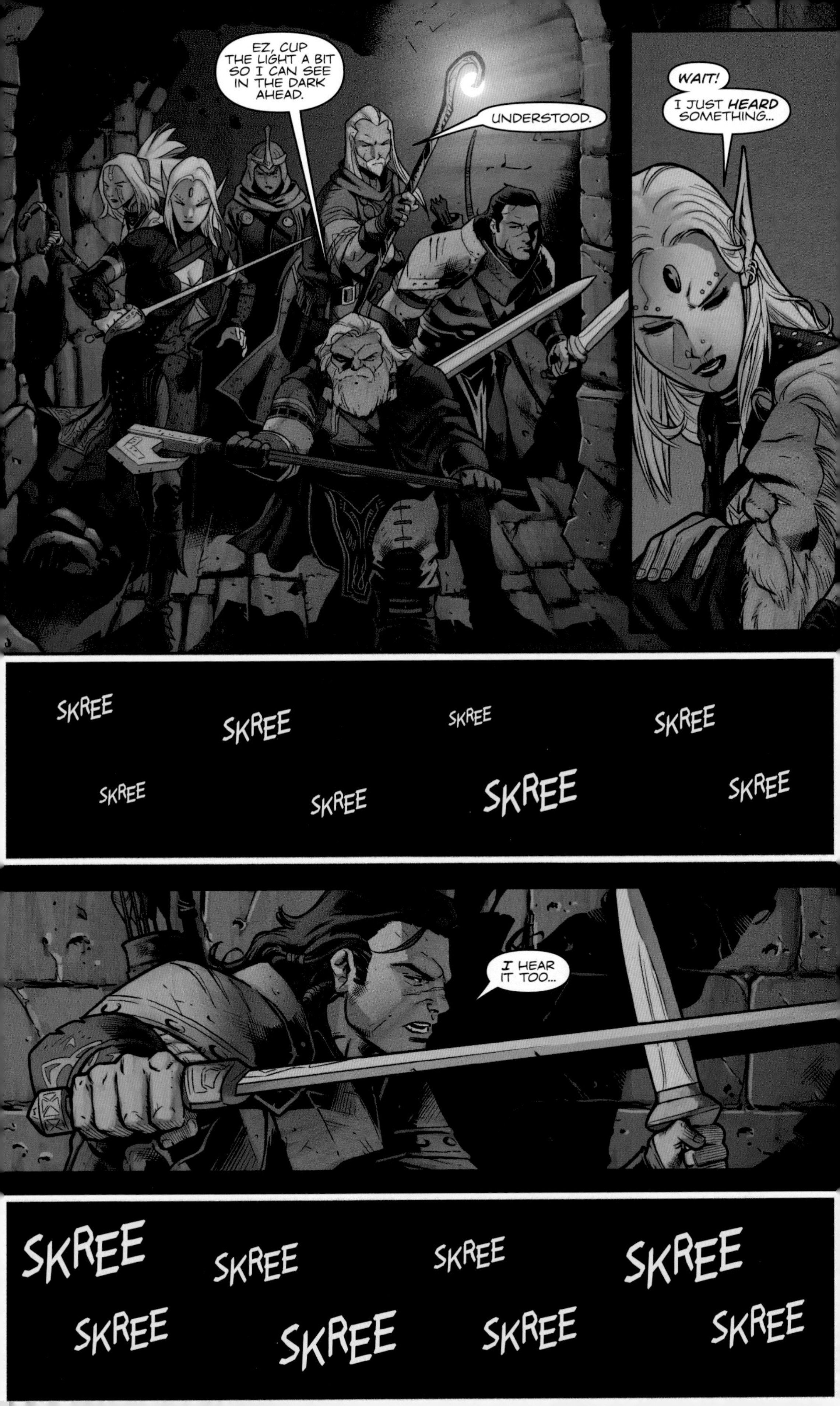

EZ, CUP THE LIGHT A BIT SO I CAN SEE IN THE DARK AHEAD.
UNDERSTOOD.
WAIT!
I JUST **HEARD** SOMETHING...
SKREE SKREE SKREE SKREE
SKREE SKREE SKREE SKREE
I HEAR IT TOO...
SKREE SKREE SKREE SKREE
SKREE SKREE SKREE SKREE

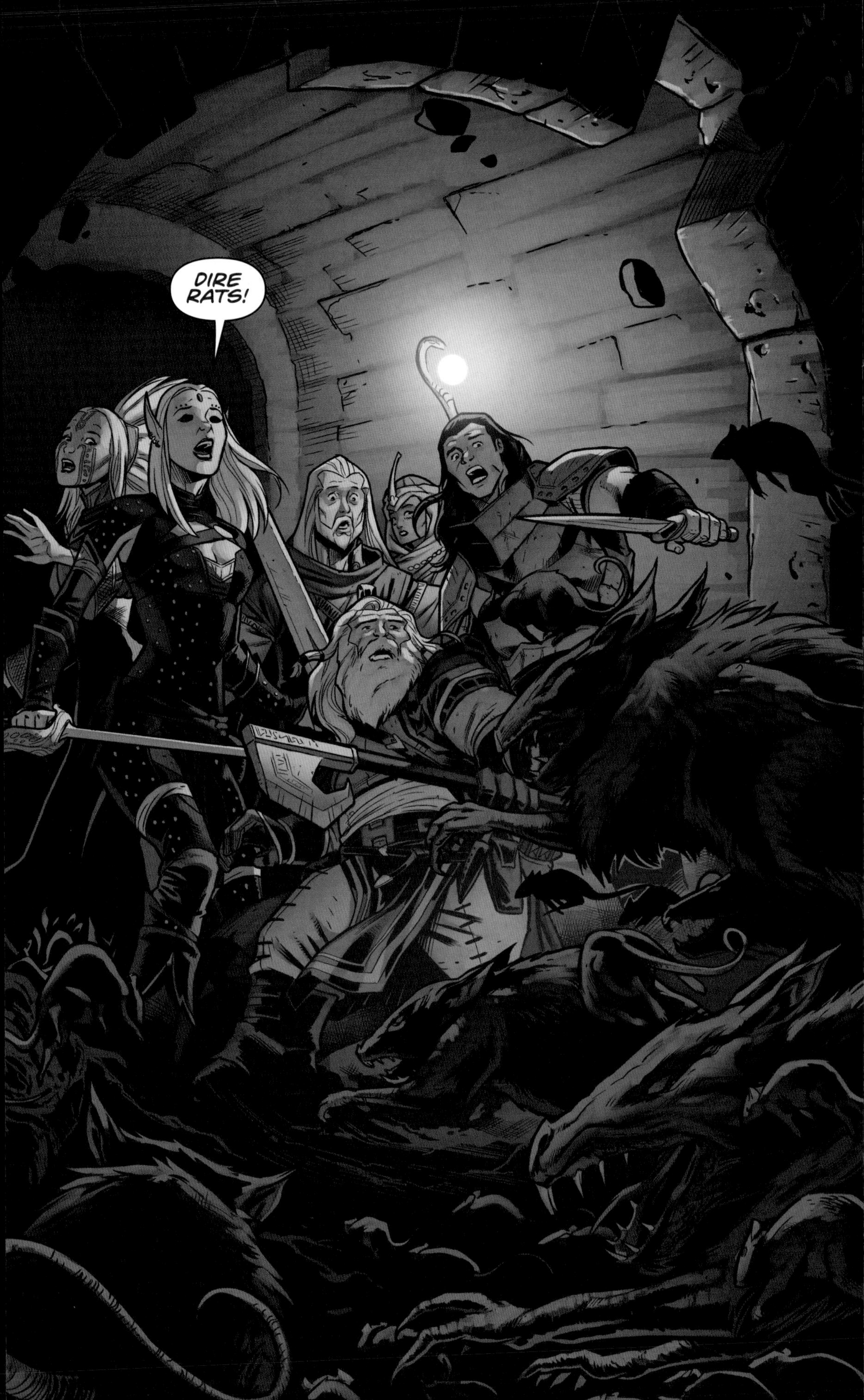
DIRE RATS!

CHAPTER 5

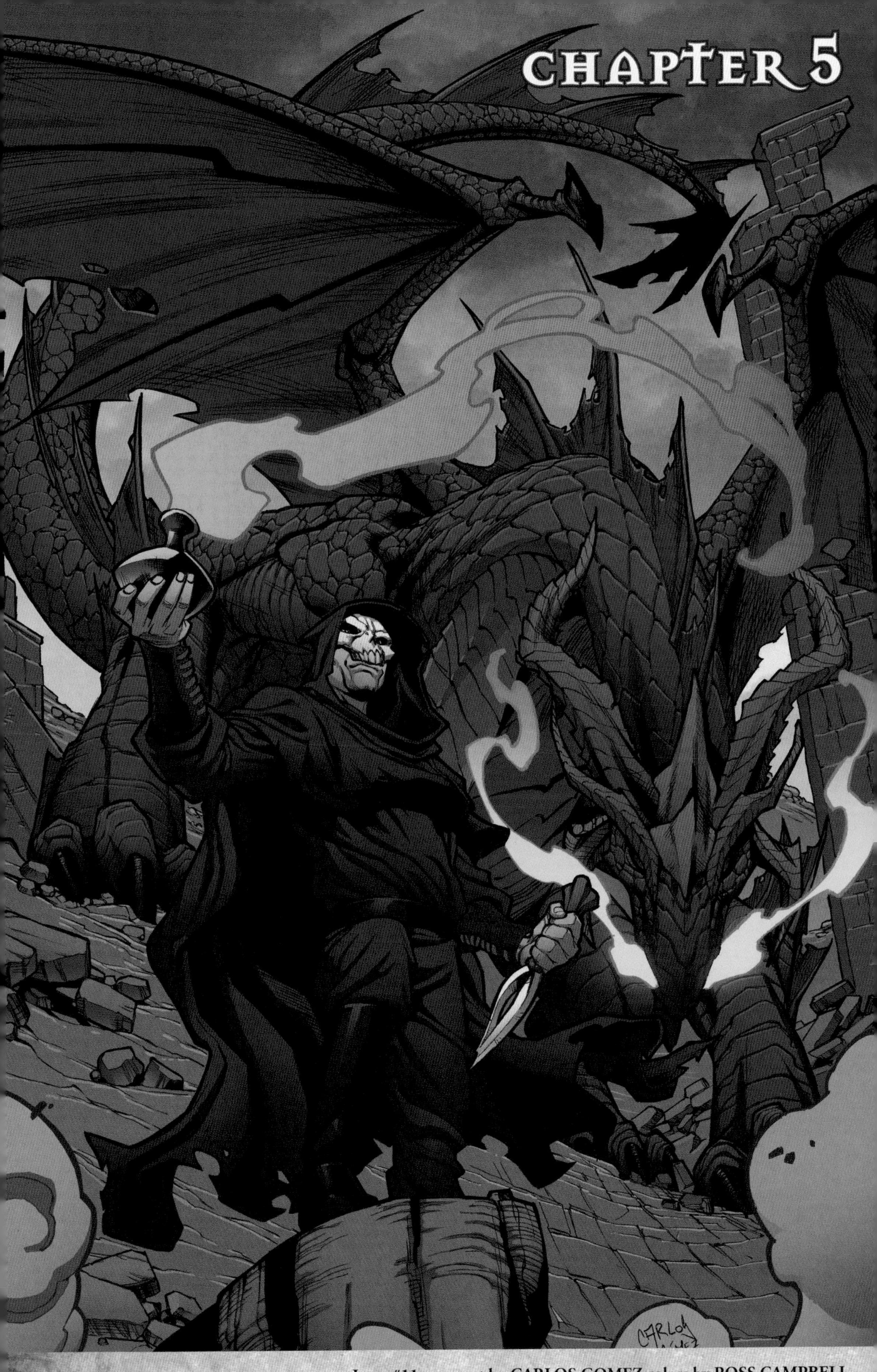

Issue #11 cover art by CARLOS GOMEZ colors by ROSS CAMPBELL

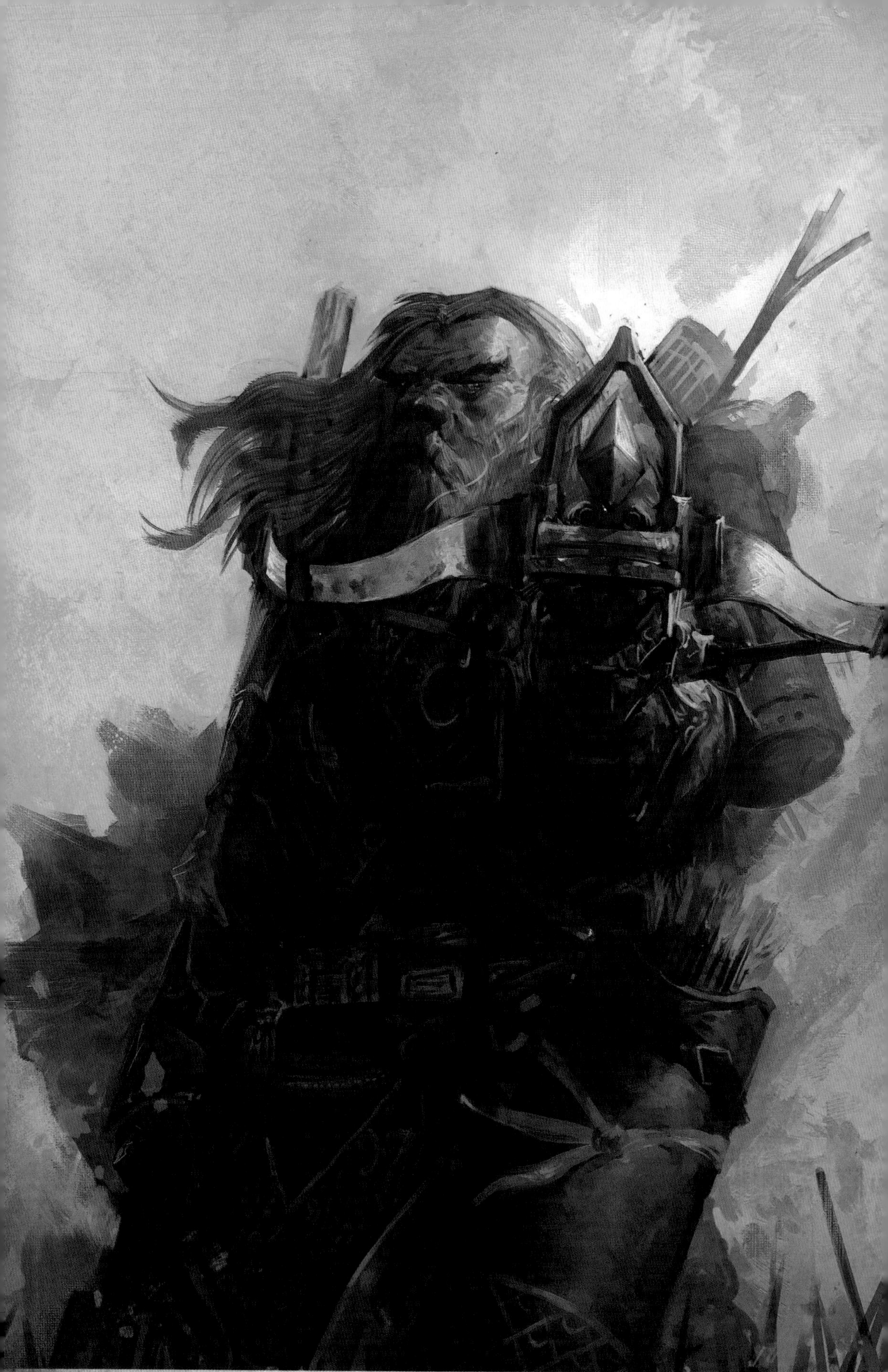
Issue #11 cover art by JORGE FARAS

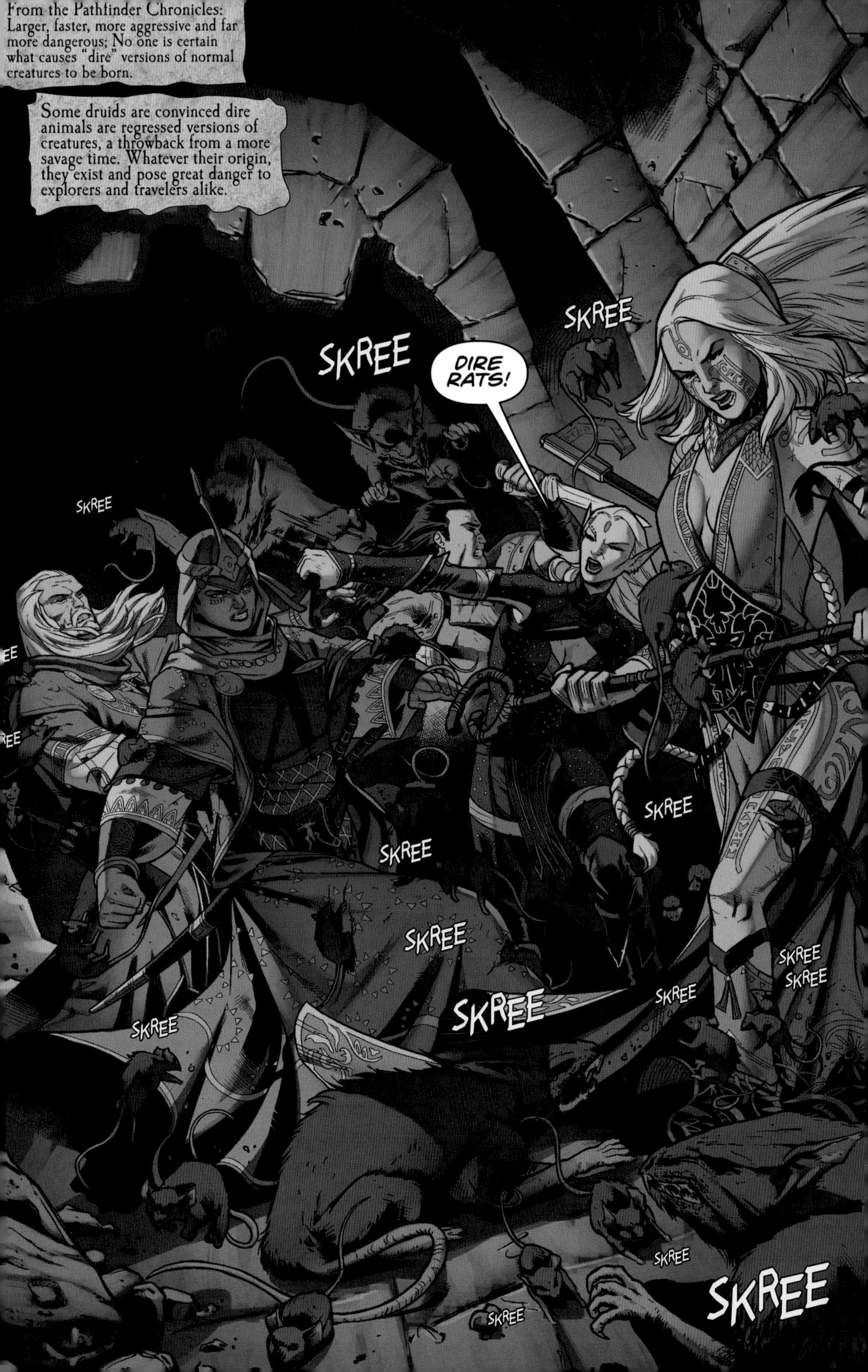
From the Pathfinder Chronicles:
Larger, faster, more aggressive and far more dangerous; No one is certain what causes "dire" versions of normal creatures to be born.
Some druids are convinced dire animals are regressed versions of creatures, a throwback from a more savage time. Whatever their origin, they exist and pose great danger to explorers and travelers alike.
SKREE
SKREE
DIRE RATS!
SKREE
SKREE
SKREE
SKREE
SKREE
SKREE
SKREE
SKREE
SKREE
SKREE
SKREE
SKREE

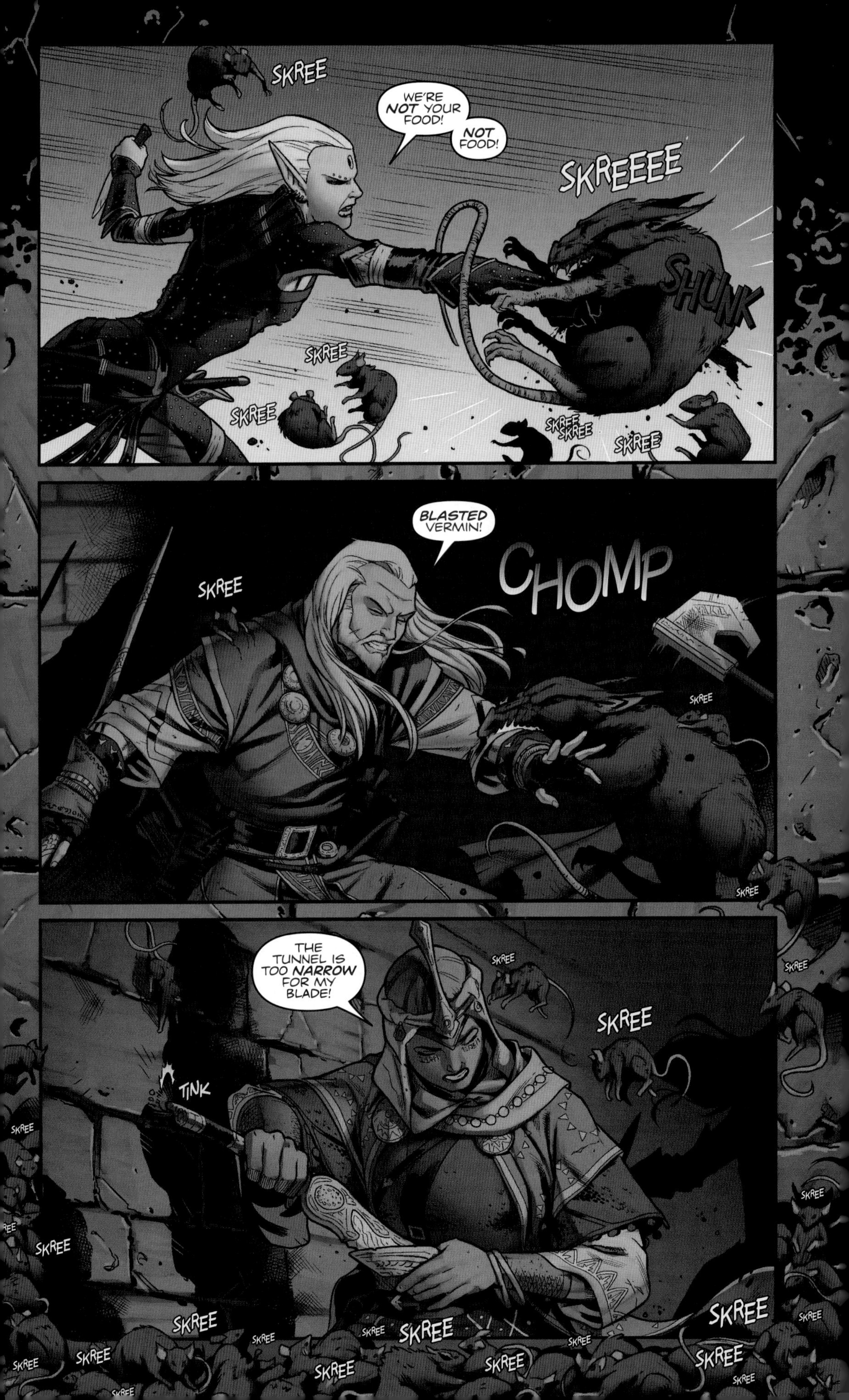
SKREE
WE'RE NOT YOUR FOOD!
NOT FOOD!
SKREEEE
SHUNK
SKREE
SKREE
SKREE SKREE
SKREE
BLASTED VERMIN!
CHOMP
SKREE
SKREE
SKREE
THE TUNNEL IS TOO NARROW FOR MY BLADE!
SKREE
SKREE
SKREE
TINK
SKREE
SKREE
SKREE
SKREE
SKREE
SKREE
SKREE
SKREE
SKREE
SKREE
SKREE
SKREE
SKREE
SKREE

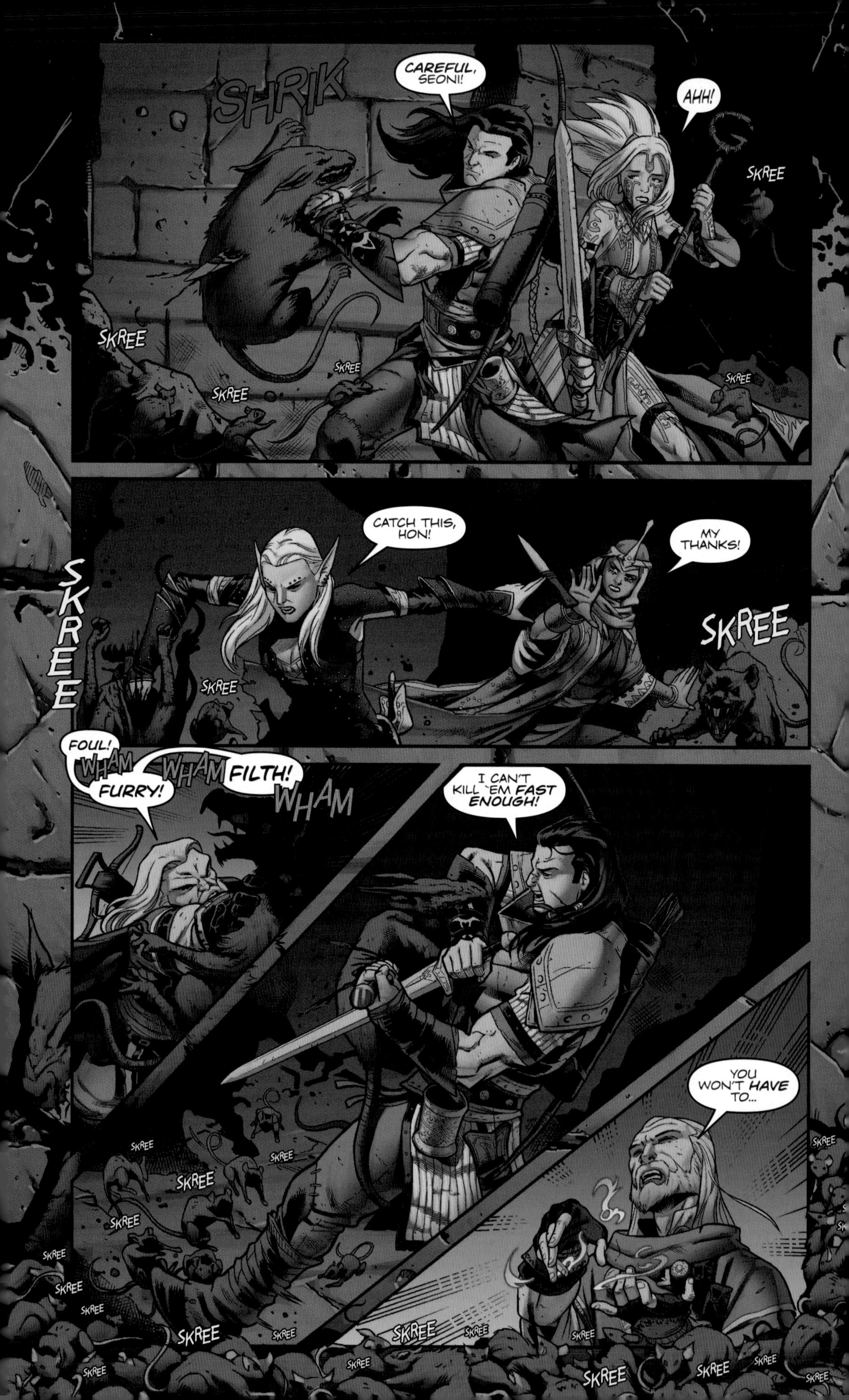

SHRIK
CAREFUL, SEONI!
AHH!
SKREE
SKREE
SKREE
SKREE
SKREE
CATCH THIS, HON!
MY THANKS!
SKREE
SKREE
SKREE
FOUL!
WHAM
FURRY!
WHAM
FILTH!
WHAM
I CAN'T KILL 'EM FAST ENOUGH!
YOU WON'T HAVE TO...
SKREE
SKREE
SKREE
SKREE
SKREE
SKREE
SKREE
SKREE
SKREE
SKREE
SKREE
SKREE
SKREE
SKREE
SKREE
SKREE
SKREE

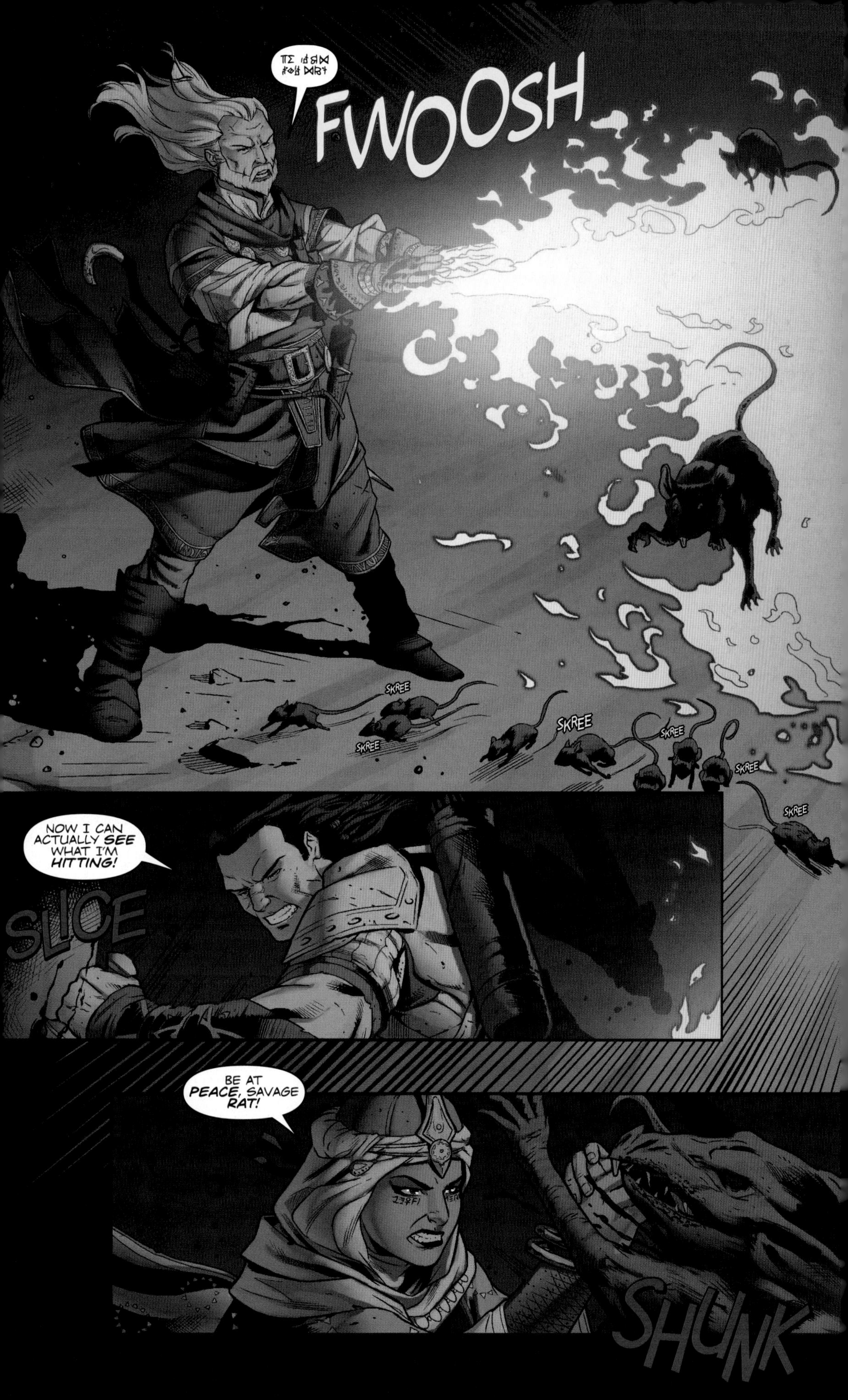
FWOOSH
SKREE
SKREE
SKREE
SKREE
SKREE
SKREE
NOW I CAN ACTUALLY SEE WHAT I'M HITTING!
SLICE
BE AT PEACE, SAVAGE RAT!
SHUNK

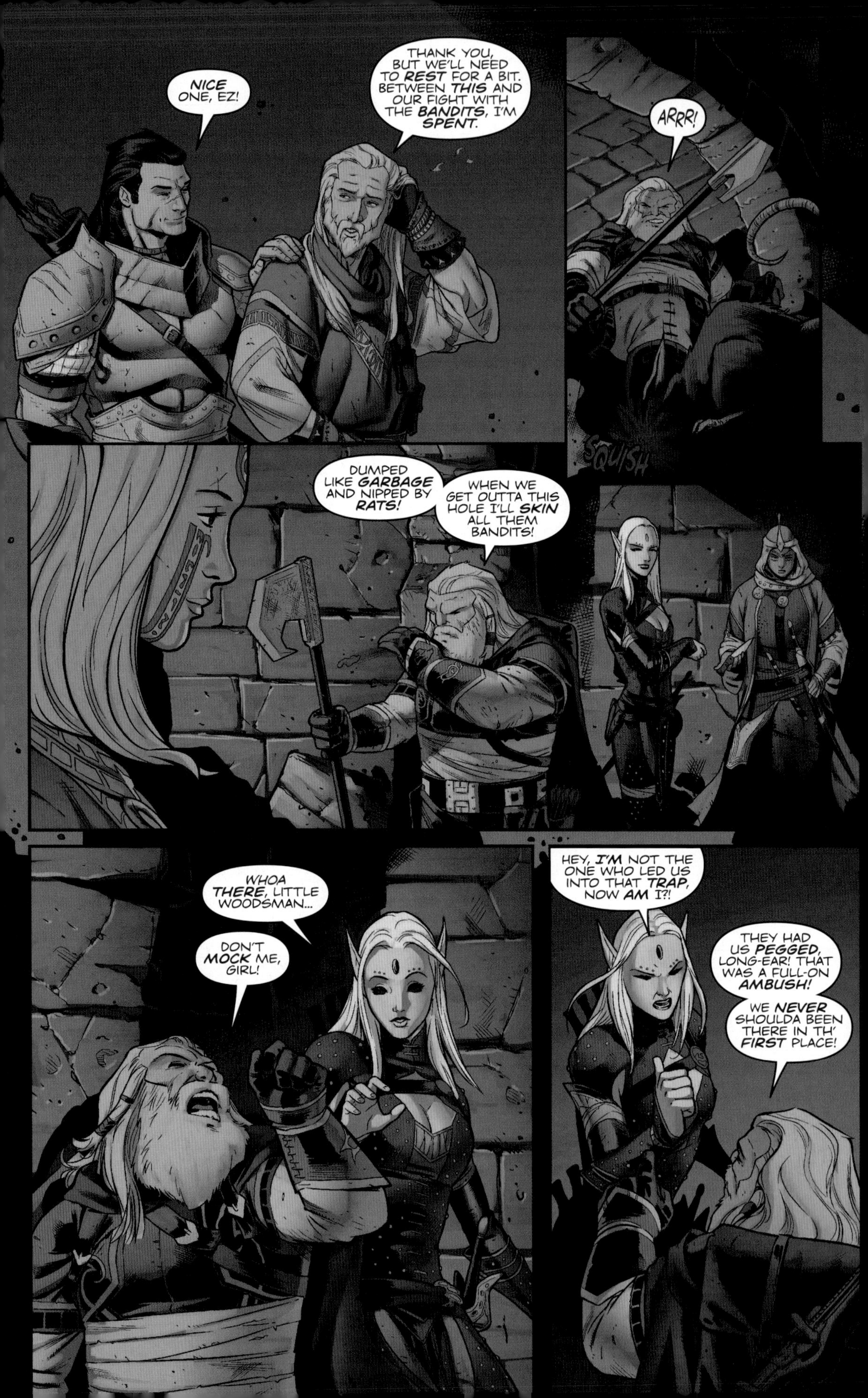
NICE ONE, EZ!
THANK YOU, BUT WE'LL NEED TO REST FOR A BIT. BETWEEN THIS AND OUR FIGHT WITH THE BANDITS, I'M SPENT.
ARRR!
SQUISH
DUMPED LIKE GARBAGE AND NIPPED BY RATS!
WHEN WE GET OUTTA THIS HOLE I'LL SKIN ALL THEM BANDITS!
WHOA THERE, LITTLE WOODSMAN...
DON'T MOCK ME, GIRL!
HEY, I'M NOT THE ONE WHO LED US INTO THAT TRAP, NOW AM I?!
THEY HAD US PEGGED, LONG-EAR! THAT WAS A FULL-ON AMBUSH!
WE NEVER SHOULDA BEEN THERE IN TH' FIRST PLACE!

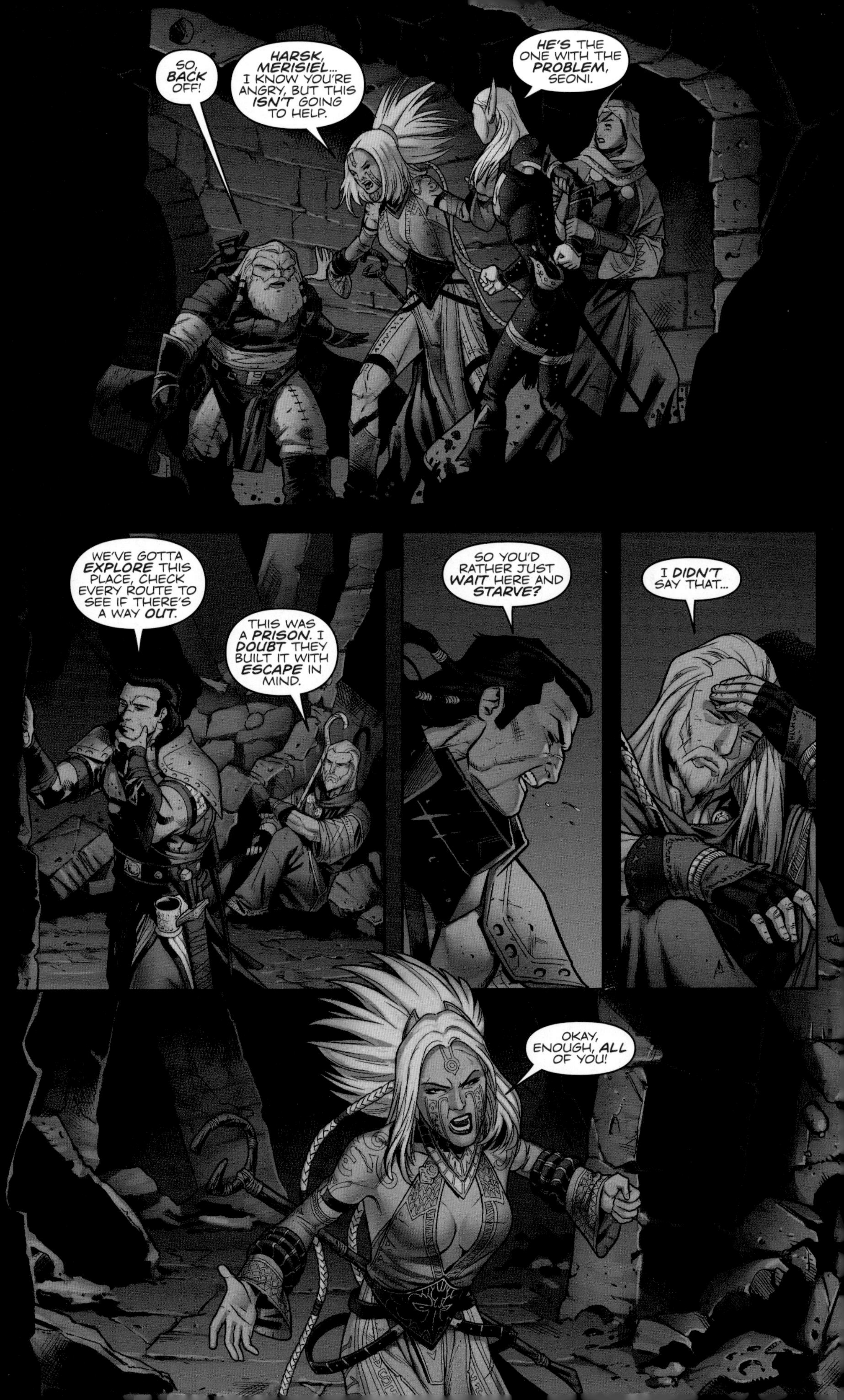
SO, BACK OFF!
HARSK, MERISIEL... I KNOW YOU'RE ANGRY, BUT THIS ISN'T GOING TO HELP.
HE'S THE ONE WITH THE PROBLEM, SEONI.
WE'VE GOTTA EXPLORE THIS PLACE, CHECK EVERY ROUTE TO SEE IF THERE'S A WAY OUT.
THIS WAS A PRISON. I DOUBT THEY BUILT IT WITH ESCAPE IN MIND.
SO YOU'D RATHER JUST WAIT HERE AND STARVE?
I DIDN'T SAY THAT...
OKAY, ENOUGH, ALL OF YOU!

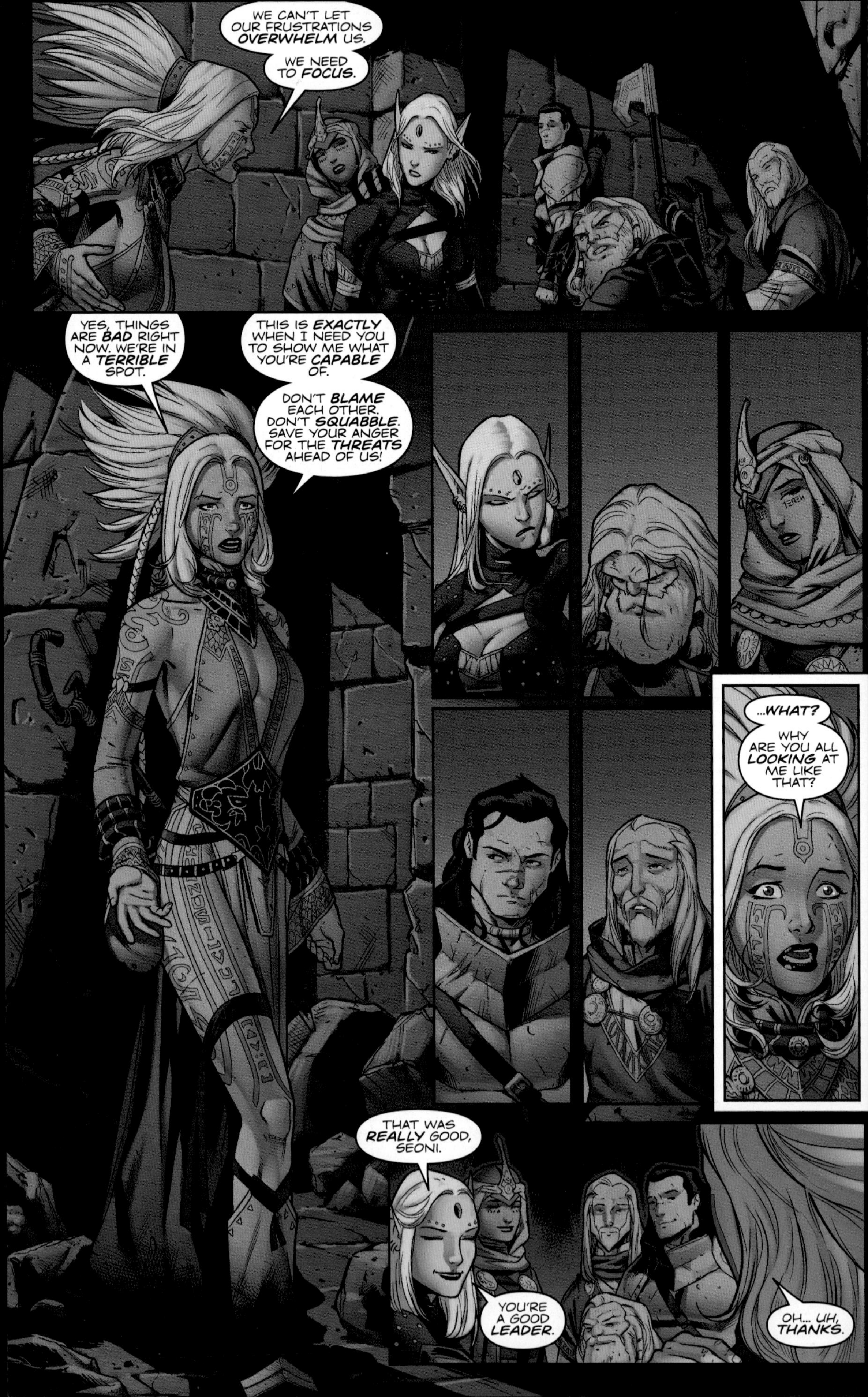
WE CAN'T LET OUR FRUSTRATIONS OVERWHELM US.
WE NEED TO FOCUS.
YES, THINGS ARE BAD RIGHT NOW. WE'RE IN A TERRIBLE SPOT.
THIS IS EXACTLY WHEN I NEED YOU TO SHOW ME WHAT YOU'RE CAPABLE OF.
DON'T BLAME EACH OTHER. DON'T SQUABBLE. SAVE YOUR ANGER FOR THE THREATS AHEAD OF US!
...WHAT?
WHY ARE YOU ALL LOOKING AT ME LIKE THAT?
THAT WAS REALLY GOOD, SEONI.
YOU'RE A GOOD LEADER.
OH... UH, THANKS.

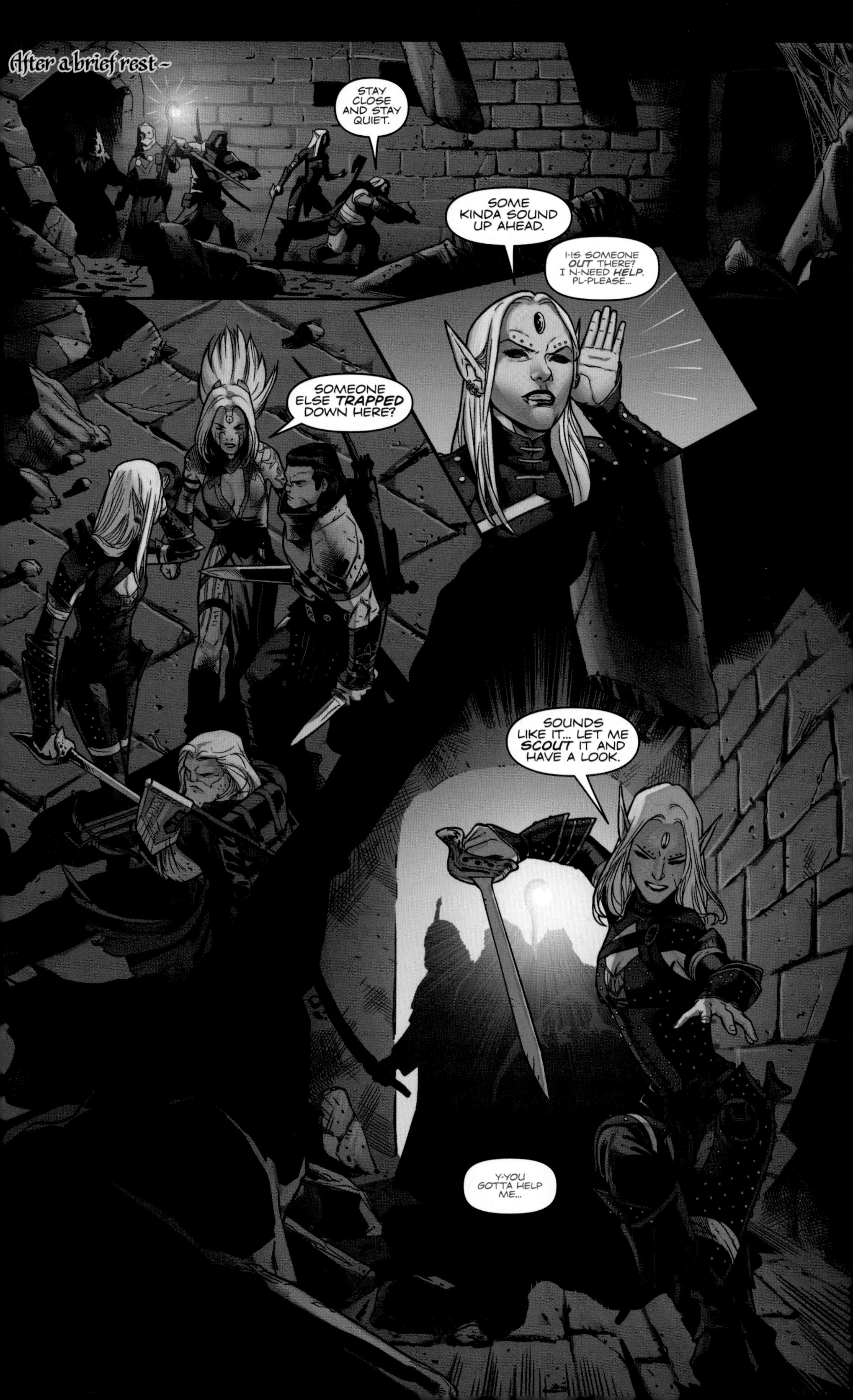
After a brief rest ~
STAY CLOSE AND STAY QUIET.
SOME KINDA SOUND UP AHEAD.
I-IS SOMEONE OUT THERE? I N-NEED HELP. PL-PLEASE...
SOMEONE ELSE TRAPPED DOWN HERE?
SOUNDS LIKE IT... LET ME SCOUT IT AND HAVE A LOOK.
Y-YOU GOTTA HELP ME...

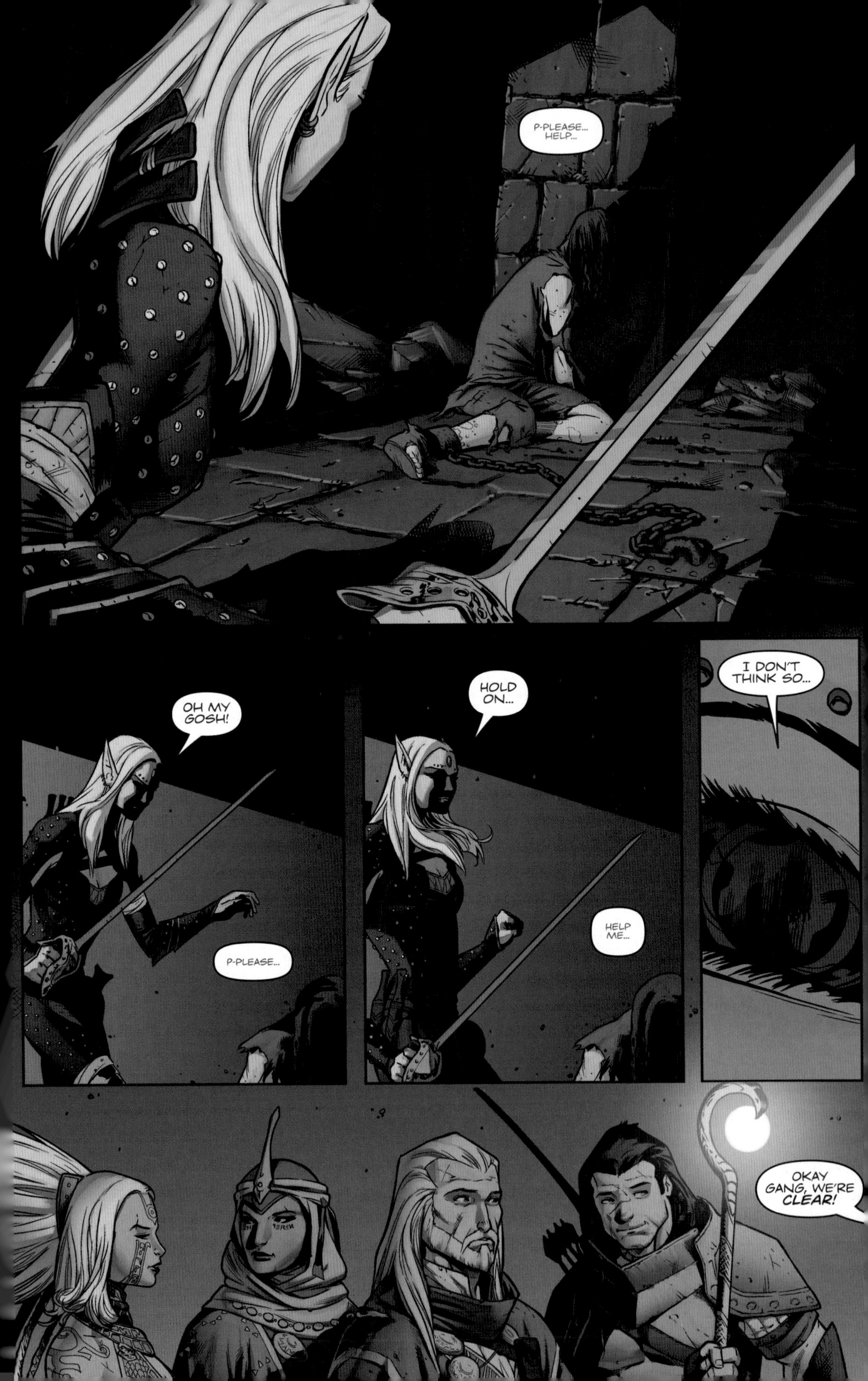
P-PLEASE... HELP...
OH MY GOSH!
P-PLEASE...
HOLD ON...
HELP ME...
I DON'T THINK SO...
OKAY GANG, WE'RE CLEAR!

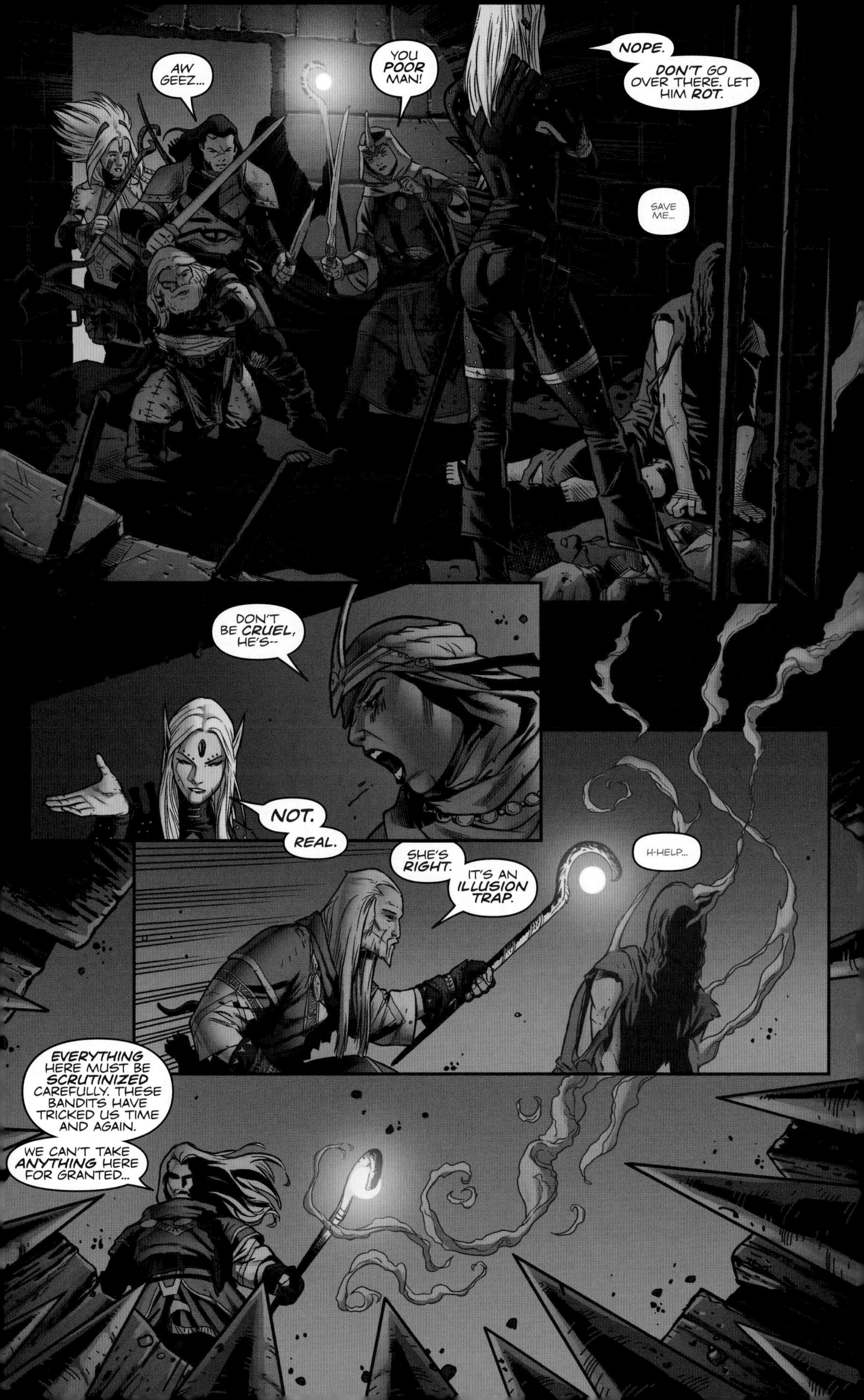
AW GEEZ...
YOU POOR MAN!
NOPE.
DON'T GO OVER THERE. LET HIM ROT.
SAVE ME...
DON'T BE CRUEL, HE'S--
NOT.
REAL.
SHE'S RIGHT.
IT'S AN ILLUSION TRAP.
H-HELP...
EVERYTHING HERE MUST BE SCRUTINIZED CAREFULLY. THESE BANDITS HAVE TRICKED US TIME AND AGAIN.
WE CAN'T TAKE ANYTHING HERE FOR GRANTED...

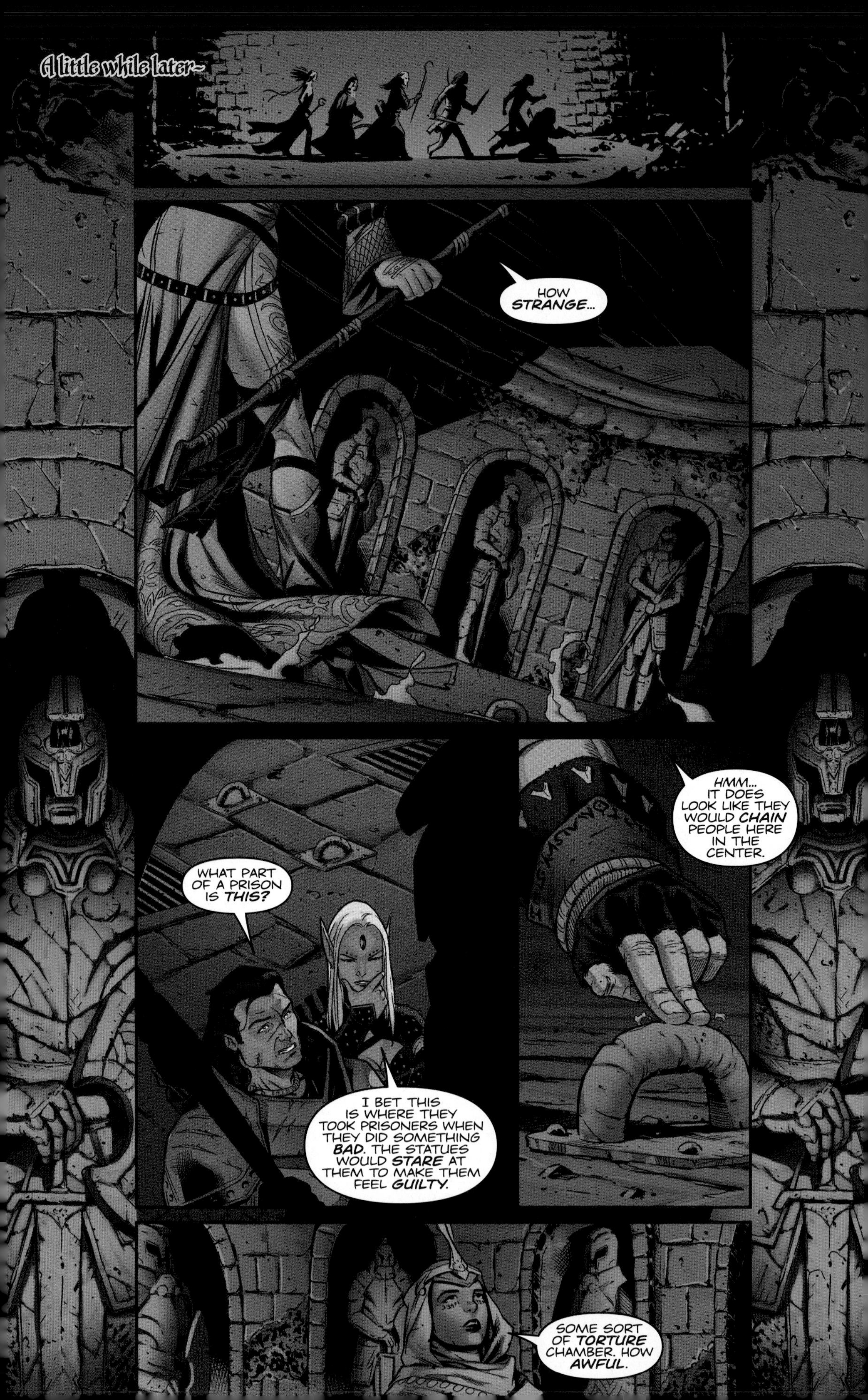
A little while later~
HOW STRANGE...
WHAT PART OF A PRISON IS THIS?
I BET THIS IS WHERE THEY TOOK PRISONERS WHEN THEY DID SOMETHING BAD. THE STATUES WOULD STARE AT THEM TO MAKE THEM FEEL GUILTY.
HMM... IT DOES LOOK LIKE THEY WOULD CHAIN PEOPLE HERE IN THE CENTER.
SOME SORT OF TORTURE CHAMBER. HOW AWFUL.

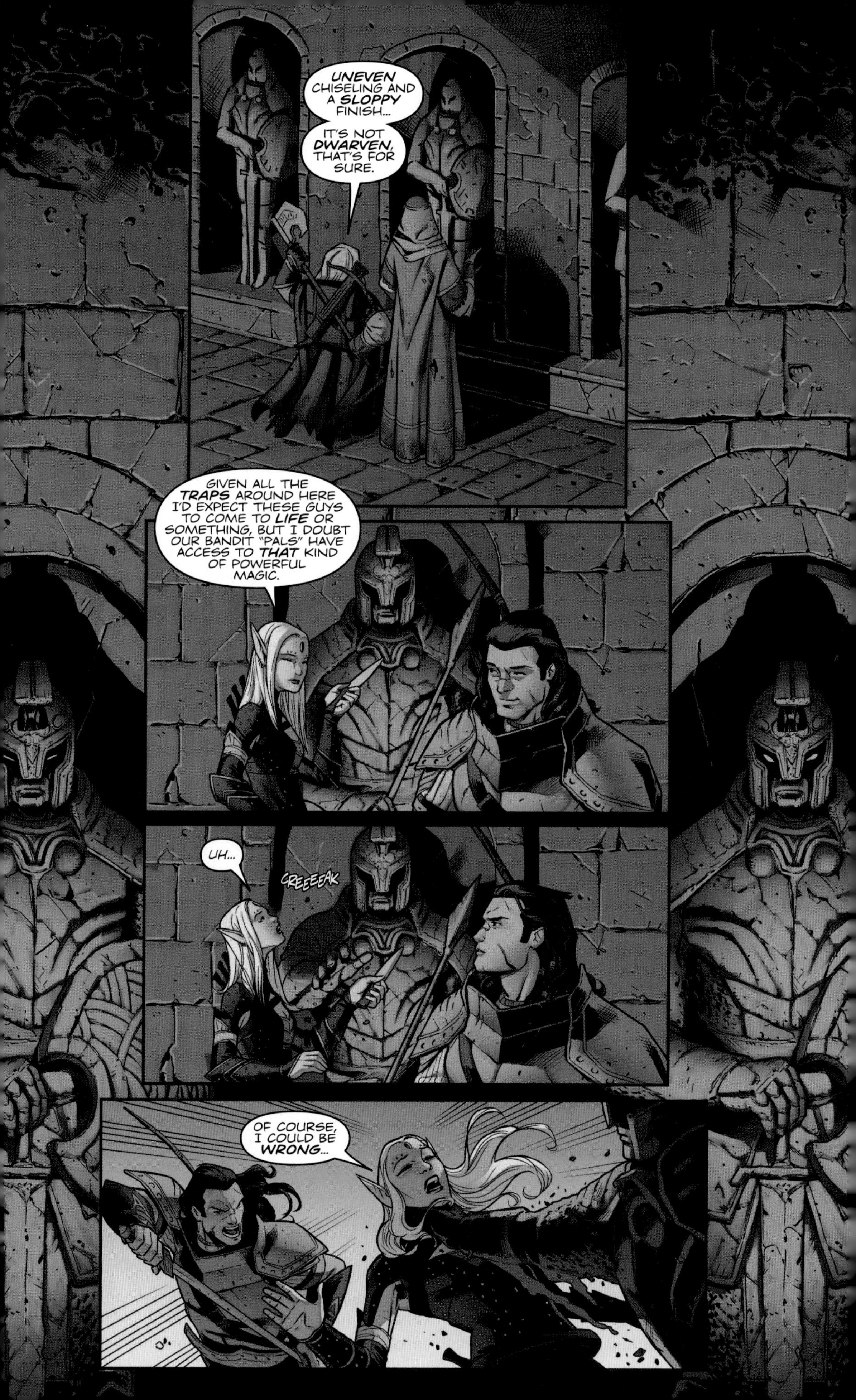
UNEVEN CHISELING AND A SLOPPY FINISH...
IT'S NOT DWARVEN, THAT'S FOR SURE.
GIVEN ALL THE TRAPS AROUND HERE I'D EXPECT THESE GUYS TO COME TO LIFE OR SOMETHING, BUT I DOUBT OUR BANDIT "PALS" HAVE ACCESS TO THAT KIND OF POWERFUL MAGIC.
UH...
CREEEEAK
OF COURSE, I COULD BE WRONG...

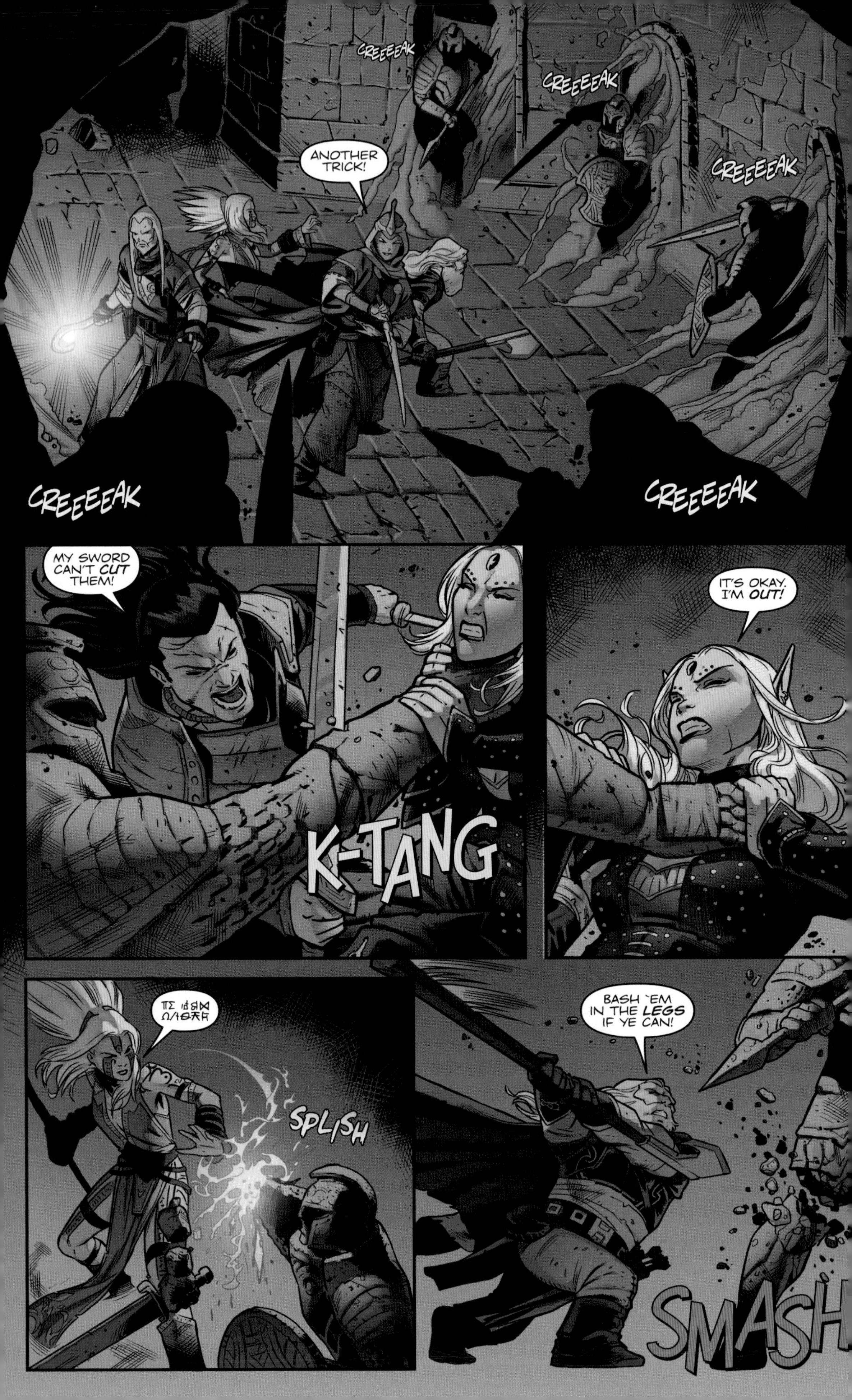
CREEEEAK
CREEEEAK
ANOTHER TRICK!
CREEEEEAK
CREEEEEAK
CREEEEAK
MY SWORD CAN'T CUT THEM!
K-TANG
IT'S OKAY. I'M OUT!
SPLISH
BASH `EM IN THE LEGS IF YE CAN!
SMASH

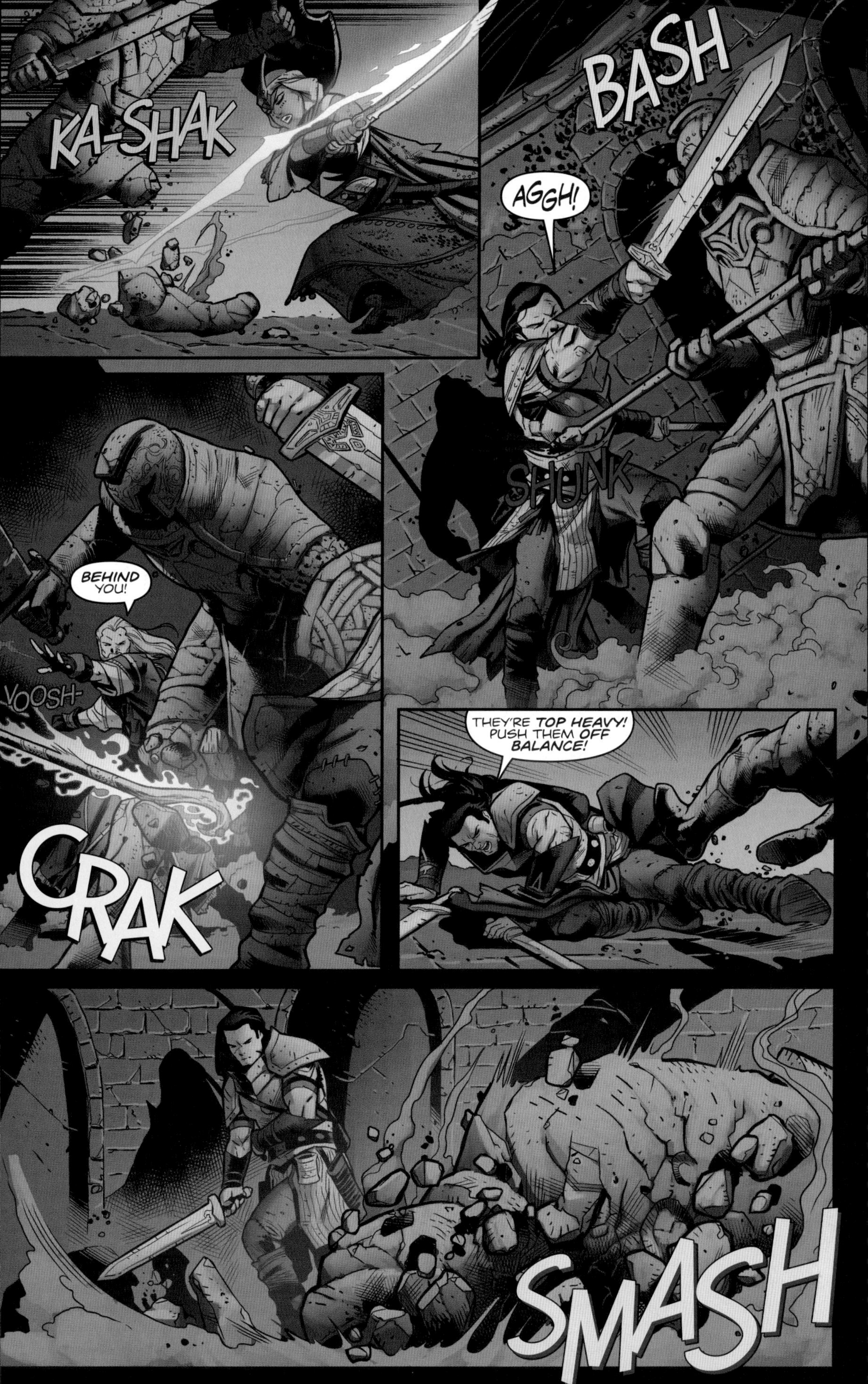
KA-SHAK
BASH
AGGH!
SHUNK
BEHIND YOU!
VOOSH-
CRAK
THEY'RE TOP HEAVY! PUSH THEM OFF BALANCE!
SMASH

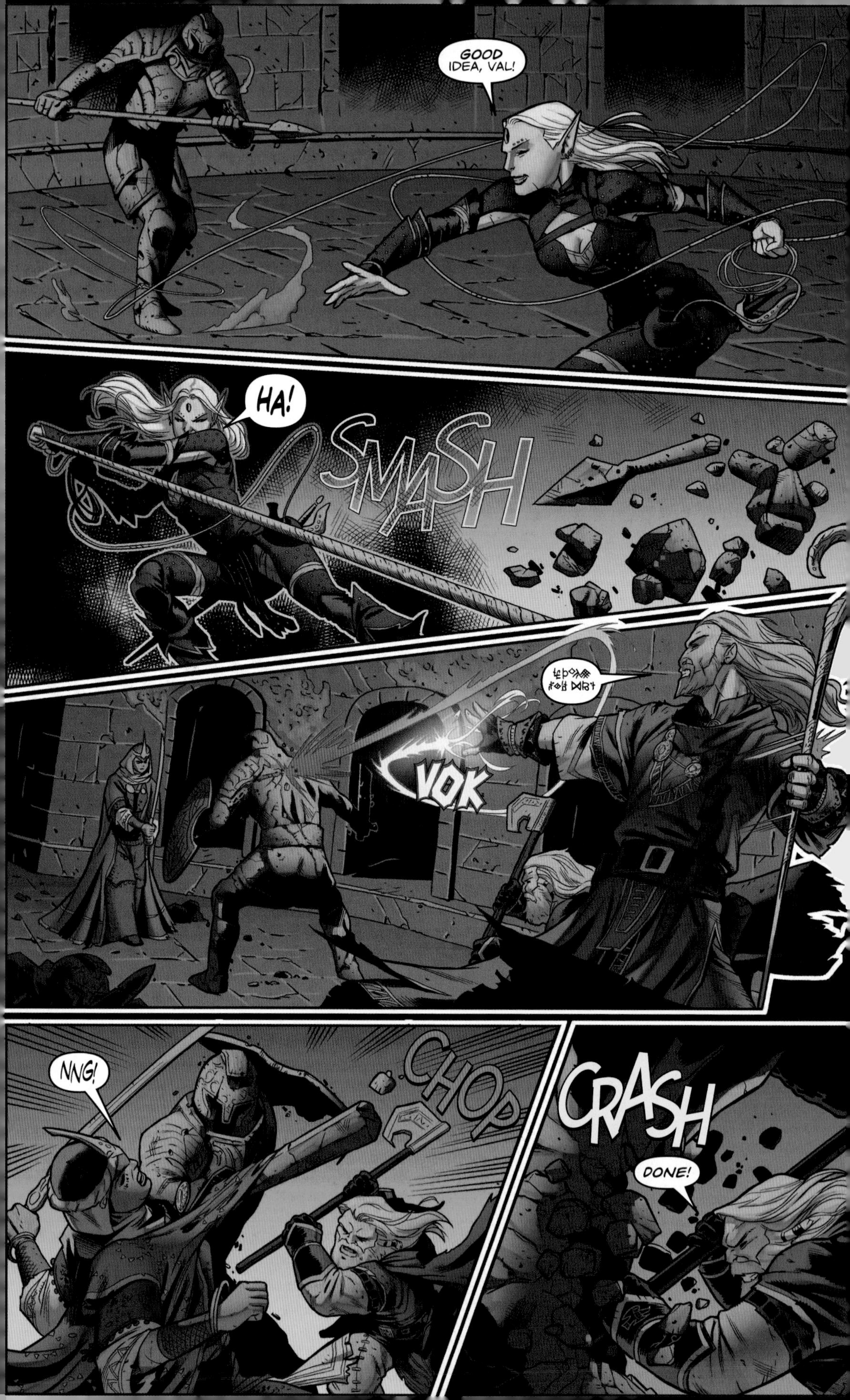
GOOD IDEA, VAL!
HA!
SMASH
VOK
NNG!
CHOP
CRASH
DONE!

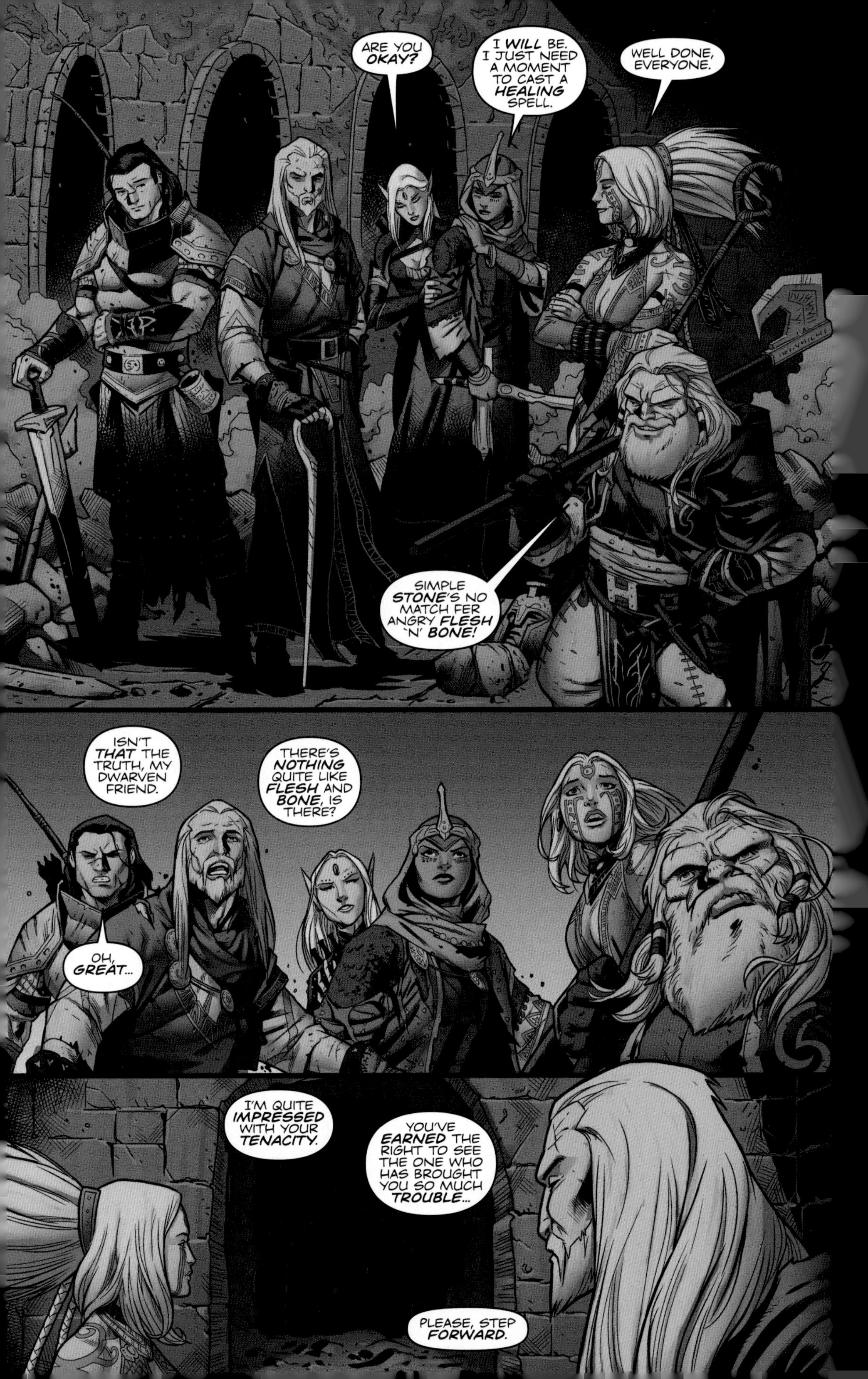
ARE YOU OKAY?
I WILL BE. I JUST NEED A MOMENT TO CAST A HEALING SPELL.
WELL DONE, EVERYONE.
SIMPLE STONE'S NO MATCH FER ANGRY FLESH 'N' BONE!
ISN'T THAT THE TRUTH, MY DWARVEN FRIEND.
THERE'S NOTHING QUITE LIKE FLESH AND BONE, IS THERE?
OH, GREAT...
I'M QUITE IMPRESSED WITH YOUR TENACITY.
YOU'VE EARNED THE RIGHT TO SEE THE ONE WHO HAS BROUGHT YOU SO MUCH TROUBLE...
PLEASE, STEP FORWARD.

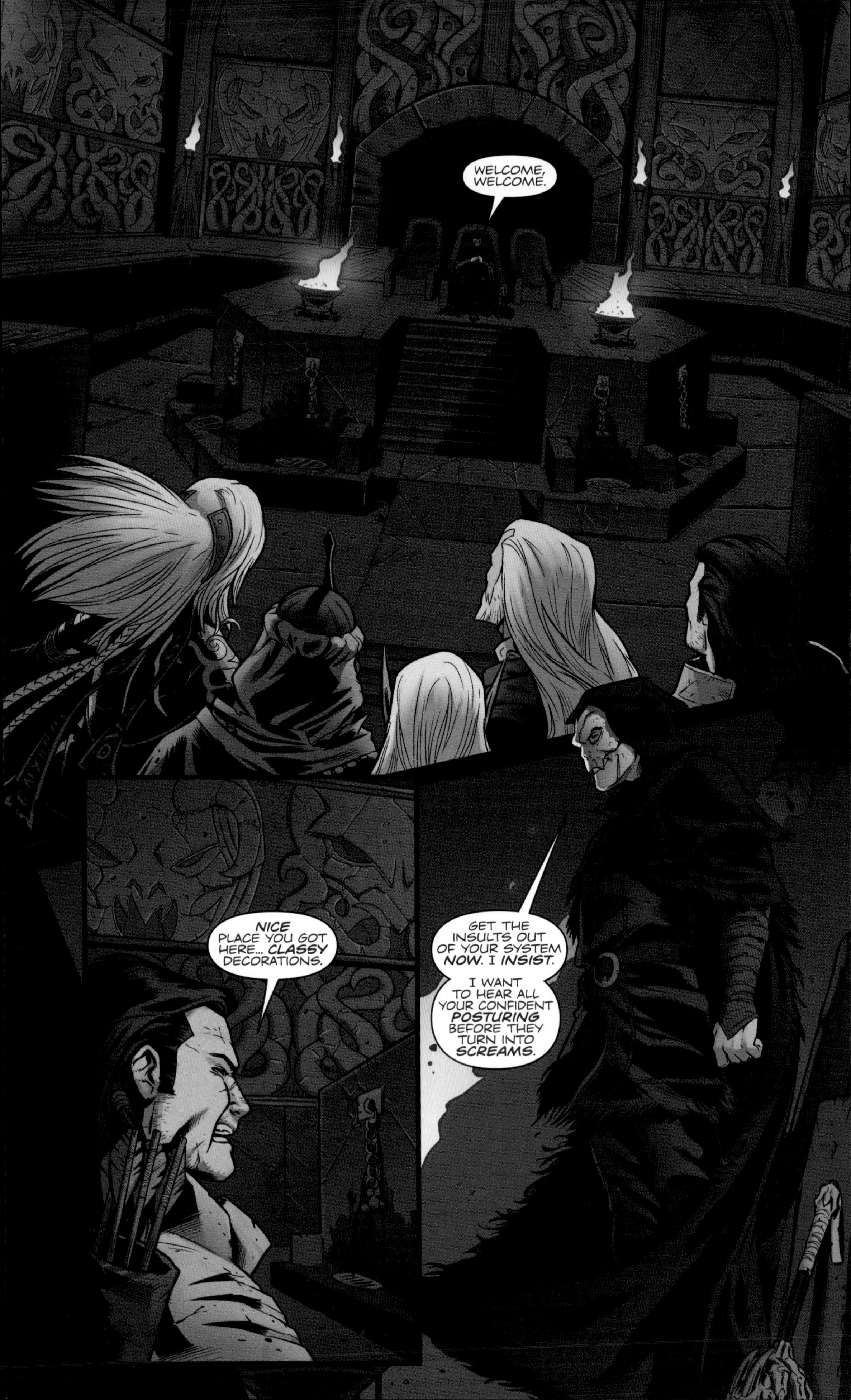
WELCOME, WELCOME.
NICE PLACE YOU GOT HERE... CLASSY DECORATIONS.
GET THE INSULTS OUT OF YOUR SYSTEM NOW. I INSIST.
I WANT TO HEAR ALL YOUR CONFIDENT POSTURING BEFORE THEY TURN INTO SCREAMS.

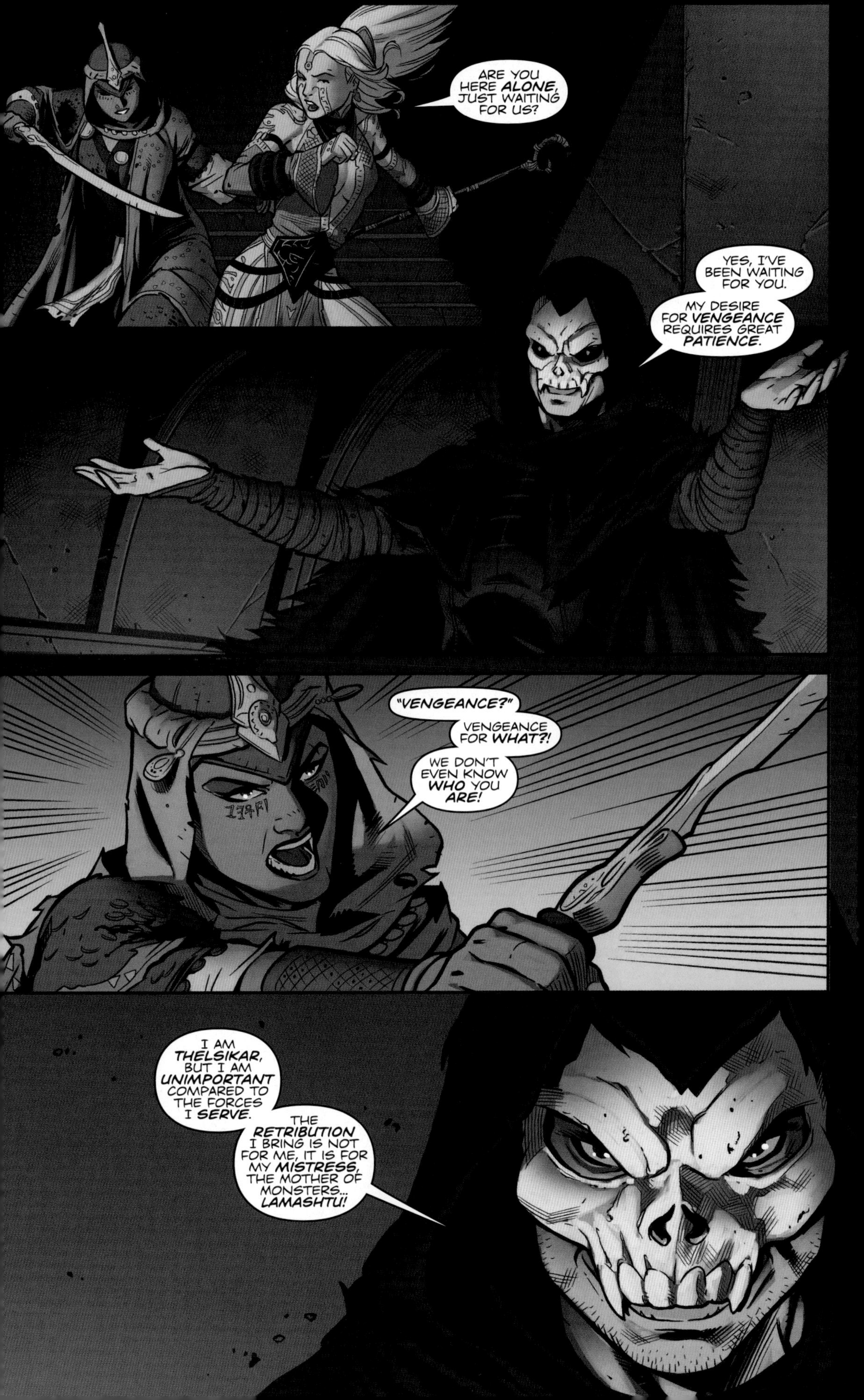
ARE YOU HERE ALONE, JUST WAITING FOR US?
YES, I'VE BEEN WAITING FOR YOU.
MY DESIRE FOR VENGEANCE REQUIRES GREAT PATIENCE.
"VENGEANCE?"
VENGEANCE FOR WHAT?!
WE DON'T EVEN KNOW WHO YOU ARE!
I AM THELSIKAR, BUT I AM UNIMPORTANT COMPARED TO THE FORCES I SERVE.
THE RETRIBUTION I BRING IS NOT FOR ME, IT IS FOR MY MISTRESS, THE MOTHER OF MONSTERS... LAMASHTU!

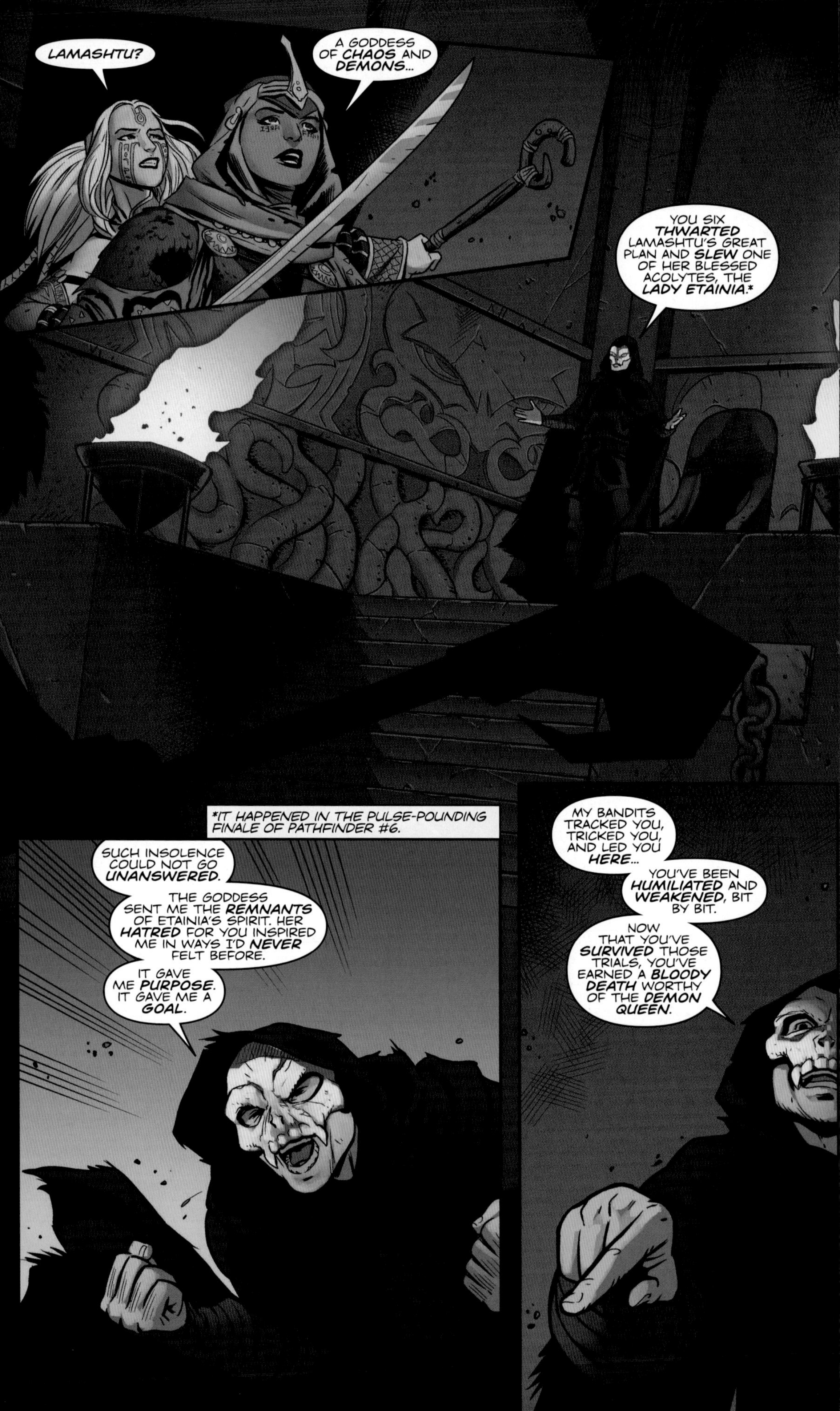
LAMASHTU?
A GODDESS OF CHAOS AND DEMONS...
YOU SIX THWARTED LAMASHTU'S GREAT PLAN AND SLEW ONE OF HER BLESSED ACOLYTES, THE LADY ETAINIA.*
*IT HAPPENED IN THE PULSE-POUNDING FINALE OF PATHFINDER #6.
SUCH INSOLENCE COULD NOT GO UNANSWERED.
THE GODDESS SENT ME THE REMNANTS OF ETAINIA'S SPIRIT. HER HATRED FOR YOU INSPIRED ME IN WAYS I'D NEVER FELT BEFORE.
IT GAVE ME PURPOSE. IT GAVE ME A GOAL.
MY BANDITS TRACKED YOU, TRICKED YOU, AND LED YOU HERE...
YOU'VE BEEN HUMILIATED AND WEAKENED, BIT BY BIT.
NOW THAT YOU'VE SURVIVED THOSE TRIALS, YOU'VE EARNED A BLOODY DEATH WORTHY OF THE DEMON QUEEN.

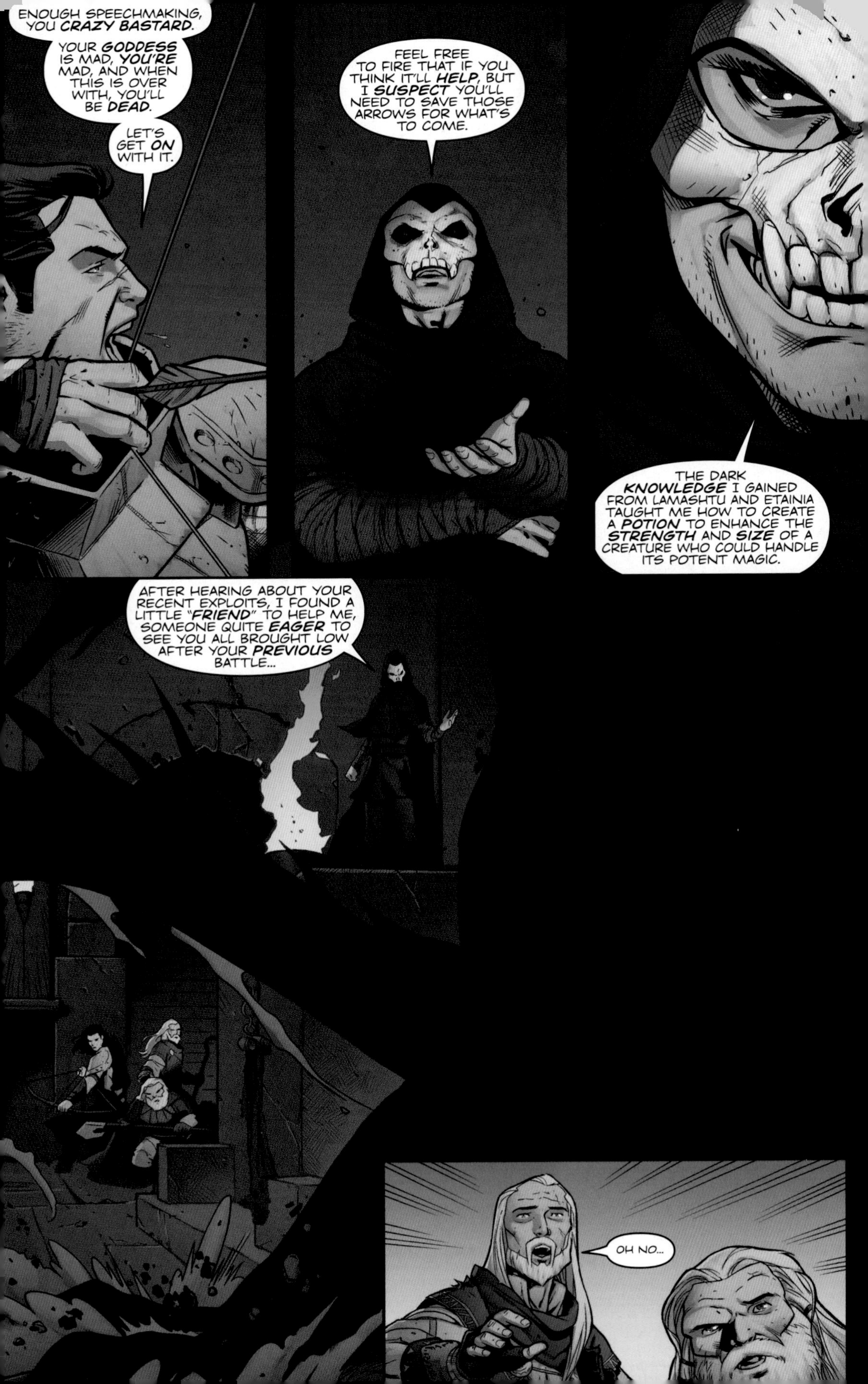
ENOUGH SPEECHMAKING, YOU CRAZY BASTARD.
YOUR GODDESS IS MAD, YOU'RE MAD, AND WHEN THIS IS OVER WITH, YOU'LL BE DEAD.
LET'S GET ON WITH IT.
FEEL FREE TO FIRE THAT IF YOU THINK IT'LL HELP, BUT I SUSPECT YOU'LL NEED TO SAVE THOSE ARROWS FOR WHAT'S TO COME.
THE DARK KNOWLEDGE I GAINED FROM LAMASHTU AND ETAINIA TAUGHT ME HOW TO CREATE A POTION TO ENHANCE THE STRENGTH AND SIZE OF A CREATURE WHO COULD HANDLE ITS POTENT MAGIC.
AFTER HEARING ABOUT YOUR RECENT EXPLOITS, I FOUND A LITTLE "FRIEND" TO HELP ME, SOMEONE QUITE EAGER TO SEE YOU ALL BROUGHT LOW AFTER YOUR PREVIOUS BATTLE...
OH NO...

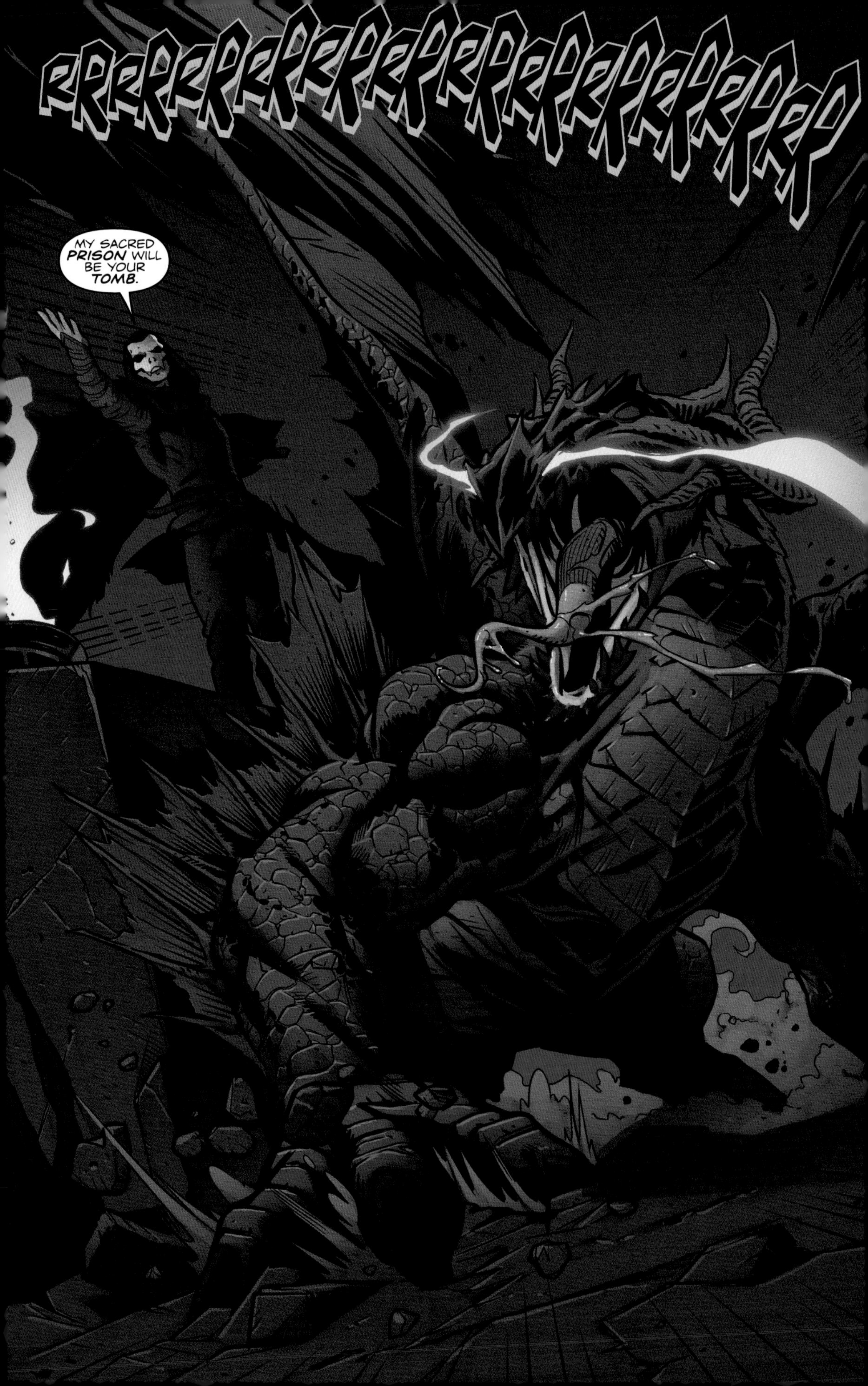
RRRRRRRRRRRRRRRRRRRRRR
MY SACRED PRISON WILL BE YOUR TOMB.

CHAPTER 6

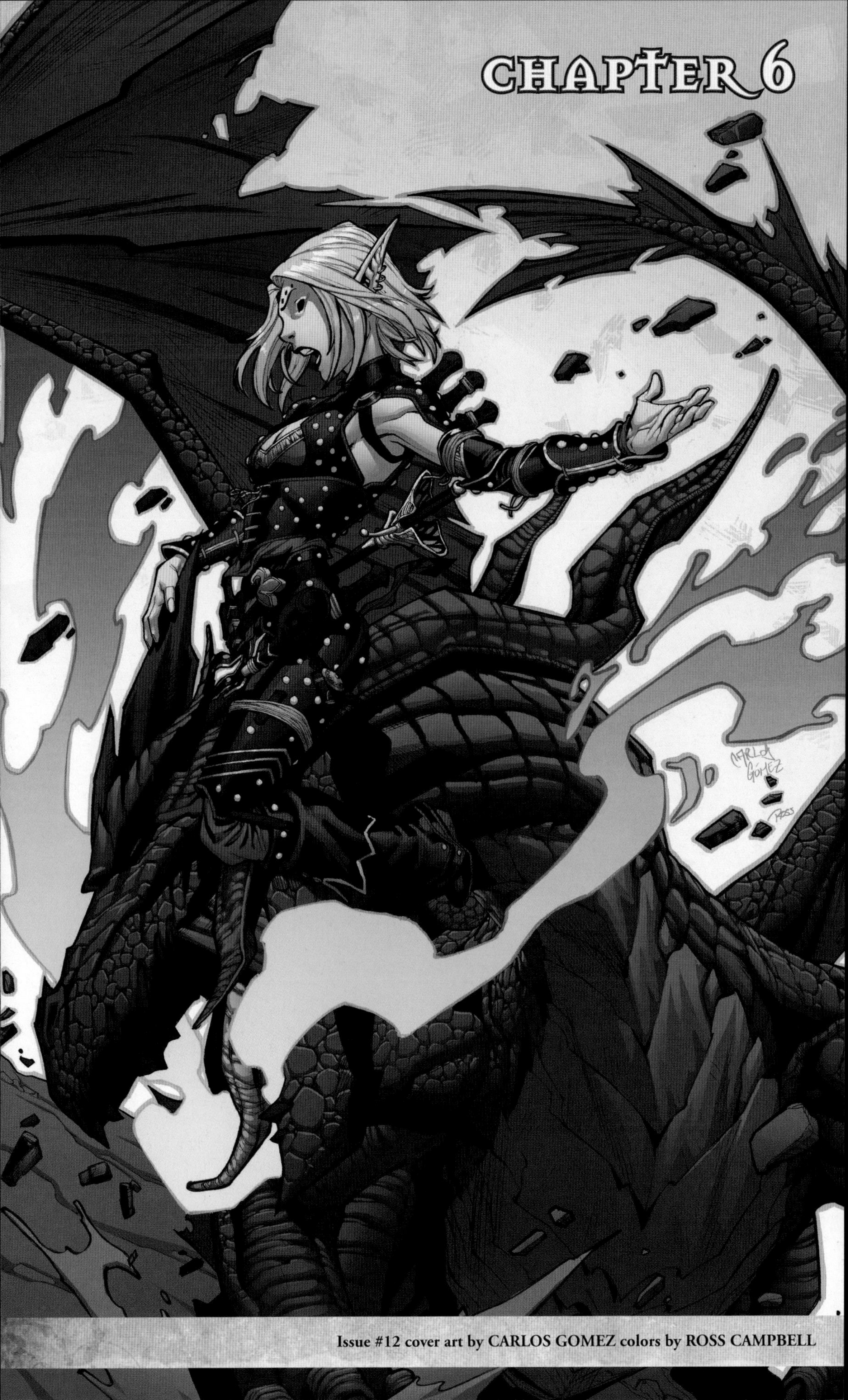
CARLOS GÓMEZ
ROSS

Issue #12 cover art by CARLOS GOMEZ colors by ROSS CAMPBELL

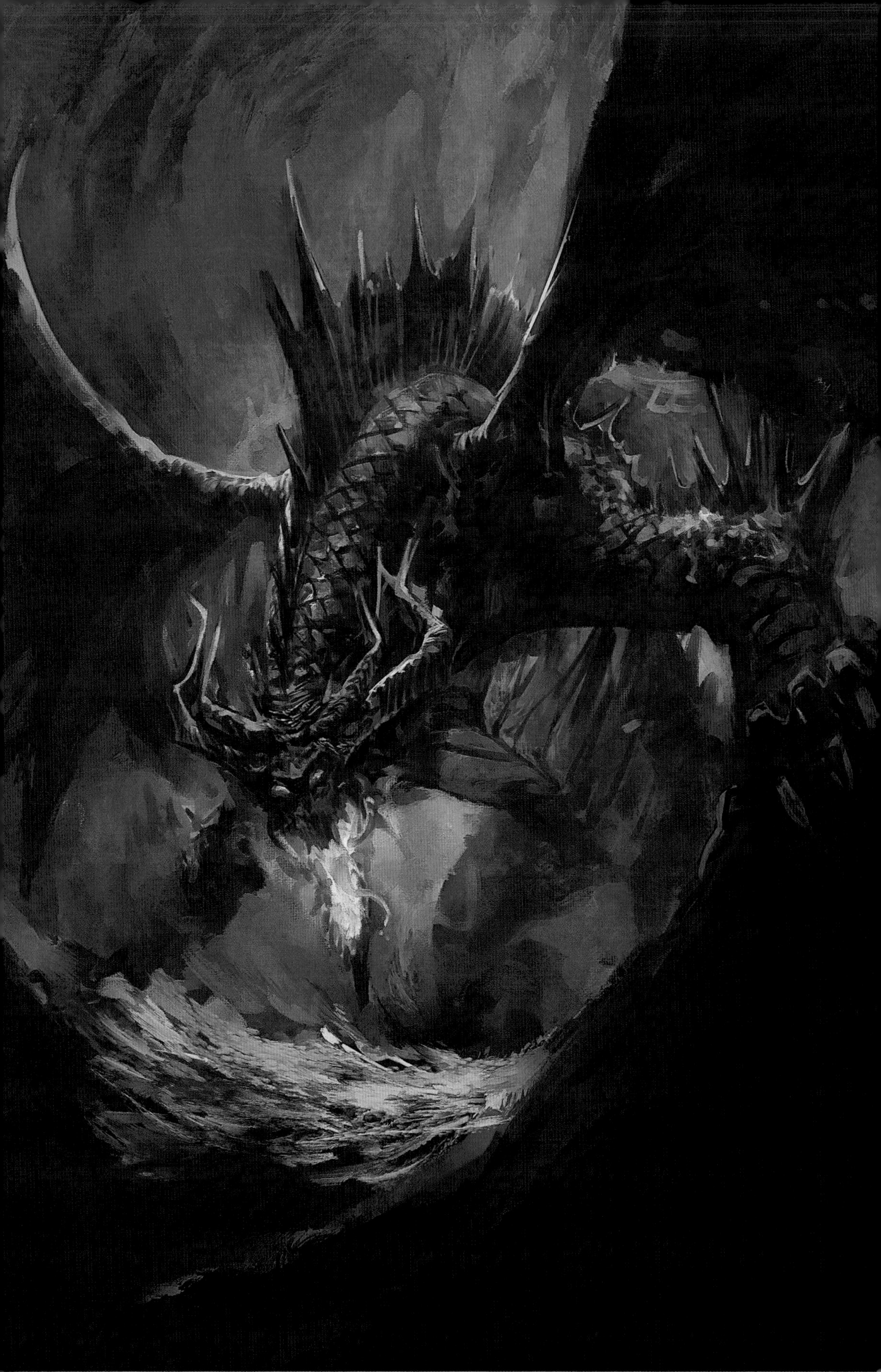

Issue #12 cover art by JORGE FARAS

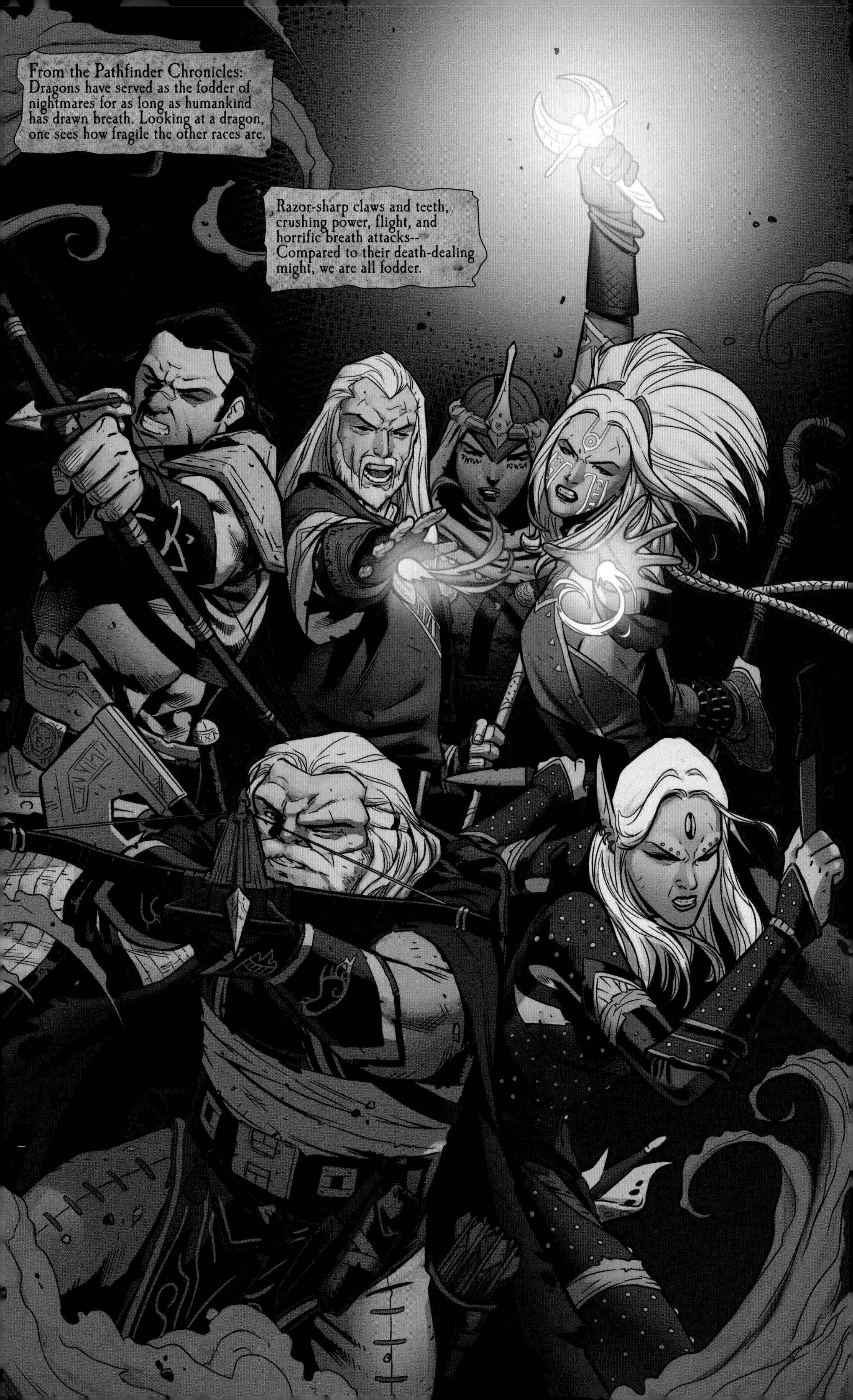
From the Pathfinder Chronicles: Dragons have served as the fodder of nightmares for as long as humankind has drawn breath. Looking at a dragon, one sees how fragile the other races are.
Razor-sharp claws and teeth, crushing power, flight, and horrific breath attacks-- Compared to their death-dealing might, we are all fodder.

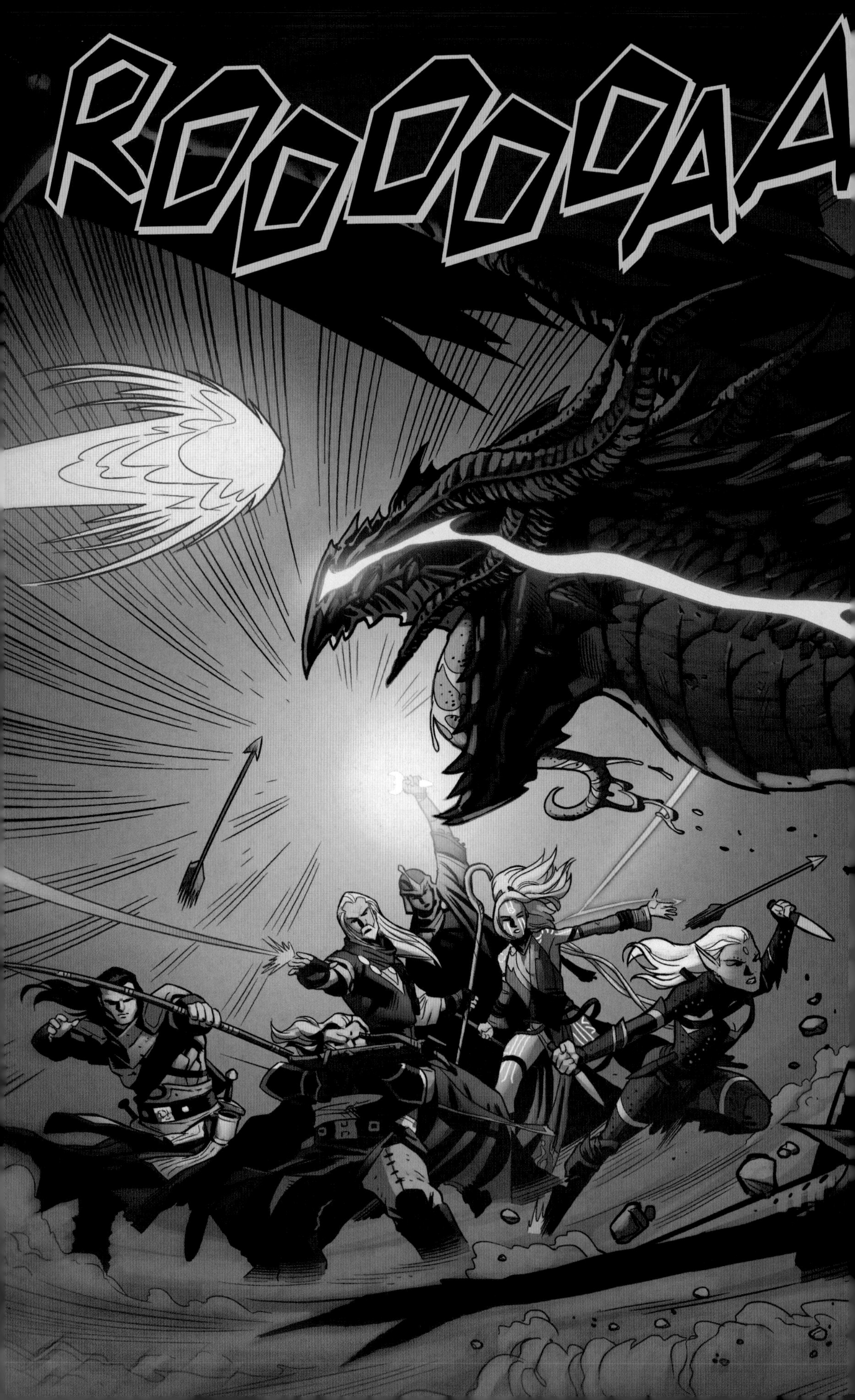
ROOOOOAA

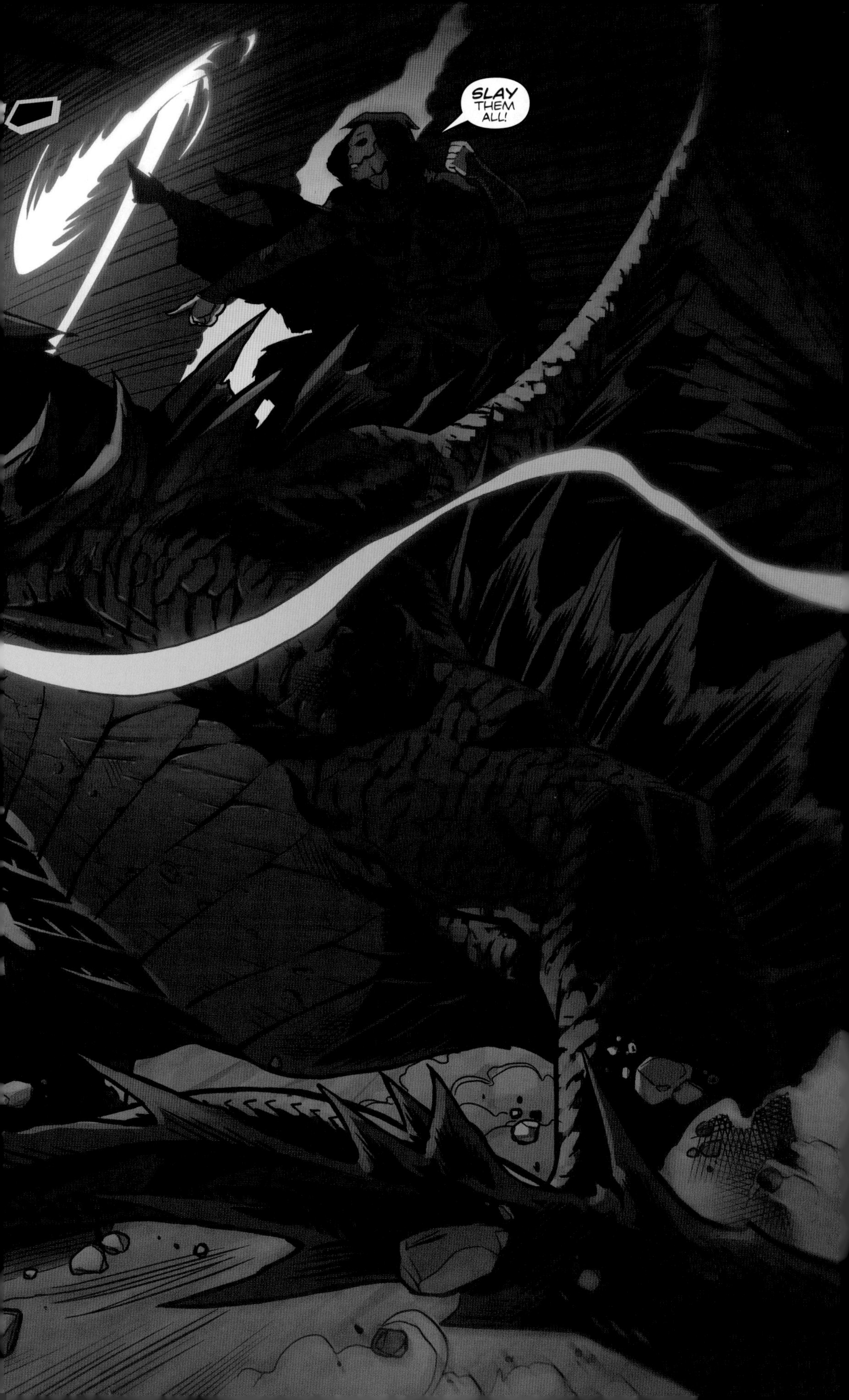
SLAY THEM ALL!

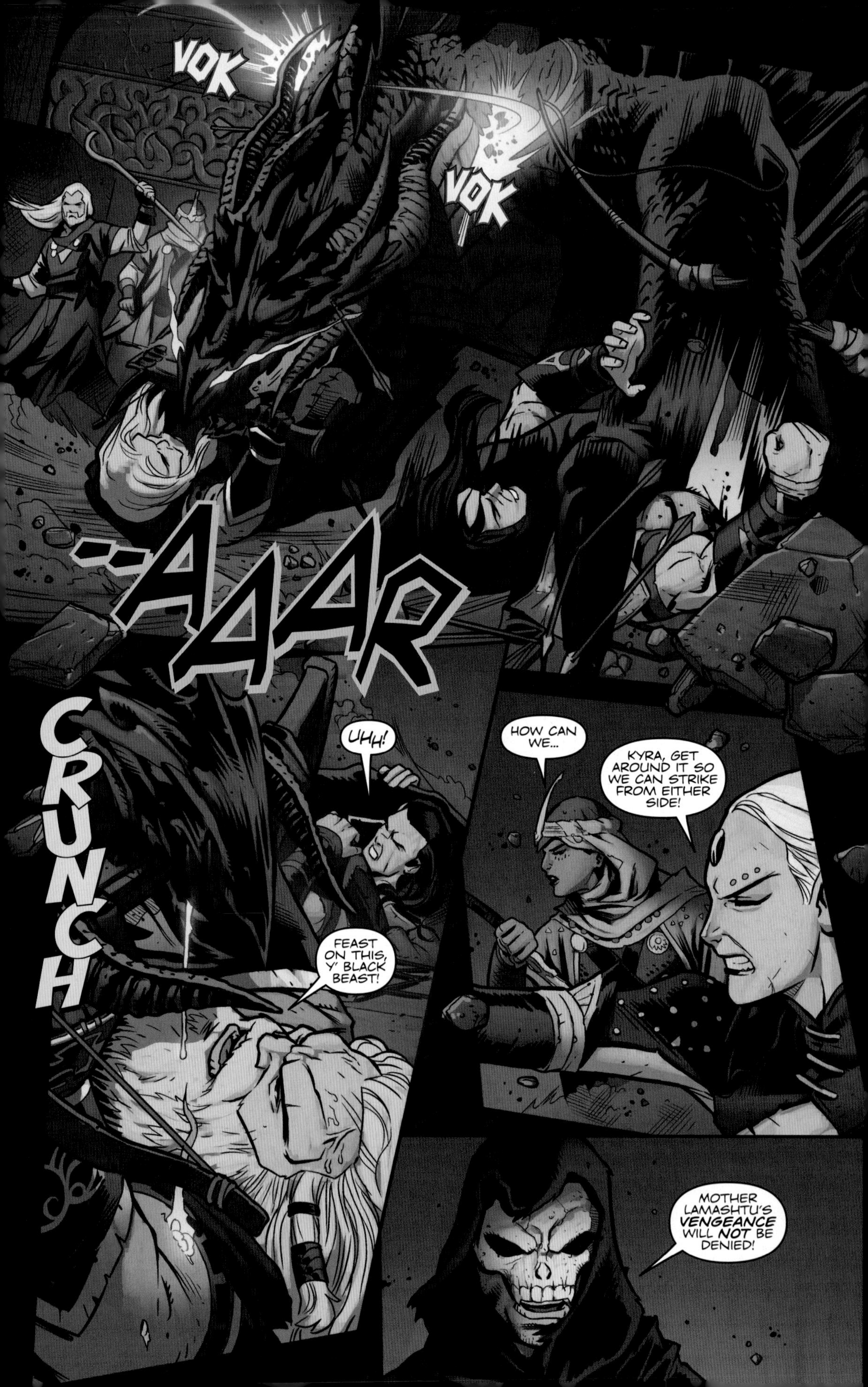
VOK
VOK
--AAAR
CRUNCH
UHH!
FEAST ON THIS, Y' BLACK BEAST!
HOW CAN WE...
KYRA, GET AROUND IT SO WE CAN STRIKE FROM EITHER SIDE!
MOTHER LAMASHTU'S VENGEANCE WILL NOT BE DENIED!

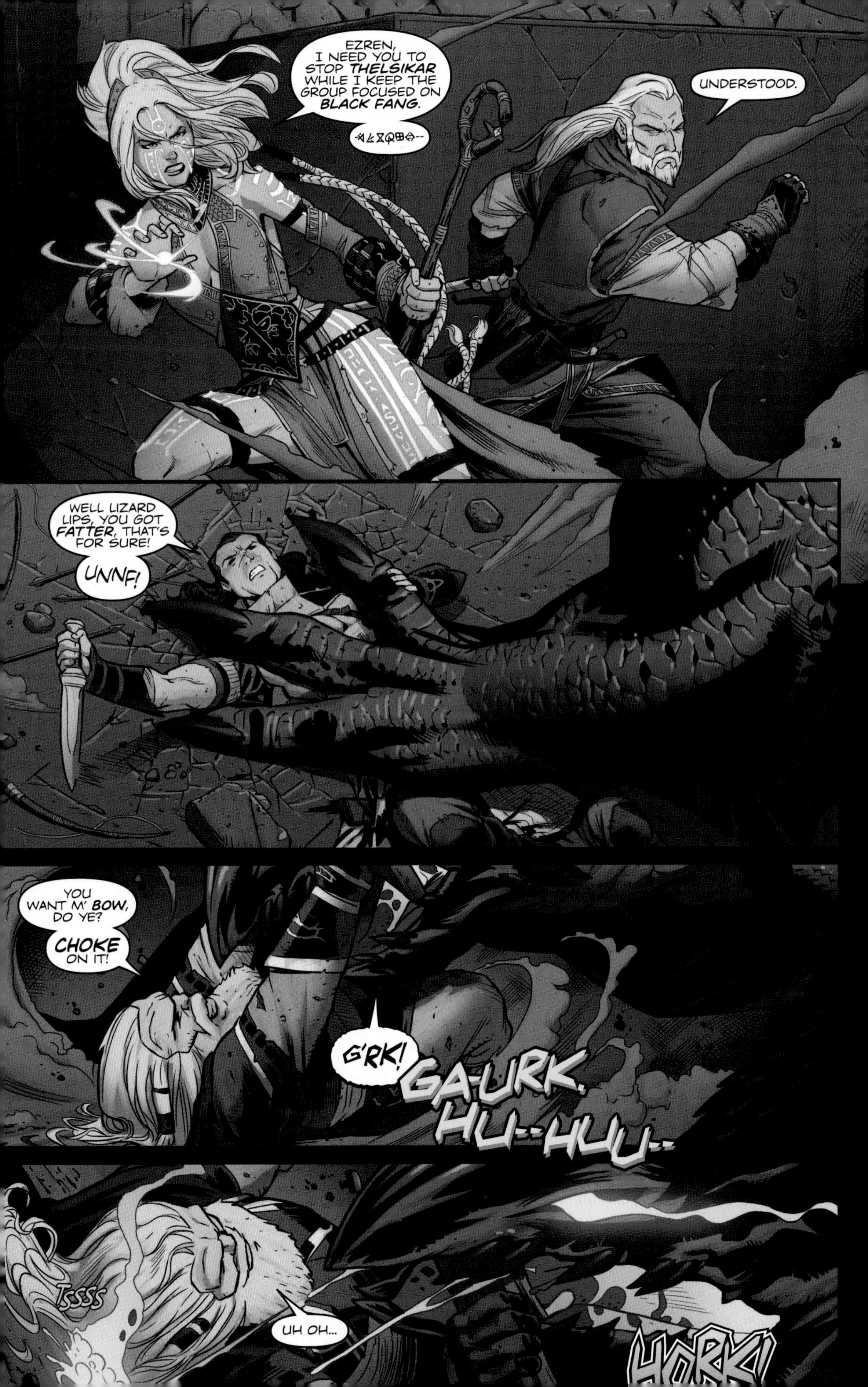

EZREN, I NEED YOU TO STOP THELSIKAR WHILE I KEEP THE GROUP FOCUSED ON BLACK FANG.
UNDERSTOOD.
WELL LIZARD LIPS, YOU GOT FATTER, THAT'S FOR SURE!
UNNF!
YOU WANT M' BOW, DO YE? CHOKE ON IT!
G'RK!
GA-URK. HU--HUU--
TSSSS
UH OH...
HORK!

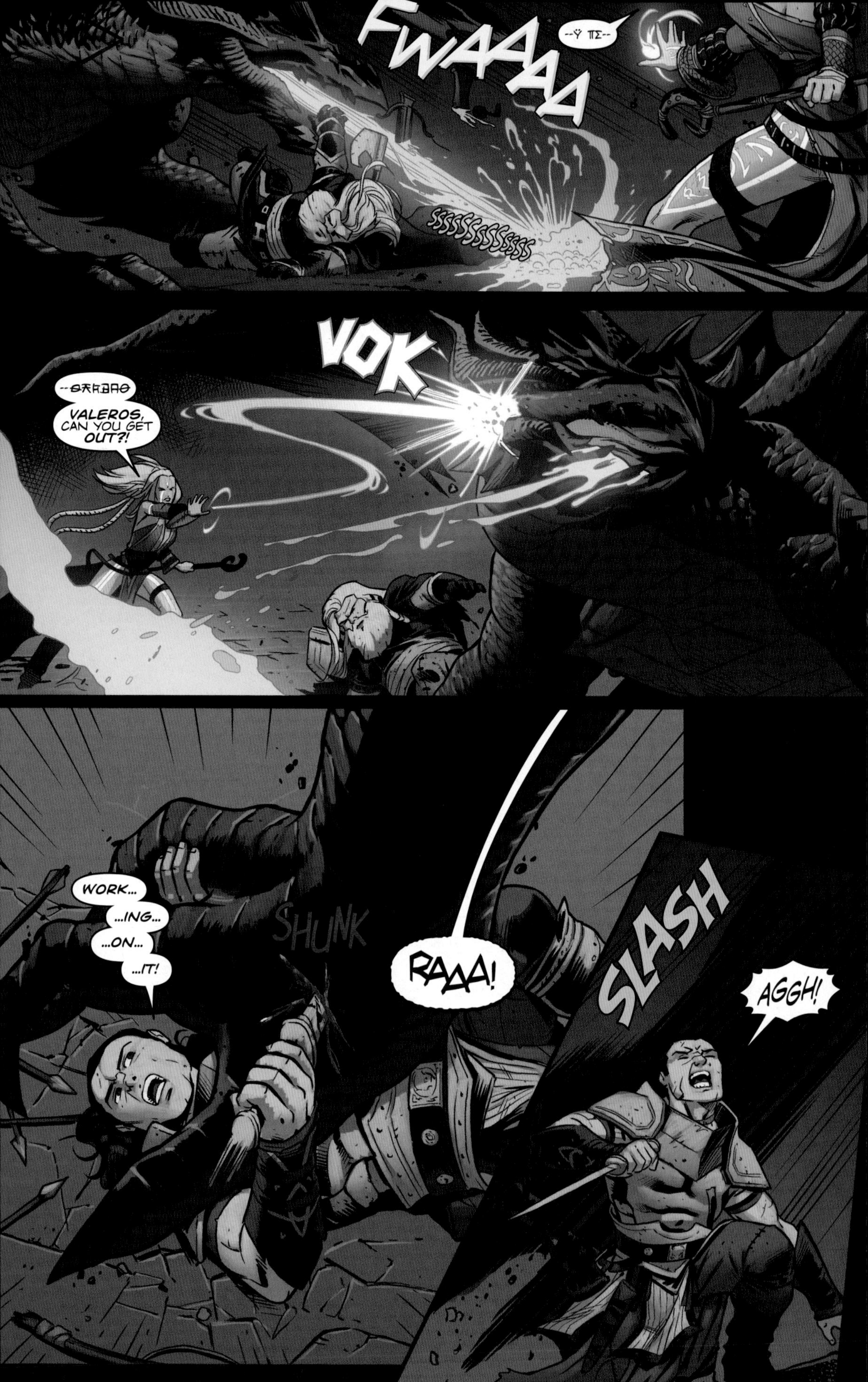
FWAAAA
SSSSSSSSSSSSS
VOK
VALEROS, CAN YOU GET OUT?!
WORK...
...ING...
...ON...
...IT!
SHUNK
RAAA!
SLASH
AGGH!

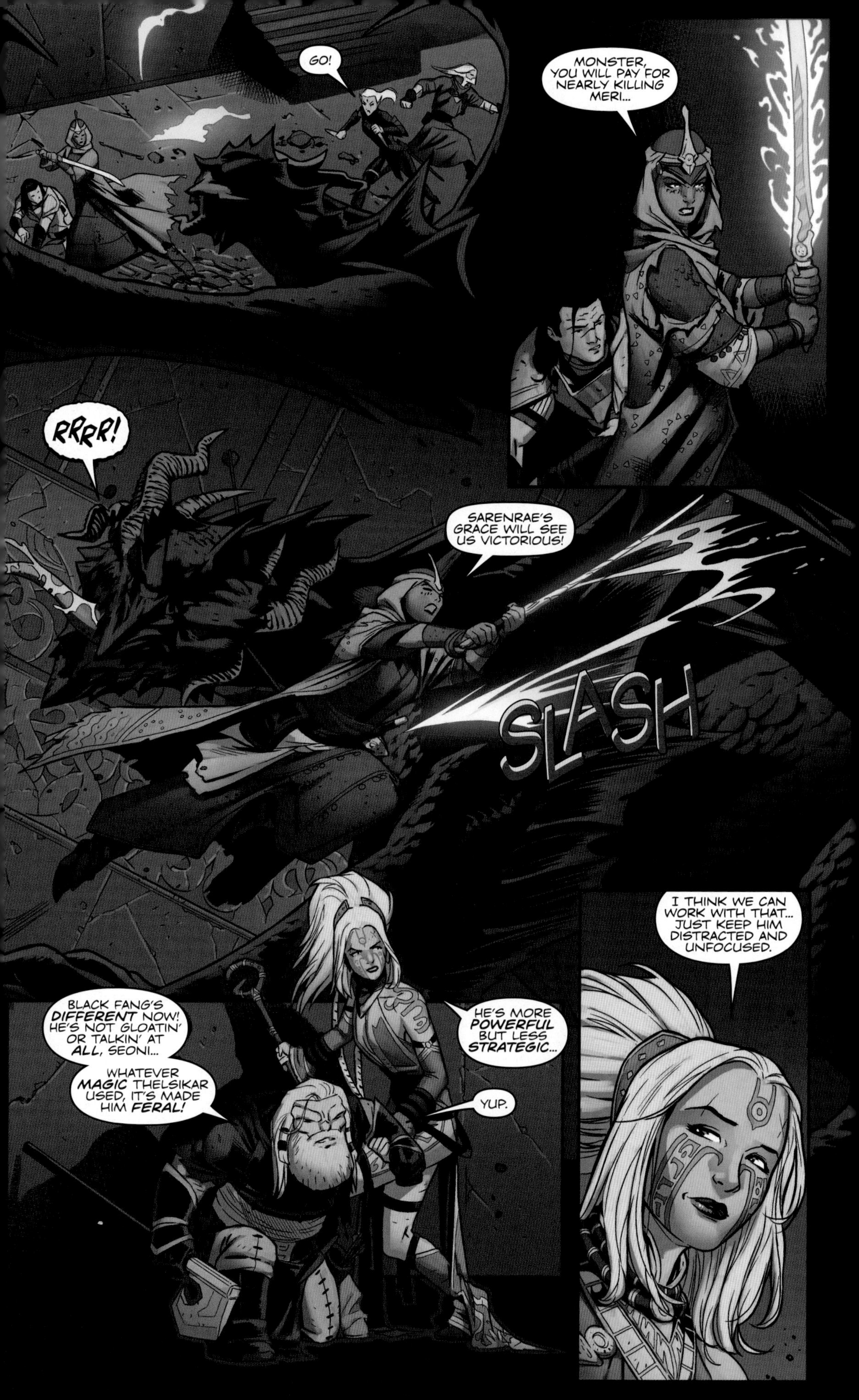
GO!
MONSTER, YOU WILL PAY FOR NEARLY KILLING MERI...
RRRR!
SARENRAE'S GRACE WILL SEE US VICTORIOUS!
SLASH
BLACK FANG'S DIFFERENT NOW! HE'S NOT GLOATIN' OR TALKIN' AT ALL, SEONI...
WHATEVER MAGIC THELSIKAR USED, IT'S MADE HIM FERAL!
HE'S MORE POWERFUL BUT LESS STRATEGIC...
YUP.
I THINK WE CAN WORK WITH THAT... JUST KEEP HIM DISTRACTED AND UNFOCUSED.

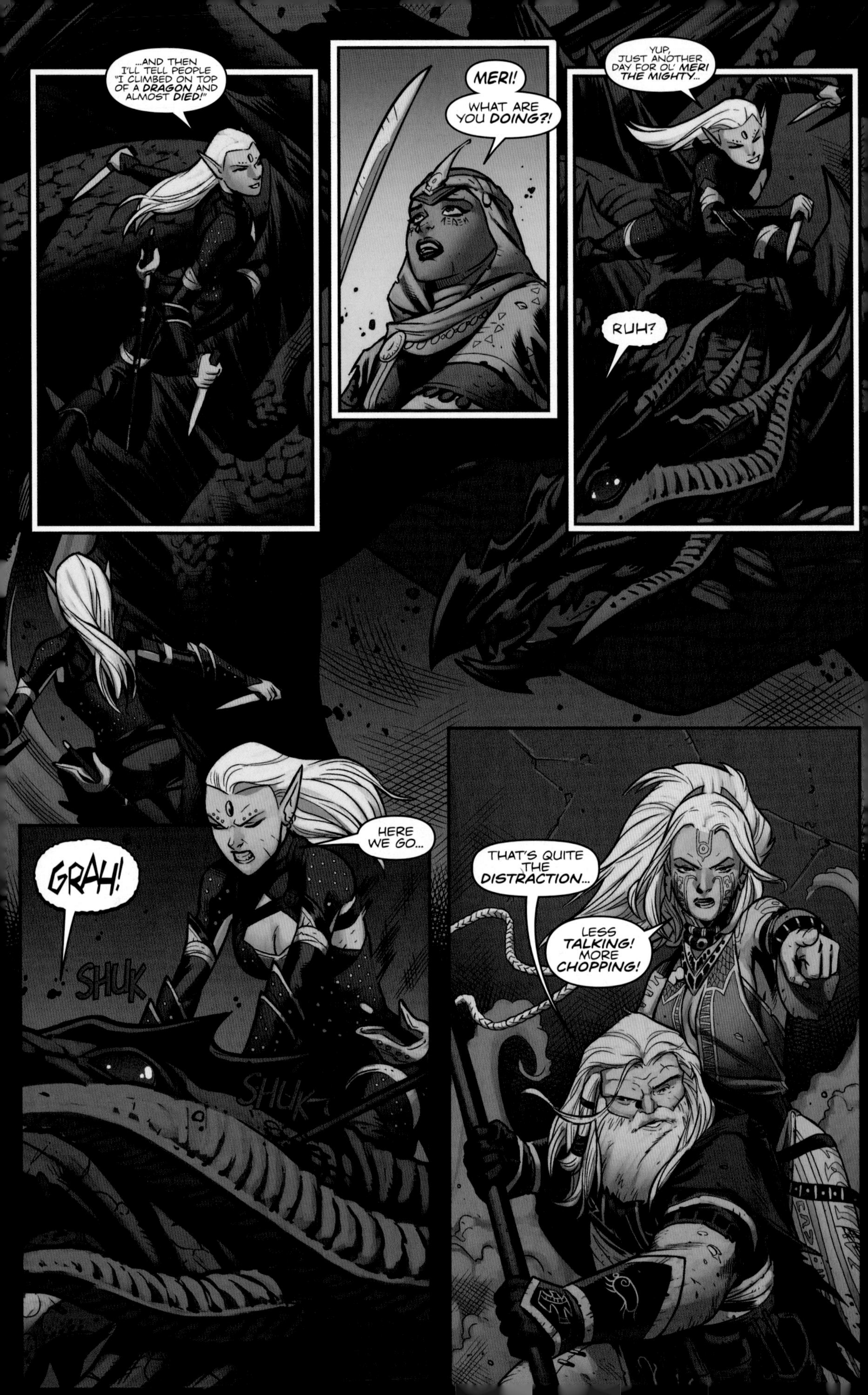

...AND THEN I'LL TELL PEOPLE "I CLIMBED ON TOP OF A DRAGON AND ALMOST DIED!"
MERI!
WHAT ARE YOU DOING?!
YUP, JUST ANOTHER DAY FOR OL' MERI THE MIGHTY...
RUH?
HERE WE GO...
GRAH!
SHUK
SHUK
THAT'S QUITE THE DISTRACTION...
LESS TALKING! MORE CHOPPING!

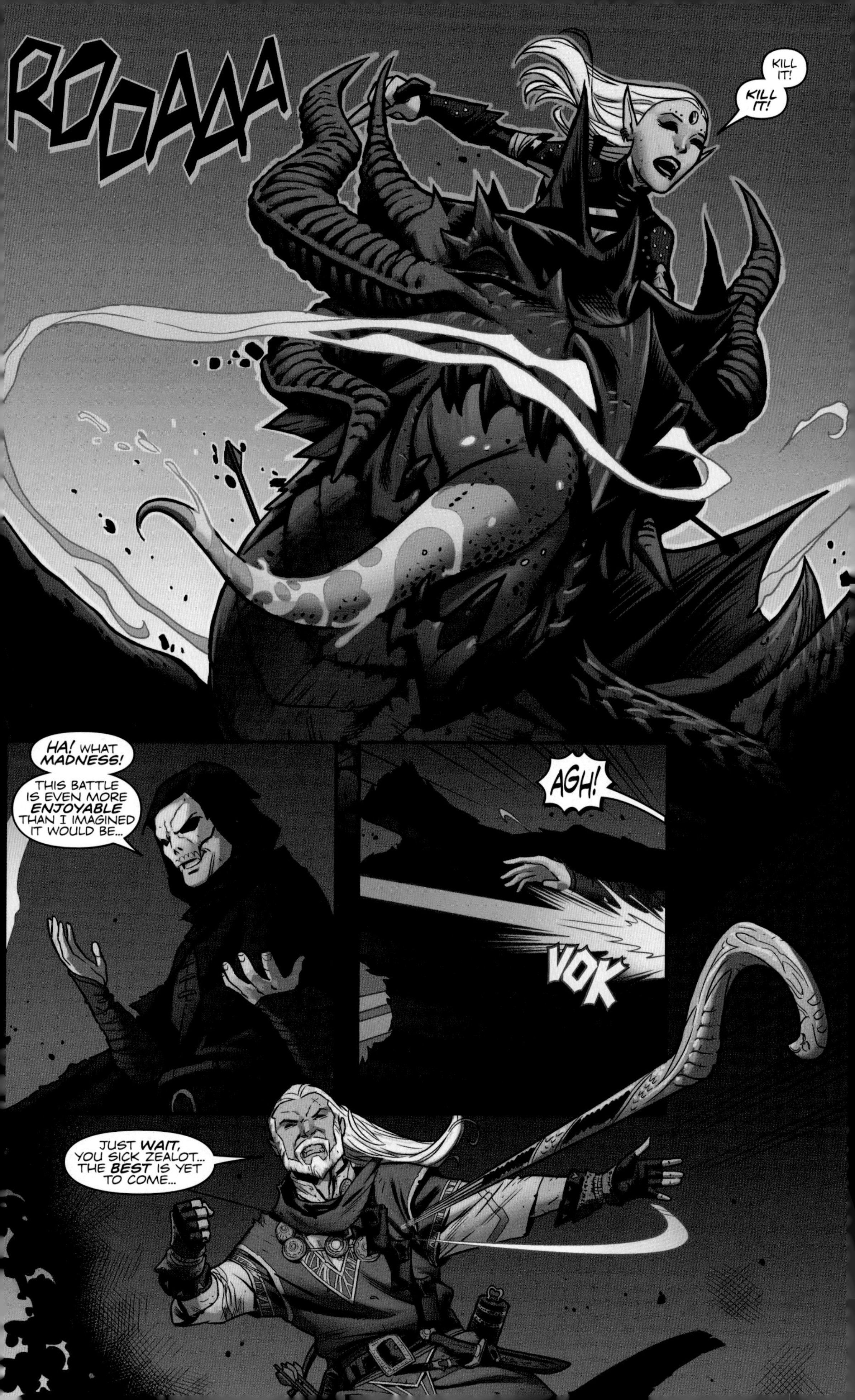
ROOAAA
KILL IT!
KILL IT!
HA! WHAT MADNESS!
THIS BATTLE IS EVEN MORE ENJOYABLE THAN I IMAGINED IT WOULD BE...
AGH!
VOK
JUST WAIT, YOU SICK ZEALOT... THE BEST IS YET TO COME...

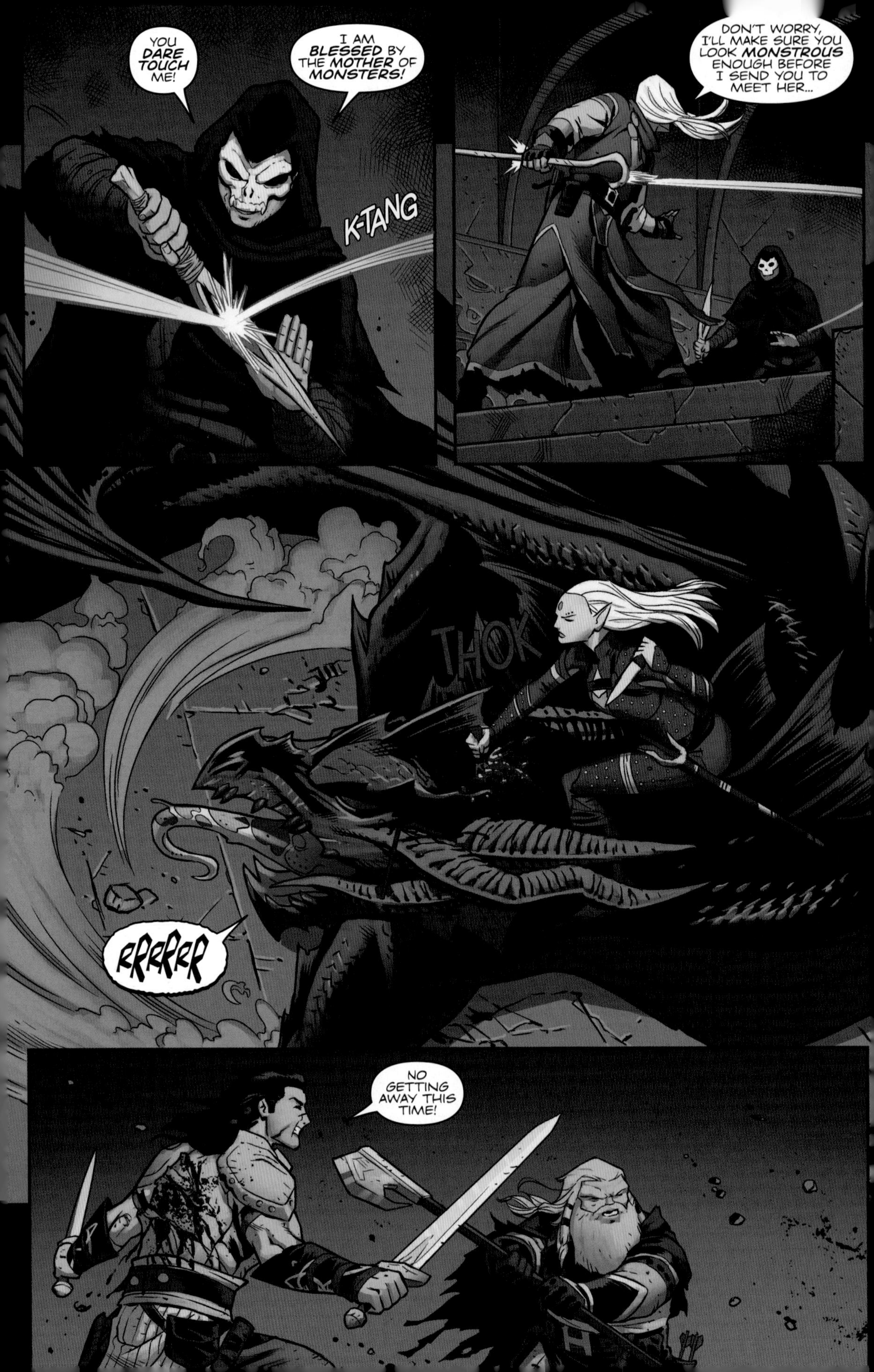
YOU DARE TOUCH ME!
I AM BLESSED BY THE MOTHER OF MONSTERS!
K-TANG
DON'T WORRY, I'LL MAKE SURE YOU LOOK MONSTROUS ENOUGH BEFORE I SEND YOU TO MEET HER...
THOK
RRRRRR
NO GETTING AWAY THIS TIME!

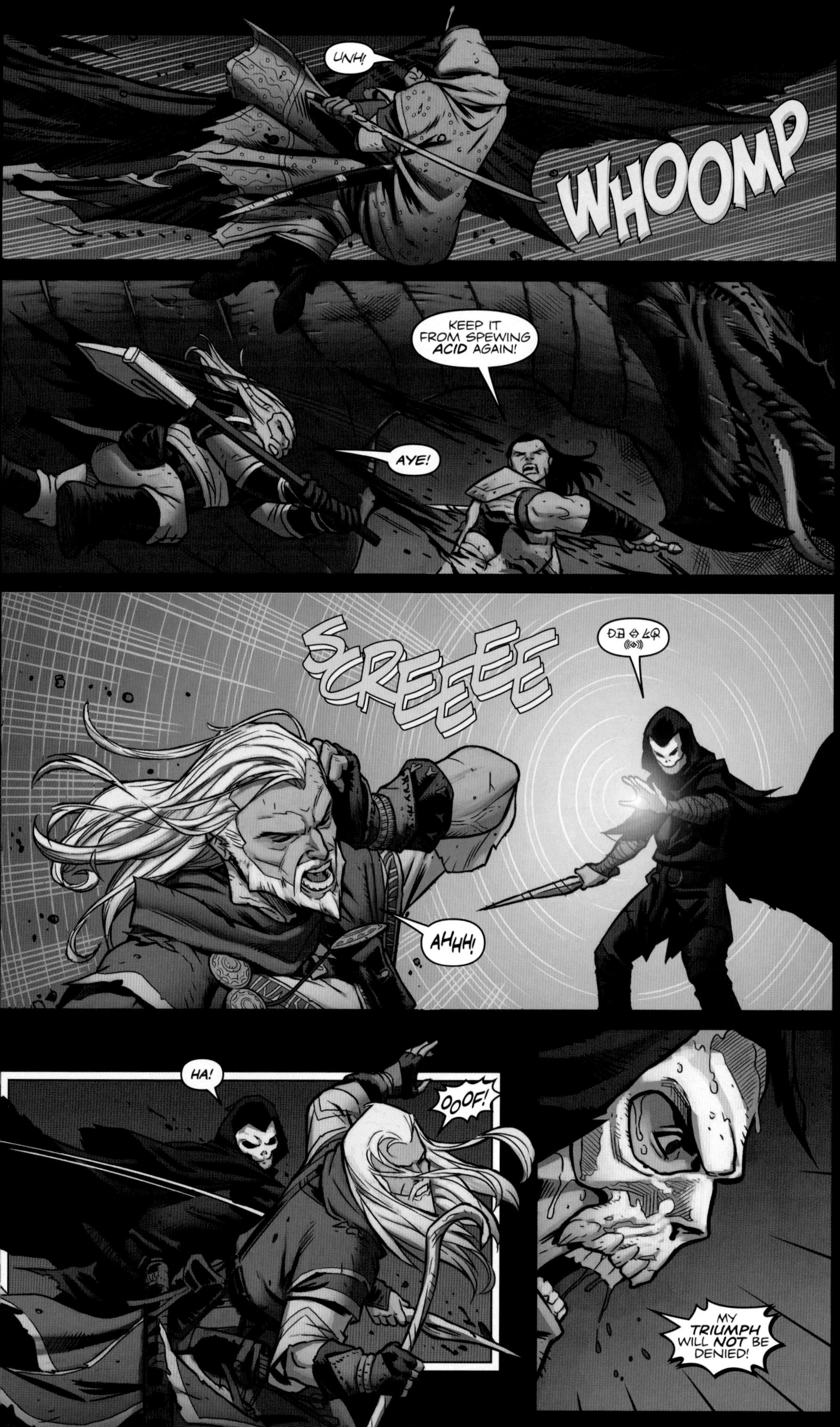
UNH!
WHOOMP
KEEP IT FROM SPEWING ACID AGAIN!
AYE!
SCREEEEE
AHHH!
HA!
OOOF!
MY TRIUMPH WILL NOT BE DENIED!

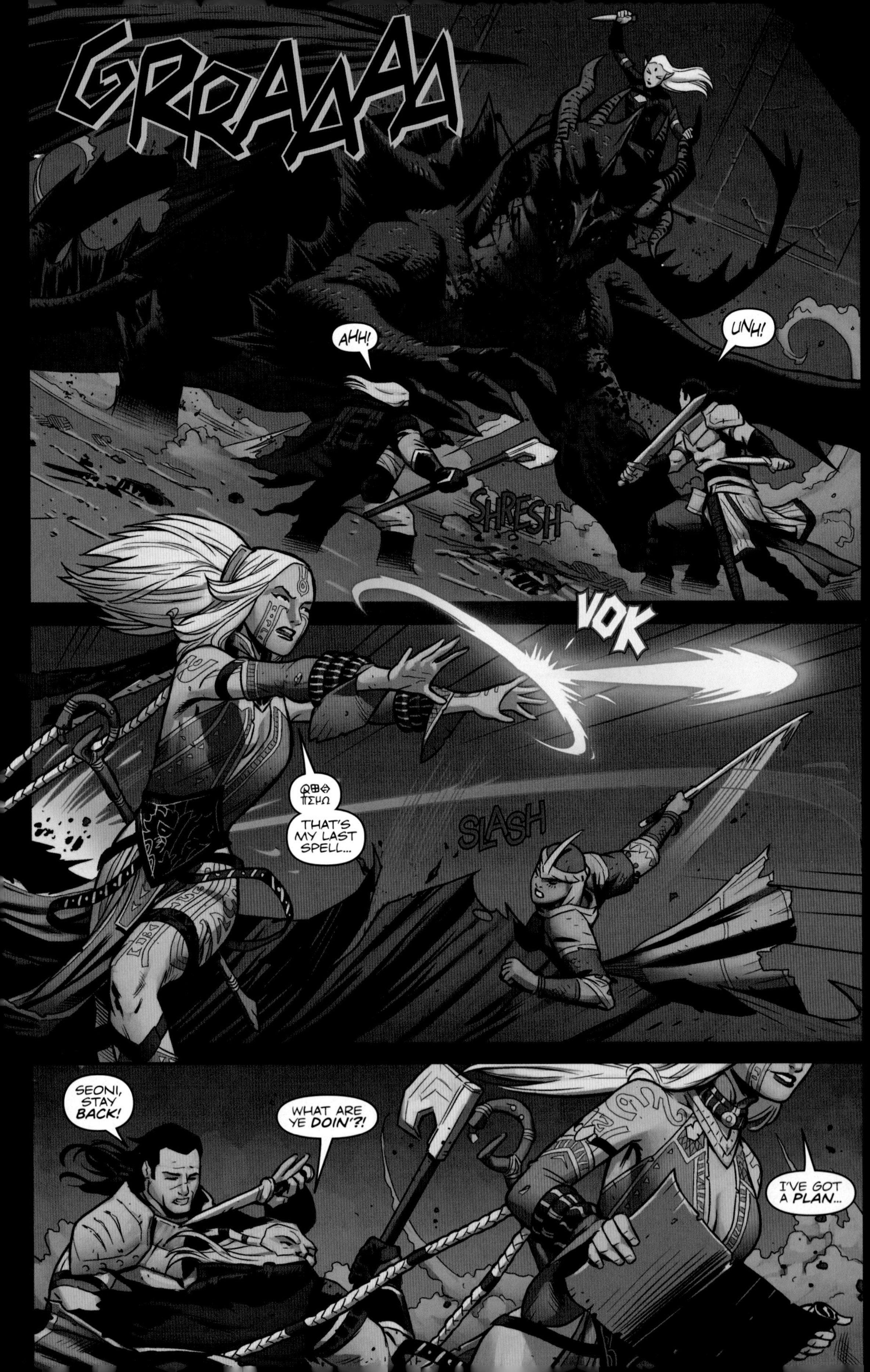
GRRAAAA
AHH!
UNH!
SHRESH
VOK
THAT'S MY LAST SPELL...
SLASH
SEONI, STAY BACK!
WHAT ARE YE DOIN'?!
I'VE GOT A PLAN...

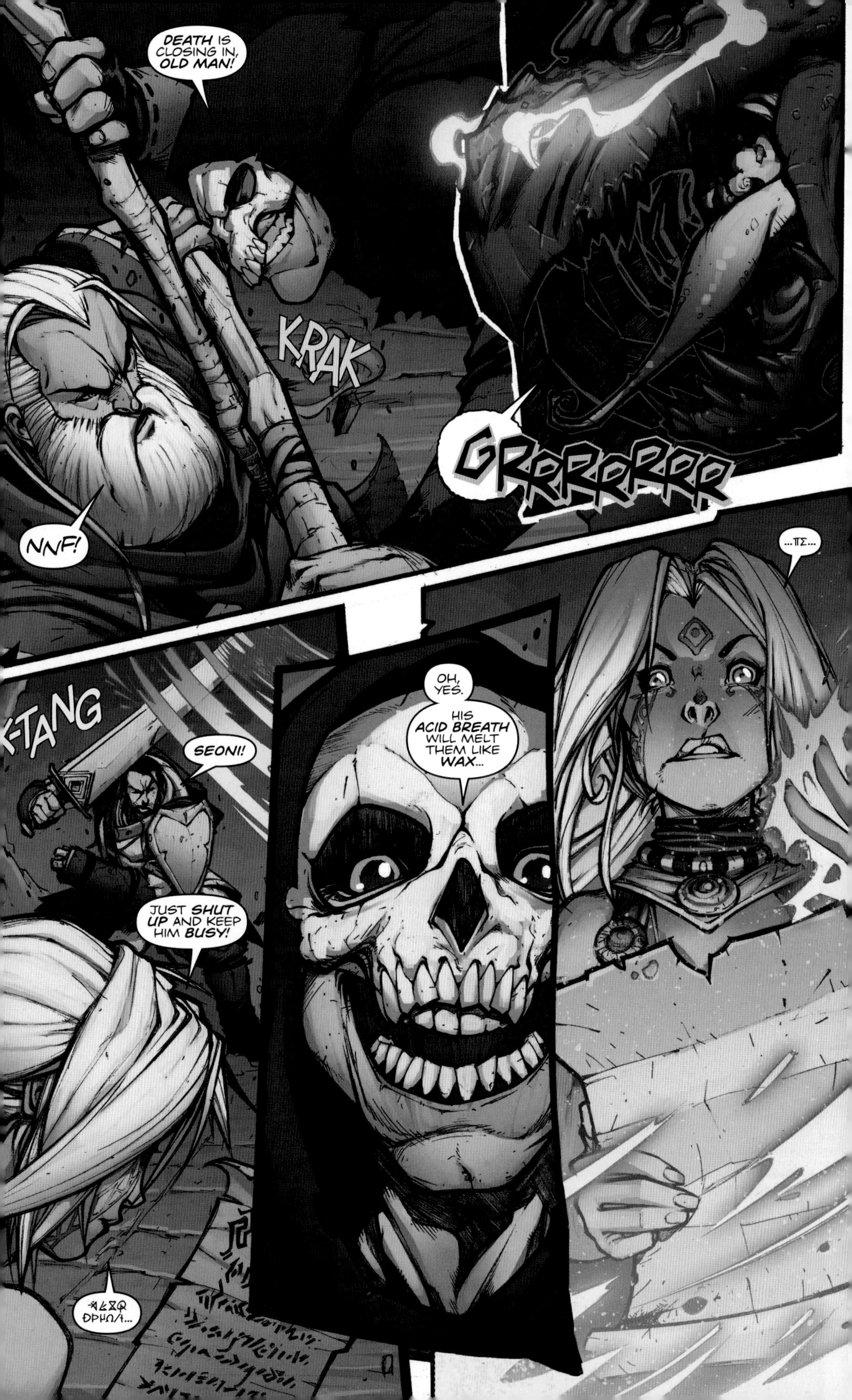
DEATH IS CLOSING IN, OLD MAN!
KRAK
NNF!
GRRRRRRR
...ΠΣ...
-TANG
SEONI!
JUST SHUT UP AND KEEP HIM BUSY!
OH, YES.
HIS ACID BREATH WILL MELT THEM LIKE WAX...

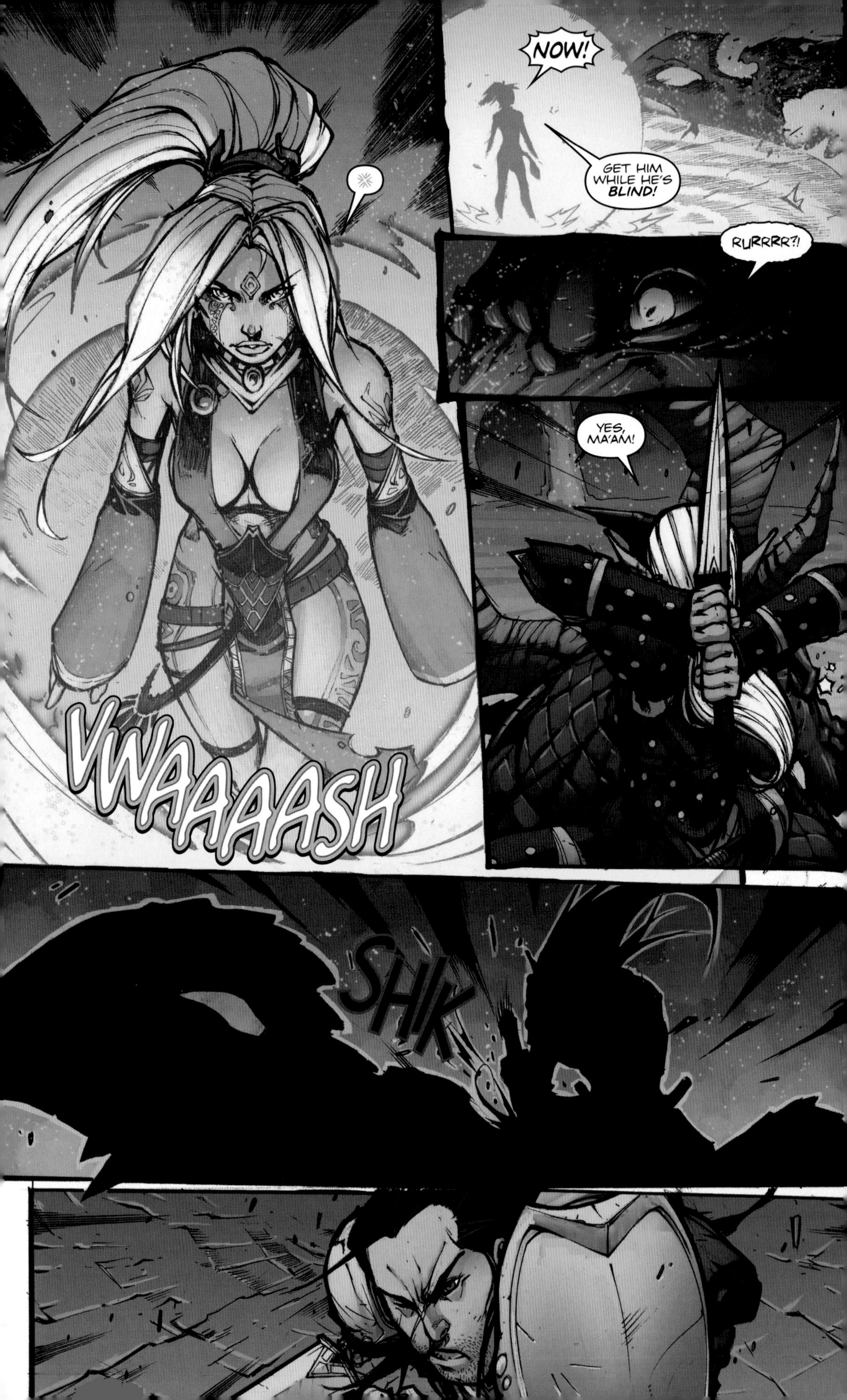
NOW!
GET HIM WHILE HE'S BLIND!
RURRRR?!
YES, MA'AM!
VWAAAAASH
SHIK

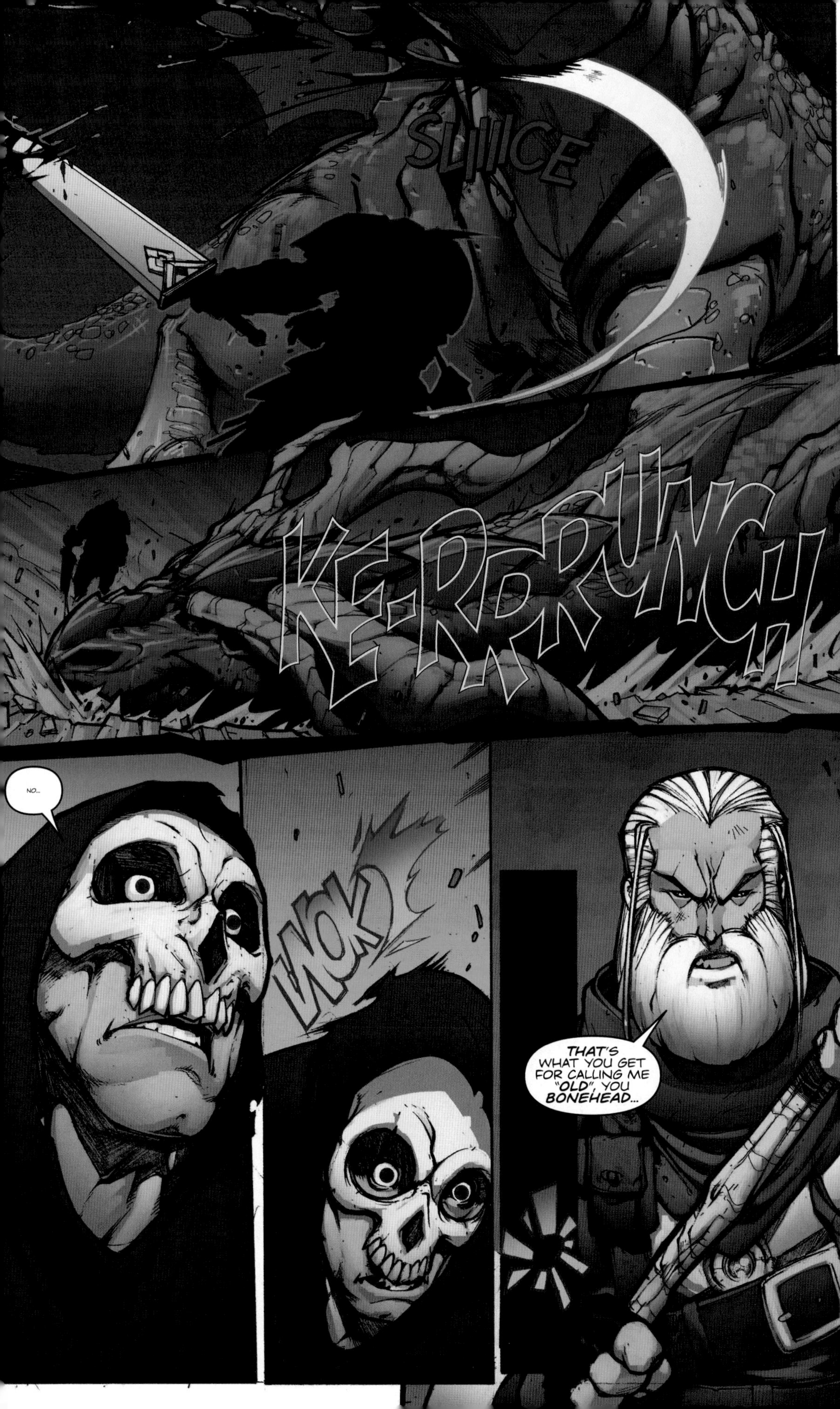
SLIIICE
KE-RRRUNCH
NO...
WOK
THAT'S WHAT YOU GET FOR CALLING ME "OLD", YOU BONEHEAD...

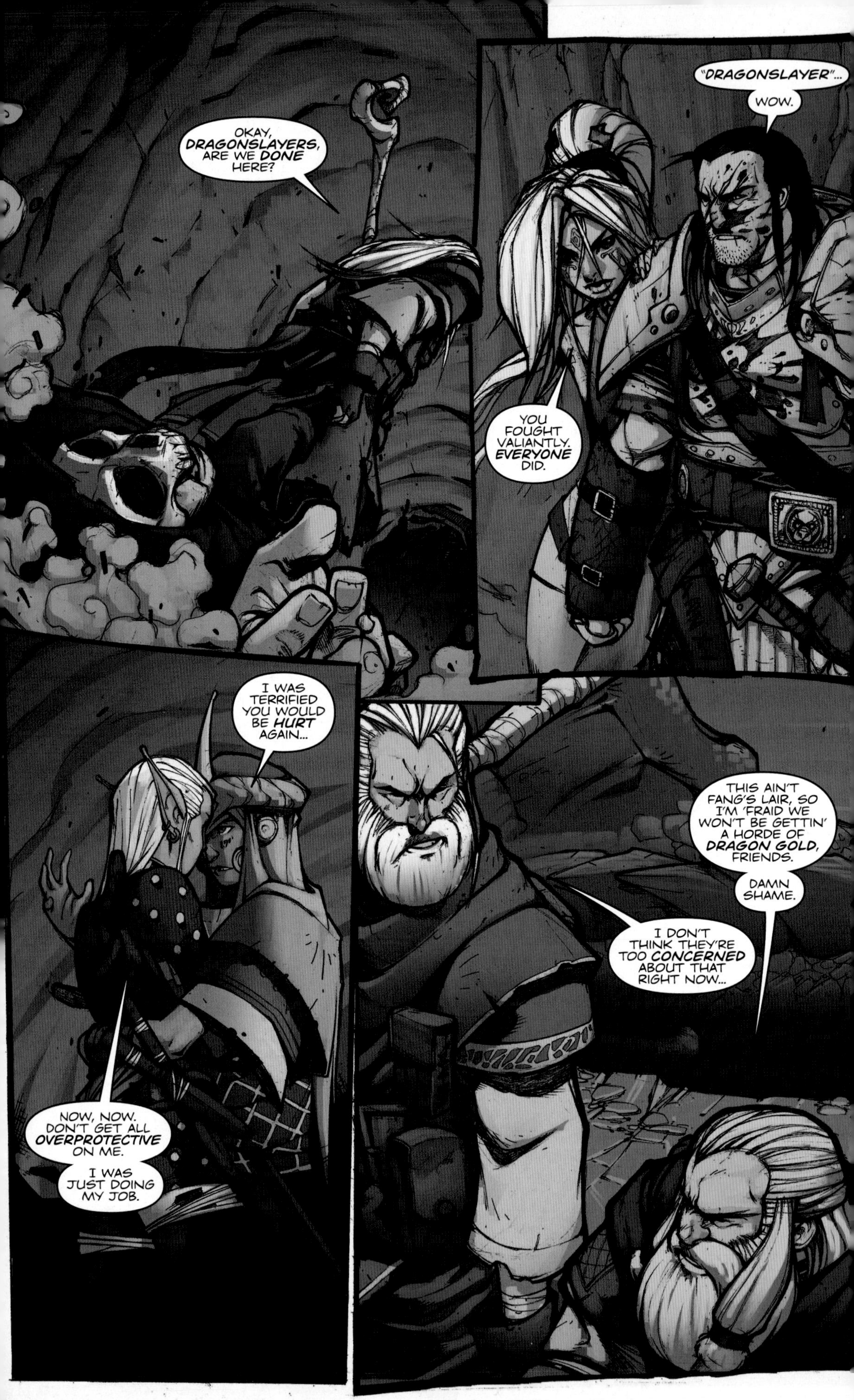
OKAY, DRAGONSLAYERS, ARE WE DONE HERE?
"DRAGONSLAYER"...
WOW.
YOU FOUGHT VALIANTLY. EVERYONE DID.
I WAS TERRIFIED YOU WOULD BE HURT AGAIN...
NOW, NOW. DON'T GET ALL OVERPROTECTIVE ON ME.
I WAS JUST DOING MY JOB.
THIS AIN'T FANG'S LAIR, SO I'M 'FRAID WE WON'T BE GETTIN' A HORDE OF DRAGON GOLD, FRIENDS.
DAMN SHAME.
I DON'T THINK THEY'RE TOO CONCERNED ABOUT THAT RIGHT NOW...

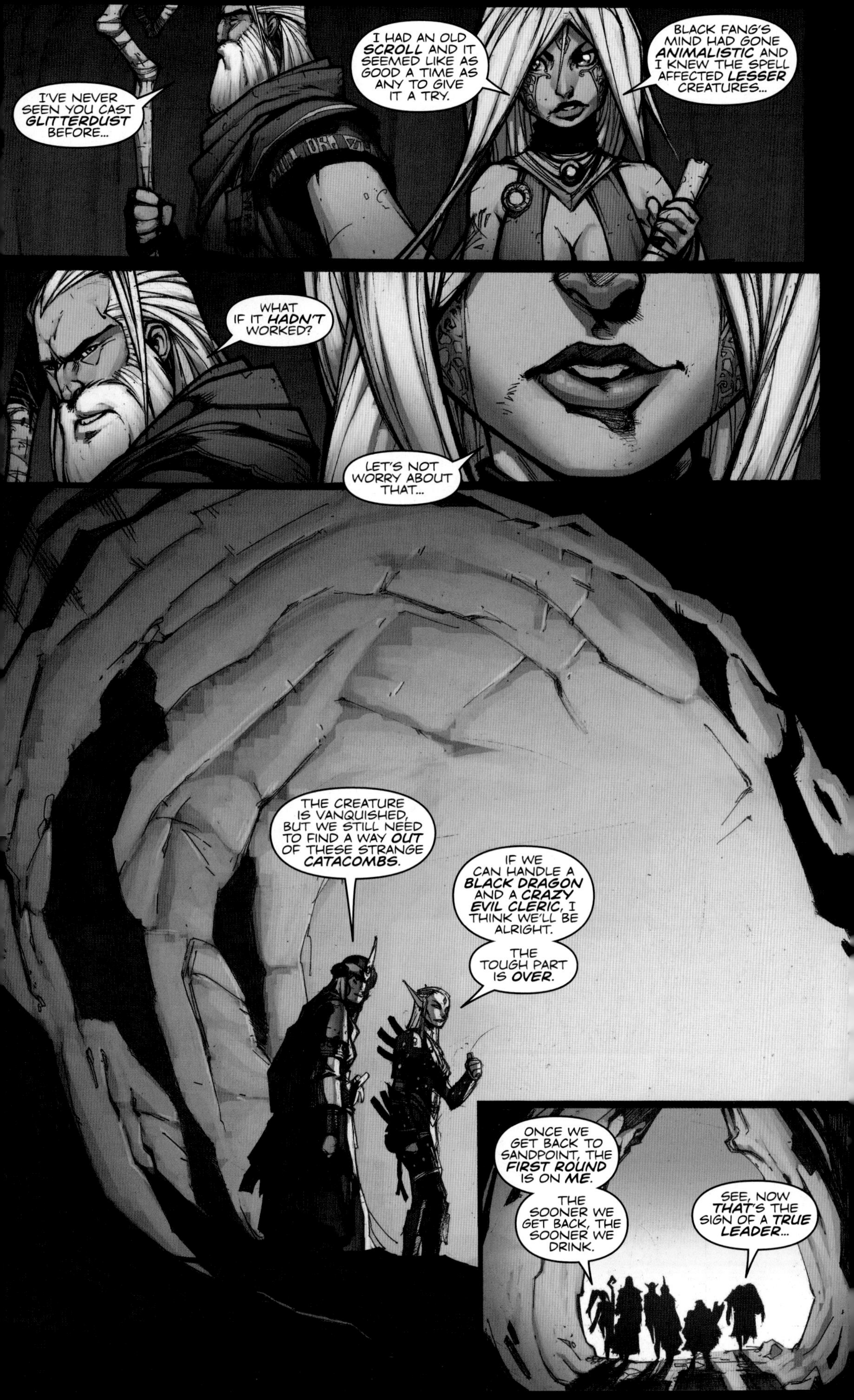
I'VE NEVER SEEN YOU CAST GLITTERDUST BEFORE...
I HAD AN OLD SCROLL AND IT SEEMED LIKE AS GOOD A TIME AS ANY TO GIVE IT A TRY.
BLACK FANG'S MIND HAD GONE ANIMALISTIC AND I KNEW THE SPELL AFFECTED LESSER CREATURES...
WHAT IF IT HADN'T WORKED?
LET'S NOT WORRY ABOUT THAT...
THE CREATURE IS VANQUISHED, BUT WE STILL NEED TO FIND A WAY OUT OF THESE STRANGE CATACOMBS.
IF WE CAN HANDLE A BLACK DRAGON AND A CRAZY EVIL CLERIC, I THINK WE'LL BE ALRIGHT.
THE TOUGH PART IS OVER.
ONCE WE GET BACK TO SANDPOINT, THE FIRST ROUND IS ON ME.
THE SOONER WE GET BACK, THE SOONER WE DRINK.
SEE, NOW THAT'S THE SIGN OF A TRUE LEADER...

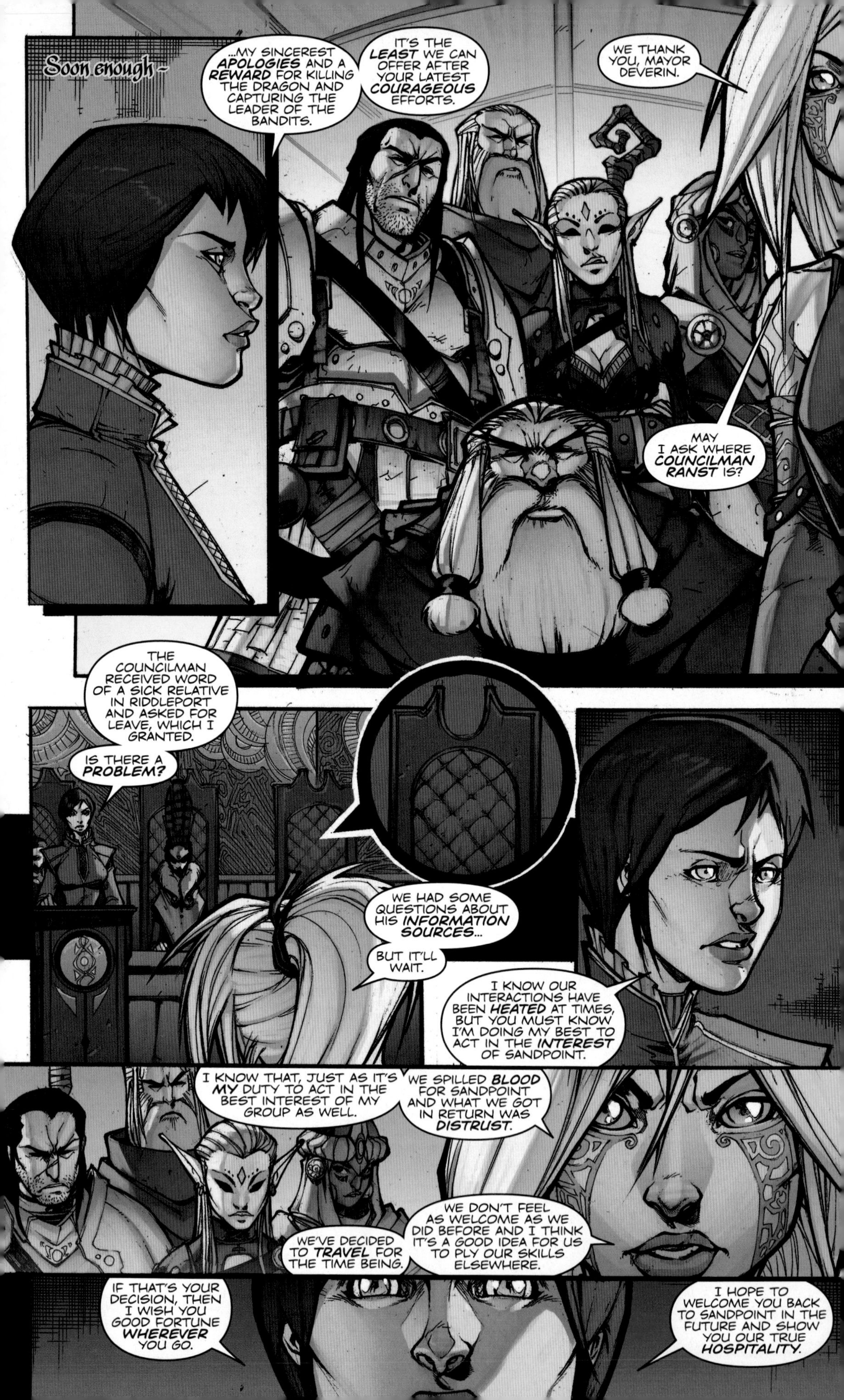
Soon enough ~
...MY SINCEREST APOLOGIES AND A REWARD FOR KILLING THE DRAGON AND CAPTURING THE LEADER OF THE BANDITS.
IT'S THE LEAST WE CAN OFFER AFTER YOUR LATEST COURAGEOUS EFFORTS.
WE THANK YOU, MAYOR DEVERIN.
MAY I ASK WHERE COUNCILMAN RANST IS?
THE COUNCILMAN RECEIVED WORD OF A SICK RELATIVE IN RIDDLEPORT AND ASKED FOR LEAVE, WHICH I GRANTED.
IS THERE A PROBLEM?
WE HAD SOME QUESTIONS ABOUT HIS INFORMATION SOURCES...
BUT IT'LL WAIT.
I KNOW OUR INTERACTIONS HAVE BEEN HEATED AT TIMES, BUT YOU MUST KNOW I'M DOING MY BEST TO ACT IN THE INTEREST OF SANDPOINT.
I KNOW THAT, JUST AS IT'S MY DUTY TO ACT IN THE BEST INTEREST OF MY GROUP AS WELL.
WE SPILLED BLOOD FOR SANDPOINT AND WHAT WE GOT IN RETURN WAS DISTRUST.
WE'VE DECIDED TO TRAVEL FOR THE TIME BEING.
WE DON'T FEEL AS WELCOME AS WE DID BEFORE AND I THINK IT'S A GOOD IDEA FOR US TO PLY OUR SKILLS ELSEWHERE.
IF THAT'S YOUR DECISION, THEN I WISH YOU GOOD FORTUNE WHEREVER YOU GO.
I HOPE TO WELCOME YOU BACK TO SANDPOINT IN THE FUTURE AND SHOW YOU OUR TRUE HOSPITALITY.

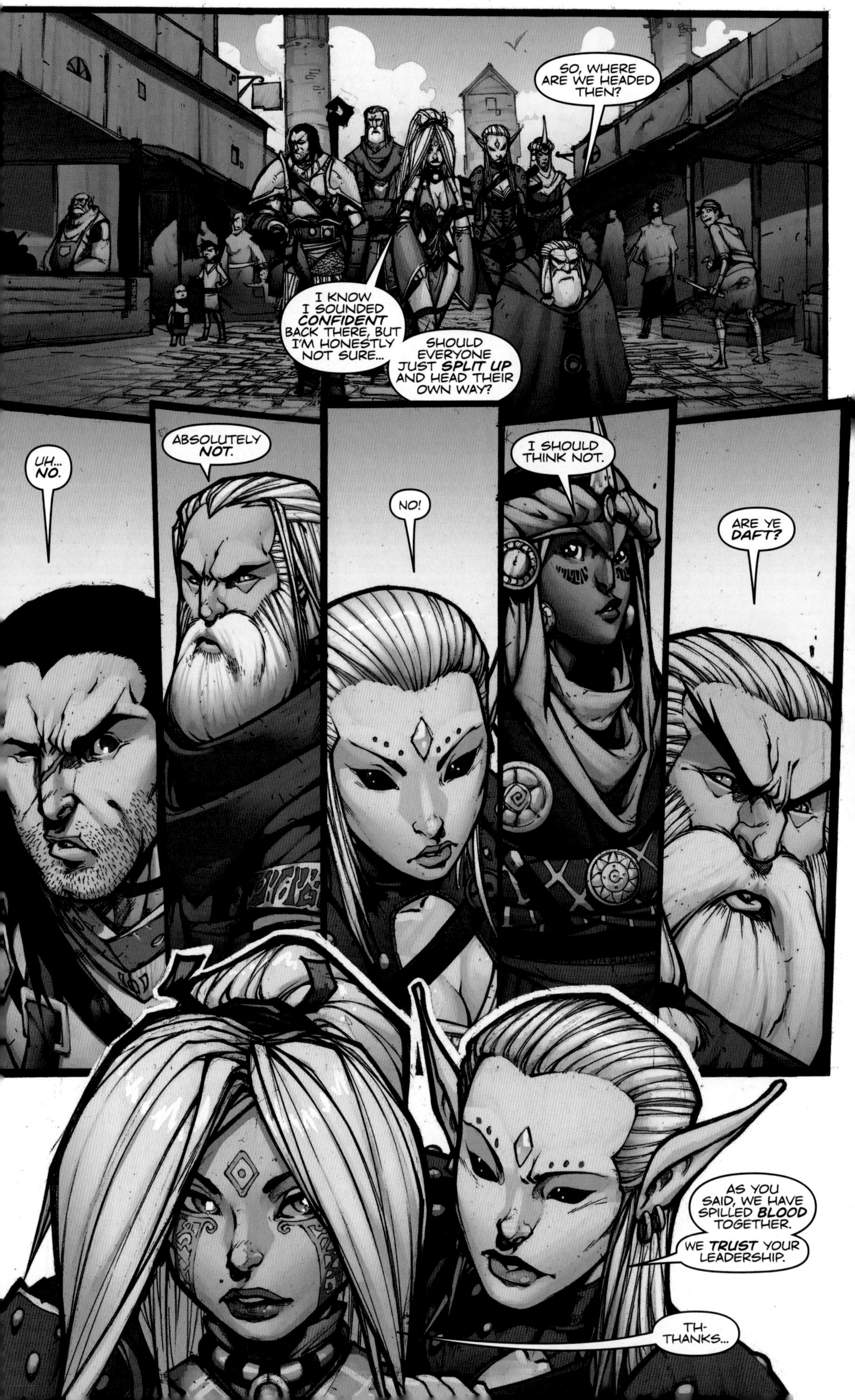
SO, WHERE ARE WE HEADED THEN?
I KNOW I SOUNDED CONFIDENT BACK THERE, BUT I'M HONESTLY NOT SURE...
SHOULD EVERYONE JUST SPLIT UP AND HEAD THEIR OWN WAY?
UH... NO.
ABSOLUTELY NOT.
NO!
I SHOULD THINK NOT.
ARE YE DAFT?
AS YOU SAID, WE HAVE SPILLED BLOOD TOGETHER.
WE TRUST YOUR LEADERSHIP.
TH-THANKS...

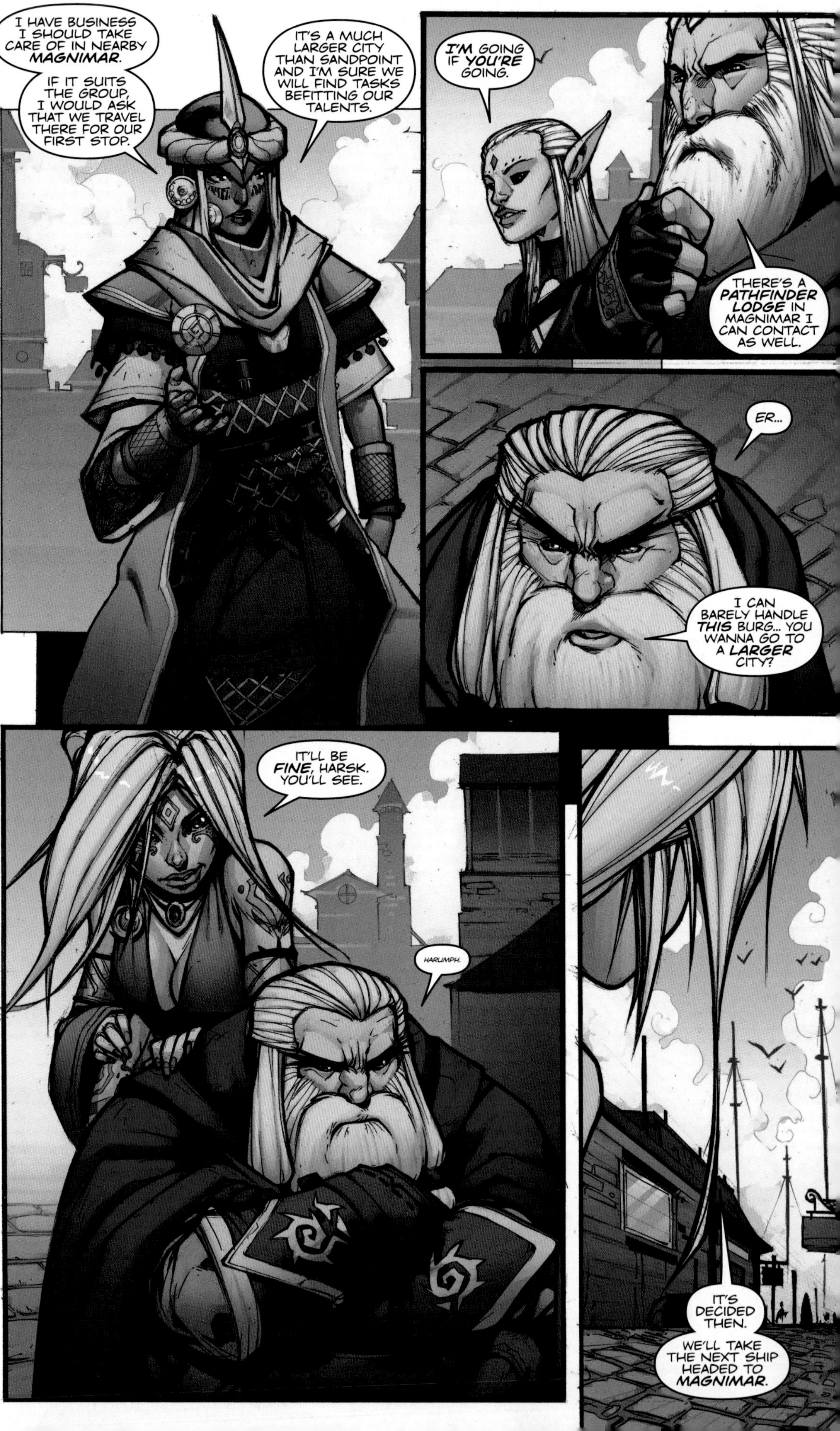

I HAVE BUSINESS I SHOULD TAKE CARE OF IN NEARBY MAGNIMAR.
IF IT SUITS THE GROUP, I WOULD ASK THAT WE TRAVEL THERE FOR OUR FIRST STOP.
IT'S A MUCH LARGER CITY THAN SANDPOINT AND I'M SURE WE WILL FIND TASKS BEFITTING OUR TALENTS.
I'M GOING IF YOU'RE GOING.
THERE'S A PATHFINDER LODGE IN MAGNIMAR I CAN CONTACT AS WELL.
ER...
I CAN BARELY HANDLE THIS BURG... YOU WANNA GO TO A LARGER CITY?
IT'LL BE FINE, HARSK. YOU'LL SEE.
HARUMPH.
IT'S DECIDED THEN.
WE'LL TAKE THE NEXT SHIP HEADED TO MAGNIMAR.

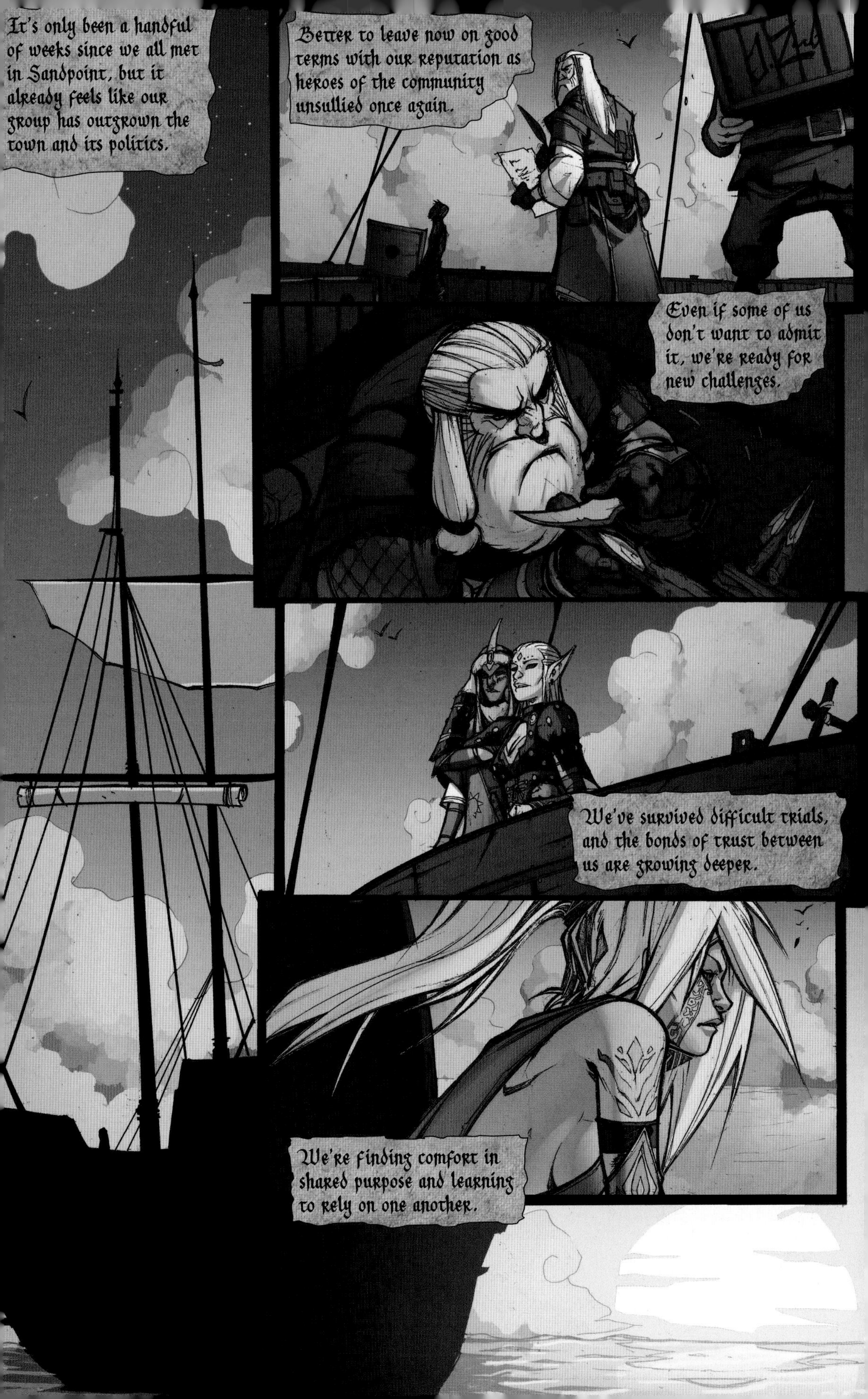
It's only been a handful of weeks since we all met in Sandpoint, but it already feels like our group has outgrown the town and its politics.
Better to leave now on good terms with our reputation as heroes of the community unsullied once again.
Even if some of us don't want to admit it, we're ready for new challenges.
We've survived difficult trials, and the bonds of trust between us are growing deeper.
We're finding comfort in shared purpose and learning to rely on one another.

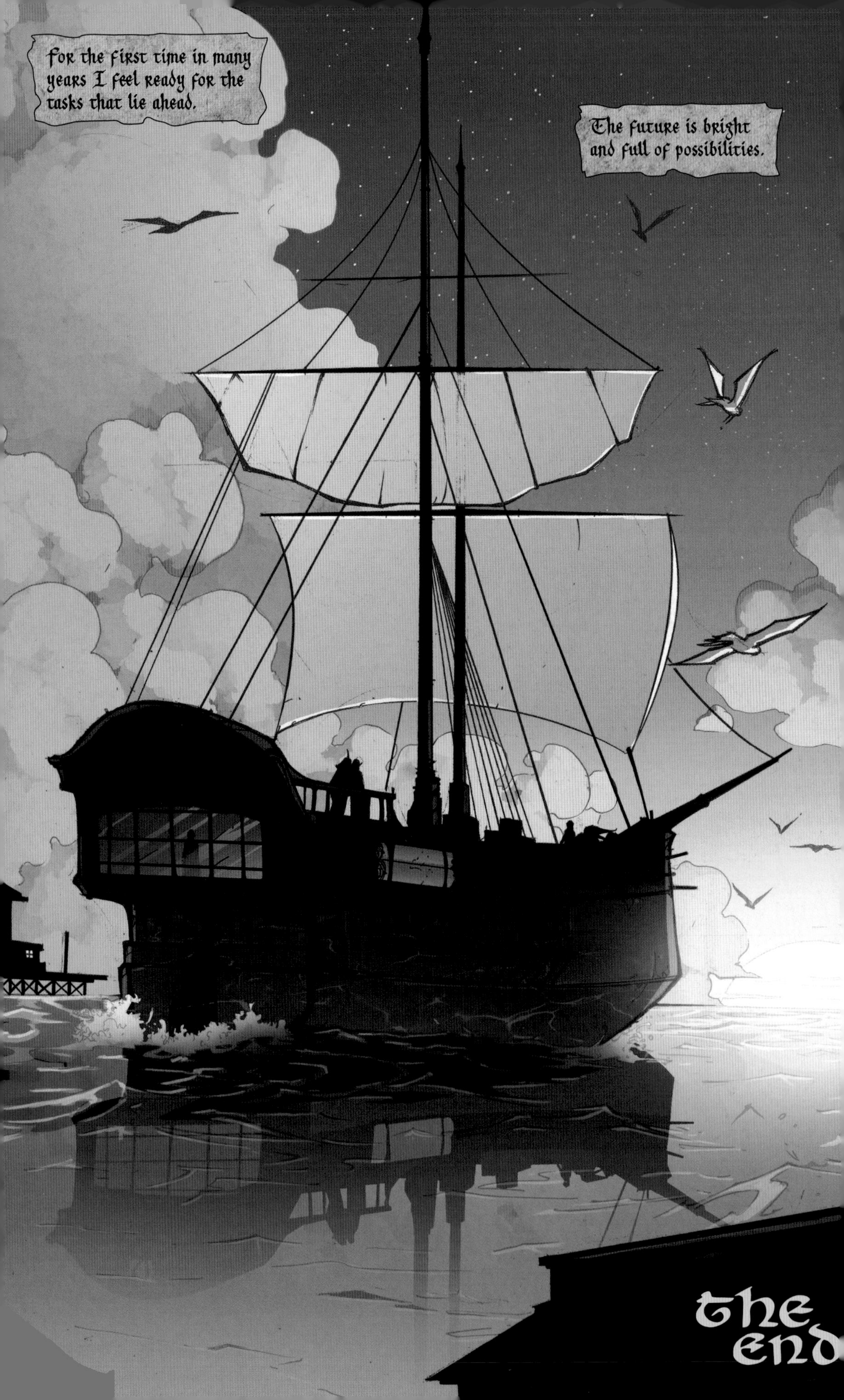
For the first time in many years I feel ready for the tasks that lie ahead.
The future is bright and full of possibilities.
The End

Night on the Town

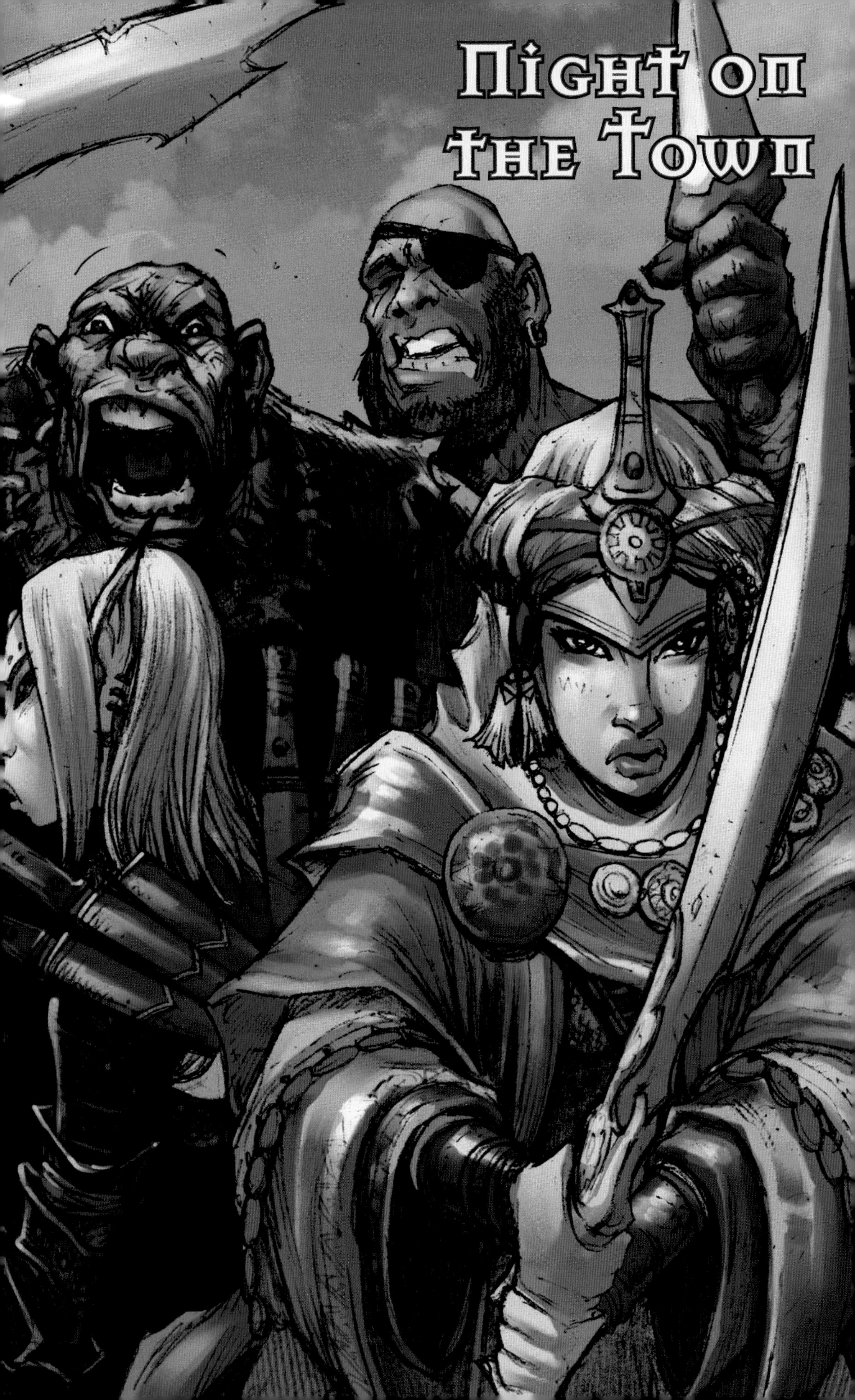

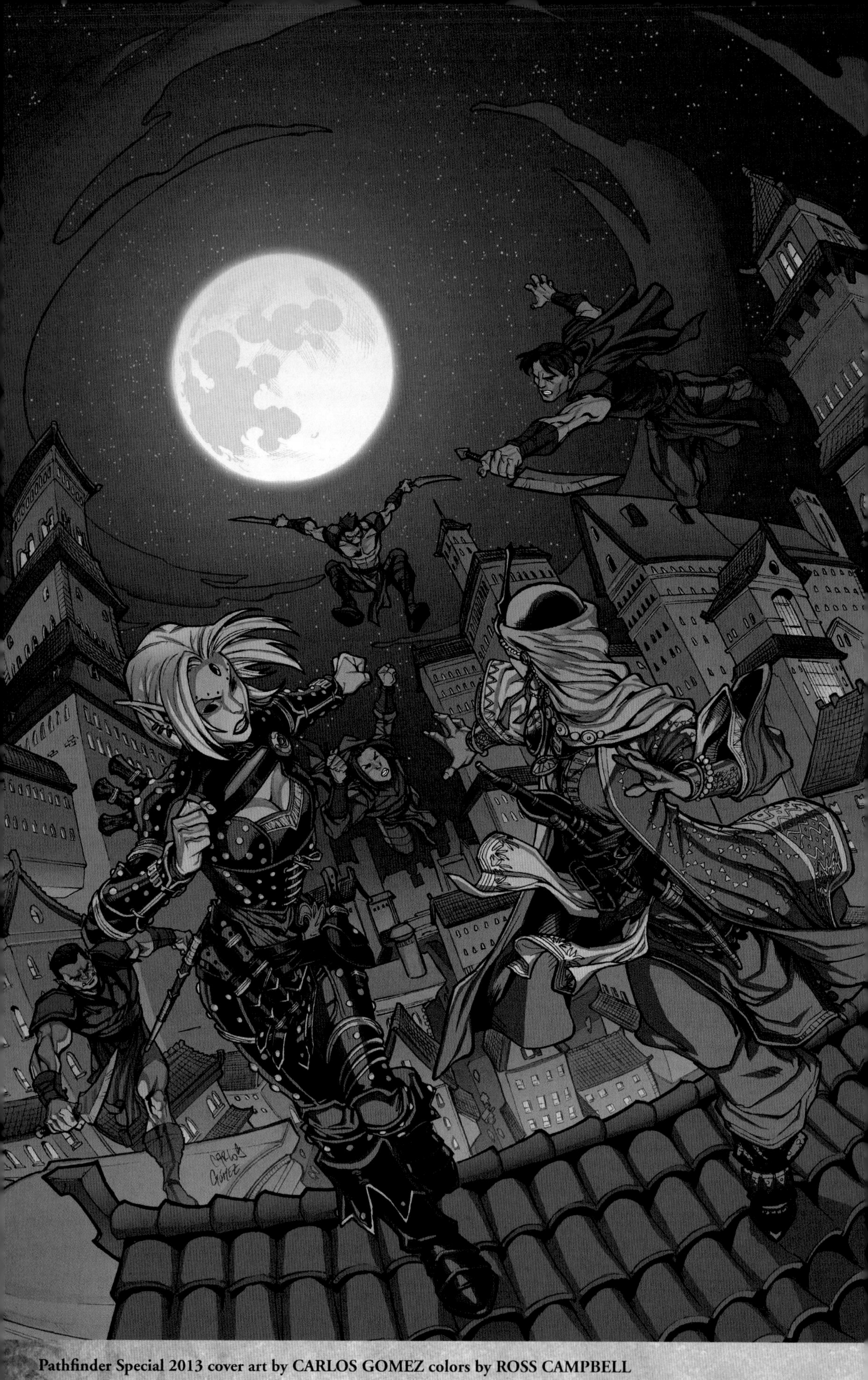

Pathfinder Special 2013 cover art by CARLOS GOMEZ colors by ROSS CAMPBELL

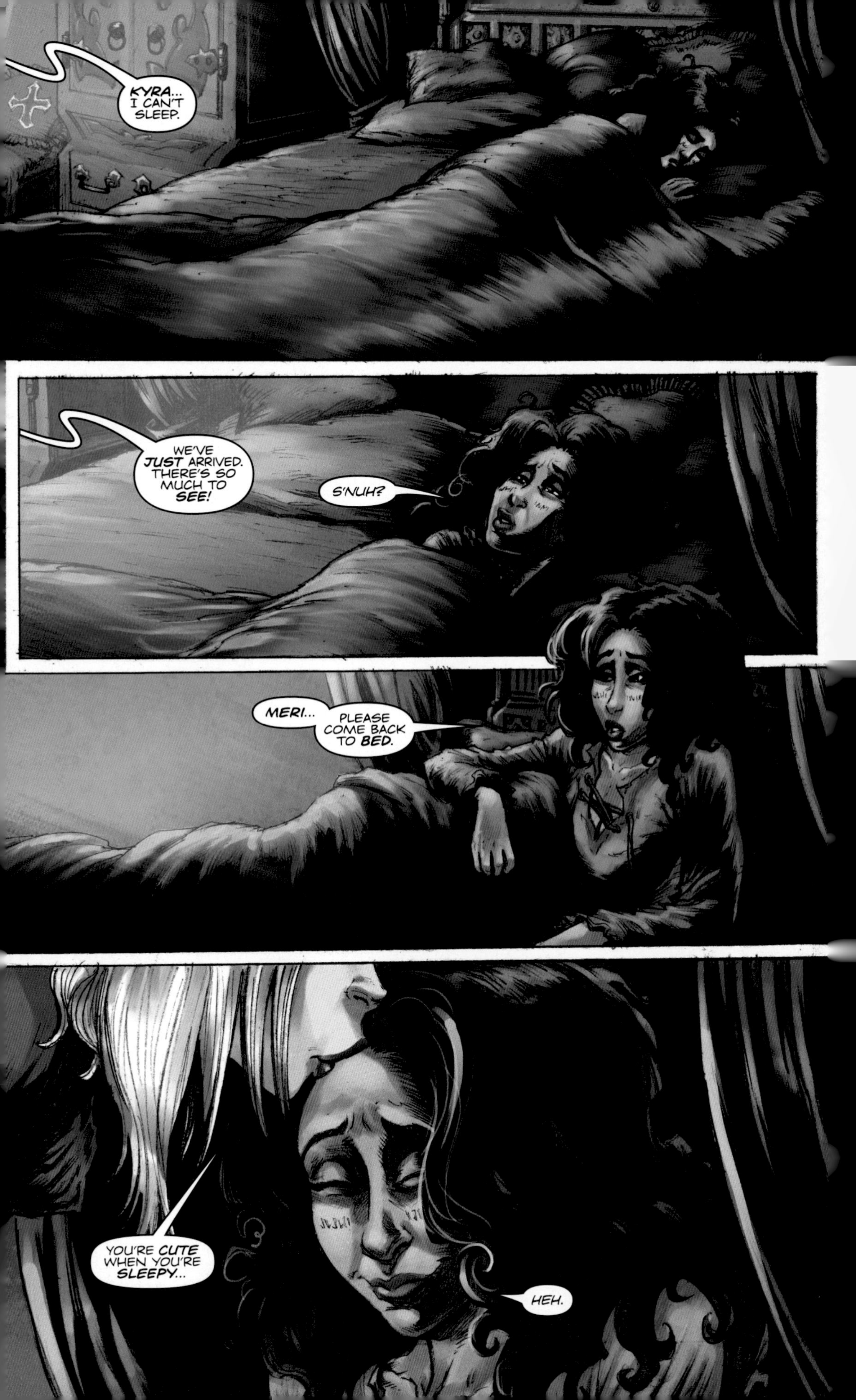
KYRA... I CAN'T SLEEP.
WE'VE JUST ARRIVED. THERE'S SO MUCH TO SEE!
S'NUH?
MERI...
PLEASE COME BACK TO BED.
YOU'RE CUTE WHEN YOU'RE SLEEPY...
HEH.

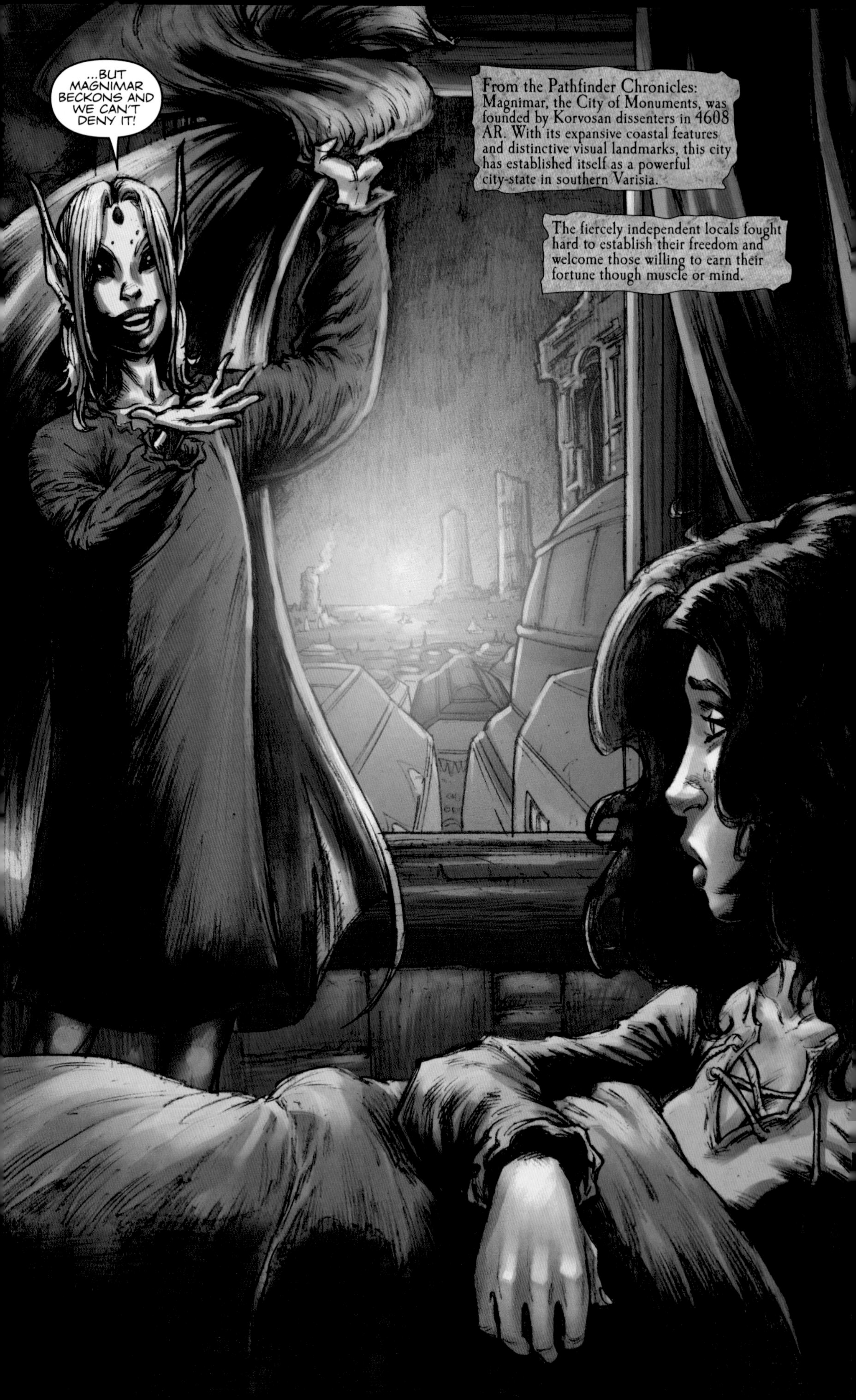
...BUT MAGNIMAR BECKONS AND WE CAN'T DENY IT!
From the Pathfinder Chronicles: Magnimar, the City of Monuments, was founded by Korvosan dissenters in 4608 AR. With its expansive coastal features and distinctive visual landmarks, this city has established itself as a powerful city-state in southern Varisia.
The fiercely independent locals fought hard to establish their freedom and welcome those willing to earn their fortune though muscle or mind.

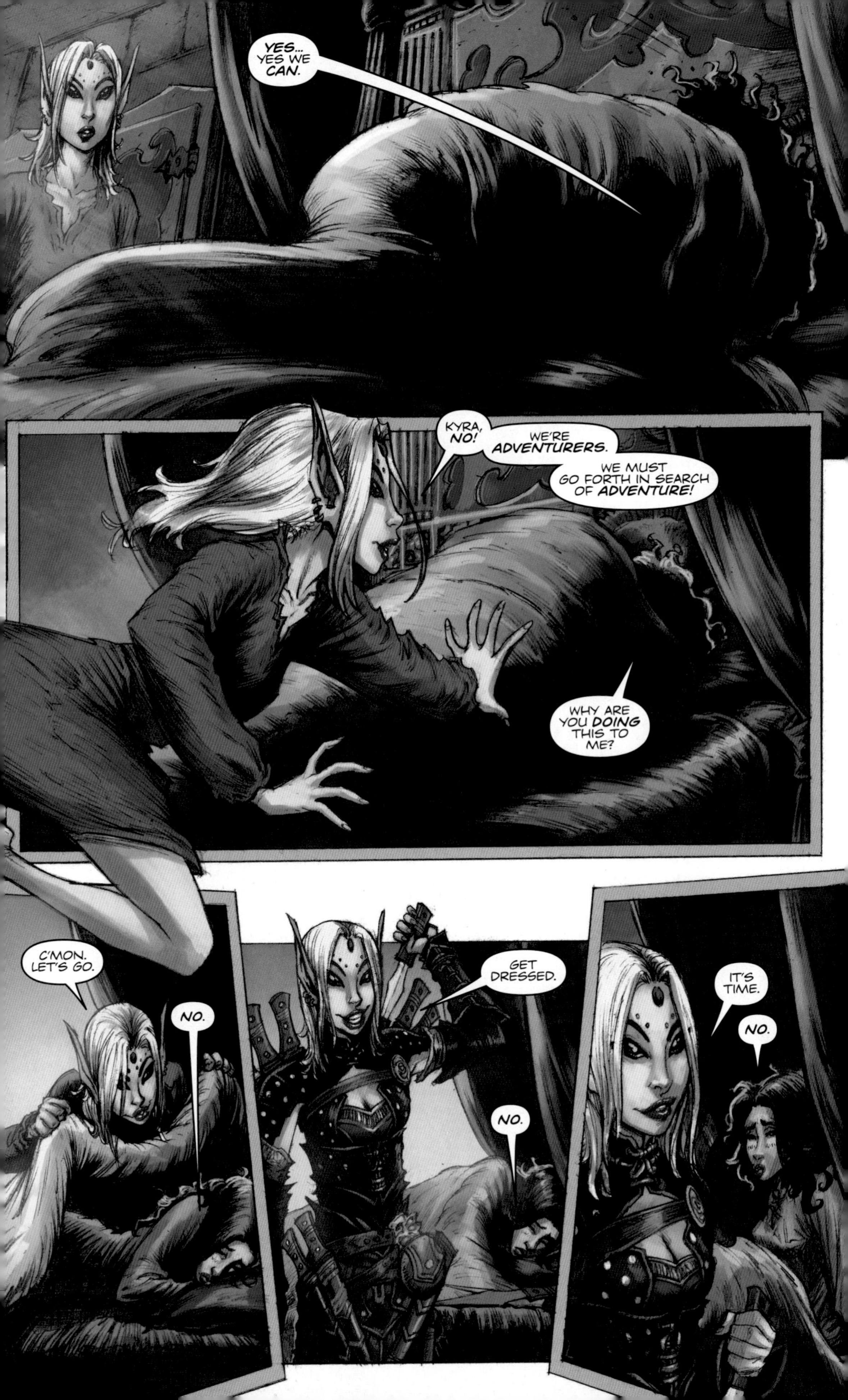
YES... YES WE CAN.
KYRA, NO!
WE'RE ADVENTURERS.
WE MUST GO FORTH IN SEARCH OF ADVENTURE!
WHY ARE YOU DOING THIS TO ME?
C'MON. LET'S GO.
NO.
GET DRESSED.
NO.
IT'S TIME.
NO.

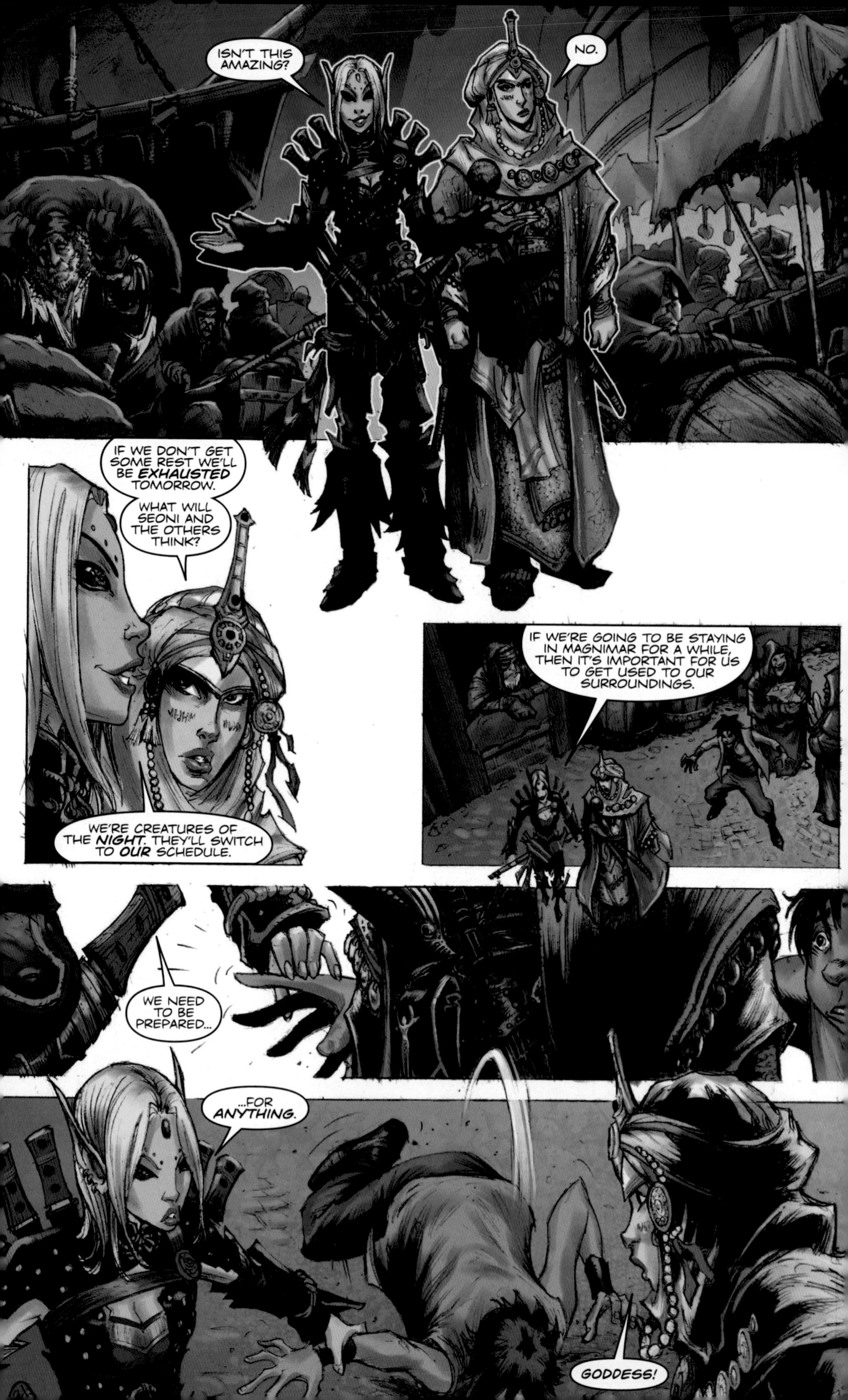
ISN'T THIS AMAZING?
NO.
IF WE DON'T GET SOME REST WE'LL BE **EXHAUSTED** TOMORROW.
WHAT WILL SEONI AND THE OTHERS THINK?
WE'RE CREATURES OF THE **NIGHT**. THEY'LL SWITCH TO **OUR** SCHEDULE.
IF WE'RE GOING TO BE STAYING IN MAGNIMAR FOR A WHILE, THEN IT'S IMPORTANT FOR US TO GET USED TO OUR SURROUNDINGS.
WE NEED TO BE PREPARED...
...FOR **ANYTHING**.
GODDESS!

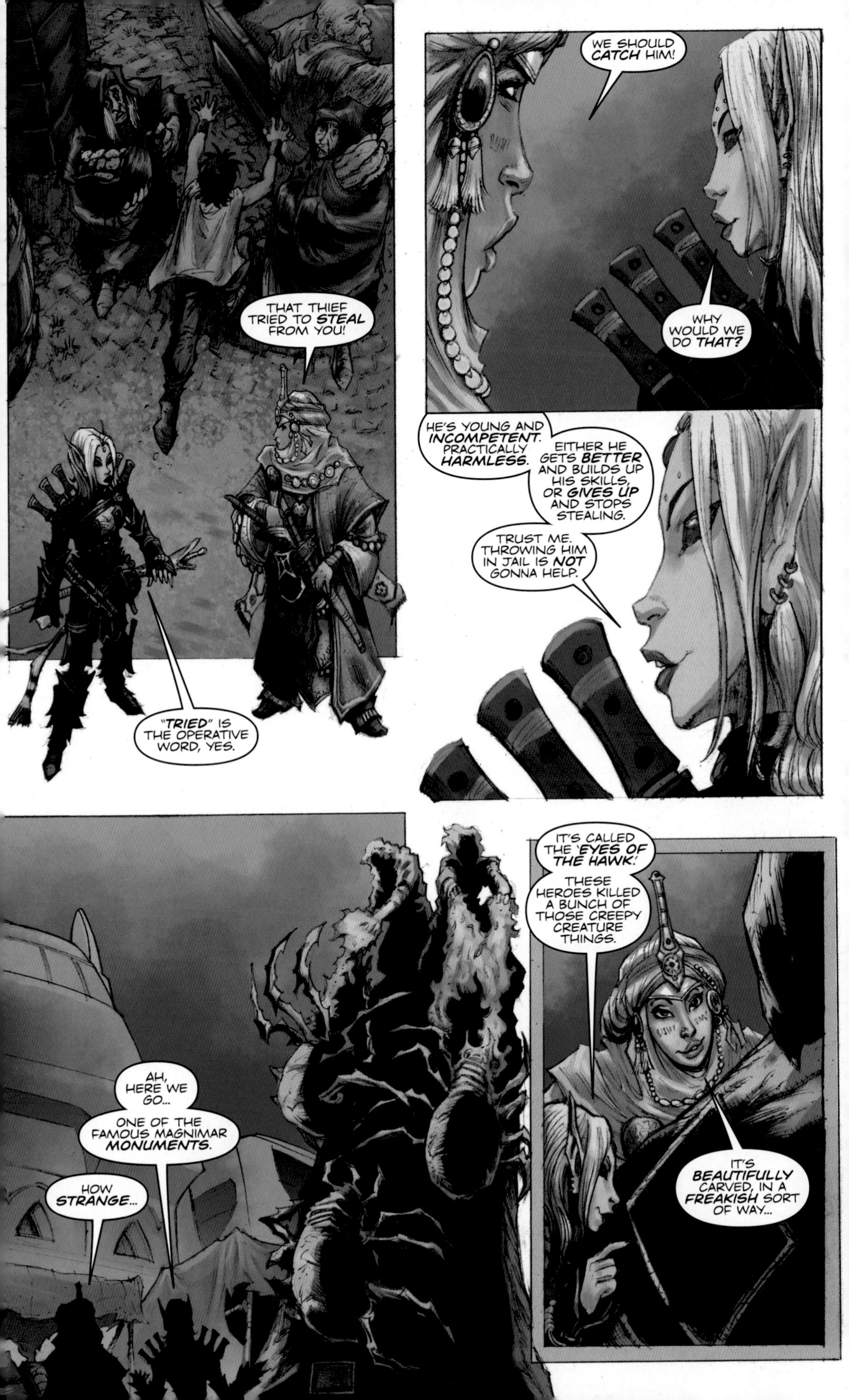
THAT THIEF TRIED TO STEAL FROM YOU!
"TRIED" IS THE OPERATIVE WORD, YES.
WE SHOULD CATCH HIM!
WHY WOULD WE DO THAT?
HE'S YOUNG AND INCOMPETENT. PRACTICALLY HARMLESS.
EITHER HE GETS BETTER AND BUILDS UP HIS SKILLS, OR GIVES UP AND STOPS STEALING.
TRUST ME. THROWING HIM IN JAIL IS NOT GONNA HELP.
AH, HERE WE GO...
ONE OF THE FAMOUS MAGNIMAR MONUMENTS.
HOW STRANGE...
IT'S CALLED THE 'EYES OF THE HAWK.'
THESE HEROES KILLED A BUNCH OF THOSE CREEPY CREATURE THINGS.
IT'S BEAUTIFULLY CARVED, IN A FREAKISH SORT OF WAY...

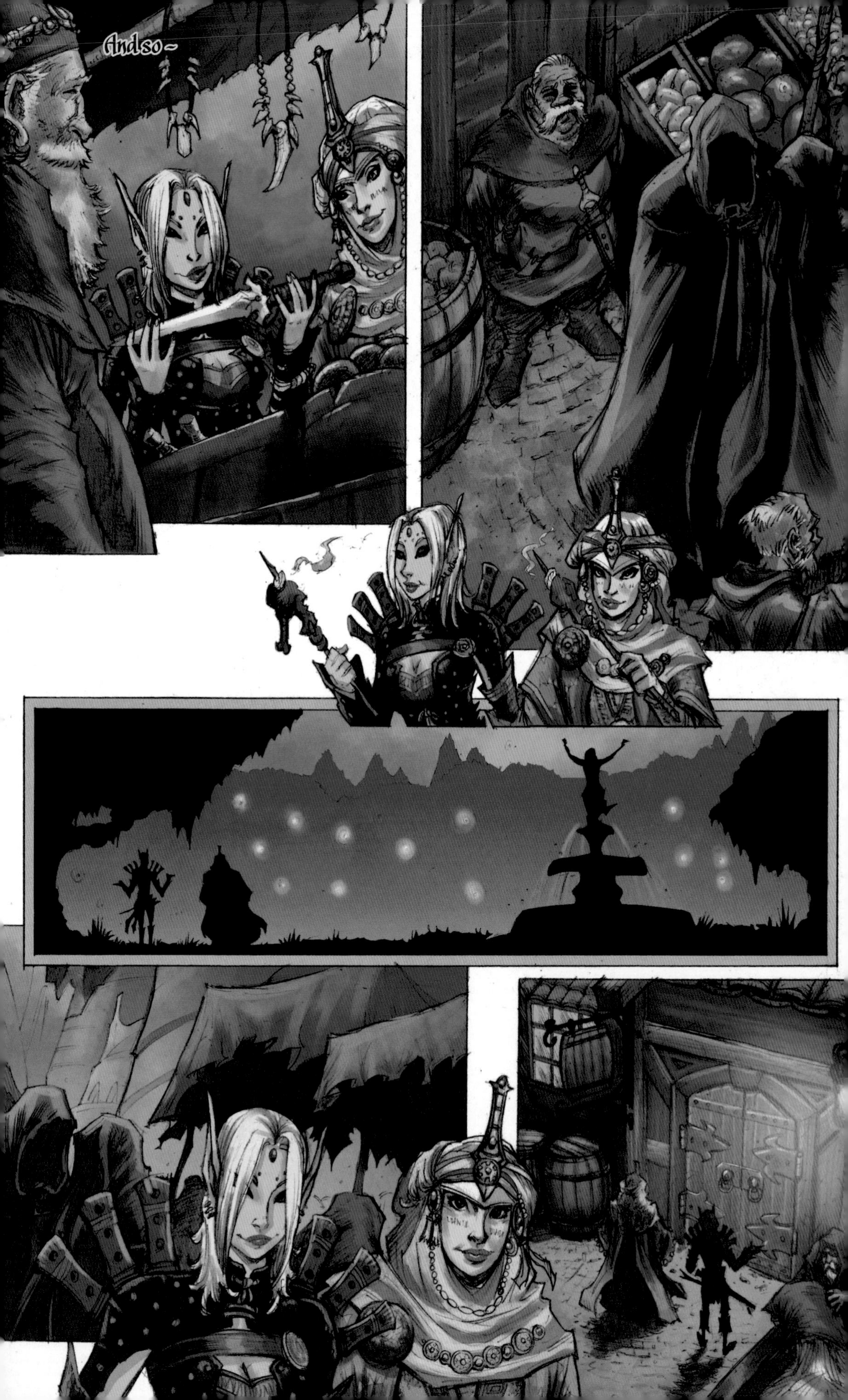
And so ~

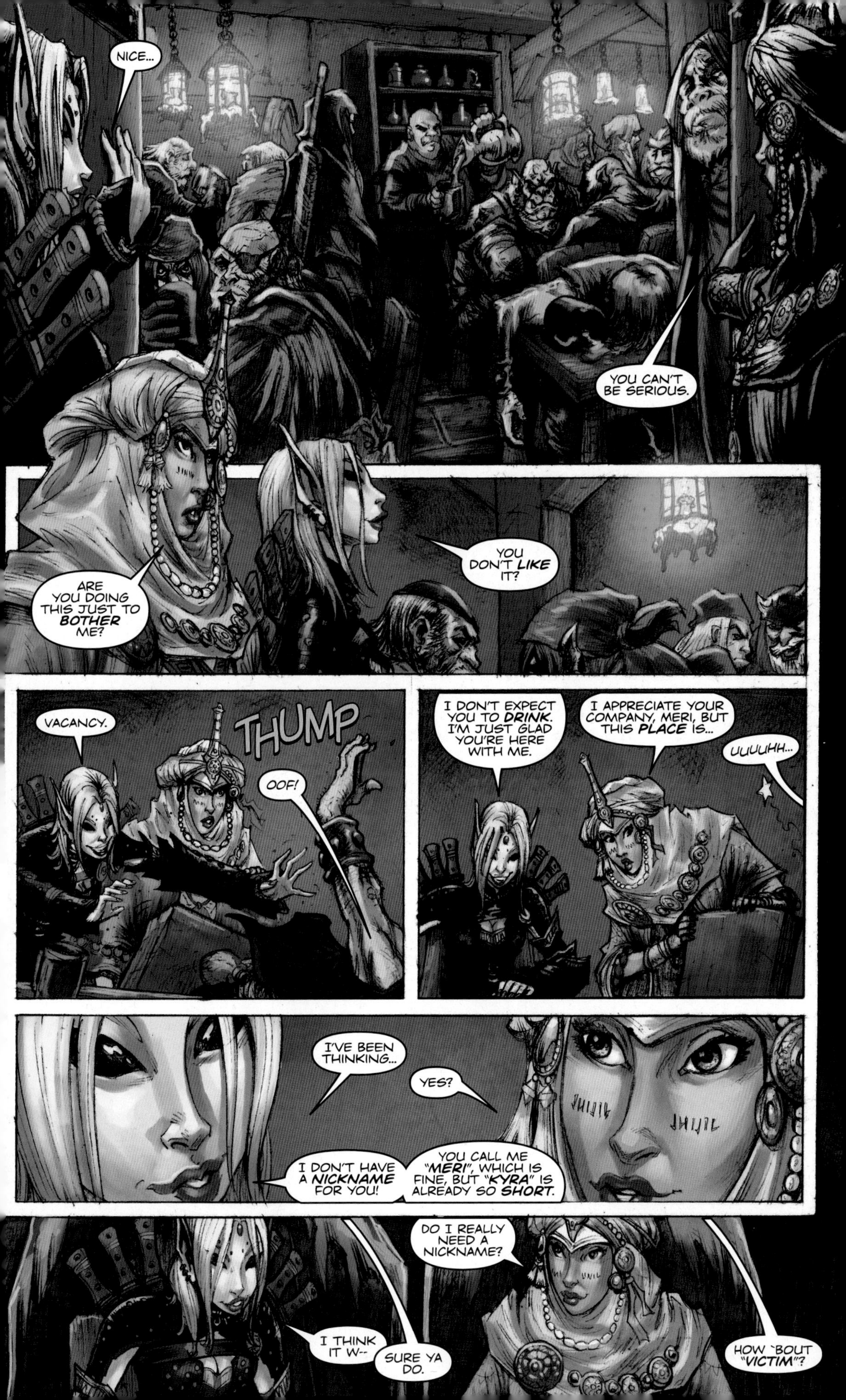
NICE...
YOU CAN'T BE SERIOUS.
ARE YOU DOING THIS JUST TO BOTHER ME?
YOU DON'T LIKE IT?
VACANCY.
THUMP
OOF!
I DON'T EXPECT YOU TO DRINK. I'M JUST GLAD YOU'RE HERE WITH ME.
I APPRECIATE YOUR COMPANY, MERI, BUT THIS PLACE IS...
UUUUHH...
I'VE BEEN THINKING...
YES?
I DON'T HAVE A NICKNAME FOR YOU!
YOU CALL ME "MERI", WHICH IS FINE, BUT "KYRA" IS ALREADY SO SHORT.
DO I REALLY NEED A NICKNAME?
I THINK IT W--
SURE YA DO.
HOW 'BOUT "VICTIM"?

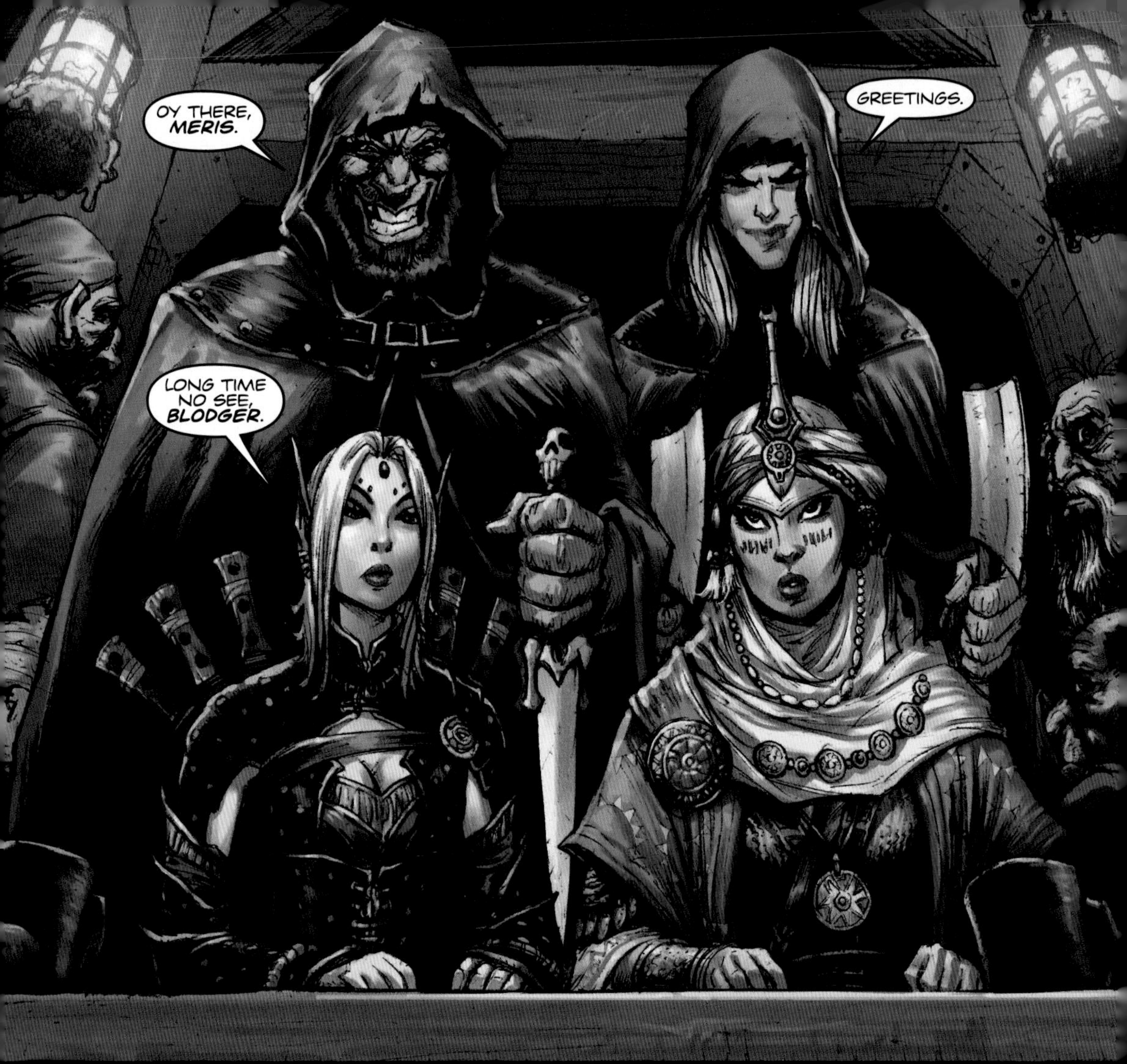
OY THERE, MERIS.
GREETINGS.
LONG TIME NO SEE, BLODGER.

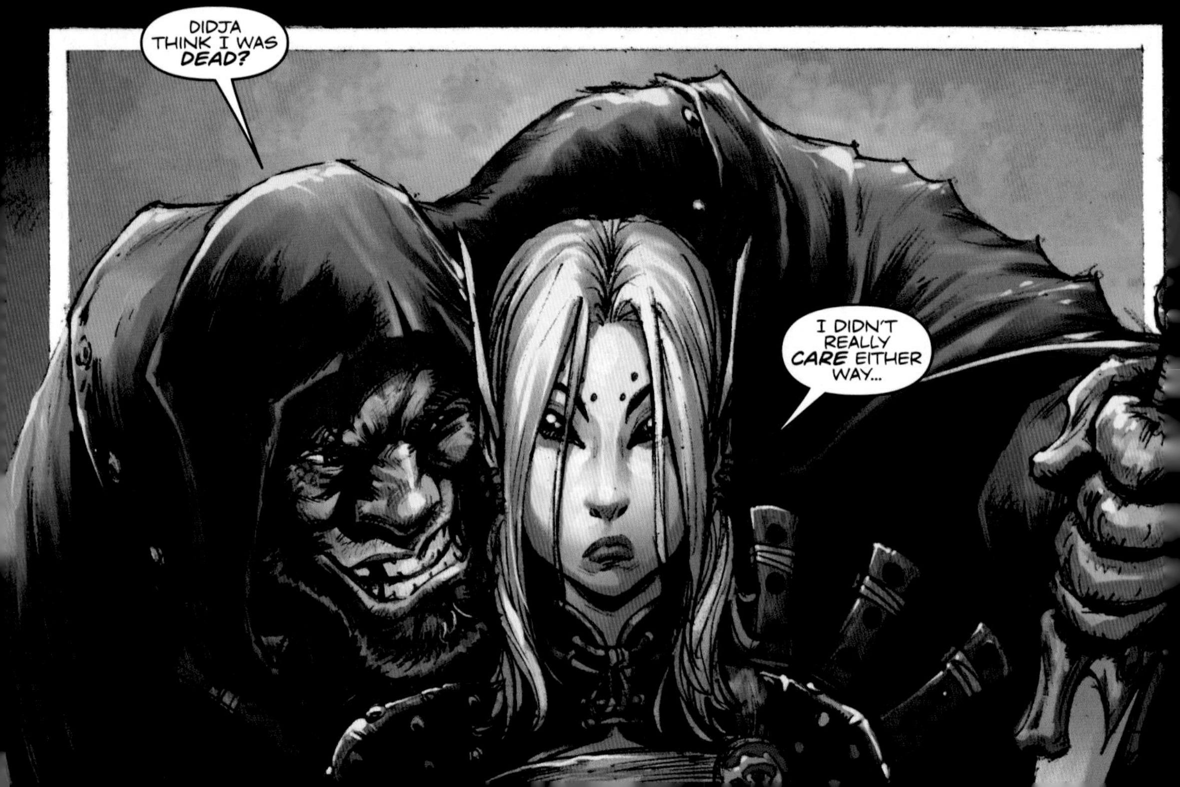
DIDJA THINK I WAS DEAD?
I DIDN'T REALLY CARE EITHER WAY...

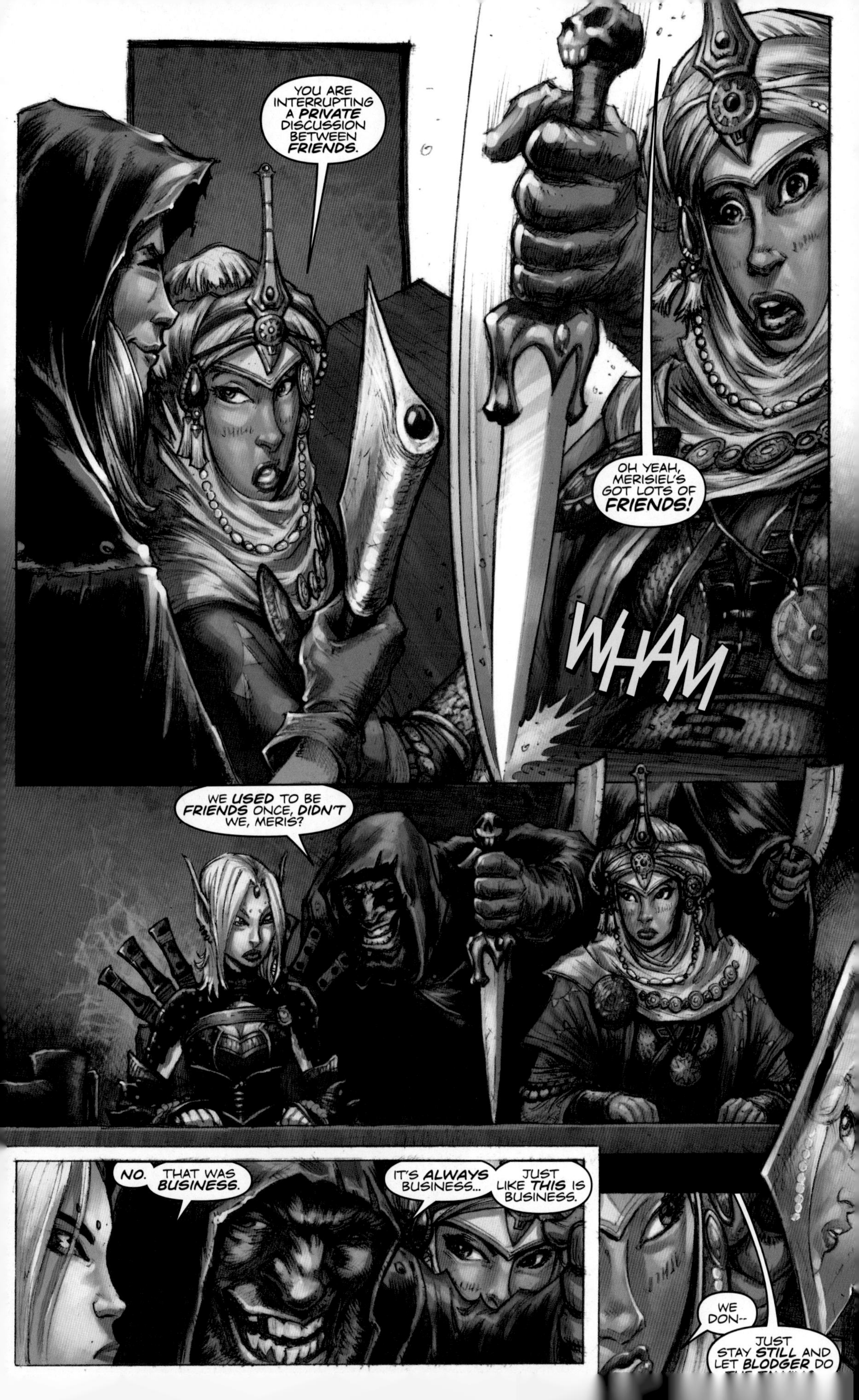
YOU ARE INTERRUPTING A PRIVATE DISCUSSION BETWEEN FRIENDS.
OH YEAH, MERISIEL'S GOT LOTS OF FRIENDS!
WHAM
WE USED TO BE FRIENDS ONCE, DIDN'T WE, MERIS?
NO. THAT WAS BUSINESS.
IT'S ALWAYS BUSINESS...
JUST LIKE THIS IS BUSINESS.
WE DON--
JUST STAY STILL AND LET BLODGER DO

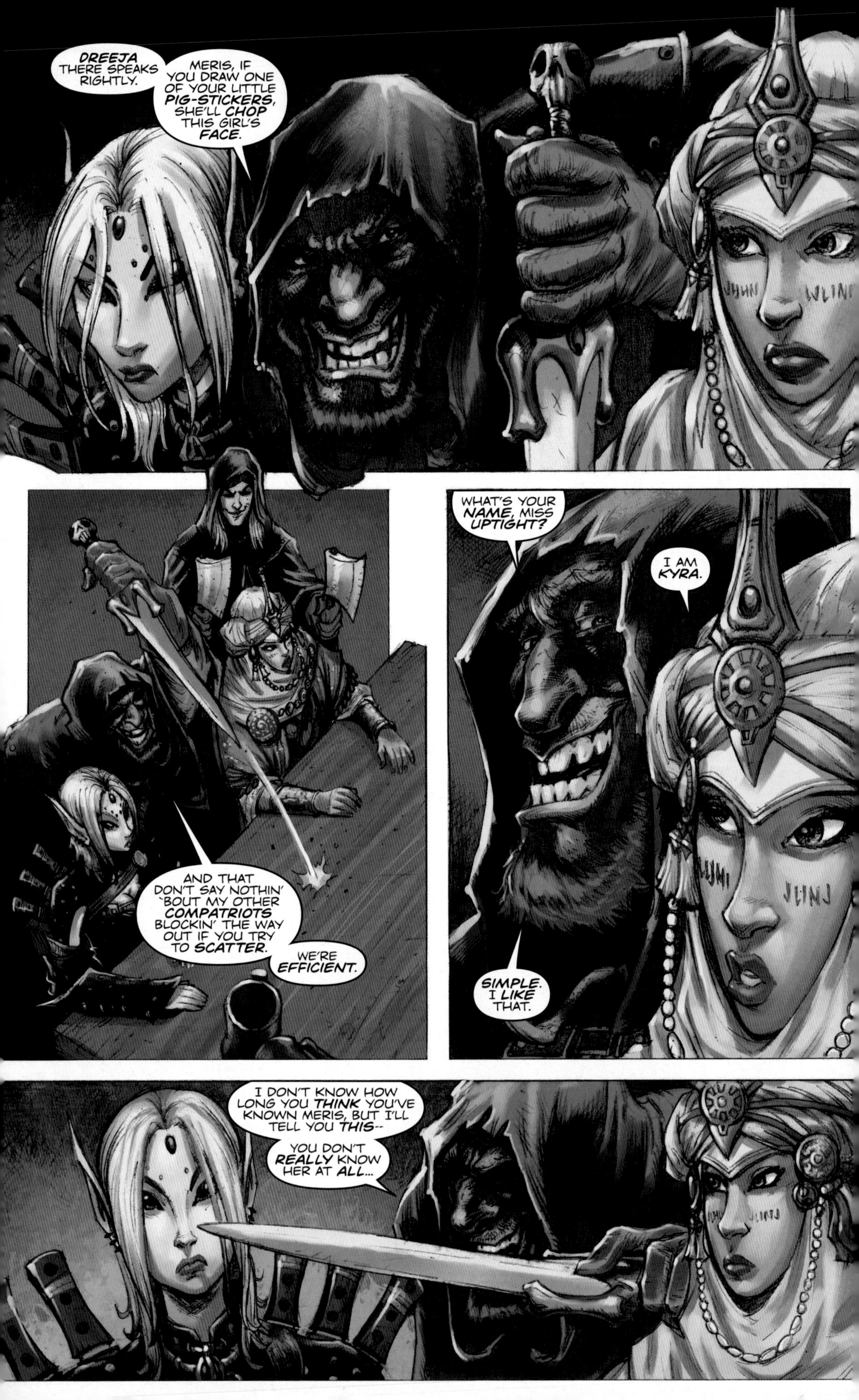
DREEJA THERE SPEAKS RIGHTLY.
MERIS, IF YOU DRAW ONE OF YOUR LITTLE PIG-STICKERS, SHE'LL CHOP THIS GIRL'S FACE.
AND THAT DON'T SAY NOTHIN' 'BOUT MY OTHER COMPATRIOTS BLOCKIN' THE WAY OUT IF YOU TRY TO SCATTER.
WE'RE EFFICIENT.
WHAT'S YOUR NAME, MISS UPTIGHT?
I AM KYRA.
SIMPLE. I LIKE THAT.
I DON'T KNOW HOW LONG YOU THINK YOU'VE KNOWN MERIS, BUT I'LL TELL YOU THIS--
YOU DON'T REALLY KNOW HER AT ALL...

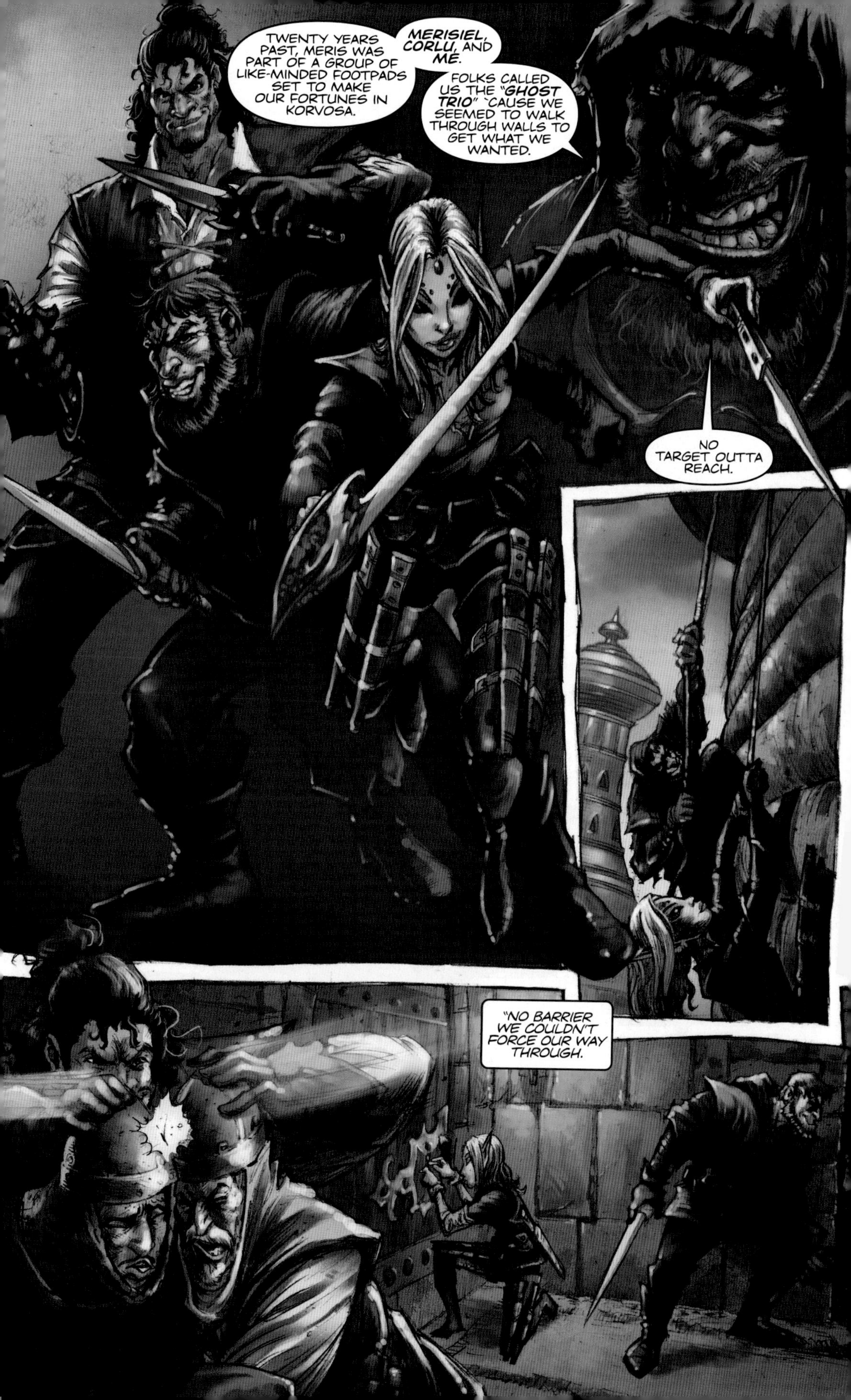
TWENTY YEARS PAST, MERIS WAS PART OF A GROUP OF LIKE-MINDED FOOTPADS SET TO MAKE OUR FORTUNES IN KORVOSA.
MERISIEL, CORLU, AND ME.
FOLKS CALLED US THE "GHOST TRIO" 'CAUSE WE SEEMED TO WALK THROUGH WALLS TO GET WHAT WE WANTED.
NO TARGET OUTTA REACH.
"NO BARRIER WE COULDN'T FORCE OUR WAY THROUGH.

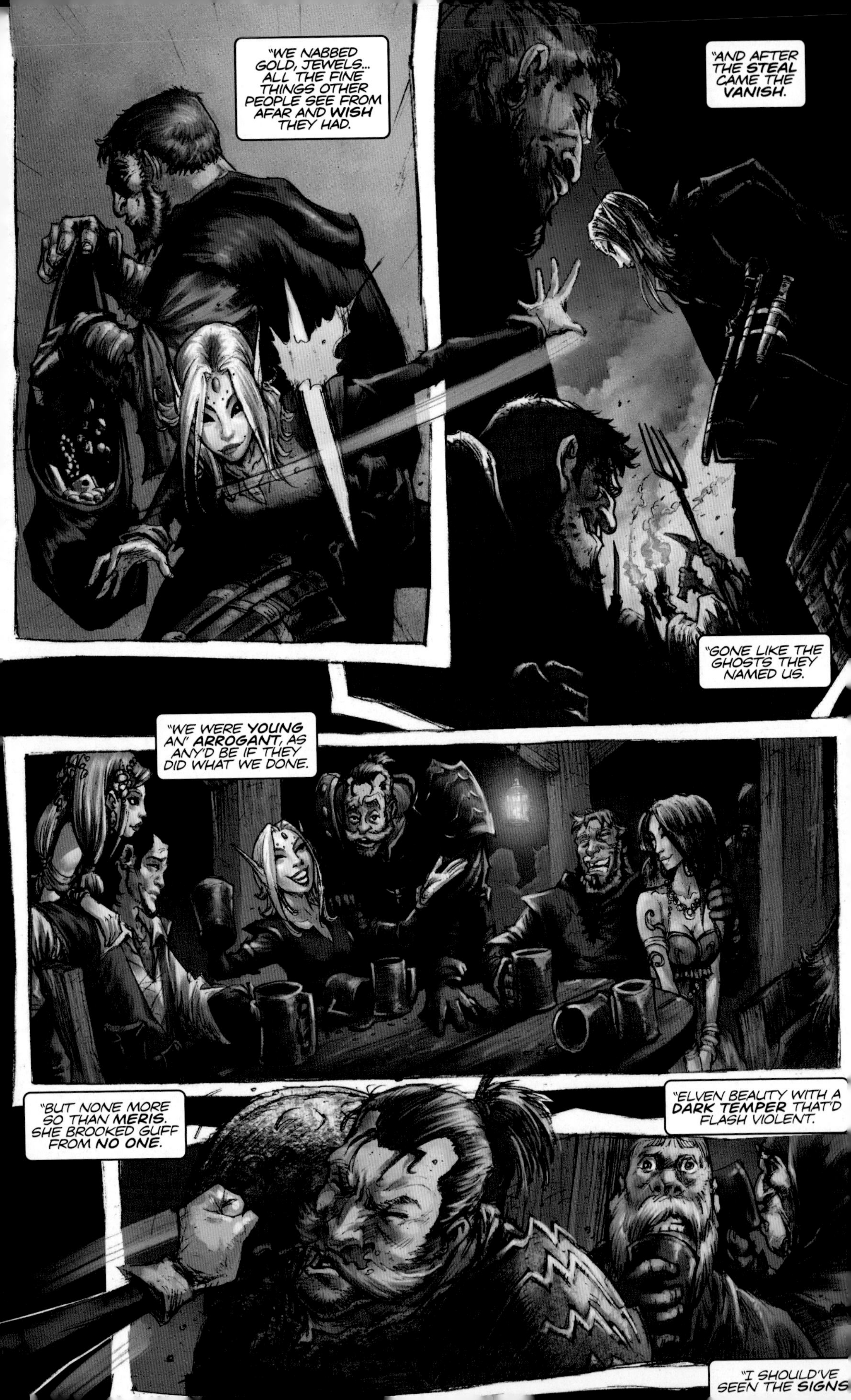
"WE NABBED GOLD, JEWELS... ALL THE FINE THINGS OTHER PEOPLE SEE FROM AFAR AND **WISH** THEY HAD.
"AND AFTER THE **STEAL** CAME THE **VANISH**.
"GONE LIKE THE GHOSTS THEY NAMED US.
"WE WERE **YOUNG** AN' **ARROGANT**, AS ANY'D BE IF THEY DID WHAT WE DONE.
"BUT NONE MORE SO THAN **MERIS**. SHE BROOKED GUFF FROM **NO ONE**.
"ELVEN BEAUTY WITH A **DARK TEMPER** THAT'D FLASH VIOLENT.
"I SHOULD'VE SEEN THE **SIGNS**

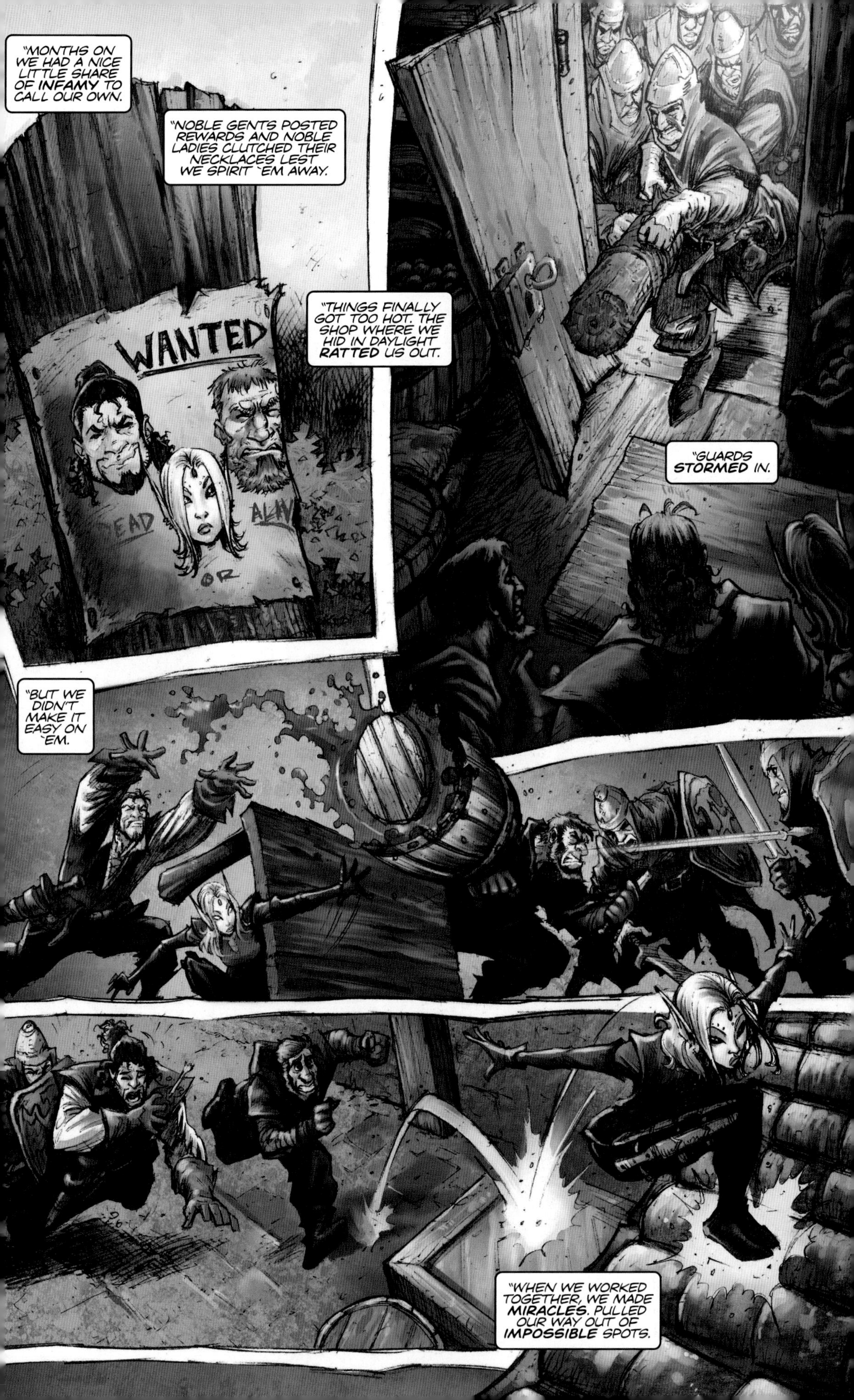
"MONTHS ON WE HAD A NICE LITTLE SHARE OF INFAMY TO CALL OUR OWN.
"NOBLE GENTS POSTED REWARDS AND NOBLE LADIES CLUTCHED THEIR NECKLACES LEST WE SPIRIT 'EM AWAY.
WANTED
DEAD OR ALIVE
"THINGS FINALLY GOT TOO HOT. THE SHOP WHERE WE HID IN DAYLIGHT RATTED US OUT.
"GUARDS STORMED IN.
"BUT WE DIDN'T MAKE IT EASY ON 'EM.
"WHEN WE WORKED TOGETHER, WE MADE MIRACLES. PULLED OUR WAY OUT OF IMPOSSIBLE SPOTS.

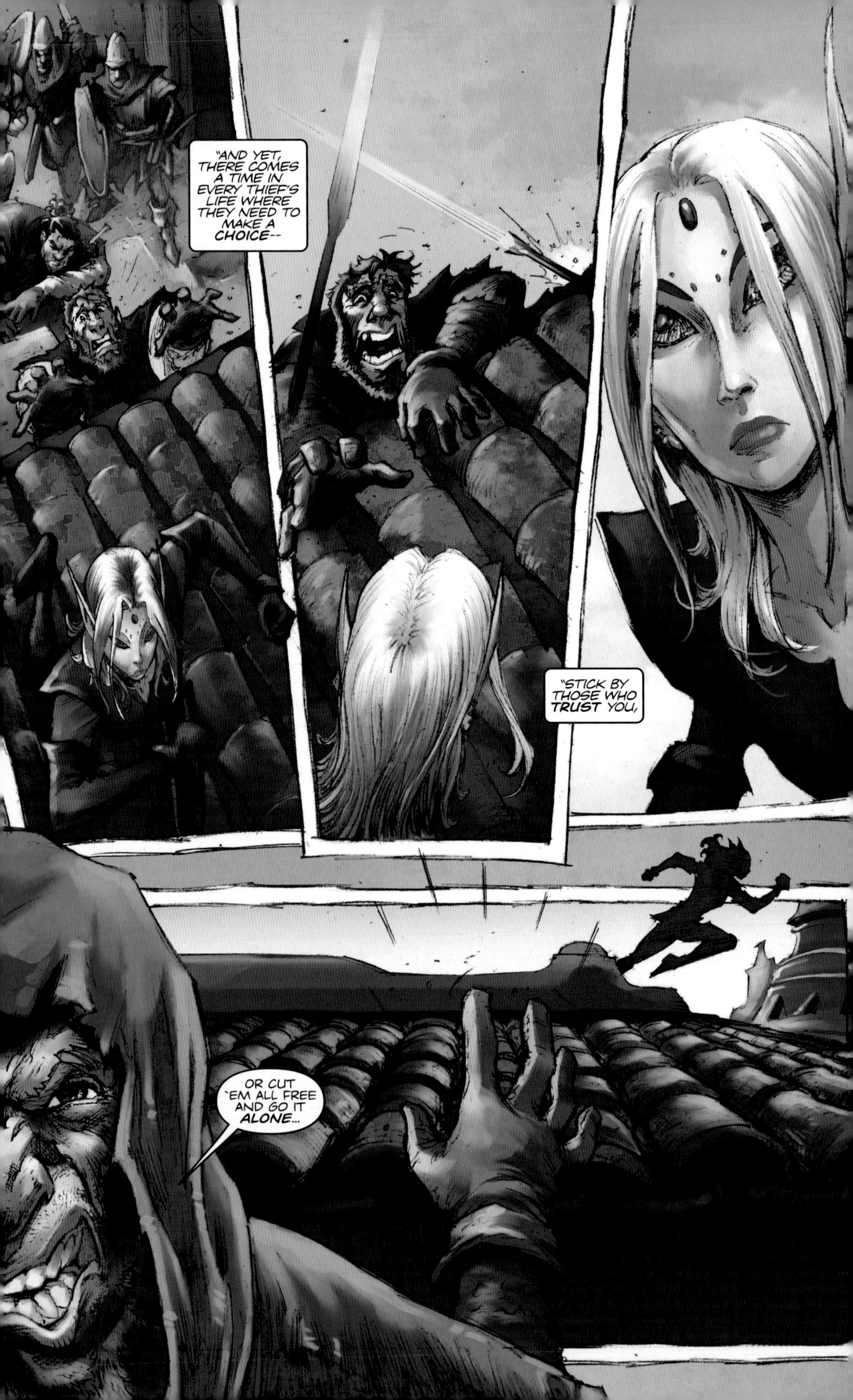
"AND YET, THERE COMES A TIME IN EVERY THIEF'S LIFE WHERE THEY NEED TO MAKE A CHOICE--
"STICK BY THOSE WHO TRUST YOU,
OR CUT `EM ALL FREE AND GO IT ALONE...

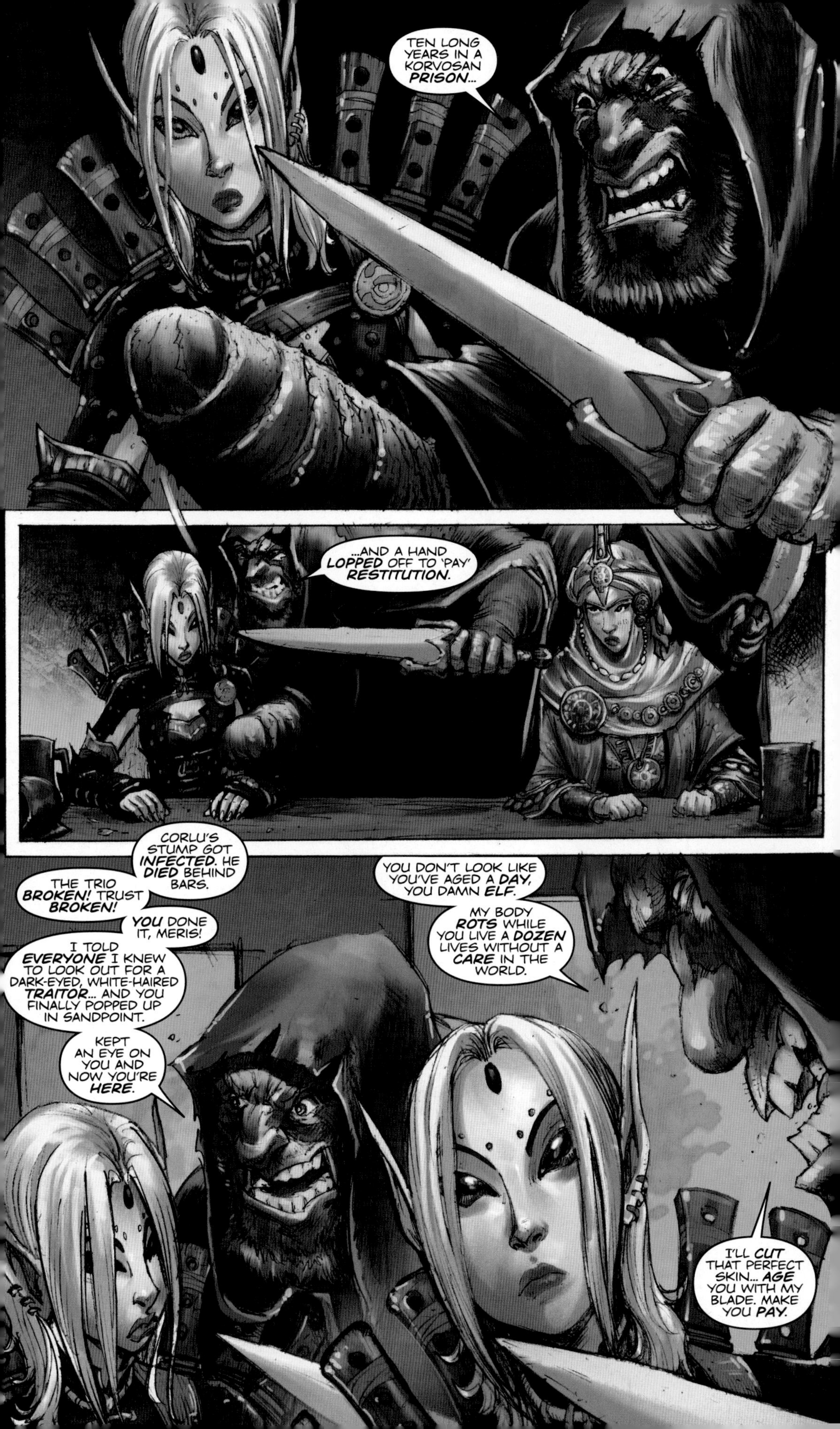
TEN LONG YEARS IN A KORVOSAN PRISON...
...AND A HAND LOPPED OFF TO 'PAY' RESTITUTION.
CORLU'S STUMP GOT INFECTED. HE DIED BEHIND BARS.
THE TRIO BROKEN! TRUST BROKEN!
YOU DONE IT, MERIS!
I TOLD EVERYONE I KNEW TO LOOK OUT FOR A DARK-EYED, WHITE-HAIRED TRAITOR... AND YOU FINALLY POPPED UP IN SANDPOINT.
KEPT AN EYE ON YOU AND NOW YOU'RE HERE.
YOU DON'T LOOK LIKE YOU'VE AGED A DAY, YOU DAMN ELF.
MY BODY ROTS WHILE YOU LIVE A DOZEN LIVES WITHOUT A CARE IN THE WORLD.
I'LL CUT THAT PERFECT SKIN... AGE YOU WITH MY BLADE. MAKE YOU PAY.

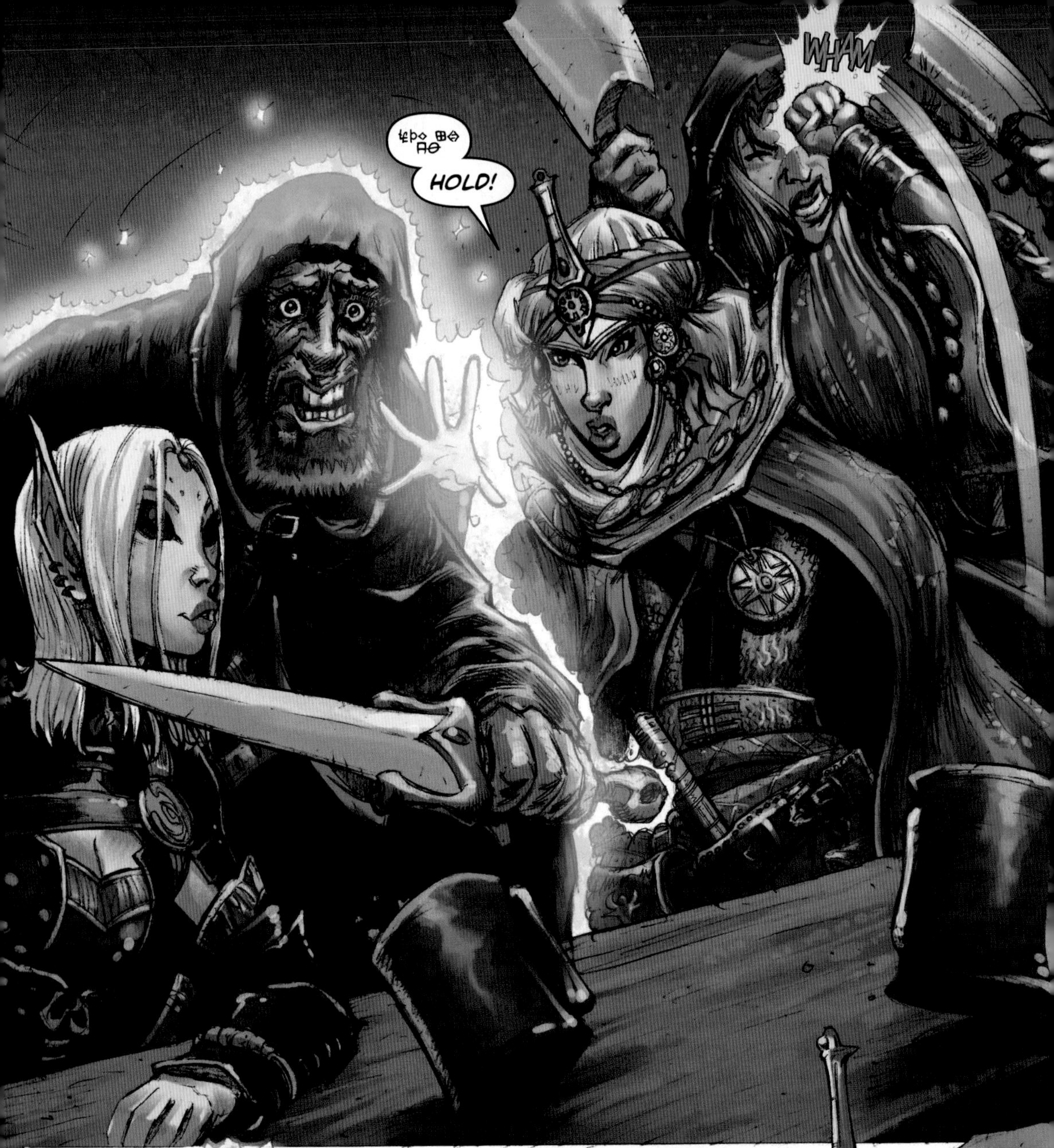
WHAM
HOLD!

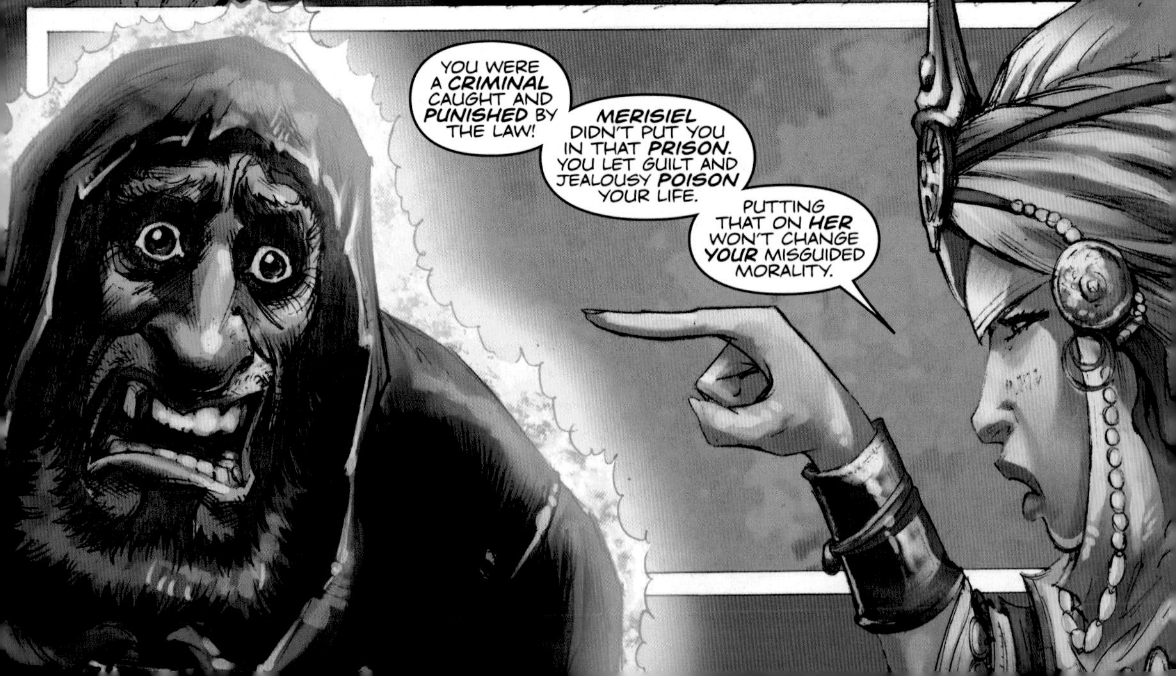
YOU WERE A **CRIMINAL** CAUGHT AND **PUNISHED** BY THE LAW!
MERISIEL DIDN'T PUT YOU IN THAT **PRISON**. YOU LET GUILT AND JEALOUSY **POISON** YOUR LIFE.
PUTTING THAT ON **HER** WON'T CHANGE **YOUR** MISGUIDED MORALITY.

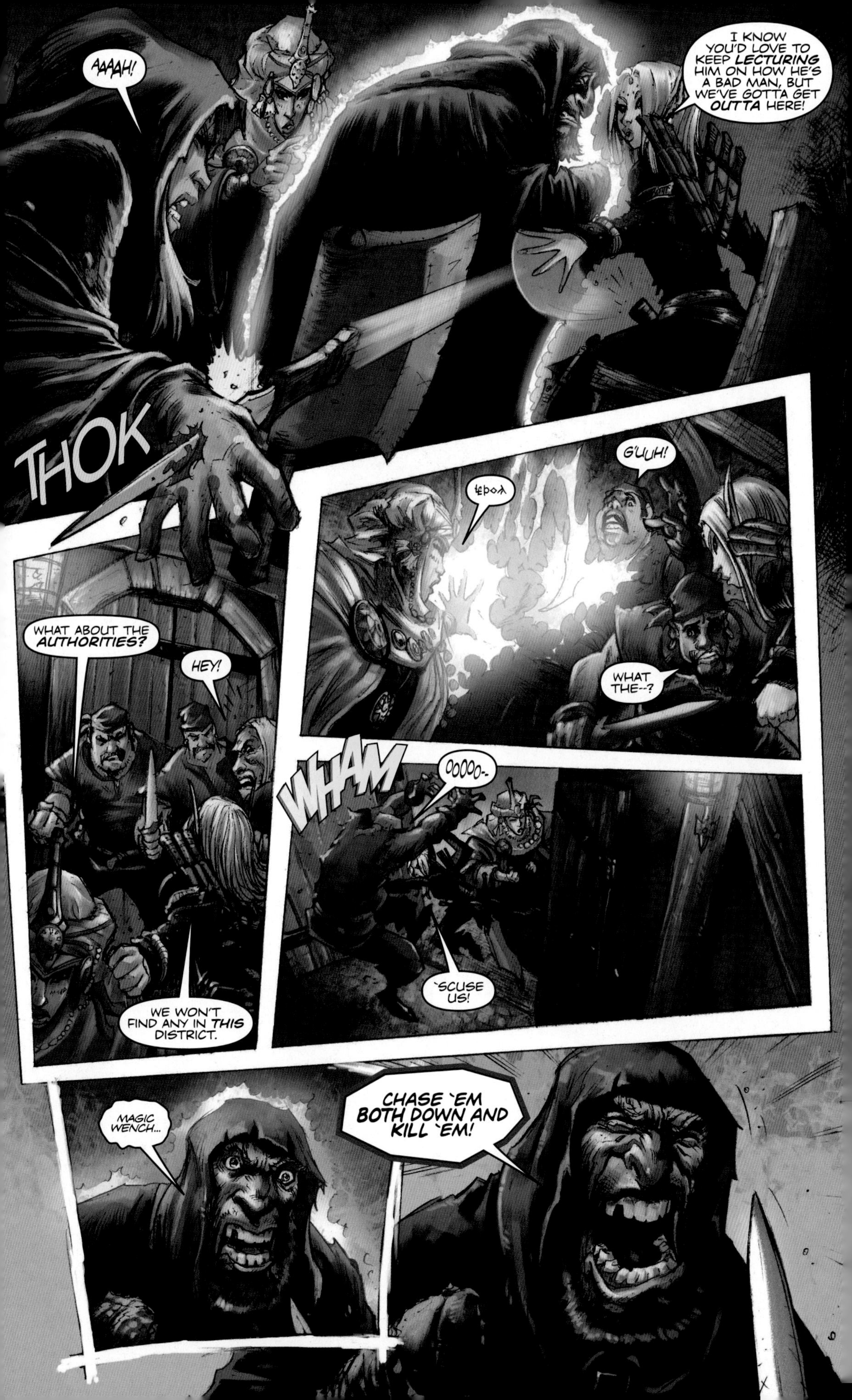
AAAAH!
I KNOW YOU'D LOVE TO KEEP LECTURING HIM ON HOW HE'S A BAD MAN, BUT WE'VE GOTTA GET OUTTA HERE!
THOK
WHAT ABOUT THE AUTHORITIES?
HEY!
WE WON'T FIND ANY IN THIS DISTRICT.
G'UUH!
WHAT THE--?
WHAM
OOOOO-.
`SCUSE US!
MAGIC WENCH...
CHASE `EM BOTH DOWN AND KILL `EM!

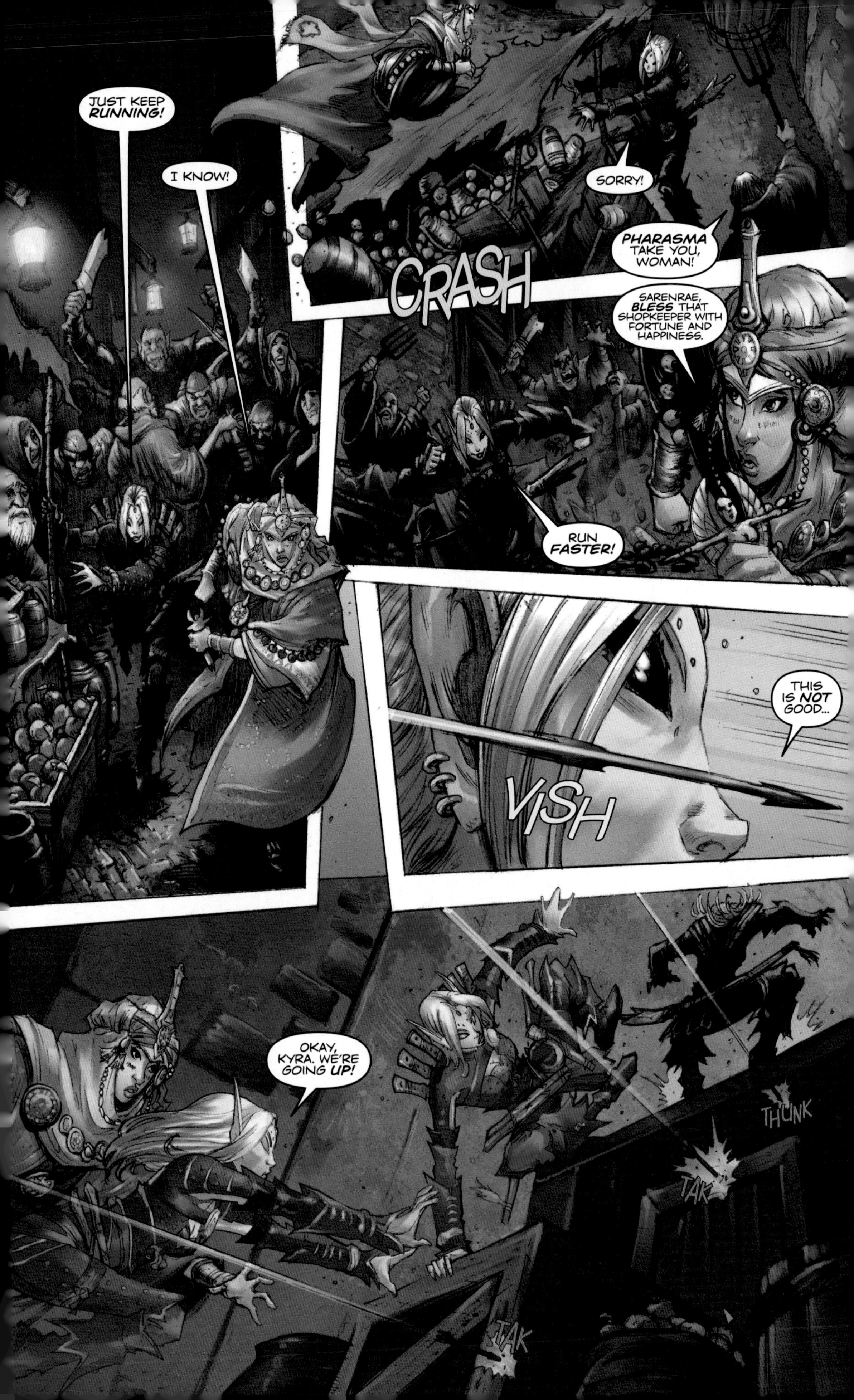
CRASH
SORRY!
PHARASMA TAKE YOU, WOMAN!
SARENRAE, BLESS THAT SHOPKEEPER WITH FORTUNE AND HAPPINESS.
JUST KEEP RUNNING!
I KNOW!
RUN FASTER!
THIS IS NOT GOOD...
VISH
OKAY, KYRA. WE'RE GOING UP!
THUNK
TAK
TAK

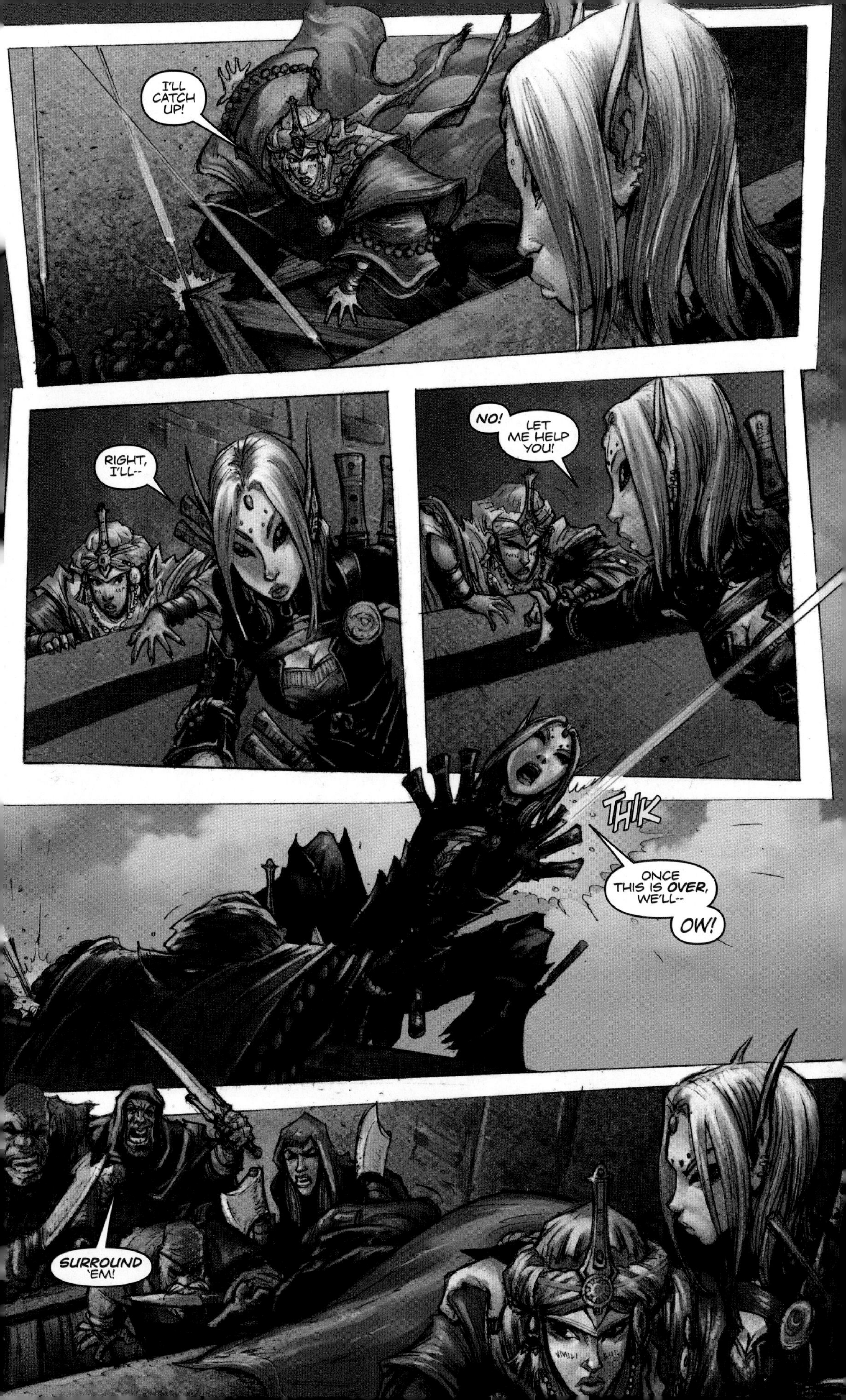
I'LL CATCH UP!
RIGHT, I'LL--
NO!
LET ME HELP YOU!
THIK
ONCE THIS IS OVER, WE'LL--
OW!
SURROUND 'EM!

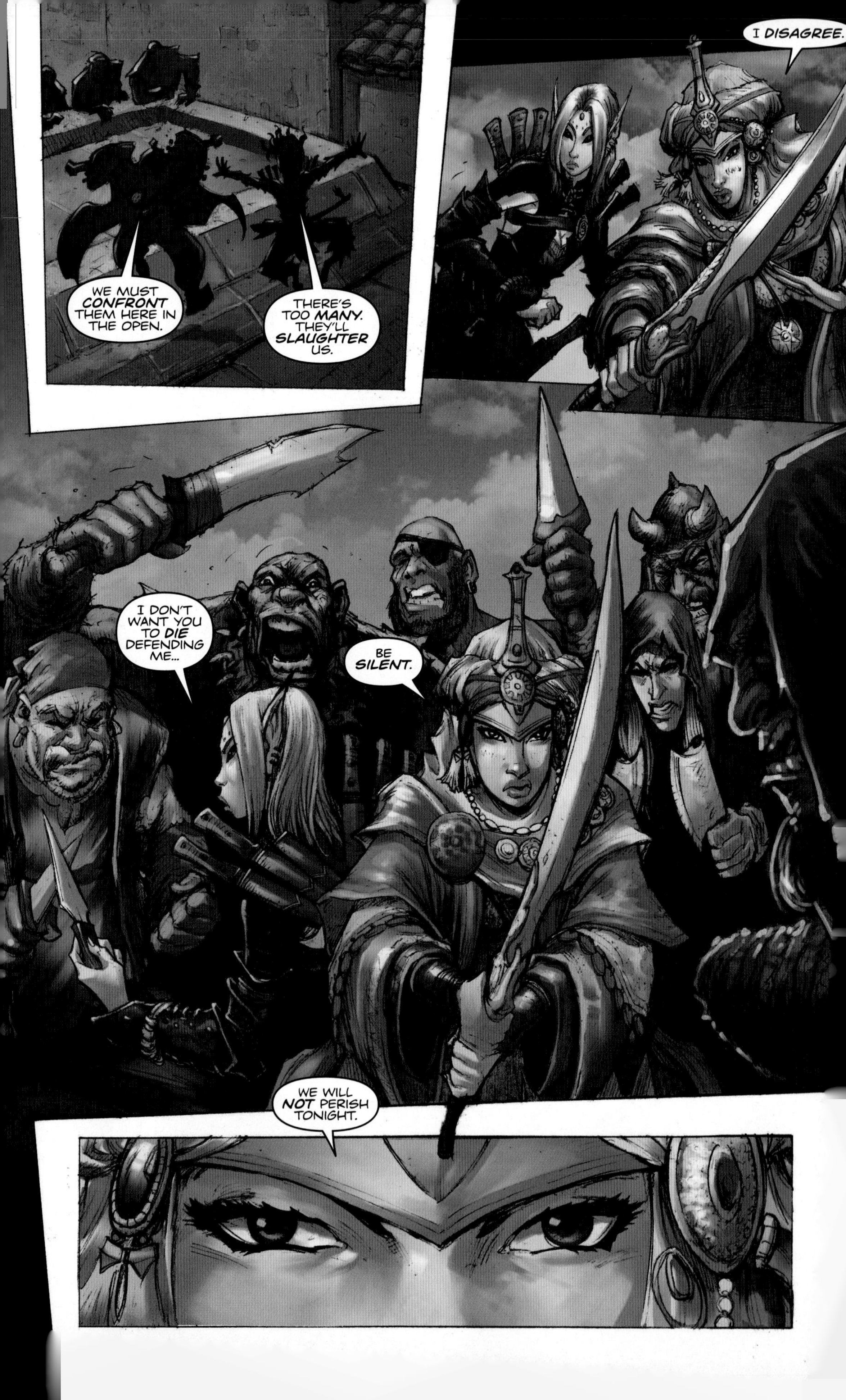
WE MUST CONFRONT THEM HERE IN THE OPEN.
THERE'S TOO MANY. THEY'LL SLAUGHTER US.
I DISAGREE.
I DON'T WANT YOU TO DIE DEFENDING ME...
BE SILENT.
WE WILL NOT PERISH TONIGHT.

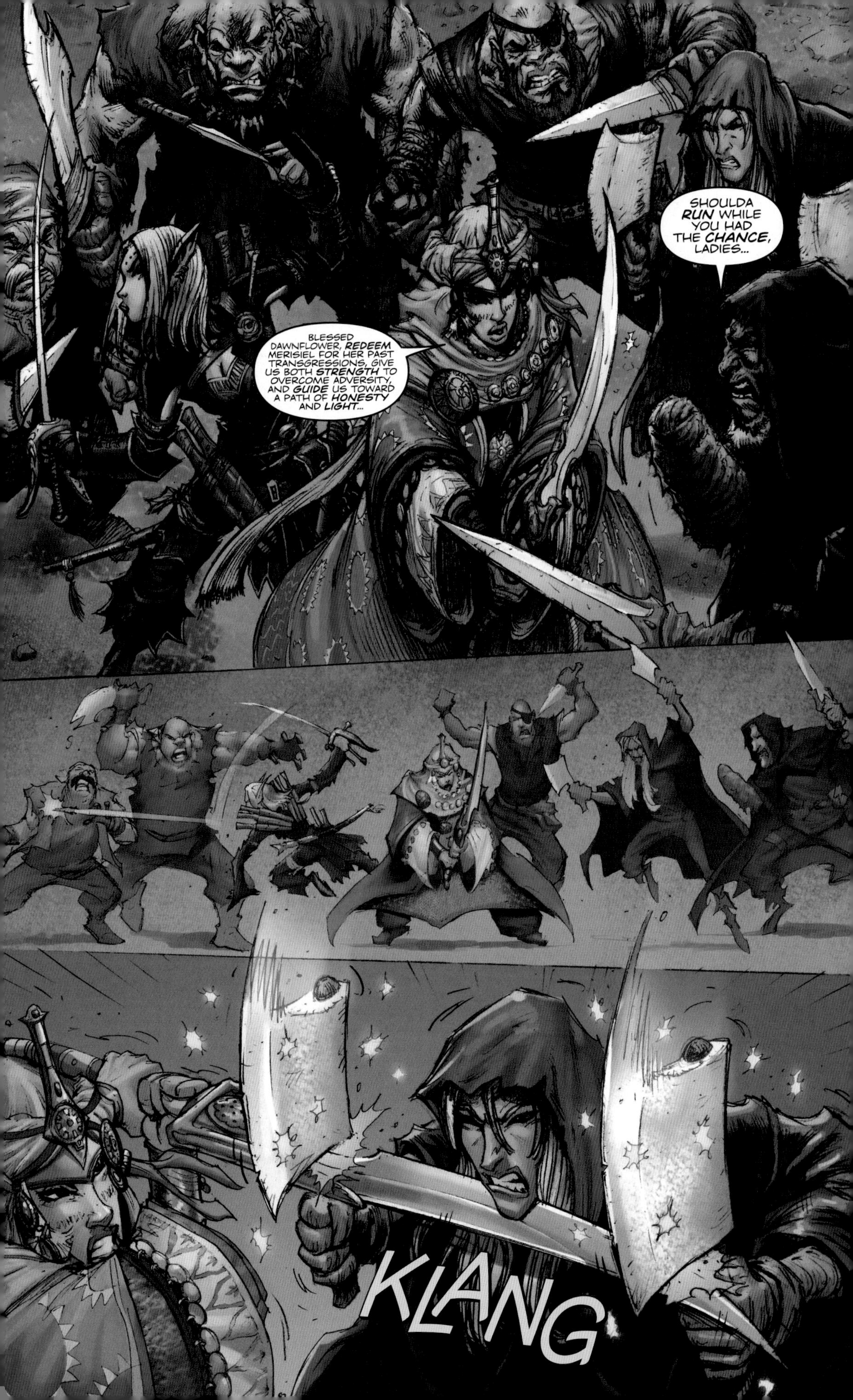
BLESSED DAWNFLOWER, REDEEM MERISIEL FOR HER PAST TRANSGRESSIONS, GIVE US BOTH STRENGTH TO OVERCOME ADVERSITY, AND GUIDE US TOWARD A PATH OF HONESTY AND LIGHT...
SHOULDA RUN WHILE YOU HAD THE CHANCE, LADIES...
KLANG

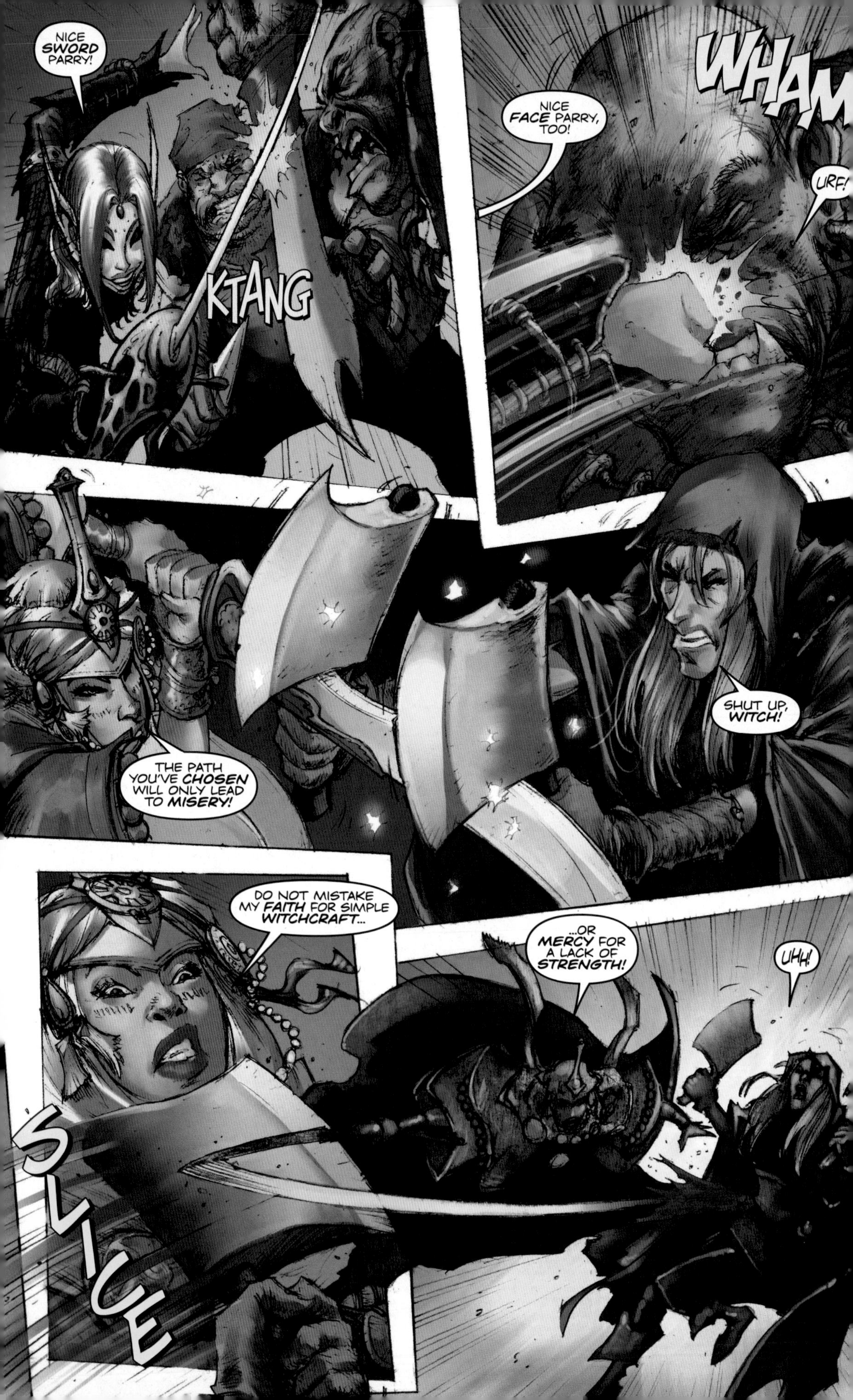
NICE SWORD PARRY!
KTANG
NICE FACE PARRY, TOO!
WHAM
URF!
THE PATH YOU'VE CHOSEN WILL ONLY LEAD TO MISERY!
SHUT UP, WITCH!
DO NOT MISTAKE MY FAITH FOR SIMPLE WITCHCRAFT...
...OR MERCY FOR A LACK OF STRENGTH!
UHH!
SLICE

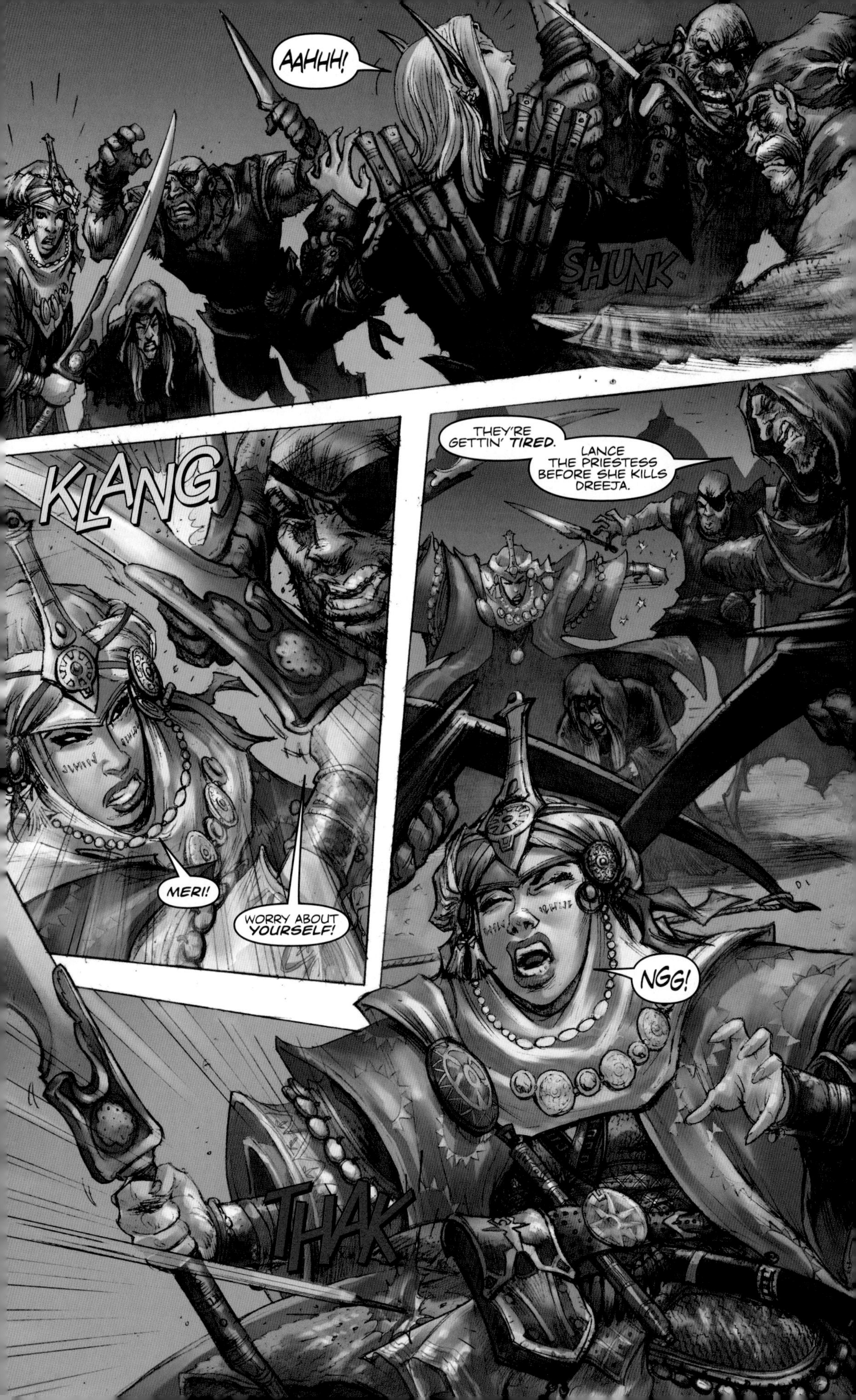
AAHHH!
SHUNK
KLANG
MERI!
WORRY ABOUT YOURSELF!
THEY'RE GETTIN' TIRED.
LANCE THE PRIESTESS BEFORE SHE KILLS DREEJA.
NGG!
THAK

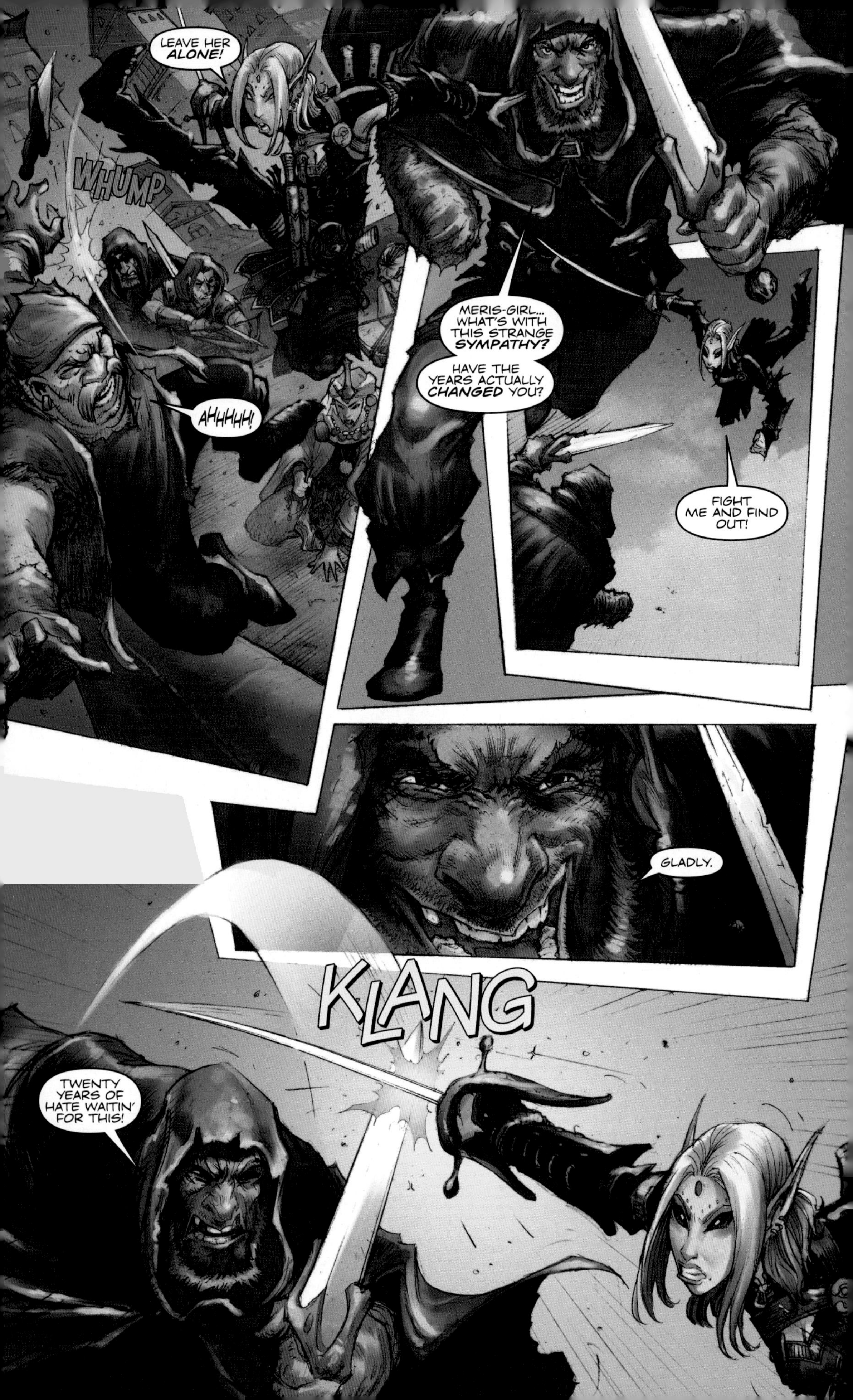
LEAVE HER ALONE!
WHUMP
AHHHHH!
MERIS-GIRL... WHAT'S WITH THIS STRANGE SYMPATHY?
HAVE THE YEARS ACTUALLY CHANGED YOU?
FIGHT ME AND FIND OUT!
GLADLY.
KLANG
TWENTY YEARS OF HATE WAITIN' FOR THIS!

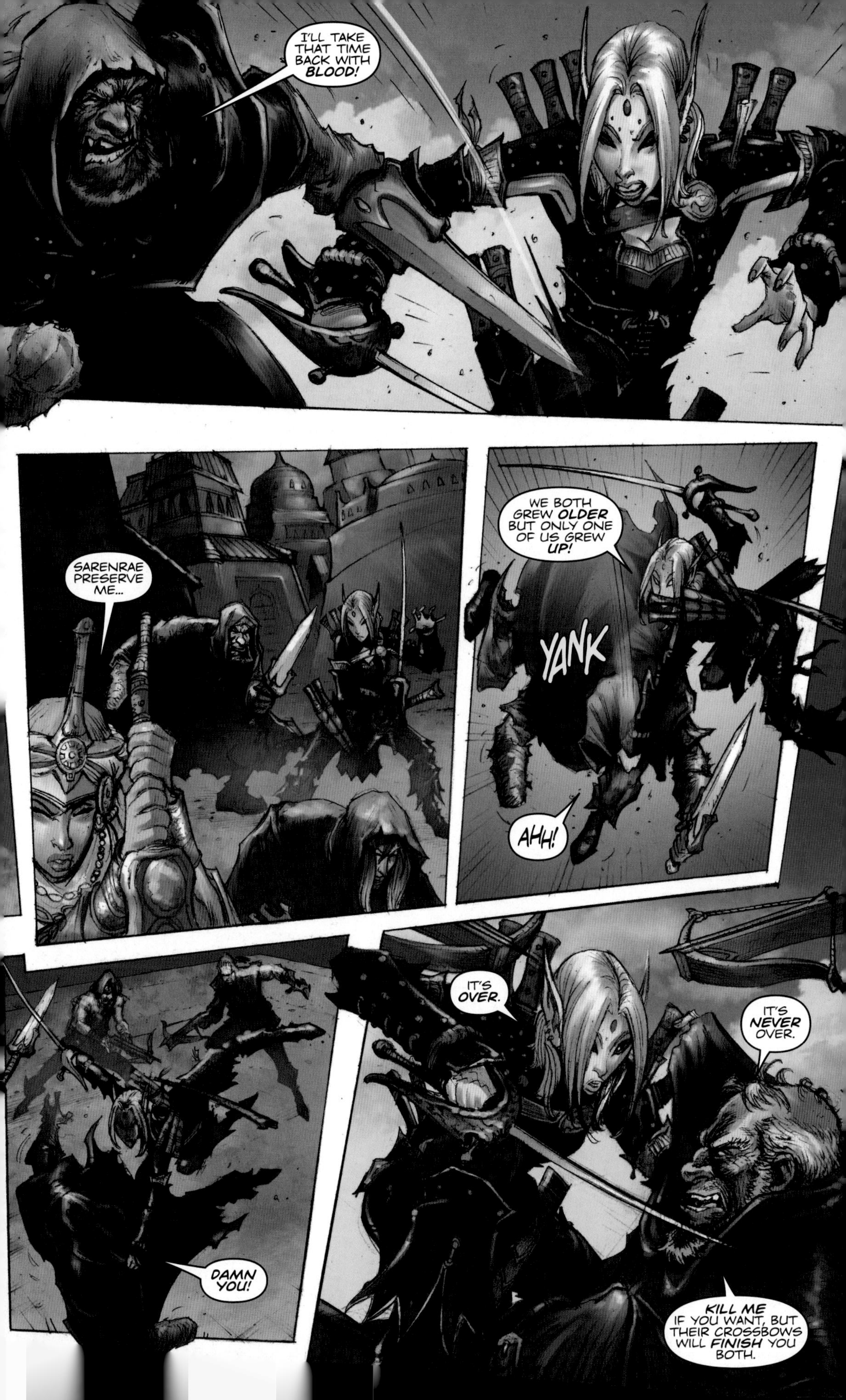
I'LL TAKE THAT TIME BACK WITH BLOOD!
SARENRAE PRESERVE ME...
WE BOTH GREW OLDER BUT ONLY ONE OF US GREW UP!
YANK
AHH!
DAMN YOU!
IT'S OVER.
IT'S NEVER OVER.
KILL ME IF YOU WANT, BUT THEIR CROSSBOWS WILL FINISH YOU BOTH.

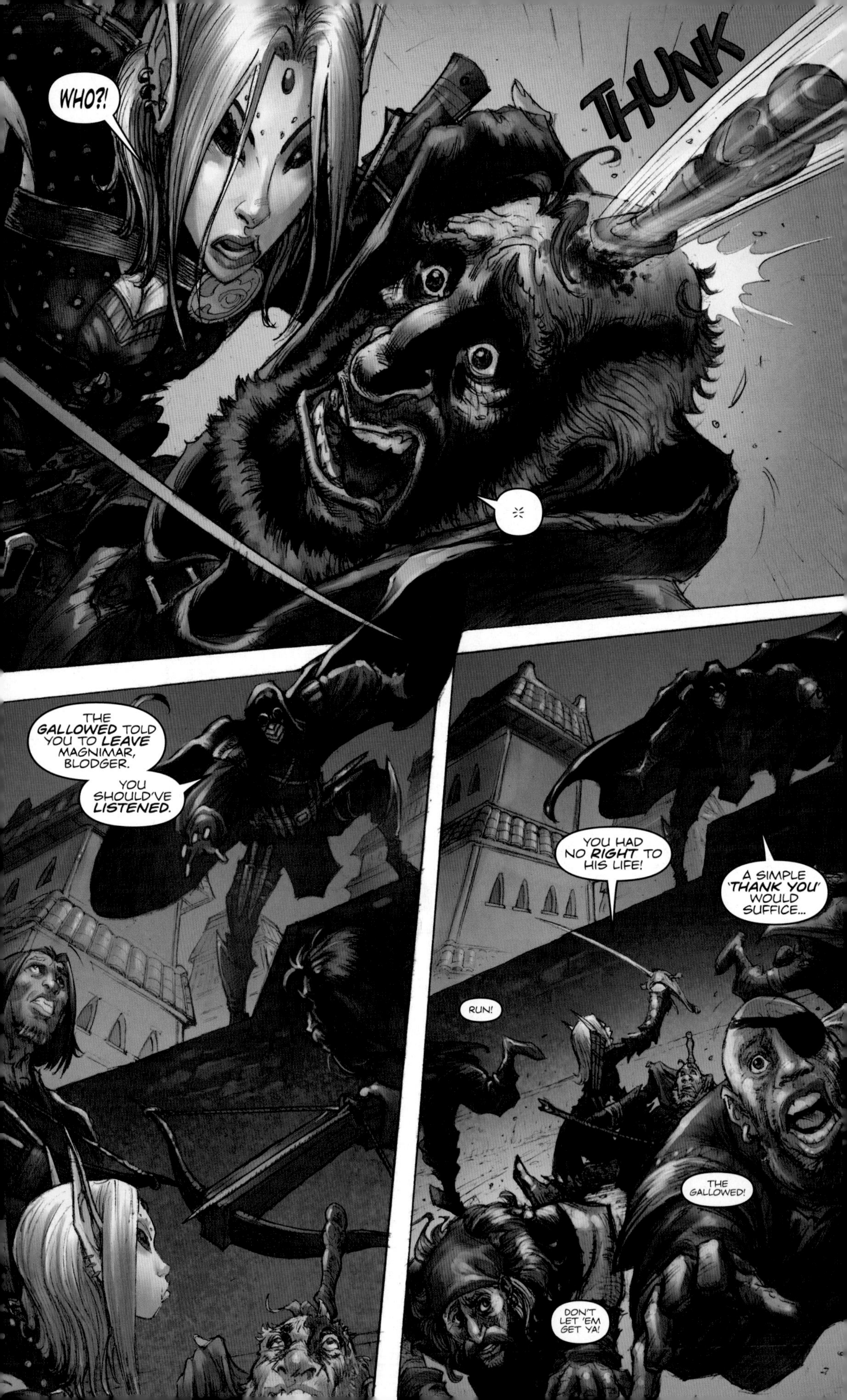
WHO?!
THUNK
THE GALLOWED TOLD YOU TO LEAVE MAGNIMAR, BLODGER.
YOU SHOULD'VE LISTENED.
YOU HAD NO RIGHT TO HIS LIFE!
A SIMPLE 'THANK YOU' WOULD SUFFICE...
RUN!
THE GALLOWED!
DON'T LET 'EM GET YA!

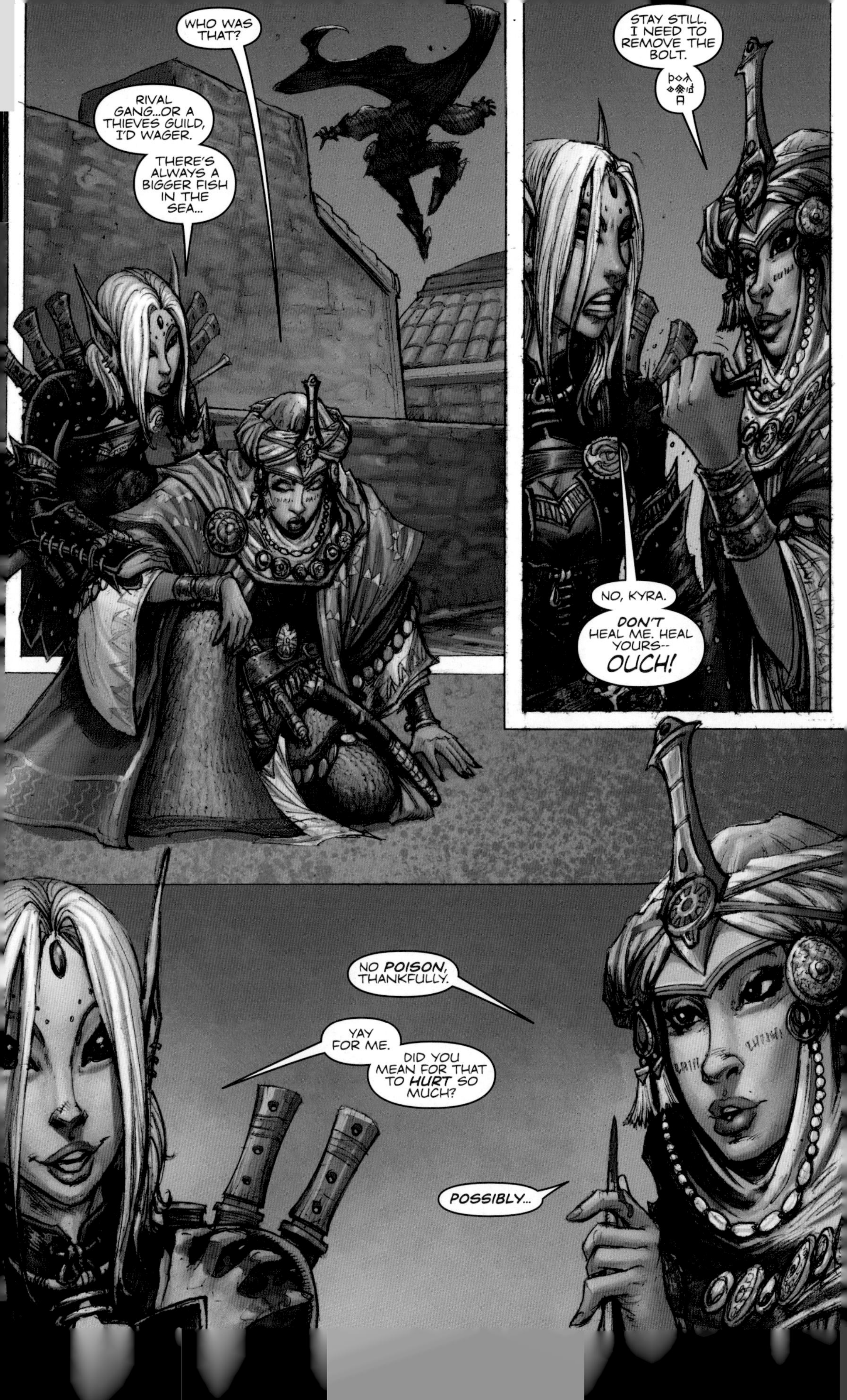
WHO WAS THAT?
RIVAL GANG...OR A THIEVES GUILD, I'D WAGER.
THERE'S ALWAYS A BIGGER FISH IN THE SEA...
STAY STILL. I NEED TO REMOVE THE BOLT.
NO, KYRA.
DON'T HEAL ME. HEAL YOURS--OUCH!
NO POISON, THANKFULLY.
YAY FOR ME.
DID YOU MEAN FOR THAT TO HURT SO MUCH?
POSSIBLY...

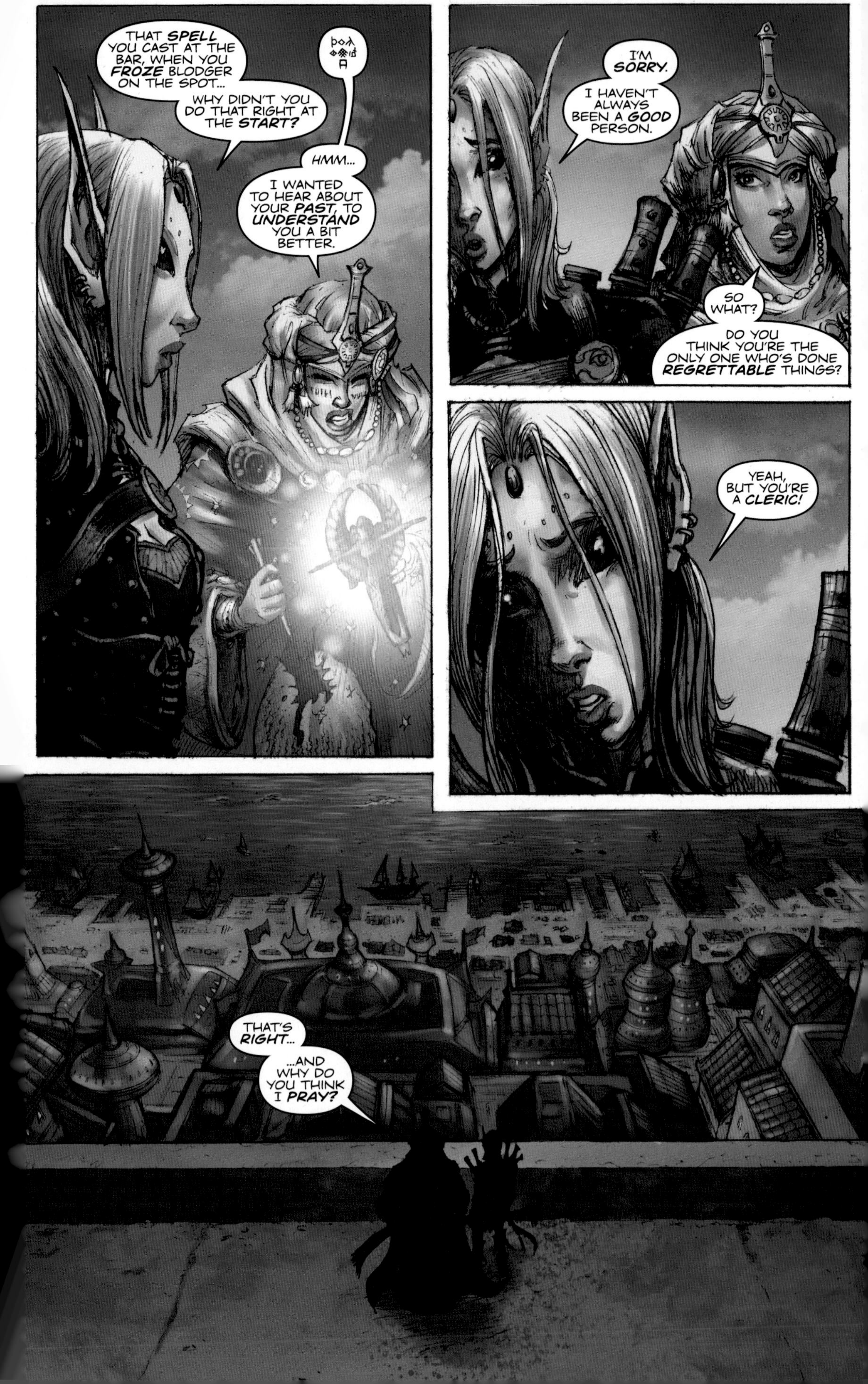
THAT **SPELL** YOU CAST AT THE BAR, WHEN YOU **FROZE** BLODGER ON THE SPOT...
WHY DIDN'T YOU DO THAT RIGHT AT THE **START?**
HMM...
I WANTED TO HEAR ABOUT YOUR **PAST**, TO **UNDERSTAND** YOU A BIT BETTER.
I'M **SORRY**.
I HAVEN'T ALWAYS BEEN A **GOOD** PERSON.
SO WHAT?
DO YOU THINK YOU'RE THE ONLY ONE WHO'S DONE **REGRETTABLE** THINGS?
YEAH, BUT YOU'RE A **CLERIC!**
THAT'S **RIGHT**...
...AND WHY DO YOU THINK I **PRAY?**

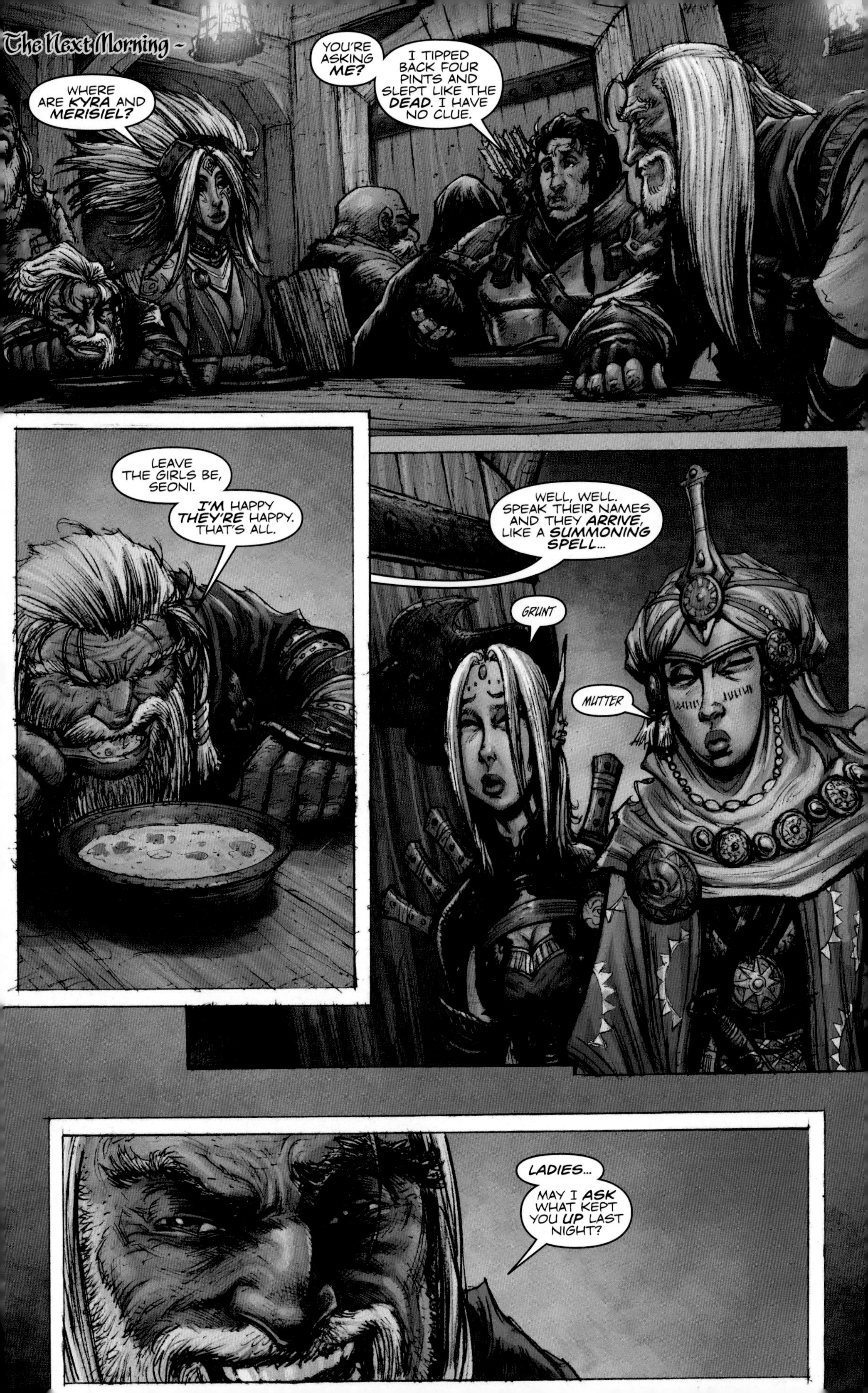
The Next Morning ~
WHERE ARE KYRA AND MERISIEL?
YOU'RE ASKING ME?
I TIPPED BACK FOUR PINTS AND SLEPT LIKE THE DEAD. I HAVE NO CLUE.
LEAVE THE GIRLS BE, SEONI.
I'M HAPPY THEY'RE HAPPY. THAT'S ALL.
WELL, WELL. SPEAK THEIR NAMES AND THEY ARRIVE, LIKE A SUMMONING SPELL...
GRUNT
MUTTER
LADIES...
MAY I ASK WHAT KEPT YOU UP LAST NIGHT?

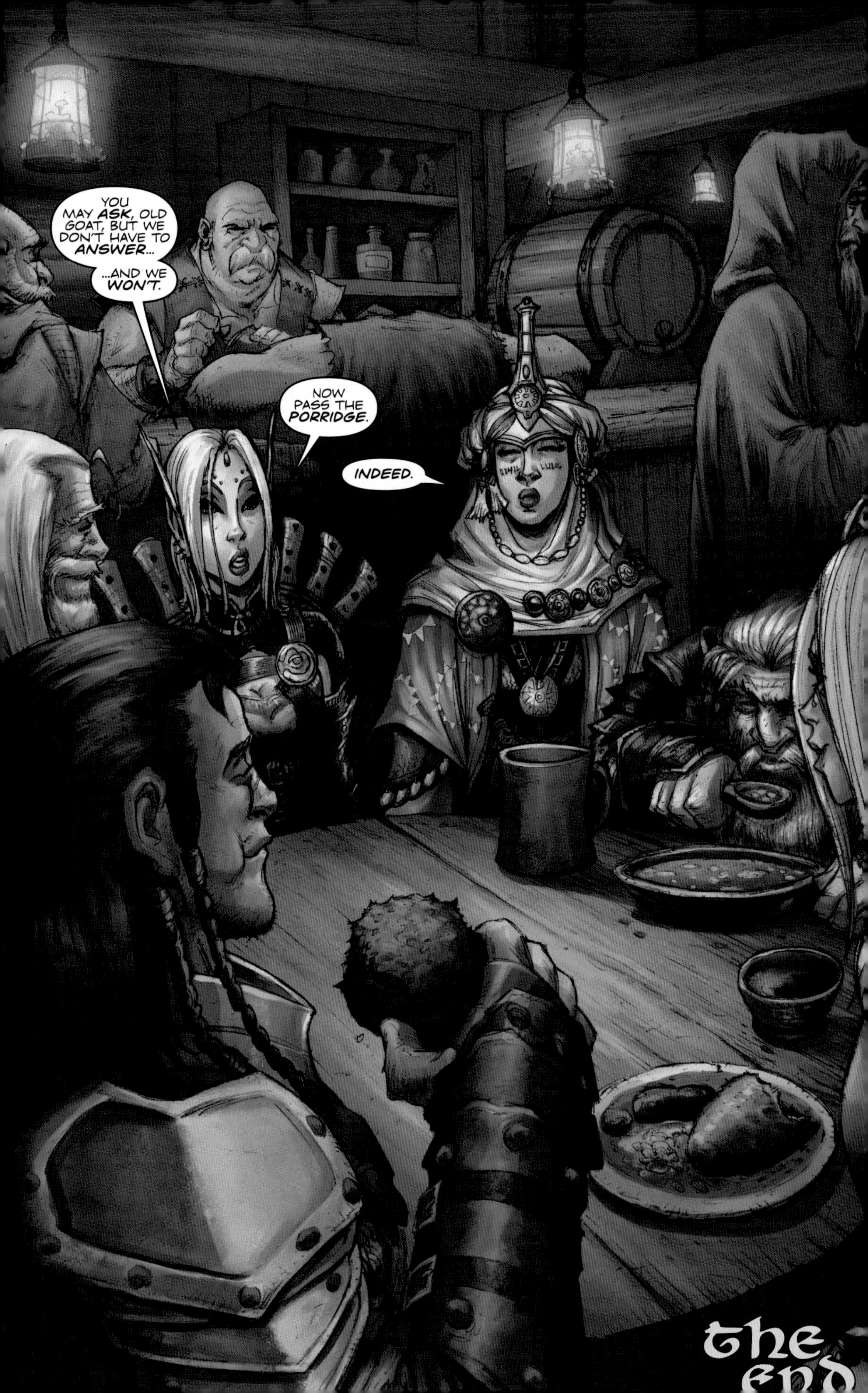
YOU MAY ASK, OLD GOAT, BUT WE DON'T HAVE TO ANSWER...
...AND WE WON'T.
NOW PASS THE PORRIDGE.
INDEED.
the end

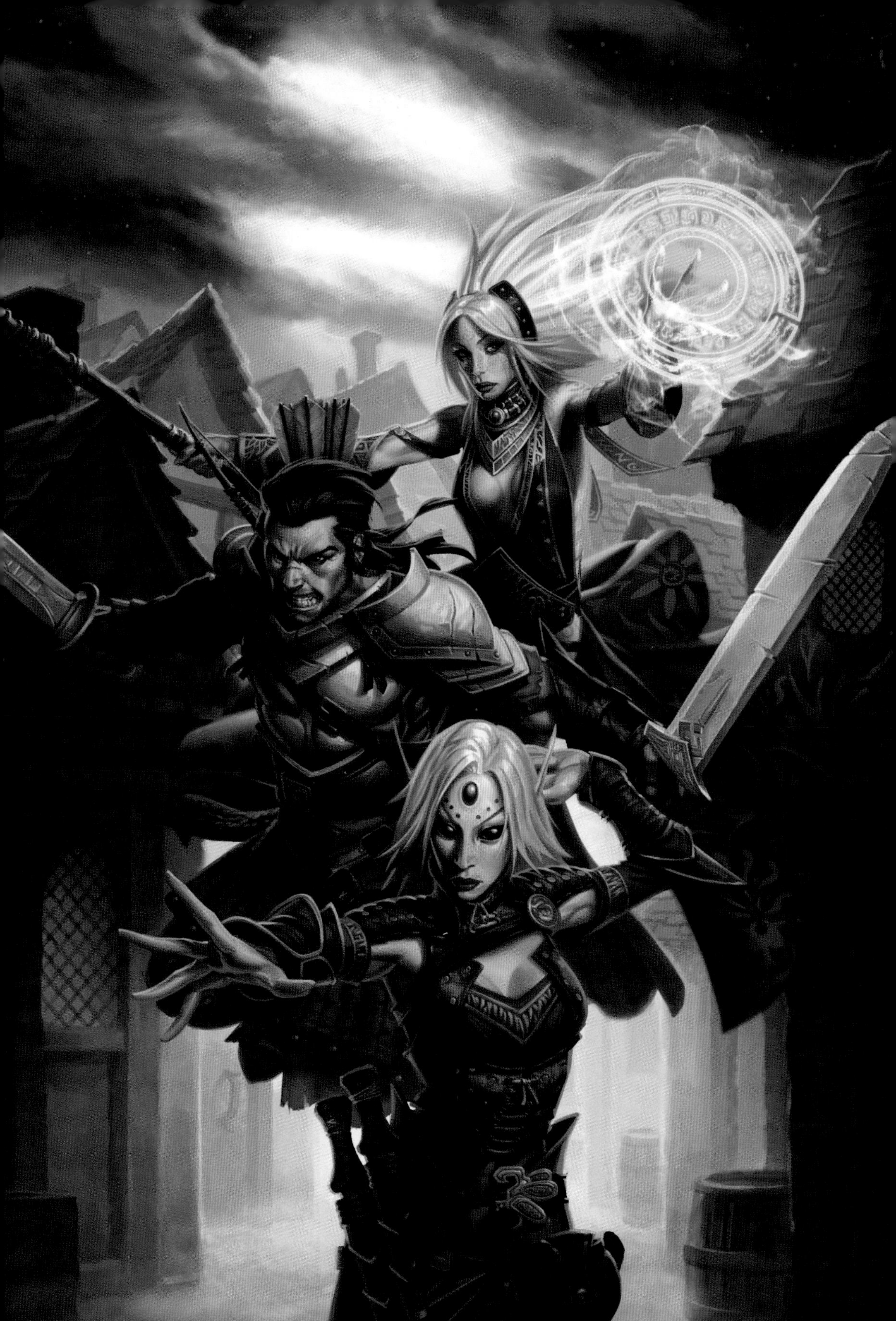

Issue #7 Paizo exclusive cover by MIKE CAPPROTTI

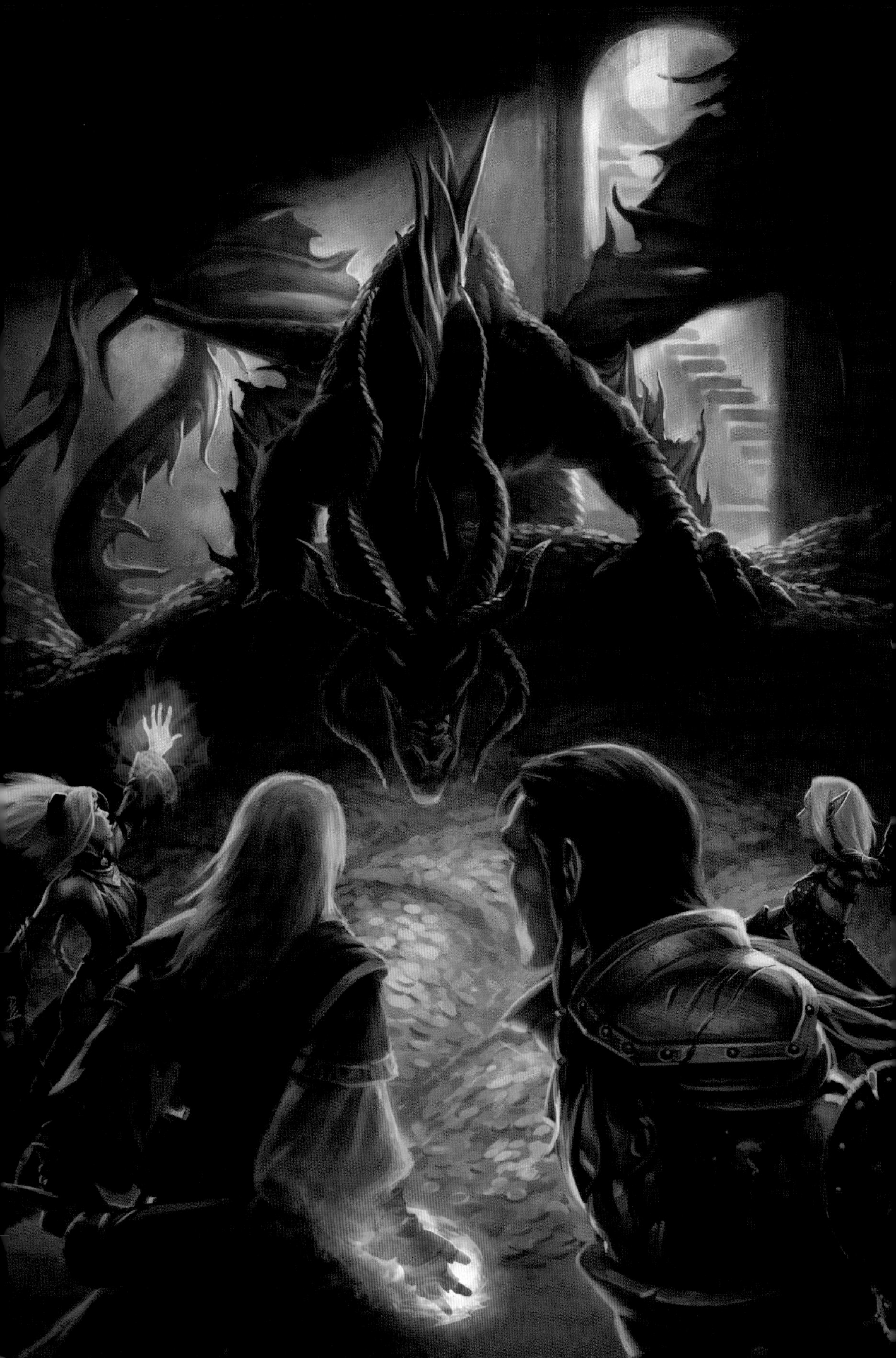

Issue #7 Paizo exclusive cover by MIKE CAPPROTTI

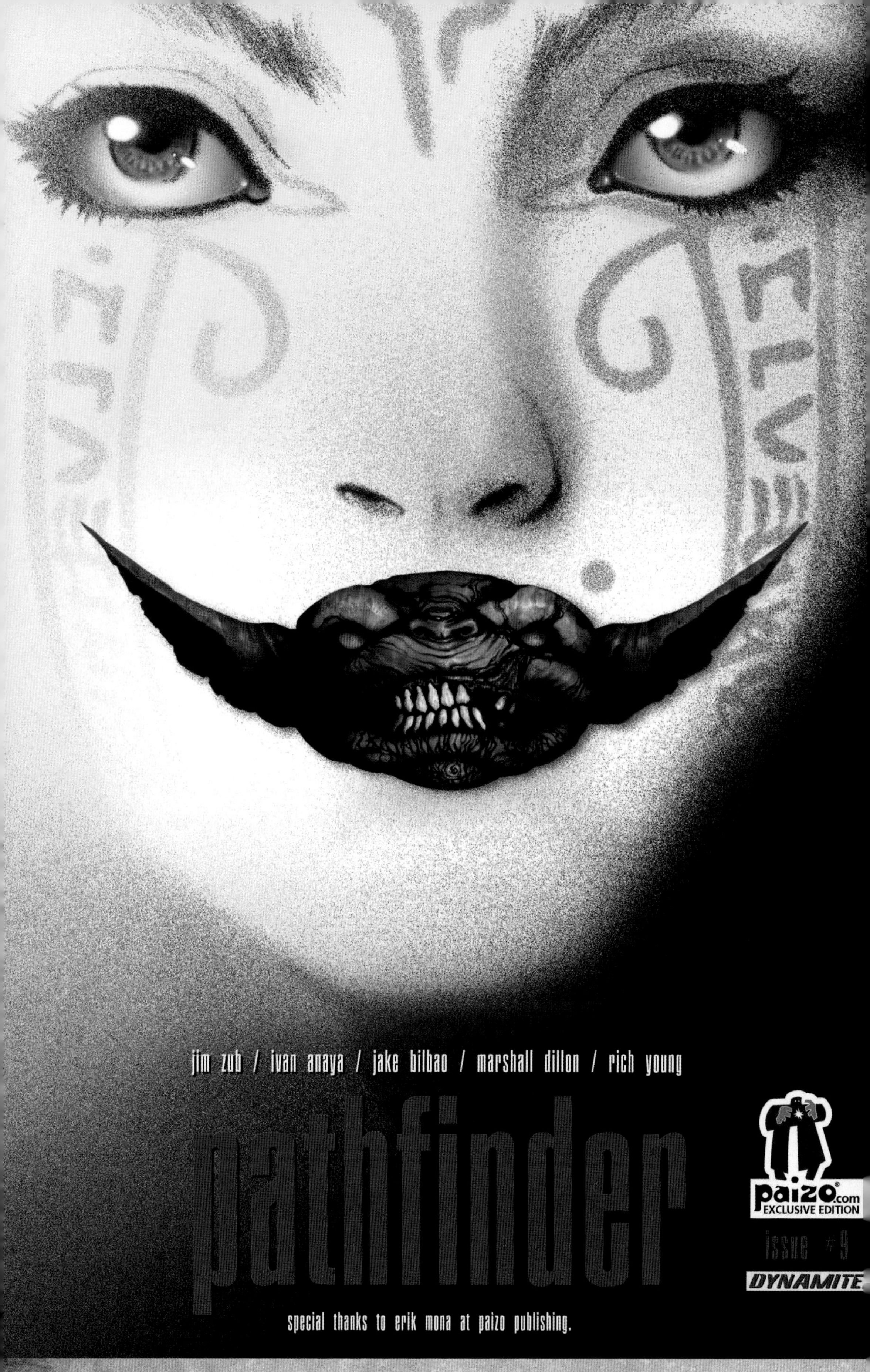
jim zub / ivan anaya / jake bilbao / marshall dillon / rich young
pathfinder
paizo.com EXCLUSIVE EDITION
issue #9
DYNAMITE
special thanks to erik mona at paizo publishing.

Issue #9 Paizo exclusive cover by SEBASTIAN CICHON

PATHFINDER

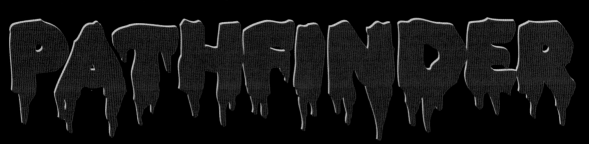

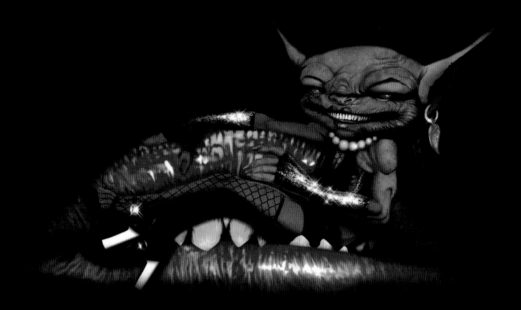

DYNAMITE ENTERTAINMENT PRESENTS "PATHFINDER" No. 10 WRITTEN BY JIM ZUB ILLUSTRATED BY SEAN IZAAKSE
COLORED BY ROSS CAMPBELL LETTERED BY MARSHALL DILLON EDITED BY RICH YOUNG
SPECIAL THANKS TO ERIK MONA AT PAIZO PUBLISHING.

DYNAMITE

paizo.com EXCLUSIVE EDITION

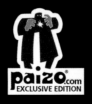

Issue #10 Paizo exclusive cover by SEBASTIAN CICHON

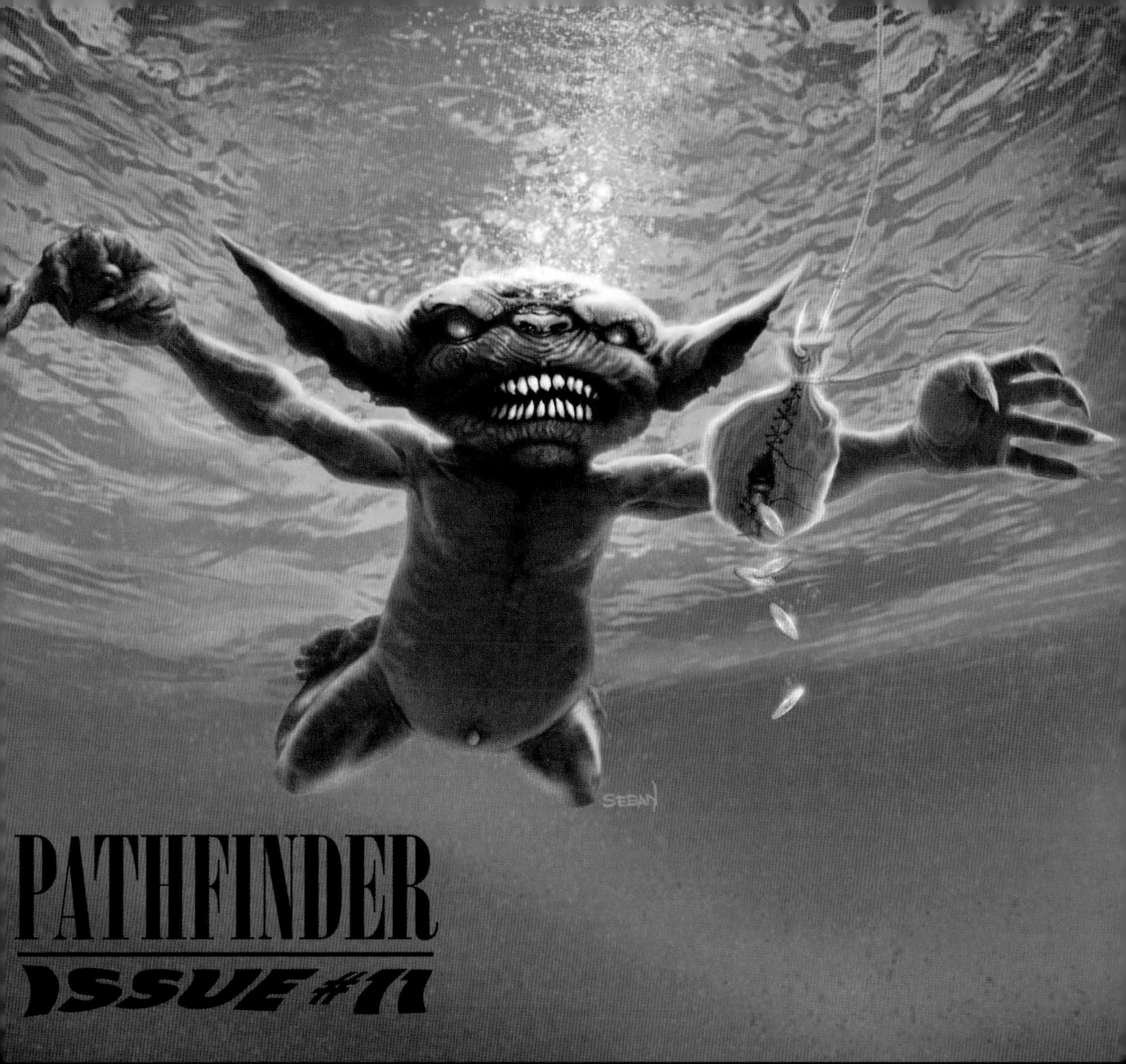
SEBAN
PATHFINDER
ISSUE #11

SPECIAL THANKS TO ERIK MONA AT PAIZO PUBLISHING

DYNAMITE®

Issue #11 Paizo exclusive cover by SEBASTIAN CICHON

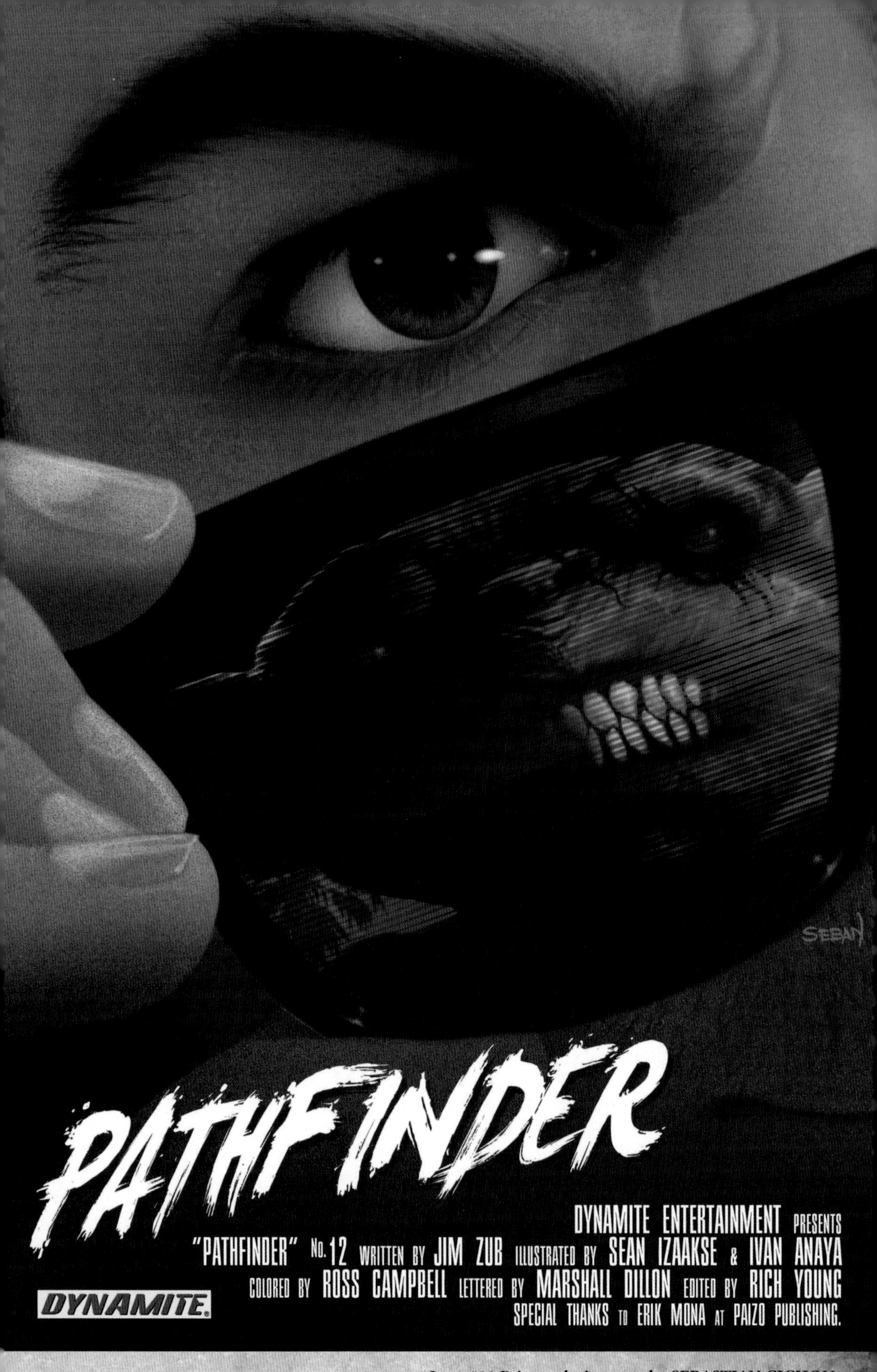
PATHFINDER
DYNAMITE ENTERTAINMENT PRESENTS
"PATHFINDER" No.12 WRITTEN BY JIM ZUB ILLUSTRATED BY SEAN IZAAKSE & IVAN ANAYA
COLORED BY ROSS CAMPBELL LETTERED BY MARSHALL DILLON EDITED BY RICH YOUNG
SPECIAL THANKS TO ERIK MONA AT PAIZO PUBLISHING.
DYNAMITE

Issue #11 Paizo exclusive cover by SEBASTIAN CICHON

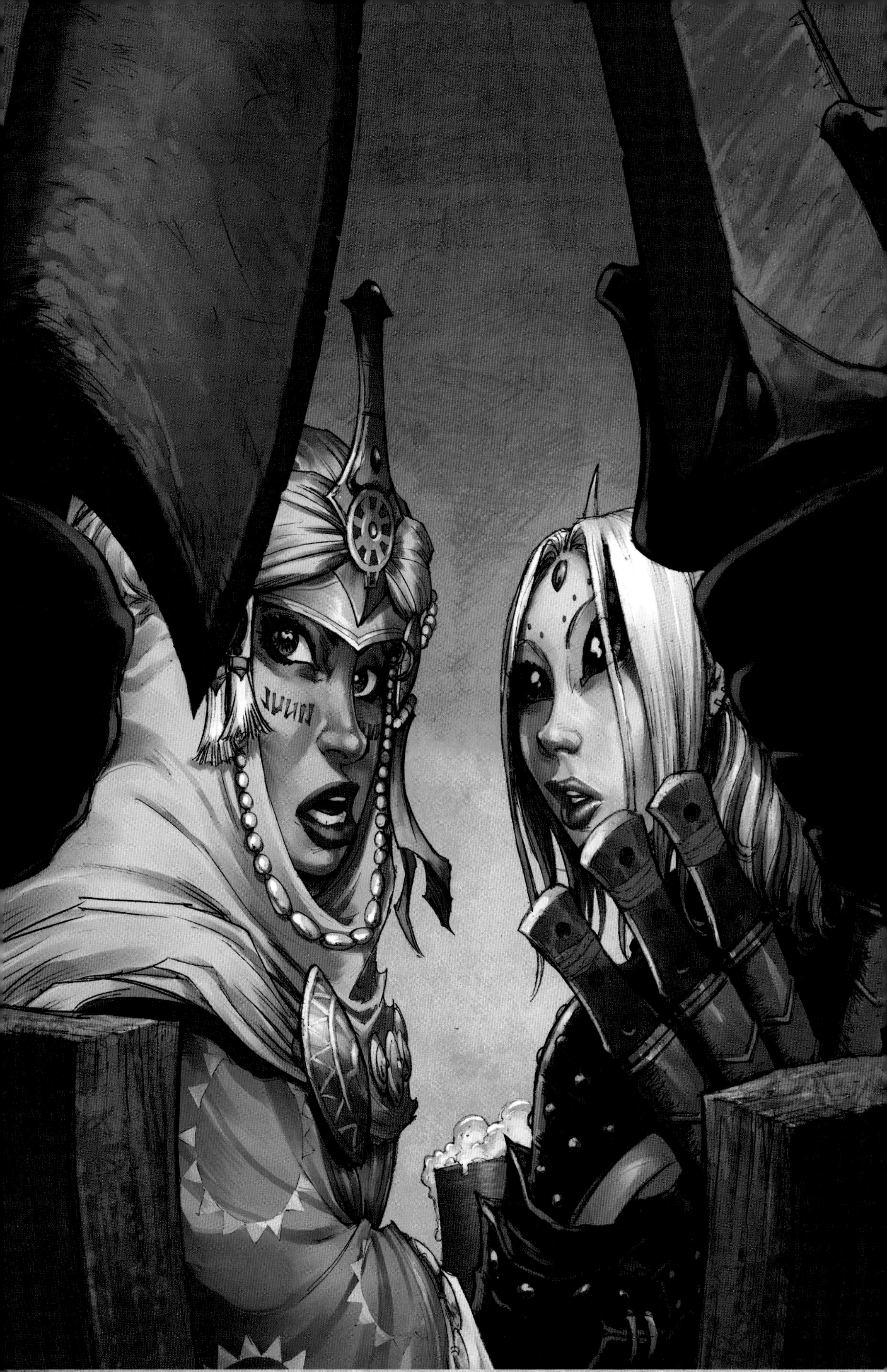

Pathfinder Special 2013 Paizo exclusive cover art by KEVIN STOKES colors by MOHAN

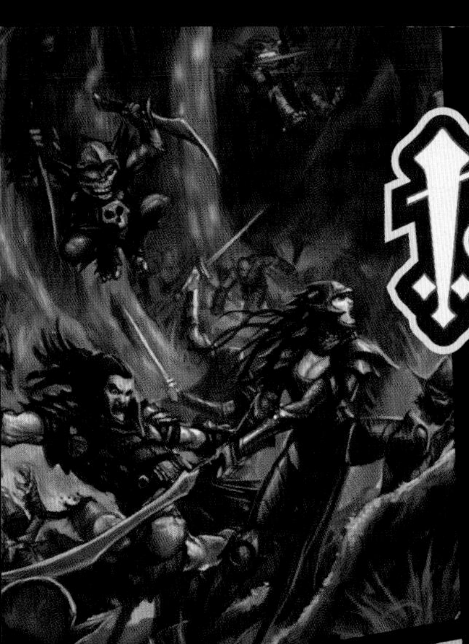

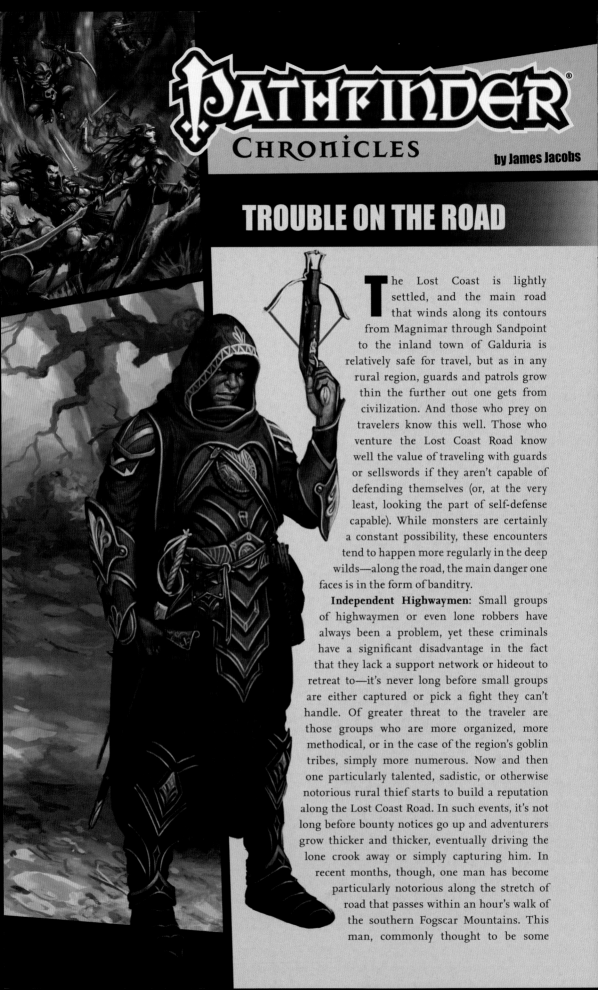

PATHFINDER® CHRONICLES

by James Jacobs

TROUBLE ON THE ROAD

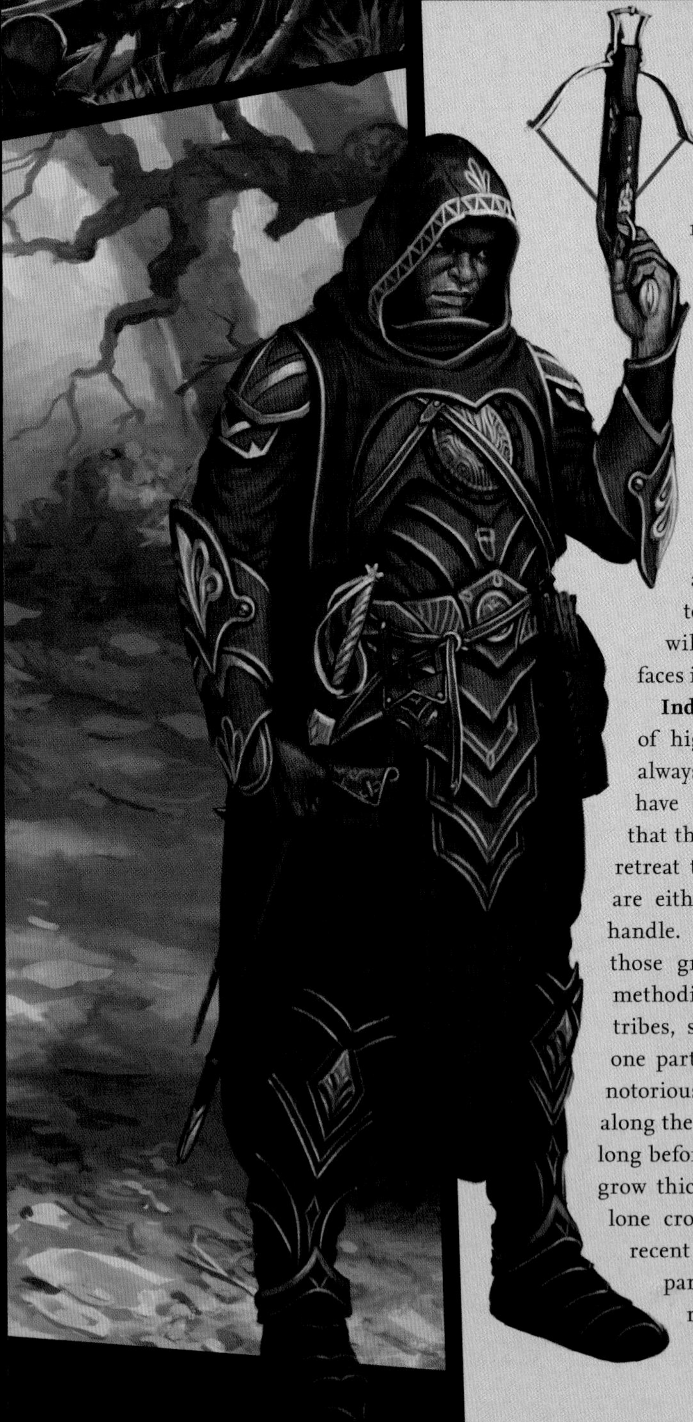

The Lost Coast is lightly settled, and the main road that winds along its contours from Magnimar through Sandpoint to the inland town of Galduria is relatively safe for travel, but as in any rural region, guards and patrols grow thin the further out one gets from civilization. And those who prey on travelers know this well. Those who venture the Lost Coast Road know well the value of traveling with guards or sellswords if they aren't capable of defending themselves (or, at the very least, looking the part of self-defense capable). While monsters are certainly a constant possibility, these encounters tend to happen more regularly in the deep wilds—along the road, the main danger one faces is in the form of banditry.

Independent Highwaymen: Small groups of highwaymen or even lone robbers have always been a problem, yet these criminals have a significant disadvantage in the fact that they lack a support network or hideout to retreat to—it's never long before small groups are either captured or pick a fight they can't handle. Of greater threat to the traveler are those groups who are more organized, more methodical, or in the case of the region's goblin tribes, simply more numerous. Now and then one particularly talented, sadistic, or otherwise notorious rural thief starts to build a reputation along the Lost Coast Road. In such events, it's not long before bounty notices go up and adventurers grow thicker and thicker, eventually driving the lone crook away or simply capturing him. In recent months, though, one man has become particularly notorious along the stretch of road that passes within an hour's walk of the southern Fogscar Mountains. This man, commonly thought to be some

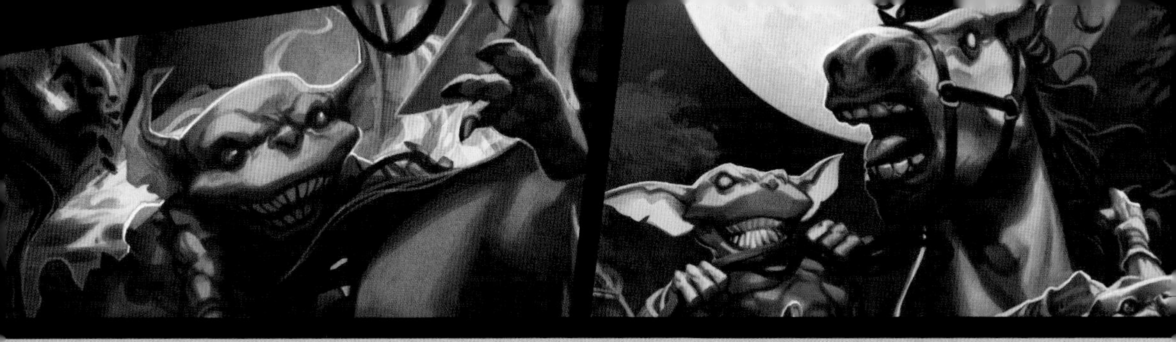

sort of elf or even, possibly, an aasimar, dresses in audacious colors (he favors reds and deep purples) yet is incredibly stealthy. He specifically targets groups that appear to have affiliations with arcanists, ignoring money and art when magical items and spellbooks are to be had. Self-styled as the Crimson Cad, this unique robber has particularly vexed the town of Galduria, where the bounty for his capture recently crested 2,000 gold coins. Rumors that the Crimson Cad is in fact a bitter ex-student from Galduria's Twilight Academy (one of the most famous schools of magic in all of Varisia) would certainly explain the bandit's apparent obsession with magic, and the town's eagerness to spare no expense for his eventual and hopefully swift capture.

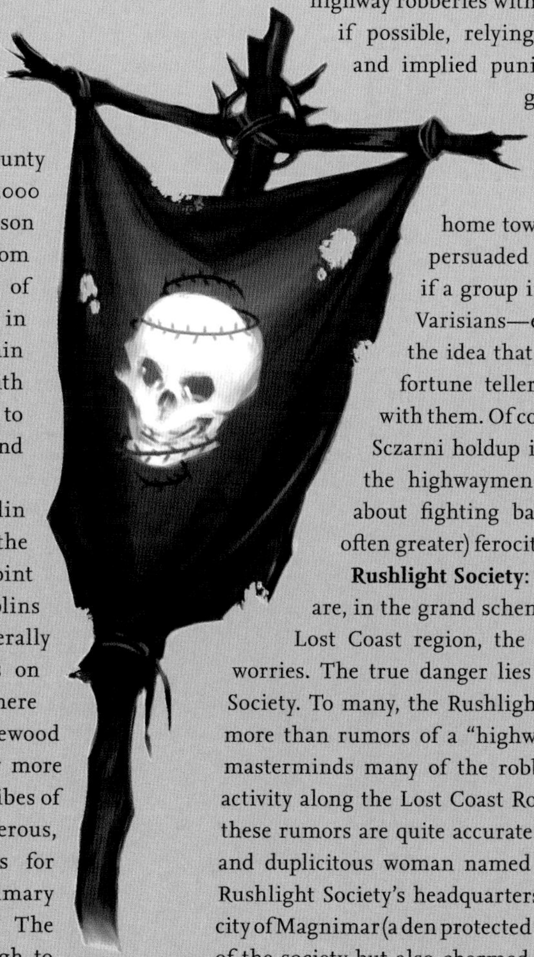

Goblin Bandits: Numerous goblin tribes dwell in the wilds alongside the Lost Coast Road. Between Sandpoint and Magnimar, the Licktoad Goblins of Brinestump Marsh are generally too timid to mount many raids on travelers, but north and east, where the road passes between Nettlewood and Mosswood, the goblins grow more bold. The various goblin family-tribes of Mosswood are certainly more numerous, and competition between tribes for raiding prizes seems to be a primary driver for attacks on caravans. The presence of horses is often enough to prevent a goblin attack, for such animals are known to frighten goblins terribly—although when a tribe of goblins is desperate enough for treasure, no amount of horses can hold them back.

Sczarni Highwaymen: The Varisian criminals and hoodlums known as the Sczarni deny having any involvement in highway robbery, often even as they're performing it. A group of Sczarni could well appear to be little more than a fellow group of travelers approaching on the road until they pass you by, at which point they might almost apologetically ask for "trail tax" for use of the road. Yet as apologetic as they might sound, smiles of delight are never far from their expressions, and knives and saps are never far from their hands. The Sczarni prefer to conduct their highway robberies without physical violence if possible, relying heavily on threats and implied punishments to get the goods. They typically don't prey upon travelers within a day's walk of their home towns, and can often be persuaded to look the other way if a group includes many fellow Varisians—especially if they get the idea that a harrower or other fortune teller or sorcerer travels with them. Of course, if an attempted Sczarni holdup is met with violence, the highwaymen are never hesitant about fighting back with equal (and often greater) ferocity.

Rushlight Society: Goblins and Sczarni are, in the grand scheme of banditry in the Lost Coast region, the least of a traveler's worries. The true danger lies with the Rushlight Society. To many, the Rushlight Society is nothing more than rumors of a "highwayman's guild" that masterminds many of the robberies and criminal activity along the Lost Coast Road, but in this case, these rumors are quite accurate. Led by a charming and duplicitous woman named Miior Duvanti, the Rushlight Society's headquarters is hidden near the city of Magnimar (a den protected not only by members of the society but also charmed ettercaps, bugbears, and even a marsh giant witch). Originally founded by Korvosan sympathizers eager to support and even increase the dangers of robbery in western Varisia (one of many attempts by Korvosa to undermine the stability of their primary regional rivals), even the smaller bandit groups don't fully understand the society's goals. And as of late, the same can be said for its Korvosan supporters, as the Rushlight Society increasingly seeks anonymity and independence to pursue its own goals without being manipulated or directed by the distant city's interests.

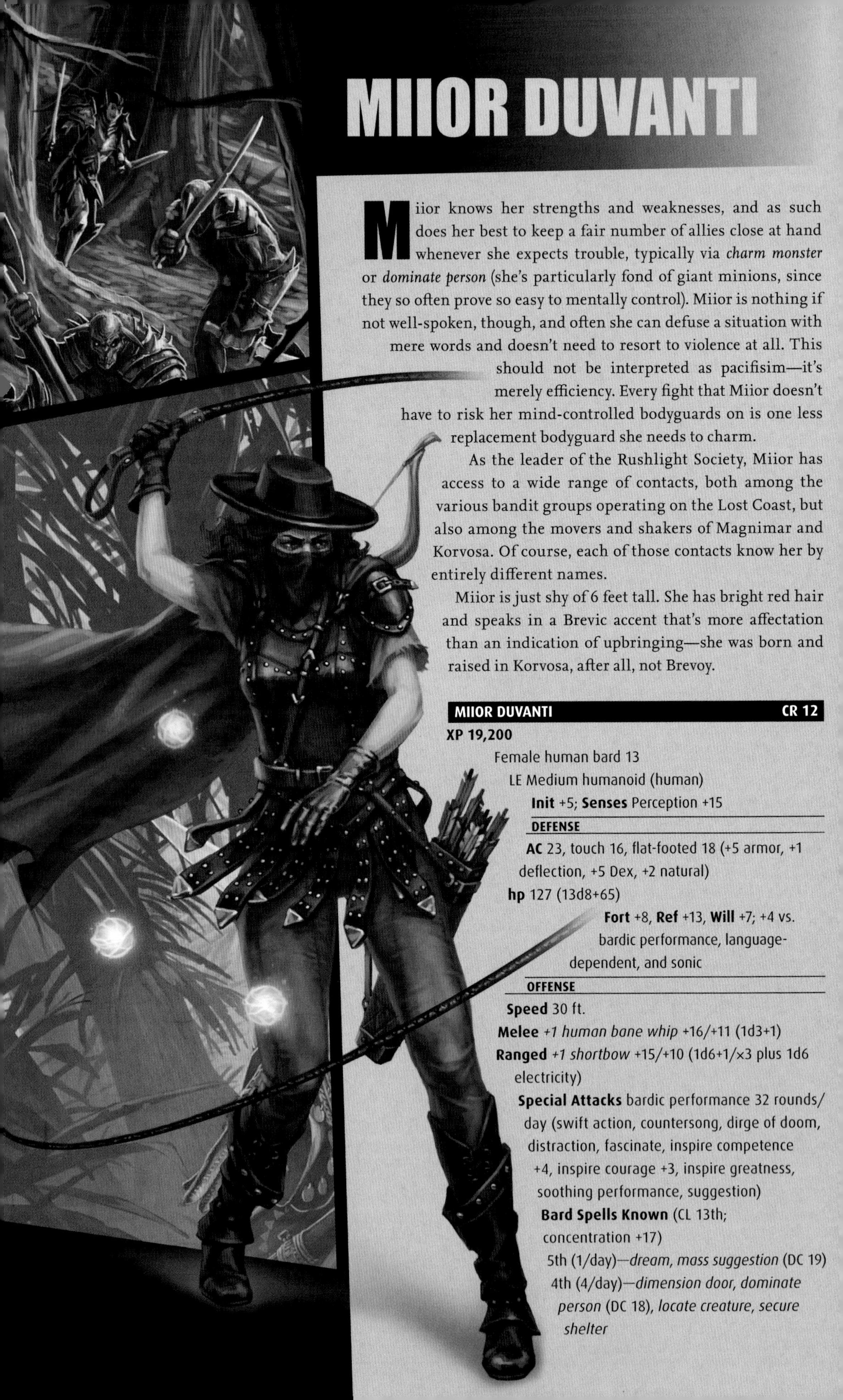

MIIOR DUVANTI

Miior knows her strengths and weaknesses, and as such does her best to keep a fair number of allies close at hand whenever she expects trouble, typically via *charm monster* or *dominate person* (she's particularly fond of giant minions, since they so often prove so easy to mentally control). Miior is nothing if not well-spoken, though, and often she can defuse a situation with mere words and doesn't need to resort to violence at all. This should not be interpreted as pacifisim—it's merely efficiency. Every fight that Miior doesn't have to risk her mind-controlled bodyguards on is one less replacement bodyguard she needs to charm.

As the leader of the Rushlight Society, Miior has access to a wide range of contacts, both among the various bandit groups operating on the Lost Coast, but also among the movers and shakers of Magnimar and Korvosa. Of course, each of those contacts know her by entirely different names.

Miior is just shy of 6 feet tall. She has bright red hair and speaks in a Brevic accent that's more affectation than an indication of upbringing—she was born and raised in Korvosa, after all, not Brevoy.

MIIOR DUVANTI **CR 12**

XP 19,200

Female human bard 13

LE Medium humanoid (human)

Init +5; **Senses** Perception +15

DEFENSE

AC 23, touch 16, flat-footed 18 (+5 armor, +1 deflection, +5 Dex, +2 natural)

hp 127 (13d8+65)

Fort +8, **Ref** +13, **Will** +7; +4 vs. bardic performance, language-dependent, and sonic

OFFENSE

Speed 30 ft.

Melee *+1 human bane whip* +16/+11 (1d3+1)

Ranged *+1 shortbow* +15/+10 (1d6+1/×3 plus 1d6 electricity)

Special Attacks bardic performance 32 rounds/day (swift action, countersong, dirge of doom, distraction, fascinate, inspire competence +4, inspire courage +3, inspire greatness, soothing performance, suggestion)

Bard Spells Known (CL 13th; concentration +17)

5th (1/day)—*dream, mass suggestion* (DC 19)

4th (4/day)—*dimension door, dominate person* (DC 18), *locate creature, secure shelter*

3rd (5/day)—*charm monster* (DC 17), *dispel magic, displacement, haste,
speak with animals*

2nd (6/day)—*cat's grace, invisibility, mirror image, suggestion* (DC 16),
whispering wind

1st (6/day)—*charm person* (DC 15), *cure light wounds, identify, silent
image* (DC 15), *undetectable alignment, unseen servant*

0 (at will)—*dancing lights, ghost sound* (DC 14), *know direction, message,
prestidigitation, summon instrument*

TACTICS

Before Combat Before she enters combat, Miior makes sure to cast *cat's
grace* and *unseen servant*.

During Combat Miior utilizes inspire courage on the first round of combat
and relies upon her allies (charmed, dominated, and otherwise) to keep
the foes busy for the first few rounds of combat while she casts spells—
mirror image first, *displacement* second, followed by *mass suggestion* to
try to get as many foes as possible to engage in some mindless, repetitive
task for the spell's duration (she's particularly fond of suggesting that
foes meticulously search the surrounding area for additional enemies that
could be lying in wait, or to move about the area cleaning the place up in
order to ensure that there's nothing on the ground that could cause foes
to stumble in combat—anything to limit the number of foes in a combat
who can legitimately take part in the battle). Her minions know to leave
those affected by this spell alone and to help her focus on any who resist
the spell's effects—once only victims of *mass suggestion* remain, she and
her allies focus on one foe at a time in order to maintain control of the
combat. When she enters combat, she always does so with Arcane Strike
and Combat Expertise and focuses her attacks on humans if she can. With
these two feats plus inspire courage in effect, Miior's AC gains a +3 dodge
bonus and her melee attacks with her whip resolve at +16/+11 (1d3+7). She
uses her *unseen servant* to hold weapons, carry potions, or otherwise aid
in combat so she doesn't have to waste time on move actions. She's also
fond of ordering it to open and close doors or otherwise inconvenience the
enemy. Miior uses dimension door to escape combat and heal if reduced to
fewer than 30 hp; she re-casts *mirror image* and *displacement* if necessary
before returning to the fight.

Morale Miior always keeps one *dimension door* handy for escape—if she is
out of healing magic, she uses this spell to get as far away from the battle
as possible before fleeing on foot and plotting revenge.

STATISTICS

Str 10, **Dex** 20, **Con** 18, **Int** 13, **Wis** 8, **Cha** 18

Base Atk +9; **CMB** +14, **CMD** 25

Feats Agile Maneuvers, Arcane Strike, Combat Expertise, Craft Magic Arms and
Armor, Craft Wondrous Item, Dodge, Weapon Finesse, Weapon Focus (whip),
Whip Mastery*

Skills Acrobatics +26, Bluff +20, Disguise +20, Diplomacy +20, Handle Animal +20,
Intimidate +20, Knowledge (local) +23, Perception +15, Perform (act) +20,
Perform (oratory) +20, Perform (wind) +20, Sense Motive +20, Stealth +26

Languages Common, Varisian

SQ bardic knowledge +6, jack-of-all-trades (use any skill), lore master 2/day,
versatile performance (act, oratory, dance)

Other Gear *+2 studded leather, +1 human bane whip*, mwk shortbow with
10 *+1 shock arrows* and 10 cold iron arrows, *amulet of natural armor +2,
belt of mighty constitution +4, headband of alluring charisma +2, ring of
protection +1, boots of elvenkind, cloak of elvenkind*, 225 gp

* This feat is from *Ultimate Combat*

PATHFINDER

CHRONICLES

by James Jacobs

DRAGONS OF THE SANDPOINT HINTERLANDS

Varisia is no stranger to dragons, but until relatively recently, the dragons of the region have not had cause to mix with civilization, for their lairs have been remote and hidden. As Varisia attracts more and more settlers and as civilization spreads, though, there comes the inevitable clashes with these ancient creatures and the region's newcomers.

The Lost Coast is no exception. In fact, several dragons dwell in the vicinity known as the Sandpoint Hinterlands, yet very few of the town's citizens realize this. Stories and rumors of dragon sightings pop up now and then, but most of the locals discount these as attempts to get attention or cases of mistaken identity—strangely enough, most of Sandpoint is more prone to believe in sightings of the famed Sandpoint Devil than they are in sightings of dragons, despite the fact that a certain number of supposed Sandpoint Devil sightings were likely to be misidentifications of dragons in flight in a foggy night.

While some of the dragons in the region are either passing through or periodic visitors from other parts of Varisia, three dragons in particular deserve mention for the fact that they make their lairs within a day's travel of Sandpoint—of these three, only the young upstart Black Fang has recently come to the attention of farmers and travelers in the region.

Black Fang: The young adult black dragon called Black Fang once dwelt with his older sister Scarhorn (see below), but after he outstayed his welcome, Black Fang was forced to seek a new home. Seething with frustration at losing the lair he had increasingly started to think of as his own, Black Fang constantly mulls over various plans to strike back against Scarhorn, but since the older and much larger dragon has already taught Black Fang numerous humiliating lessons about her superiority in all things combat-related, Black Fang has begrudgingly set his plans for retaking the lair aside for now. Unlike the other two dragons listed below, Black Fang combines a dangerous combination of youthful arrogance and inexperience—he increasingly has little compunctions about hunting close to home, and with each successful raid on a farm, goblin tribe, or lone traveler, it's only a matter of time before he becomes audacious enough to attack Sandpoint itself. Possible alliances with other villainous conspirators or secret organizations in the region (such as the cult of Lamashtu) only increases his temerity.

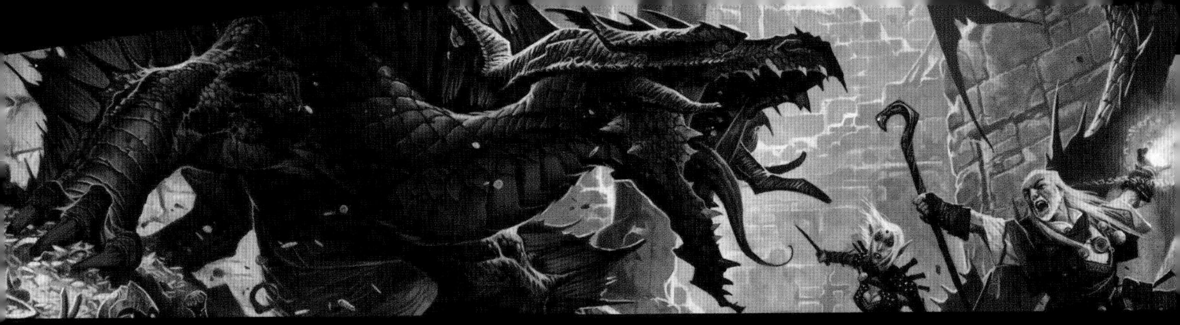

Scarhorn: Just over a mile and a half out to sea to the northwest of Sandpoint lies the bowl-shaped island known as Dragon's Punchbowl. The island's rugged ridges rise nearly fifty feet from the sea, and are plainly visible from Sandpoint, yet few approach the rocky island itself. Wyverns have long roosted in the rocky bluffs that surround the island's central lake, dragon-like beasts that are only too eager to swoop out and attack any boat that comes within a few thousand feet of the shore. Fishing in the waters around the island is said to be particularly good, yet none in recent years have dared to test these rumors, for more compelling rumors persist in saying that the wyverns are merely scavengers compared to the beast that actually dwells within the central lake. Known to the Varisian travelers of the Lost Coast as Scarhorn, stories of this old black dragon go back for hundreds of years, centuries before Sandpoint's founding—before the arrival of southern colonists along the Lost Coast itself, in fact. Scarhorn is presented in detail on the following pages.

Tiruvinn: Before Ameiko Kaijitsu retired early from the adventuring lifestyle to buy Sandpoint's oldest inn, the building was a relatively run-down establishment known somewhat dully as the "Sandpoint Inn." The owners were eager to sell the building and retire to Magnimar, but they may now regret that decision after Ameiko singlehandedly turned the establishment into the town's most successful business. She renamed the place the Rusty Dragon, apparently after the old iron dragon-shaped lightning rod and decoration that has graced the building's roofline for decades, but whenever anyone asks her about the choice of name, she shrugs and smirks mischievously, as if there's more to the story she's not telling. In fact, the original dragon on which the decoration was inspired by is Tiruvinn, a reclusive adult bronze dragon that has dwelt in a hidden sea cave a few miles north of Nettlewood. Tiruvinn once engaged with the Varisian travelers more often than he does today, but with the encroachment of civilization, he's grown increasingly more secretive, taking pains to disguise himself as a human whenever he's not hunting far out to sea or hidden in his home.

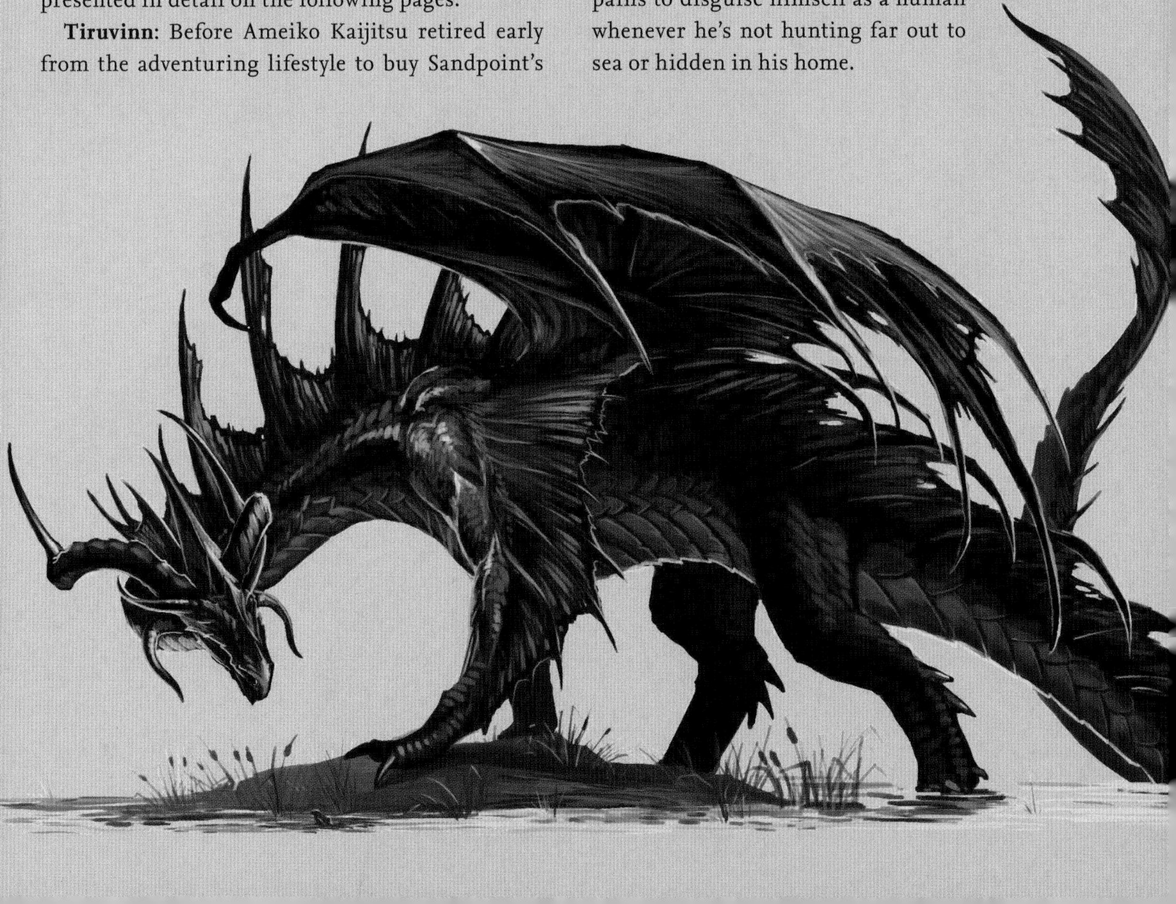

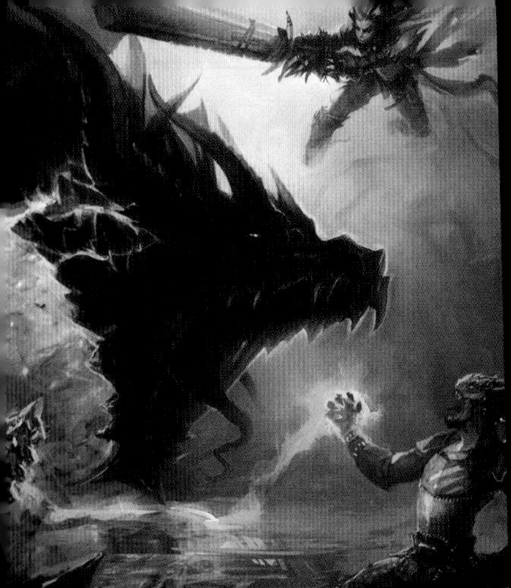

SCARHORN

The dragon known to the long-time travelers of the Lost Coast as Scarhorn has dwelt in the flooded caverns below Devil's Punchbowl for over 500 years, yet in that time she has taken pains to never hunt within a fifty-mile radius of her home. Those who have endured her predations have no idea she dwells so close to Sandpoint, which is as she likes it. For several decades, she shared her home with her younger brother Black Fang, but after he dared to attack a passing trade vessel bound for Riddleport, she knew he had to go. Black Fang survived her attempt to kill him, and now she watches with amusement from afar as her foolish younger brother slowly builds a case against himself for a need for dragonslayers.

Scarhorn was, of course, not born with the name—her true name is Auhlzodrue, but the travelers of the region have long known her by her missing horn, an old wound she suffered in a fight against a band of would-be dragonslayers who learned the hard way that underestimating a dragon's will to live is often the last mistake one will ever make. Able to breathe water and swim well, Scarhorn has made countless trips into the depths of the Varisian Gulf to scavenge for treasures among the sunken buildings and ruins of ancient Thassilon, using *beast shape I* or *alter self* to temporarily assume the form of fish or merfolk in order to navigate

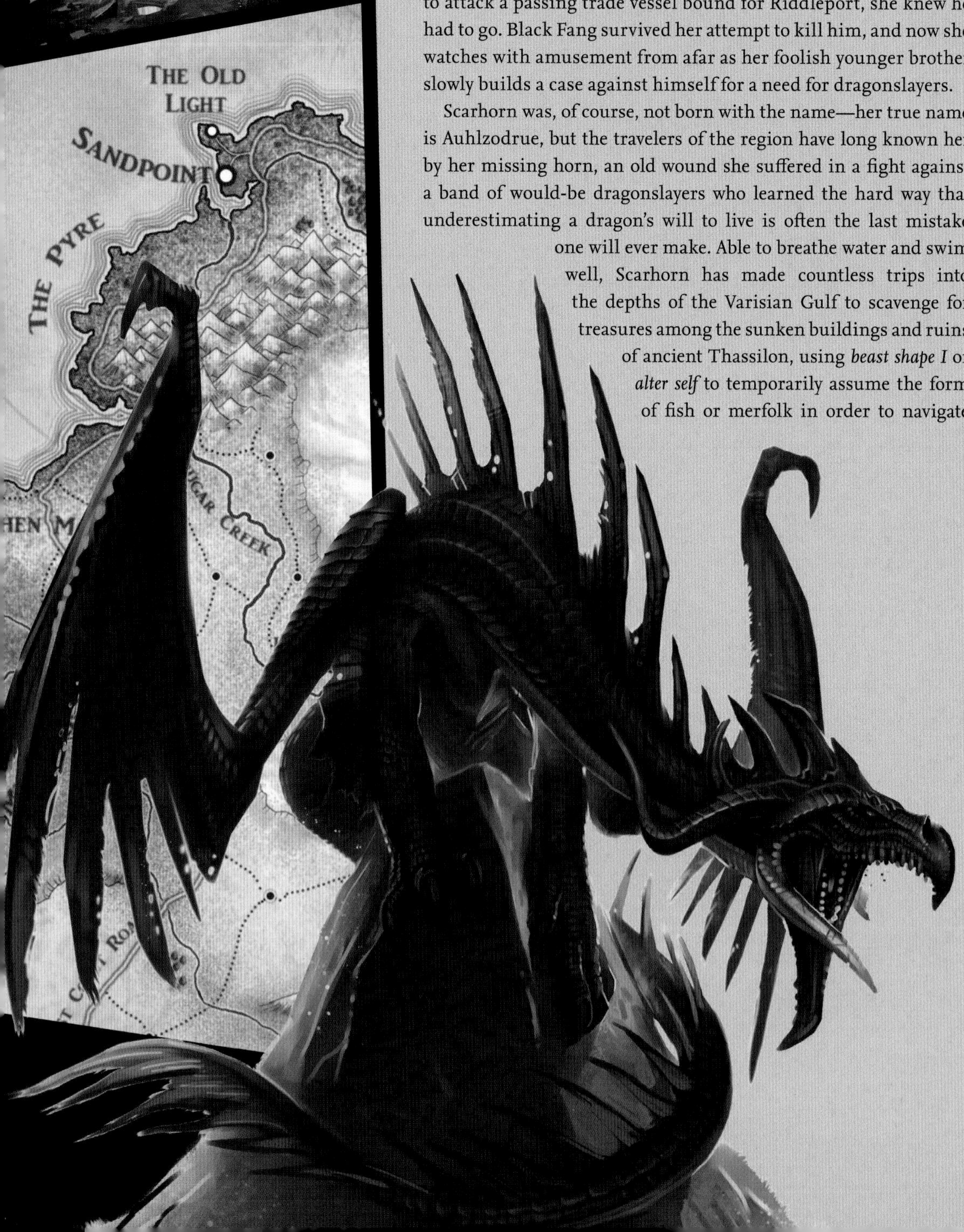

THE OLD LIGHT
SANDPOINT
THE PYRE

ruins too small for her to fit into in her true form. Her hoard reflects the fruits of these forays with its large number of exotic and ancient magical items and works of art. Her lair is guarded not only by her "pet" wyverns, but a fair number of aquatic undead monstrosities she's recruited as minions via *command undead* spells.

SCARHORN (AUHLZODRUE)   CR 14

XP 38,400

Female old black dragon (*Pathfinder RPG Bestiary* 92)

CE Huge dragon (water)

Init +4; **Senses** blindsense 60 ft., darkvision 120 ft., dragon senses; Perception +25

Aura frightful presence (240 ft., DC 25)

DEFENSE

AC 32, touch 8, flat-footed 32 (+24 natural, –2 size)

hp 225 (18d12+108)

Fort +17, **Ref** +11, **Will** +15

DR 10/magic; **Immune** acid, paralysis, sleep; **SR** 25

OFFENSE

Speed 60 ft., fly 200 ft. (poor), swim 60 ft.

Melee bite +25 (2d8+13/19–20 plus 2d6 acid), 2 claws +25 (2d6+9), 2 wings +20 (1d8+4), tail slap +20 (2d6+13)

Space 15 ft.; **Reach** 15 ft.

Special Attacks acidic bite, breath weapon (100-ft. line, 16d6 acid, Reflex DC 25 for half, usable every 1d4 rounds), crush (2d8+13, DC 25)

Spell-Like Abilities (CL 18th; concentration +21)

Constant—*speak with reptiles*

At will—*darkness, plant growth*

1/day—*corrupt water*

Sorcerer Spells Known (CL 7th; concentration +10)

3rd (5)—*beast shape I, dispel magic*

2nd (7)—*alter self, command undead* (DC 15), *locate object*

1st (7)—*alarm, charm person* (DC 14), *comprehend languages, shield, true strike*

0 (at will)—*dancing lights, detect magic, ghost sound* (DC 13), *mage hand, mending, prestidigitation, read magic*

TACTICS

During Combat Scarhorn opens a battle with her breath weapon, then moves on to making flyby attacks with Vital Strike bites. She prefers not to land and engage in melee unless she's facing only one foe—when she does, she utilizes Power Attack. If she's being hit often in combat, she'll take a round to cast *shield* on herself before resuming the battle.

Morale Scarhorn flees if reduced to fewer than 60 hit points, using *beast shape I* to throw off pursuit once she gets out of sight.

STATISTICS

Str 29, **Dex** 10, **Con** 23, **Int** 16, **Wis** 19, **Cha** 16

Base Atk +18; **CMB** +29; **CMD** 39 (43 vs. trip)

Feats Combat Expertise, Critical Focus, Flyby Attack, Improved Critical (bite), Improved Initiative, Improved Vital Strike, Power Attack, Sickening Critical, Vital Strike

Skills Appraise +24, Fly +13, Intimidate +24, Knowledge (arcana) +24, Knowledge (geography) +21, Linguistics +9, Perception +25, Spellcraft +24, Stealth +13, Swim +38

Languages Aklo, Aquan, Common, Draconic, Giant, Thassilonian, Varisian

SQ swamp stride, water breathing

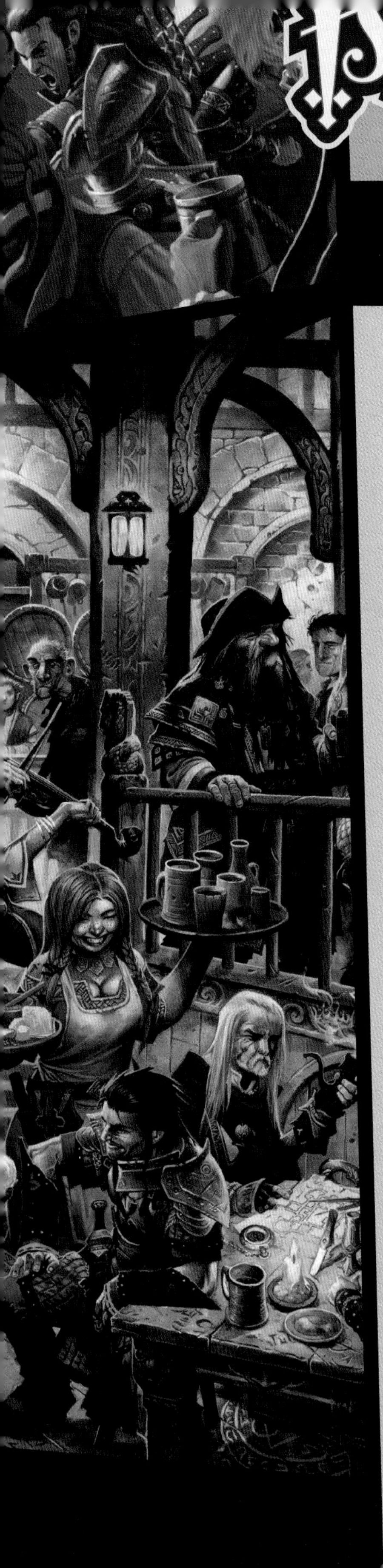

PATHFINDER® CHRONICLES

by James Jacobs

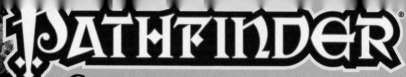

THE RUSTY DRAGON

The Rusty Dragon is Sandpoint's oldest inn, notable for the impressive (and quite rusty) iron dragon that looms on the building's roof, doubling as lightning rod and decor. The Rusty Dragon features a full-service tavern, where drinks like raspberry mead and ale along with the owner's own specialties of curried salmon and cheese-curd-stuffed artichoke hearts are quite popular. The tavern's an excellent place to meet visitors from out of town, as its proximity to the southern bridge into town makes it a logical first stop.

The common room of the Rusty Dragon is easily it's largest—it's also the first room you see when you enter by the wide front doors. A dozen tables fill the room, and a large stage for musicians, actors, orators, and others to perform upon commands one side of the room opposite a large hearth on the opposite wall. The bar runs along the wall across from the front door, running nearly the length of the common room. Other ground floor rooms include the kitchen, storage, employee rooms (including proprietor Ameiko Kaijitsu's cozy suite of personal chambers), a few rooms for private meals and meetings (these rooms are rented at a rate of 1 sp an hour), while the upper floor is taken up entirely by the Rusty Dragon's twelve guest rooms.

Staff: The Rusty Dragon is owned and run by Ameiko Kaijitsu, a beautiful and personable woman who made her fortune early in a short and successful adventuring career. While her own career was cut short by a tragedy she rarely speaks about, Ameiko is particularly fond of adventurers and her tavern welcomes such with open arms. She employes locals now and then to serve as additional help or as bouncers during the busy season, but for the most part, the tavern and inn is run by herself and one of her closest friends, the halfling woman Bethana Corwin, to whom Ameiko has promised the Tavern should she decide to move on. Bethana is as introverted and quiet as Ameiko is extroverted and chatty, and while Ameiko focuses her work on the tavern side of things, Bethana handles the maid services and room rentals.

Food: Food and drink at the Rusty Dragon are affordable; Ameiko charges standard prices (see *Pathfinder RPG Core Rulebook*, page 159) for meals, save for during festivals and other big events, where she instead charges a relatively modest 3 sp "banquet" charge and allows visitors to eat as much as they wish during their stay. These banquets invariably involve some new dish she's invented for the occasion, and while some of these become notorious failures (people still talk about the unfortunately named but delicious

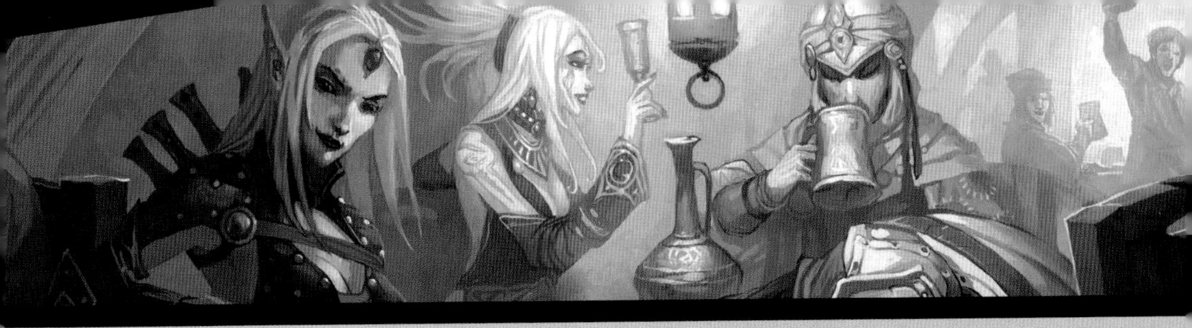

"goblin brain cookies" that ended up inflicting those who ate them with green urine for a week, and at least one local has scars from overindulging on the ill-advised "porcupine skewer" experiment), but for the most part, Ameiko's culinary creativity is met with great success.

Entertainment: Ameiko's talents extend to music, particularly at song and at stringed instruments. Her favorite instrument is an exotic samisen from her homeland—distant Minkai, a place she's never been but would some day love to visit. Yet music and song aren't the only offerings; the Rusty Dragon's stage is open to any who would wish to try a hand at any form of performance. Ameiko allows those who perform here to keep their earnings, and some whisper that this policy could have something to do with her long-standing feud with local thespian and director Cyrdak Drokkus, but the bad blood between the two seems far more significant than what this could explain. One particularly unusual open invitation at the tavern is for adventurers to hit the stage and recount tales of their daring deeds. Ameiko enjoys hearing these stories, and as long as they're real accounts (fake stories must be supported by a successful DC 20 Bluff or Perform [act] check), Ameiko grants discounts to the adventurers on rooms they rent.

Lodging: While guests are allowed to sleep on the common room floor for 1 cp, the Rusty Dragon features a dozen rooms, of which five are "luxury" rooms with their own commodes. All of the rooms have dragon-themed names, and the keys to each bear a small carving of the associated dragon. The seven smaller one-bedroom rooms are the Black, Blue, Green, Red, White, Drake, and Wyvern rooms—these can be had for a price of 5 sp (or 3 sp to a storytelling adventurer). Four of the luxury rooms are Gold, Copper, Brass, and Silver rooms. The fifth room, the Bronze Room, is generally not rented out—Ameiko keeps the Bronze Room free for special guests. Some whisper that this room is where Ameiko's mysterious paramour stays, while others maintain that the room is in fact haunted by the ghost of a traveling merchant who killed himself in the room by swallowing a *bead of force*. There are dozens of stories about who the man was, why he killed himself, and why he's haunting the room; Ameiko generally doesn't add to these tales herself, but only smiles knowingly when folks think they've figured things out. The luxury rooms are 2 gp a night (1 gp per night to adventurers who have entertained with tales of their deeds), but the Bronze Room, when it's available at Ameiko's discretion, is always free of charge.

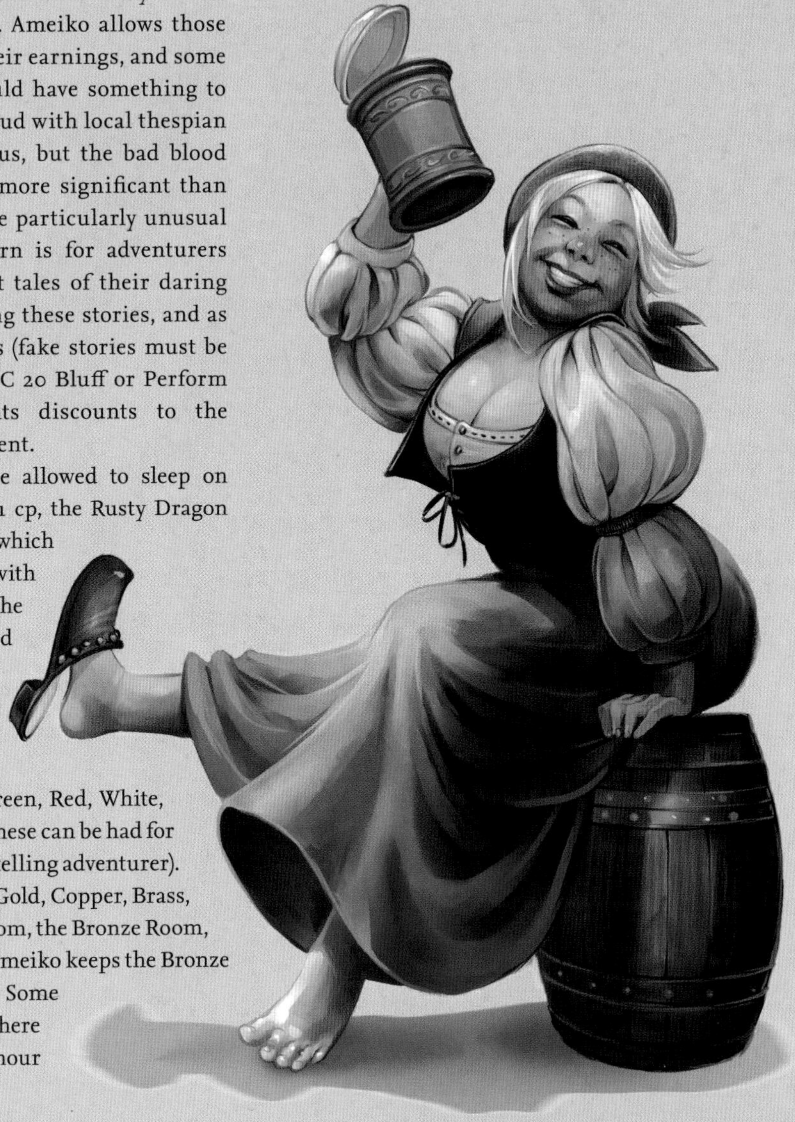

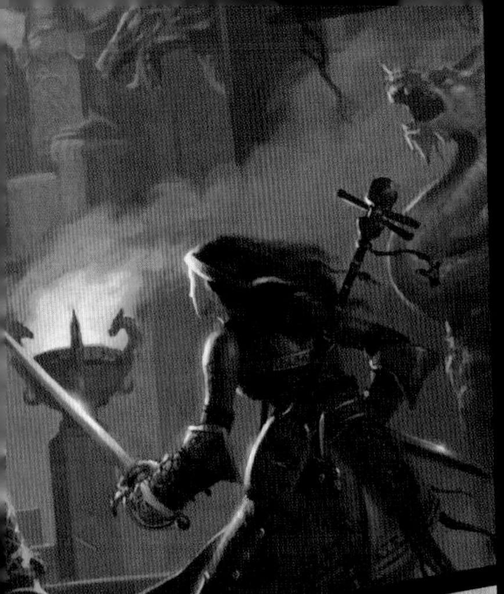

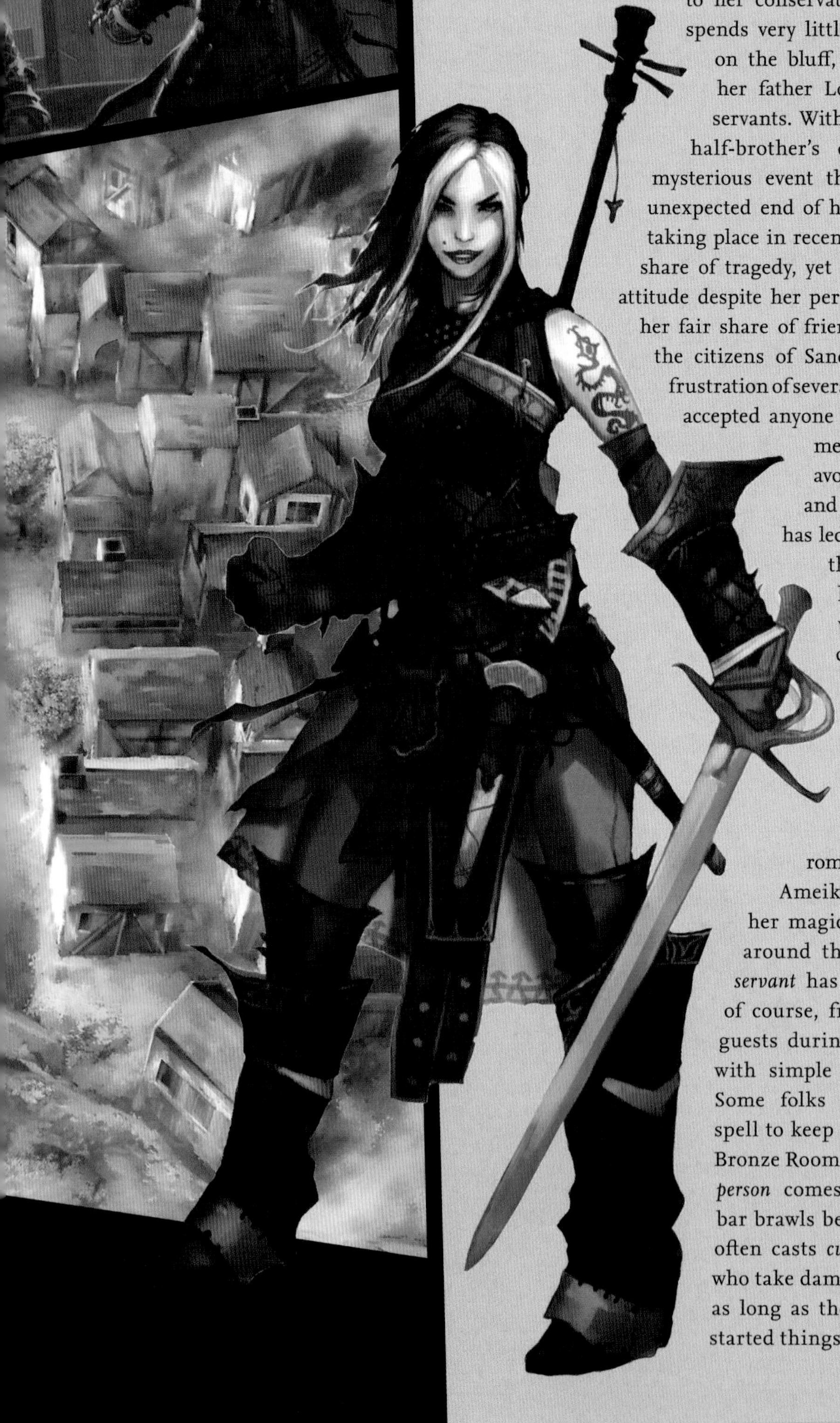

AMEIKO KAIJITSU

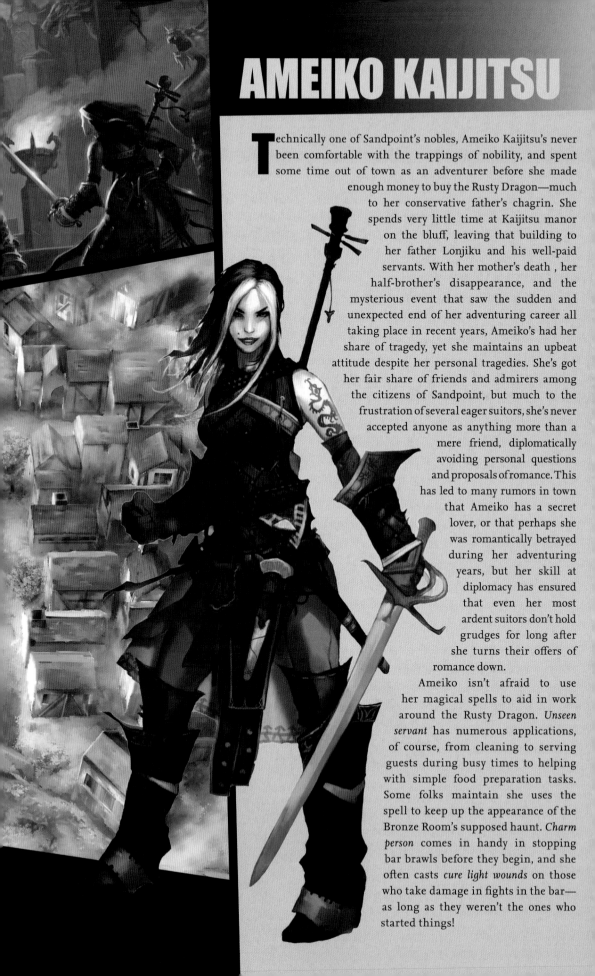

Technically one of Sandpoint's nobles, Ameiko Kaijitsu's never been comfortable with the trappings of nobility, and spent some time out of town as an adventurer before she made enough money to buy the Rusty Dragon—much to her conservative father's chagrin. She spends very little time at Kaijitsu manor on the bluff, leaving that building to her father Lonjiku and his well-paid servants. With her mother's death , her half-brother's disappearance, and the mysterious event that saw the sudden and unexpected end of her adventuring career all taking place in recent years, Ameiko's had her share of tragedy, yet she maintains an upbeat attitude despite her personal tragedies. She's got her fair share of friends and admirers among the citizens of Sandpoint, but much to the frustration of several eager suitors, she's never accepted anyone as anything more than a mere friend, diplomatically avoiding personal questions and proposals of romance. This has led to many rumors in town that Ameiko has a secret lover, or that perhaps she was romantically betrayed during her adventuring years, but her skill at diplomacy has ensured that even her most ardent suitors don't hold grudges for long after she turns their offers of romance down.

Ameiko isn't afraid to use her magical spells to aid in work around the Rusty Dragon. *Unseen servant* has numerous applications, of course, from cleaning to serving guests during busy times to helping with simple food preparation tasks. Some folks maintain she uses the spell to keep up the appearance of the Bronze Room's supposed haunt. *Charm person* comes in handy in stopping bar brawls before they begin, and she often casts *cure light wounds* on those who take damage in fights in the bar—as long as they weren't the ones who started things!

AMEIKO KAIJITSU   CR 4

Female human aristocrat 1/bard 3/rogue (rake) 1 (*Advanced Player's Guide* 134)

CG Medium humanoid (human)

Init +2; **Senses** Perception +7

DEFENSE

AC 17, touch 14, flat-footed 14 (+3 armor, +1 deflection, +2 Dex, +1 dodge)

hp 26 (5d8+5)

Fort +2, **Ref** +7, **Will** +6; +4 vs. bardic performance, language dependent, and sonic

OFFENSE

Speed 30 ft.

Melee *+1 mithral rapier* +5 (1d6+2/18–20)

Ranged dagger +4 (1d4+1/19–20)

Special Attacks bardic performance 12 rounds/day (countersong, distraction, fascinate, inspire competence +2, inspire courage +1), bravado's blade*, sneak attack +1d6

Bard Spells Known (CL 3rd; concentration +7)

   1st (4/day)—*charm person* (DC 15), *cure light wounds, feather step*, unseen servant*

   0 (at will)—*detect magic, light, mage hand, prestidigitation, summon instrument, unwitting ally** (DC 14)

TACTICS

During Combat Ameiko begins combat by activating her bardic performance. When able to strike first in a combat, Ameiko uses bravado's blade to intimidate foes instead of dealing sneak attack damage. She always uses Arcane Strike in battle (these bonuses are included in her stats above), preferring to use her rapier in a fight and to save her magic for healing after the battle if possible.

Morale Ameiko is loyal to her friends, and never abandons an ally in combat. Alone, her bravery isn't as great. When she is faced with a dangerous foe and has no allies in peril, she prefers to flee if reduced below 15 hit points.

STATISTICS

Str 10, **Dex** 14, **Con** 13, **Int** 12, **Wis** 8, **Cha** 18

Base Atk +2; **CMB** +2; **CMD** 16

Feats Arcane Strike, Dodge, Iron Will, Weapon Finesse

Skills Acrobatics +10, Bluff +12, Diplomacy +12, Intimidate +12, Knowledge (arcana) +6, Knowledge (local) +8, Knowledge (nobility) +6, Knowledge (religion) +6, Perception +7, Perform (sing) +12, Perform (string) +12 (+14 with mwk samisen), Profession (tavern keeper) +4, Spellcraft +9, Stealth +10

Languages Common, Tien, Varisian

SQ bardic knowledge +1, versatile performance (string)

Combat Gear *potion of remove disease, wand of cure moderate wounds* (25 charges), *wand of identify* (40 charges); **Other Gear** *+1 leather armor, +1 mithral rapier,* daggers (3), *ring of protection +1,* belt pouch, gold signet ring worth 100 gp, masterwork samisen, silver holy symbol of Shelyn, spell component pouch, 18 pp, 3 gp

* See the *Pathfinder RPG Advanced Player's Guide.*

PATHFINDER®
CHRONICLES
by James Jacobs

MAGIC OF THE CULT OF LAMASHTU

The cult of Lamashtu has long held an interest in the Lost Coast, as certain blasphemous scriptures declare specific regions of the area sacred to the Queen of Demons. Much to the vexation of her priesthood, though, these texts—tomes with names like *Whispers from the Third Eye*, *Riddles of the Rasp*, *The Four Hides of Lawm*, or *Nightmares and other Nocturnal Pleasures*—are maddeningly vague about the exact sites of these sacred places, noting only that those among her faithful who track down these mysterious locations will be granted great power and the favor of the Mother of Monsters.

The cults organize themselves into small cells, so that should one fall to meddling do-gooders or other champions of the region, the others can not only continue their work but perhaps even take vengeance for their lost kin. At the very least, they can attempt to reclaim lost relics or regain lost shrines. A typical Lamashtan shrine on the Lost Coast consists of a small underground complex (typically a cave network), an old fort, or in some cases the ruins of an ancient Thassilonian complex from before Earthfall.

As with all cults, the Lost Coast Lamashtans often utilize specialized magic—spells the Demon Queen only grants to those who have found her sacred sites along the Lost Coast and have performed the proper prayers.

DEMON DREAM
School illusion (phantasm) [evil, mind-affecting]; **Level** cleric 6
Components V, S, DF
When the target of *demon dream* is a worshiper of a demon lord or Lamashtu, the caster has the option of making the spell function instead as a *dream* spell. Otherwise, this spell functions like *nightmare* (see *Pathfinder RPG Core Rulebook* 316), save that the subject matter of the dream always involves demons. Upon waking from a *demon dream*, the victim must make a saving throw against the spell to resist taking 1d6 points of Wisdom drain from the unsettling, madness-inducing dream—this is in addition to the damage and fatigue normally caused by the *nightmare*.

SUMMON BARGHEST I
School conjuration (summoning) [evil]; **Level** cleric 4
Casting Time 1 round
Components V, S, DF

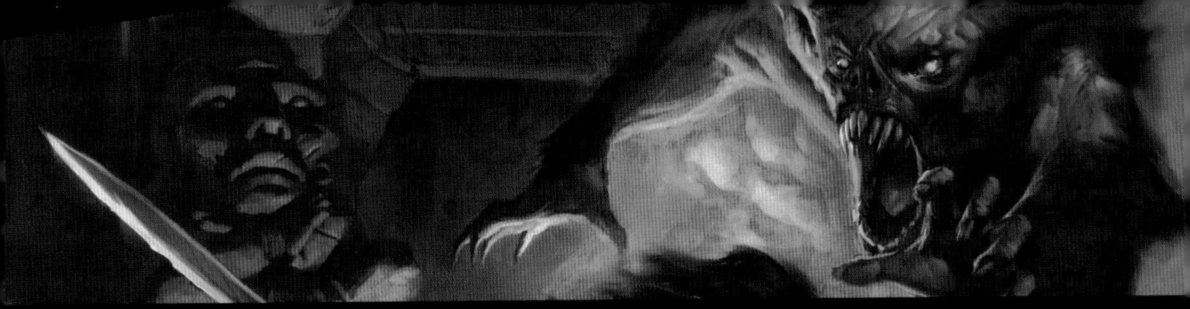

Range close (25 ft. + 5 ft./2 levels)
Duration 1 round/level (D)
Saving Throw none; **SR** no

This spell summons a barghest from the Abyssal realm of Basalfeyst to serve the caster, functioning similarly to *summon monster* save that it may only be used to summon a single barghest. Although the summoned barghest does not have the feed ability, if you are at least caster level 9th the summoned barghest appears with 2 growth points (and with it the appropriate bonuses to its attacks, CMB, saves, skill checks, hit points, and caster level).

SUMMON BARGHEST II

School conjuration (summoning) [evil]; **Level** cleric 6

This spell functions like *summon barghest I*, save that it can summon 1 greater barghest or 1d3 normal barghests with 2 growth points each.

TERATOID CARESS

School conjuration (calling) [chaotic, curse, evil]; **Level** cleric 3
Casting Time 1 standard action
Components V, S, DF
Range touch
Target 1 living non-evil creature
Duration permanent
Saving Throw Fortitude partial; **SR** yes

With a gentle caress, you infuse the creature touched with a blight of energy from the Abyss that feeds upon goodness and transforms flesh into monstrous deformity. The target can resist a teratoid caress with a successful Fortitude save, but even on a successful save, the target becomes sickened for 1 round by the vile energies.

If the target fails the save, his body becomes infected with Abyssal energy and a small portion of his body distorts and grows hideous, inflicting 2 points of Dexterity damage or 2 points of Charisma damage (50% chance of either effect). This deformity is always unsightly and offensive. Thereafter, the victim suffers a –1 penalty on all saving throws against evil effects. Worse, whenever the victim casts a good spell, channels positive energy, or offers a prayer to a good-aligned deity, the Abyssal energies seethe inside him, forcing a new Fortitude save to resist suffering an additional 1 point of Dexterity or Charisma damage. A good-aligned divine spellcaster who suffers from this curse suffers a –4 penalty on all concentration checks. This is a curse effect, but the effect can also be instantly removed with a *dispel evil* or *atonement* spell.

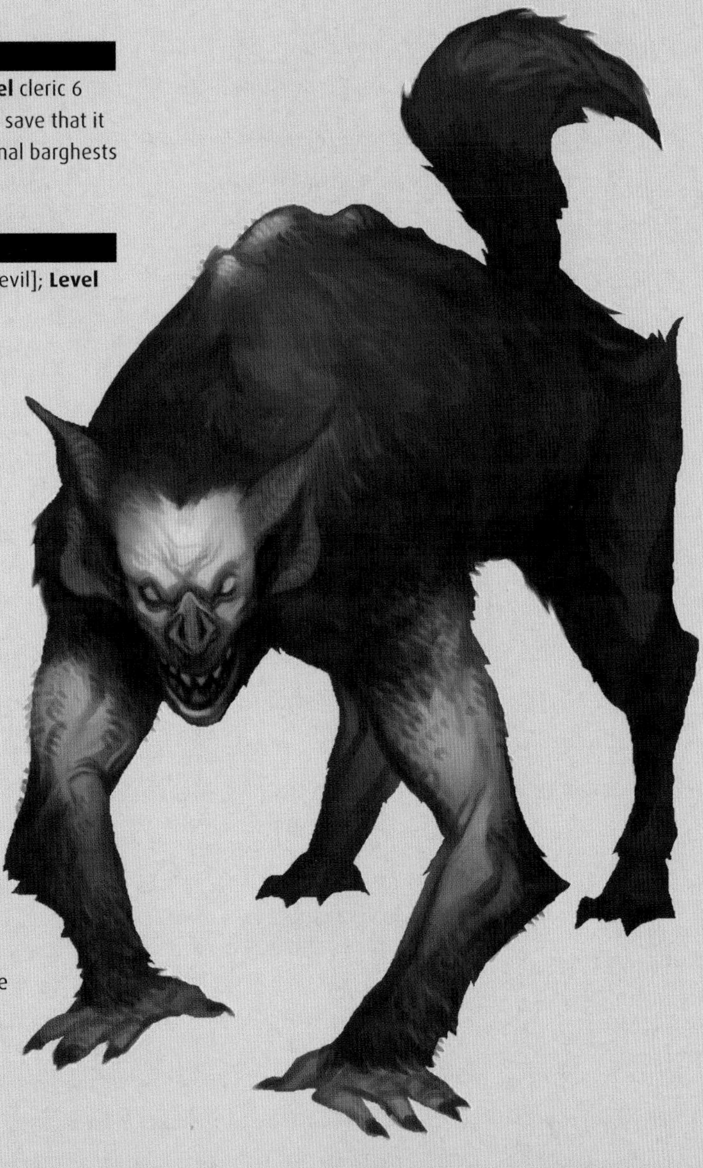

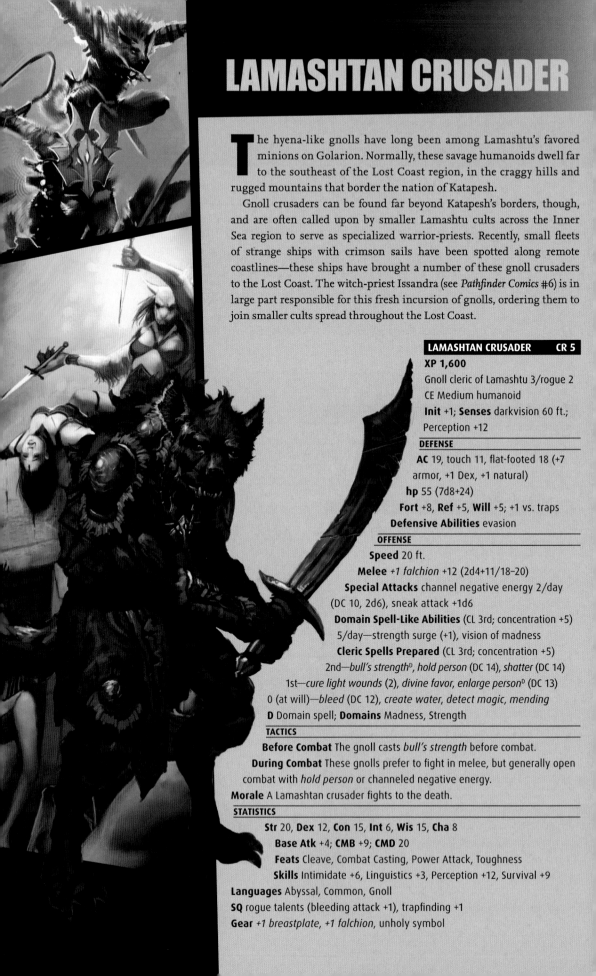

LAMASHTAN CRUSADER

The hyena-like gnolls have long been among Lamashtu's favored minions on Golarion. Normally, these savage humanoids dwell far to the southeast of the Lost Coast region, in the craggy hills and rugged mountains that border the nation of Katapesh.

Gnoll crusaders can be found far beyond Katapesh's borders, though, and are often called upon by smaller Lamashtu cults across the Inner Sea region to serve as specialized warrior-priests. Recently, small fleets of strange ships with crimson sails have been spotted along remote coastlines—these ships have brought a number of these gnoll crusaders to the Lost Coast. The witch-priest Issandra (see *Pathfinder Comics* #6) is in large part responsible for this fresh incursion of gnolls, ordering them to join smaller cults spread throughout the Lost Coast.

LAMASHTAN CRUSADER	**CR 5**

XP 1,600

Gnoll cleric of Lamashtu 3/rogue 2

CE Medium humanoid

Init +1; **Senses** darkvision 60 ft.; Perception +12

DEFENSE

AC 19, touch 11, flat-footed 18 (+7 armor, +1 Dex, +1 natural)

hp 55 (7d8+24)

Fort +8, **Ref** +5, **Will** +5; +1 vs. traps

Defensive Abilities evasion

OFFENSE

Speed 20 ft.

Melee *+1 falchion* +12 (2d4+11/18–20)

Special Attacks channel negative energy 2/day (DC 10, 2d6), sneak attack +1d6

Domain Spell-Like Abilities (CL 3rd; concentration +5)

5/day—strength surge (+1), vision of madness

Cleric Spells Prepared (CL 3rd; concentration +5)

2nd—*bull's strength*[D], *hold person* (DC 14), *shatter* (DC 14)

1st—*cure light wounds* (2), *divine favor*, *enlarge person*[D] (DC 13)

0 (at will)—*bleed* (DC 12), *create water*, *detect magic*, *mending*

D Domain spell; **Domains** Madness, Strength

TACTICS

Before Combat The gnoll casts *bull's strength* before combat.

During Combat These gnolls prefer to fight in melee, but generally open combat with *hold person* or channeled negative energy.

Morale A Lamashtan crusader fights to the death.

STATISTICS

Str 20, **Dex** 12, **Con** 15, **Int** 6, **Wis** 15, **Cha** 8

Base Atk +4; **CMB** +9; **CMD** 20

Feats Cleave, Combat Casting, Power Attack, Toughness

Skills Intimidate +6, Linguistics +3, Perception +12, Survival +9

Languages Abyssal, Common, Gnoll

SQ rogue talents (bleeding attack +1), trapfinding +1

Gear *+1 breastplate*, *+1 falchion*, unholy symbol

PRIESTESS OF LAMASHTU

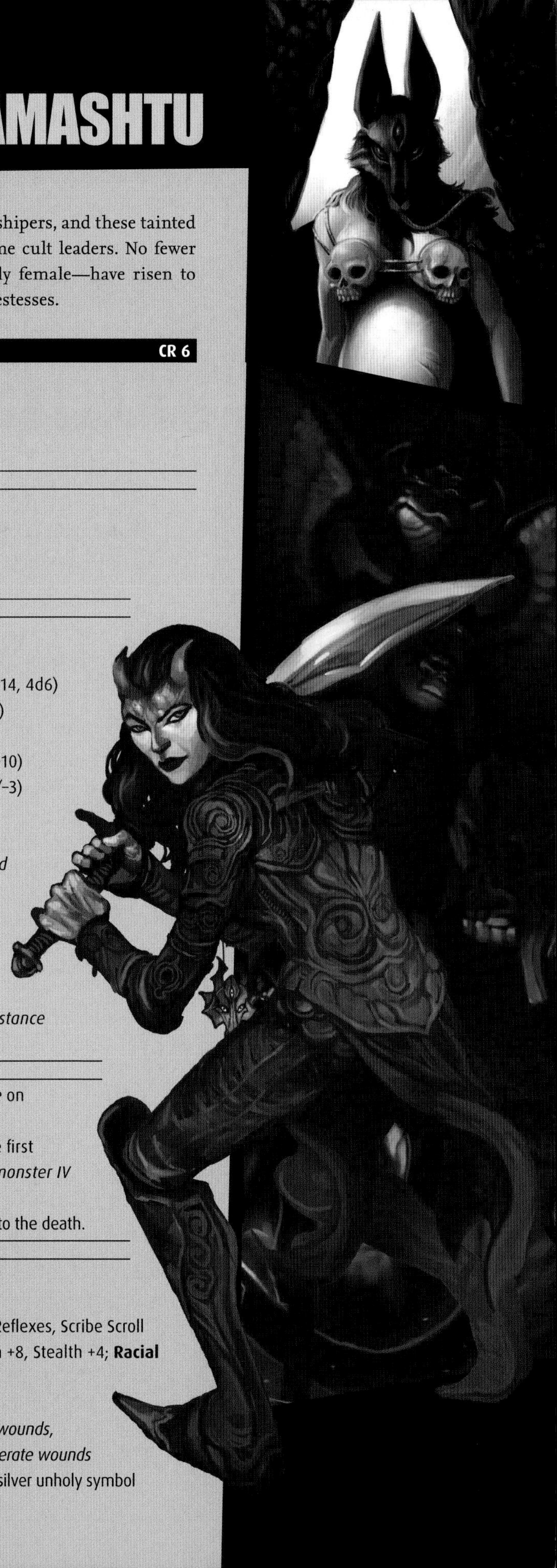

Lamashtu particularly favors her tiefling worshipers, and these tainted creatures rise swiftly in her ranks to become cult leaders. No fewer than a dozen of these tieflings—universally female—have risen to prominence in the Lost Coast region as local priestesses.

PRIESTESS OF LAMASHTU — CR 6

XP 2,400

Female tiefling cleric of Lamashtu 7

CE Medium outsider (native)

Init +4; **Senses** darkvision 60 ft.; Perception +8

DEFENSE

AC 20, touch 10, flat-footed 20 (+10 armor)

hp 63 (7d8+28)

Fort +8, **Ref** +4, **Will** +8

Resist cold 5, electricity 5, fire 5

OFFENSE

Speed 20 ft.

Melee *+1 falchion* +7 (2d4+2/18–20)

Special Attacks channel negative energy 4/day (DC 14, 4d6)

Tiefling Spell-Like Abilities (CL 7th; concentration +8)

1/day—*darkness*

Domain Spell-Like Abilities (CL 7th; concentration +10)

6/day—copycat (7 rounds), vision of madness (+3/–3)

Cleric Spells Prepared (CL 7th; concentration +10)

4th—*confusion*[D] (DC 17), *summon barghest*

3rd—*dispel magic, magic vestment, rage*[D], *teratoid caress* (DC 16)

2nd—*bear's endurance, hold person* (DC 15), *invisibility*[D], *spiritual weapon, status*

1st—*command* (DC 14), *cure light wounds* (3), *divine favor, lesser confusion*[D] (DC 14)

0 (at will)—*bleed* (DC 13), *detect magic, light, resistance*

D Domain spell; **Domains** Madness, Trickery

TACTICS

Before Combat The priestess casts *bear's endurance* on herself, along with *magic vestment* on her armor.

During Combat The priestess casts *invisibility* on the first round of combat, then proceeds to cast *summon monster IV* to summon 1d3 dretches before entering melee.

Morale A priestess of Lamashtu is fanatical, and fights to the death.

STATISTICS

Str 12, **Dex** 10, **Con** 17, **Int** 12, **Wis** 16, **Cha** 12

Base Atk +5; **CMB** +6; **CMD** 16

Feats Combat Casting, Improved Initiative, Lightning Reflexes, Scribe Scroll

Skills Bluff +10, Knowledge (religion) +11, Perception +8, Stealth +4; **Racial Modifiers** +2 Bluff, +2 Stealth

Languages Abyssal, Common, Gnoll

Combat Gear *scroll of death knell, scroll of cure serious wounds, scroll of air walk, scroll of sending, wand of cure moderate wounds* (12 charges); **Other Gear** mwk full plate, *+1 falchion*, silver unholy symbol

PATHFINDER
CHRONICLES
by James Jacobs

DUNGEONS OF THE LOST COAST

Although the Lost Coast has only recently seen the encroachment of civilization, this fog-shrouded region of Varisia's west coast has never been completely abandoned. Traveling Varisians have traditions of carving tombs for their dead among the tors of the coastline. Goblinoid creatures are fond of digging warrens into the deep. Caves riddle the region with winding networks of passageways often expanded upon by ghoulish talons or stranger, more sinister digging denizens of the dark. Some of these tunnels extend all the way down into the Darklands, where other things have long made their homes and have carved extensive dungeons from the rock. And, of course, there is always the legacy of old Thassilon—for the region was once one of that empire's most hotly contested borders. Magically preserved ruins from that pre-Earthfall empire still exist throughout the region, and it is these dungeons that hold both the greatest dangers and the most amazing treasures.

Some, but certainly not all, of the strange and mysterious dungeons scattered throughout the Sandpoint Hinterlands are summarized below. Tread with care, those who would dare delve into these secret and ruinous domains!

Bleaklow Warrens

Moors sprawl in the Sandpoint hinterlands between rugged tors and tangled woodlands. The southernmost moor of the hinterlands is Bleaklow, a desolate enough place above, yet below it is riddled with twisting, turning tunnels carved by the claws of one of the region's largest tribes of ghouls. Few permanent openings to the Bleaklow Warrens exist on the moor itself, with most opening along the steep gorges and cliffs that separate the moor from Brinestump, Foxglove River, and the sea. A large number of these tunnels are flooded, inhabited by lacedons and worse horrors, including a large number of particularly dangerous undead creatures known as trailgaunts (see next page).

The Pit

Devil's Platter, the largest rocky rise in the hinterlands, has its share of caves and crannies, but the most notorious of them all is the Pit. Believed to be a stable but immense sinkhole, the Pit drops down into obscurity, plunging into constantly fog-shrouded depths from which strange noises sometimes swell up.

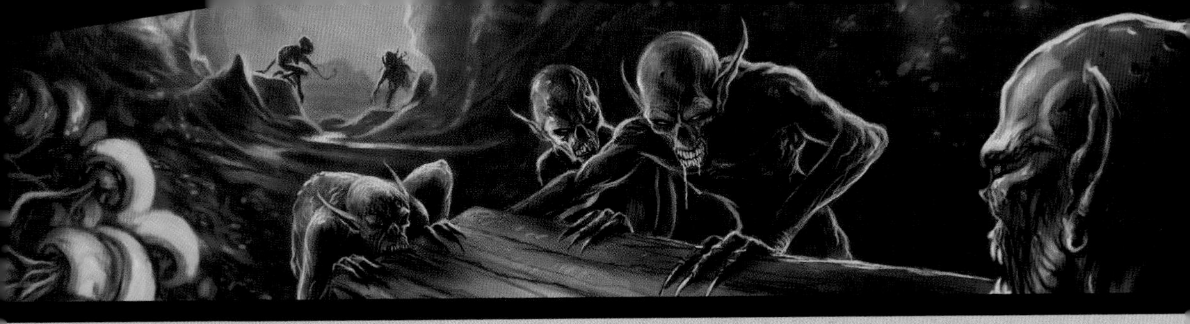

The Pit's sheer walls are networked by a series of narrow ledges connected by crude rope ladders and rickety rope bridges in place—constructions doubtfully maintained by the goblins, mites, dark folk, and other humanoids who lurk within the numerous caves that line the location's walls. These tribes of savages exist in a tenuous alliance of sorts, but most cringe in fear of what lies in the deepest caves. Whispers of fungus empires, hissing troglodyte clans, sinister derros, and a cult of demon-worshiping ghouls are common, yet the most widely-circulated story of the Pit's depths is that somewhere deep down below dwells the Sandpoint Devil itself.

Raven's Watch

The ruins of Raven's Watch are among the more recent additions to the Sandpoint Hinterlands, yet this should not be taken as an indication of safety. Originally built to serve as a prison, the fort of Raven's Watch sat on the north bank of the Turandarok River in the tors known as Ravenroost. Once Sandpoint grew large enough to support its own garrison and jail, though, the soldiers who manned Raven's Watch abandoned the fortress in favor of a more local and convenient demesne. Stories that the soldiers abandoned Raven's Watch and its underground dungeons because of a strange curse that haunted the region, or due to the way the numerous ravens who dwelt in the region seemed strangely curious, were summarily ignored by the soldiers, as were claims that they left some of their more dangerous prisoners behind to starve and rot in the cells. Certainly the aboveground portion of Raven's Watch seemed to crumble quickly, as if the tors wanted none of the edifice within them. Today, whispers that a group of bandits allied with the cult of Lamashtu have taken up residence in Raven's Watch have worried locals.

Wisher's Well

Aboveground, Wisher's Well is little more than an ancient circular stone tower, 30 feet in height. Within, the tower's floors have long since crumbled away, leaving a 100-foot-deep shaft at the tower's heart. Below, a deep pool of cold, dark water awaits any unfortunate enough to fall in. Drowning is a mercy to those who do so, though, for where this water begins, so do extensive and flooded dungeons that date back to Thassilonian times. A large number of skum and other aquatic humanoids dwell in these caves, and their croaking prayers to the "Deep Ghost" can sometimes be heard by those who listen hard at the entrance far above.

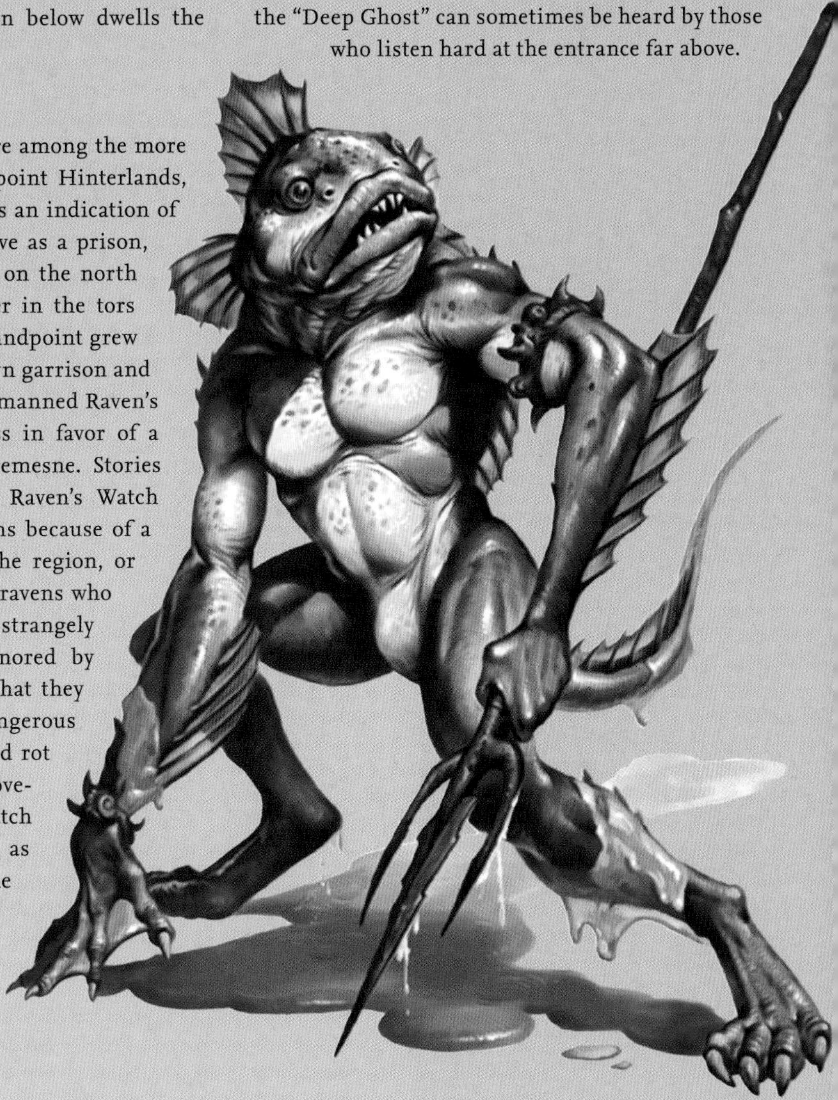

TRAILGAUNT

This pallid figure lurches forward as if it weren't entirely in control of its twitching limbs. Bugs and worms wriggle in its tangled hair, and its nails and teeth are cracked and ragged, and a low gurgle of pain and despair slops from between its dirt-caked lips.

TRAILGAUNT	CR 3

XP 800
NE Medium undead
Init +2; **Senses** darkvision 60 ft.; Perception +8

DEFENSE

AC 15, touch 8, flat-footed 15 (−2 Dex, +7 natural)
hp 25 (3d8+12)
Fort +5, **Ref** −1, **Will** +5
Defensive Abilities channel resistance +2; **DR** 5/slashing; **Immune** undead traits
Weaknesses loathing

OFFENSE

Speed 10 ft., burrow 10 ft., climb 10 ft.
Melee bite +4 (1d4+2 plus pain), 2 claws +4 (1d4+2 plus pain)
Special Attacks create spawn, mutter, vengeful strike

STATISTICS

Str 15, **Dex** 6, **Con** —, **Int** 7, **Wis** 14, **Cha** 19
Base Atk +2; **CMB** +4; **CMD** 12
Feats Improved Initiative, Step Up
Skills Climb +10, Perception +7, Stealth +7, Survival +4 (+12 following tracks);
Racial Modifiers +4 Stealth, +8 Survival following tracks
Languages Varisian
SQ sudden lunge, sure stride

ECOLOGY

Environment any wilderness land
Organization solitary, pair, or pack (3–10)
Treasure standard

SPECIAL ABILITIES

Create Spawn (Su) A humanoid creature killed by a trailgaunt becomes a trailgaunt itself at the next sunset as long as the body is both unburied and not within line of sight of a well-maintained road. Spawn so created are free-willed, and do not possess any of the abilities they had in life.

Loathing (Ex) A trailgaunt cannot cross a well-maintained road—it can burrow under it or climb over it, but cannot walk across such a barrier. A trailgaunt placed or pushed onto a well-maintained road must make a DC 15 Will save at the start of each round or be unable to take any actions.

Mutter (Su) A trailgaunt's pain-filled muttering and groaning is distressing to hear. A creature that begins its turn within 10 feet of a trailgaunt must make a successful DC 15 Will save or become shaken for 1 minute—multiple failed saving throws against a trailgaunt's mutter do not increase this effect to frightened. This is a mind-affecting sonic fear effect.

Pain (Su) A creature damaged by a trailgaunt's bite or claws must make a successful DC 15 Fortitude save to avoid being staggered by pain in their legs and feet for 1 round. Creatures in contact with the ground suffer a −1 penalty on this saving throw. The save DC is Charisma-based.

Sudden Lunge (Ex) Once per minute, a trailgaunt can lurch into a burst of

activity, gaining a speed of 40 feet for 1 round.

Sure Stride (Su) A trailgaunt's speed is never reduced by difficult terrain, and it can five foot adjust in such conditions.

Vengeful Strike (Ex) A trailgaunt particularly hates living Varisians. The undead gains a +2 bonus on all attack rolls made against Varisians, as well as on any Perception or Survival checks made against Varisians.

The dreaded trailgaunt is a form of undead unique to regions where the Varisian peoples have long traveled. Varisians regard the trailgaunt with an equal mixture of fear and pity, for as the legends go, the trailgaunt rises when a particularly depressed or rueful Varisian, typically one who has been cast out of his or her family, dies in the wild out of sight of the roads that served in life as a source of life and tradition. In death, the trailgaunt lurks in the scrub and undergrowth near well-traveled roads, watching and waiting patiently for its favored prey to pass it by—Varisian travelers. A trailgaunt follows stealthily along the roadside once it spies a victim, its natural stealth hampered by its slow movement. Rarely will a trailguant catch up with a foe on the move, but once a foe is sighted it tracks its victim relentlessly until sunrise, at which point a trailgaunt that hasn't found warm Varisian flesh to eat hunkers down in the undergrowth again to await new victims to stalk. When a trailgaunt does come upon a Varisian campsite, it lurches in to attack a foe. Curiously, trailgaunts feed only on the feet of their slain victims, and even then the flesh and bones they consume never last long, for by sunrise the foul undead vomits up its meal before staggering back into the undergrowth to await new prey. Yet a body whose feet have been hideously gnawed away is not always sure sign of a trailgaunt, for vengeful Varisians or other canny murderers have been known to hack away a victim's feet in an attempt to shift blame from a more mundane crime to one of supernatural revenge.

A trailgaunt looks like a human (or other humanoid creature) from a distance, but as soon as the undead creature lurches into motion, it becomes increasingly difficult to mistake it for anything living. Every step brings pain to a trailgaunt, causing it to stagger and thrash awkwardly and distressingly as it moves and wrenching choking cries of pain from its rotten throat. On closer inspection, the creature's bloodless flesh, filthy clothing and hair, and jagged teeth and nails leave no doubt that the thing is a horror. Trailgaunts who have risen as spawn after being slain by another of their kind lack feet, and are forced to stagger horribly upon mud-caked ragged stumps of flesh and splintered bone.

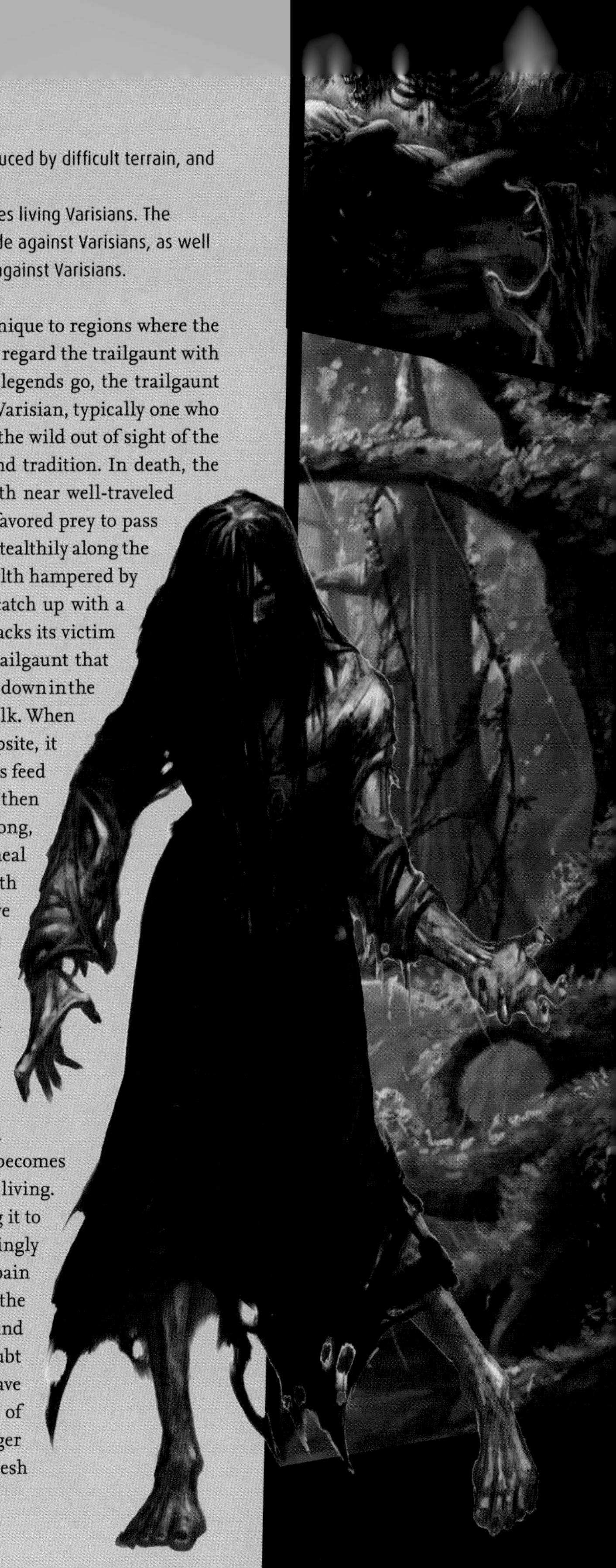

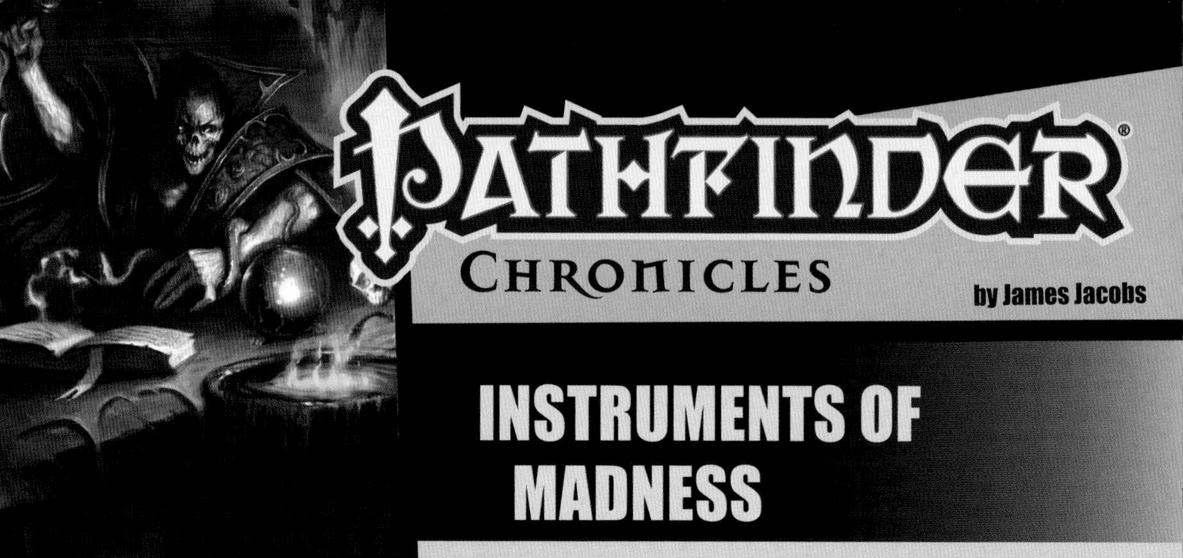

Pathfinder® Chronicles

by James Jacobs

INSTRUMENTS OF MADNESS

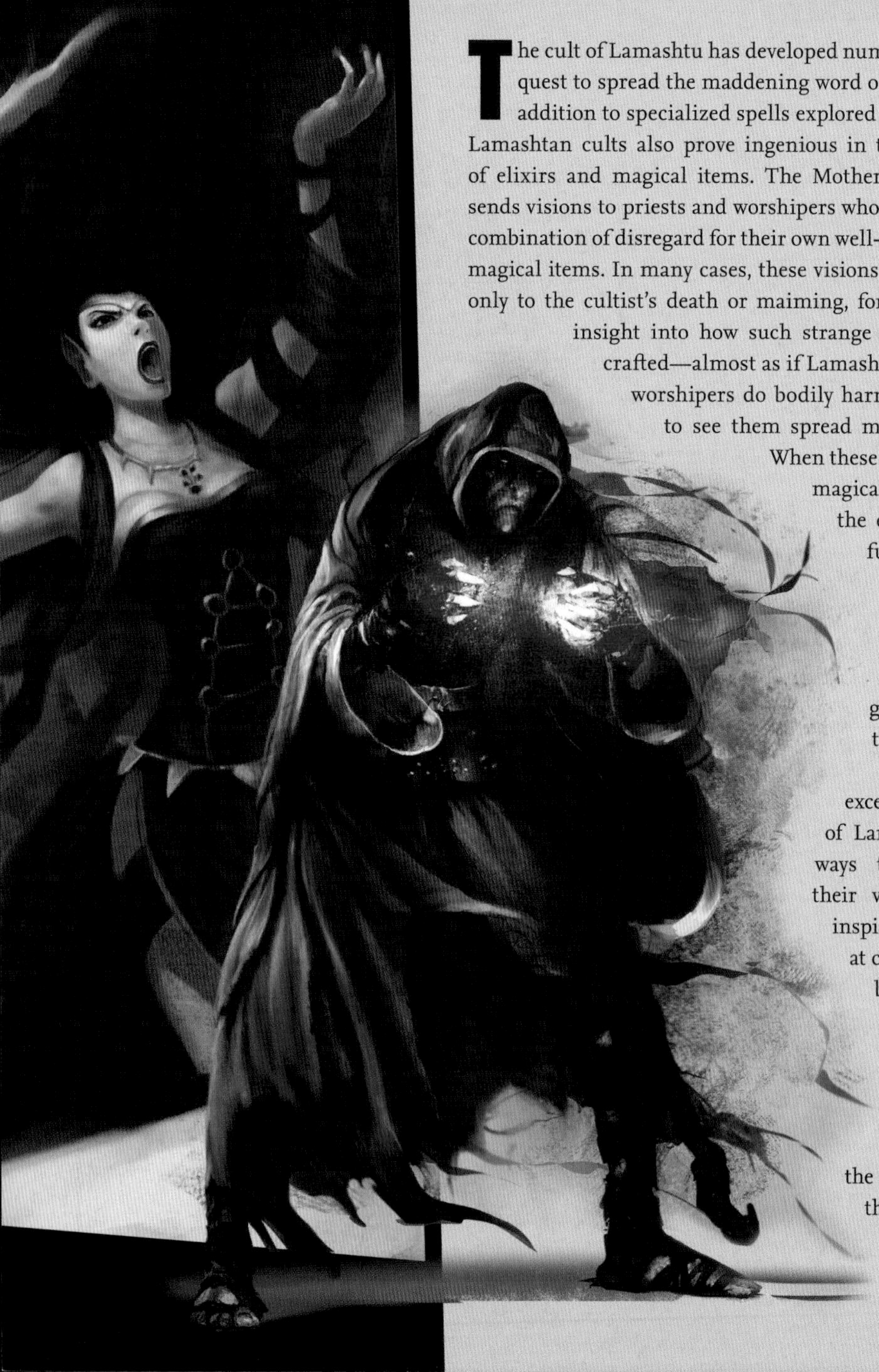

The cult of Lamashtu has developed numerous tools to aid in their quest to spread the maddening word of their demon goddess. In addition to specialized spells explored previously in these pages, Lamashtan cults also prove ingenious in the crafting and creation of elixirs and magical items. The Mother of Monsters sometimes sends visions to priests and worshipers whom she feels have the right combination of disregard for their own well-being and skill at crafting magical items. In many cases, these visions, while inspirational, lead only to the cultist's death or maiming, for the visions rarely grant insight into how such strange and exotic items can be crafted—almost as if Lamashtu is as amused to see her worshipers do bodily harm to themselves as she is to see them spread misery to their neighbors. When these visions do result in viable magical items and discoveries, the creation is almost always fueled as much by faith as by any real skill—such items cannot be duplicated by the use of item-crafting feats, and generally function only for those who create them.

There are, of course, exceptions. The most brilliant of Lamashtu's worshipers find ways to stabilize and refine their visions, mixing demonic inspiration with logic and talent at crafting. These items often become favorite regional weapons of her cultists—two such items detailed on these pages are owned by the cultist Thelsikar (the *bonespur dagger* and the *mortuary mask*), while the third (the *jackal's blade*) is an example of a much more powerful creation.

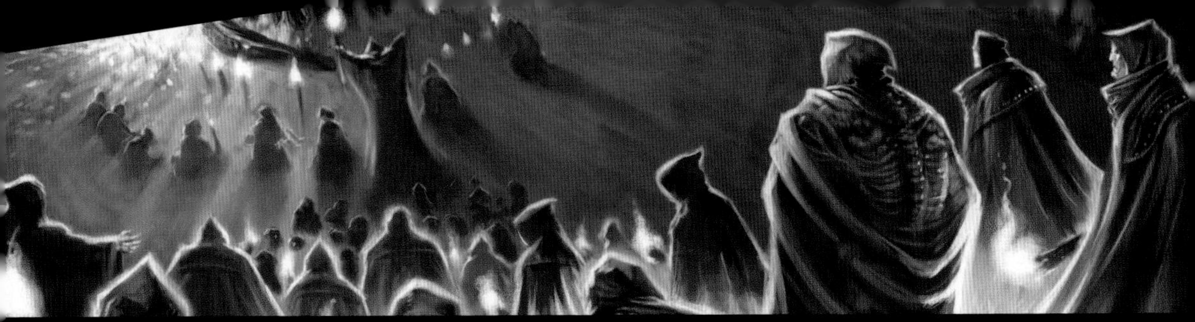

BONESPUR DAGGER

BONESPUR DAGGER		PRICE 6,302 GP
SLOT weapon	**CL** 6th	**WEIGHT** 2 lbs.
AURA moderate necromancy		

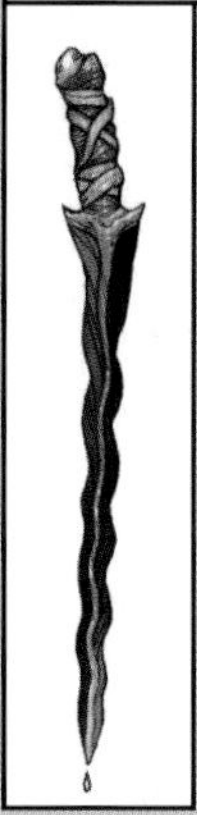

A *bonespur dagger* appears to have been crafted from a humanoid radius and ulna, sharpened to a razor edge and needle point just below where the elbow would be located and fitted with a hilt made of wood and bone. While the weapon looks fragile, the magic that infuses the grisly blade tempers and strengthens it to the level of steel. A *bonespur dagger* functions as a *+1 punching dagger,* save that on a successful critical hit, the weapon strikes bone and cracks it. The creature so struck must make a DC 15 Fortitude save to resist suffering a –2 penalty to Strength for 1 minute from this pain; penalties from multiple successful critical hits stack up to 3 times. As a curious side effect, *bonespur daggers* penetrate the damage reduction of animated skeletons and skeletal champions (but not other skeletal undead) as if they were bludgeoning weapons rather than piercing weapons.

CONSTRUCTION REQUIREMENTS	COST 3,302 GP

Craft Magic Arms and Armor; *ray of enfeeblement*

JACKAL'S BLADE

JACKAL'S BLADE		PRICE 45,375 GP
SLOT weapon	**CL** 13th	**WEIGHT** 7 lbs.
AURA strong evocation [evil]		

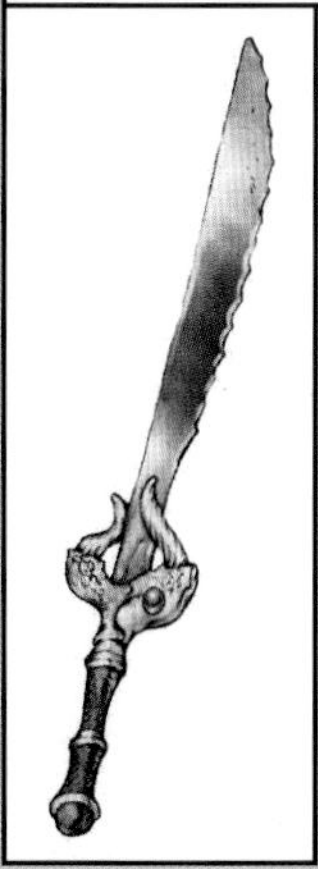

A *jackal's blade* appears as a well-used falchion. The handle looks aged and unpleasant, but despite these cosmetic features, the blade is quite sharp, functioning as a *+2 unholy falchion*. The weapon inflicts particularly grievous wounds on paladins and lawful good clerics, functioning as a *bane* weapon against such targets. It also functions as a divine focus for worshipers of Lamashtu. When used as such for casting a spell, the user gains a +4 bonus on any concentration checks needed to complete that spell.

CONSTRUCTION REQUIREMENTS	COST 22,875 GP

Craft Magic Arms and Armor, *bane, unholy blight*

MORTUARY MASK

MORTUARY MASK		PRICE 3,500 GP
SLOT face	**CL** 6th	**WEIGHT** 2 lbs.
AURA moderate necromancy		

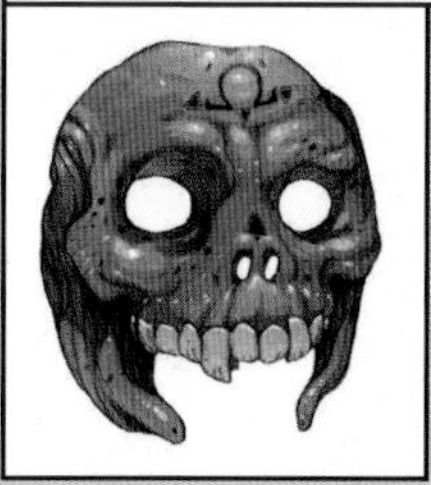

A *mortuary mask* covers the top half of the face, leaving the mouth and chin exposed. The design of this eerie mask evokes that of a human skull, although some *mortuary masks* have more canine or even demonic features. Regardless of the mask's appearance, once it is donned, a *mortuary mask* works to enhance the wearer's presence, making him or her appear more horrific and frightening and granting a resonant tone to the wearer's voice. These enhancements grant a +3 circumstance bonus on all Intimidate checks made while the mask is worn. In addition to this unnerving effect, a *mortuary mask* also grants constant *deathwatch* while it is worn, allowing the wearer to see the auras of living and dead creatures within 30 feet. The wearer loses the ability if he is blinded or cannot see (such as might occur while in darkness). Furthermore, the mask guides the wearer's hand against foes who are heavily wounded. When the wearer of a *mortuary mask* attacks a creature that has 3 or fewer hit points remaining, the wearer gains a +2 insight bonus on the attack roll.

CONSTRUCTION REQUIREMENTS	COST 1,750 GP

Craft Wondrous Item, *cause fear, deathwatch*

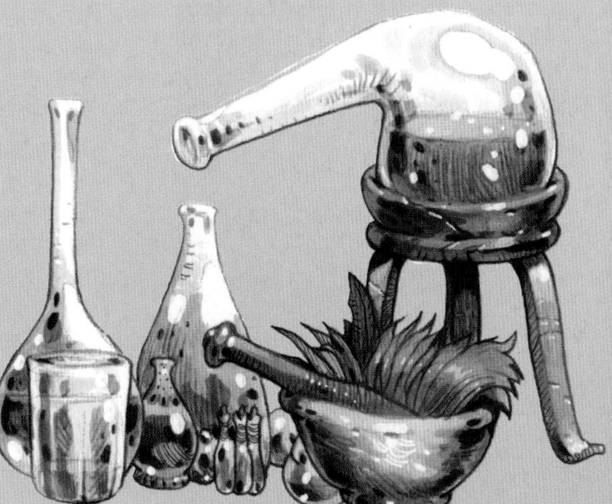

THELSIKAR

This man is clad in dark clothes and a long, black hooded robe. A skull-shaped mask further obscures his identity, while in his hand he carries a crude and sadistic-looking dagger apparently crafted from a pair of sharpened arm bones. Thelsikar has long followed the visions and nightmares he believes have been granted to him by his demon goddess Lamashtu, but until he received his vision of draconic fury, none of those visions held much in the way of power. He now believes that Lamashtu has chosen him to unleash a plague of demonic dragons on the world. With Blackfang, Thelsikar has finally secured the most important part of this plan—a dragon upon which to work his vile magic.

THELSIKAR	CR 6

XP 2,400
Human cleric of Lamashtu 7
CE Medium humanoid (human)
Init +1; **Senses** *deathwatch*, Perception +9

DEFENSE
AC 17, touch 14, flat-footed 16 (+3 armor, +3 deflection, +1 Dex)
hp 63 (7d8+28)
Fort +8, **Ref** +4, **Will** +10

OFFENSE
Speed 30 ft.
Melee *bonespur dagger* +9 (1d4+4/×3)
Special Attacks channel negative energy 2/day (DC 12, 4d6)
Domain Spell-Like Abilities (CL 7th; concentration +11)
   7/day—strength surge (+3), vision of madness (+/−3)
Cleric Spells Prepared (CL 7th; concentration +11)
   4th—*confusion*ᴰ (DC 18), *poison* (DC 18), *unholy blight* (DC 18)
   3rd—*contagion* (DC 17), *dispel magic*, *magic vestment*ᴰ, *searing light*
   2nd—*bear's endurance*, *bull's strength*ᴰ, *cure moderate wounds*, *desecrate*, *sound burst* (DC 16)
   1st—*bane* (DC 15), *command* (DC 15), *cure light wounds*, *divine favor*, *lesser confusion*ᴰ (DC 15), *shield of faith*
   0 (at will)—*bleed* (DC 14), *detect magic*, *light*, *mending*
   D Domain spell; **Domains** Madness, Strength

TACTICS
Before Combat Thelsikar enhances his leather armor with *magic vestment* well before an encounter, as soon as he suspects danger may be drawing near. He casts *bear's endurance*, *bull's strength*, and *shield of faith* before combat.

During Combat Thelsikar is rarely encountered alone, and directs his minions—be they goblins, cultists, or dragons enhanced by one of his elixirs of draconic fury—to attack foes in melee while he hangs back and begins combat using his ranged spells. Yet while spells like *confusion* and *unholy blight* can wreak havoc, it's never long before Thelsikar abandons his spells to wade into melee. His lust for battle and the feel of his knife cutting the flesh of his enemy may be his greatest weakness, and a foe who knows this can sometimes lure the cleric into battle when his spells might have been the better option.

Morale Thelsikar is supremely confident in his abilities, right up to the point where death is staring him in the face. If reduced to fewer than 10 hit points, he suddenly panics and attempts to flee. If prevented from flight, the priest begs for his life, yet if mercy is granted, he takes the first chance he can get to either turn on his captors and murder them in their sleep or flee to plot revenge.

STATISTICS

Str 16, **Dex** 13, **Con** 14, **Int** 14, **Wis** 18, **Cha** 8
Base Atk +5; **CMB** +6; **CMD** 20
Feats Brew Potion, Combat Casting, Craft Wondrous Item, Skill Focus (Craft [alchemy]), Toughness
Skills Craft (alchemy) +15, Intimidate +2, Knowledge (arcana) +12, Knowledge (religion) +12, Linguistics +7, Perception +9, Spellcraft +12
Languages Abyssal, Common, Draconic, Goblin, Varisian
SQ vision of draconic fury
Combat Gear *potion of cure moderate wounds* (3), *potion of rage*; **Other Gear** mwk leather armor, *cloak of resistance +1, bonespur dagger, mortuary mask*, unholy symbol of Lamashtu

SPECIAL ABILITIES

Vision of Draconic Fury (Su) Thelsikar has been granted a singular vision by his dark goddess, Lamashtu—divine inspiration on how to craft a potent *elixir of draconic fury*. It takes Thelsikar 2d6 weeks to brew a single dose of this elixir, and the rare ingredients cost 10,000 gp per dose, ensuring that, for now, he cannot afford to brew any more of these elixirs. (He hopes to earn more funds as thanks from the first dragon who he chooses to grace with the elixir.) Once brewed, a dose of the elixir remains potent only for 7 days, after which the unstable magical drink decays into a noxious black sludge that has no beneficial effects whatsoever. A dragon who drinks a fresh *elixir of draconic fury* must make a successful DC 25 Fortitude save or take 1d6 points of Intelligence damage. On a successful save, the dragon still takes the Intelligence damage but gains a +4 enhancement bonus to Strength, Constitution, and its natural armor bonus for 1 hour. Thelsikar continues to work at enhancing the elixir, but has yet to determine a method of extending its life or negating its befuddling side effect.

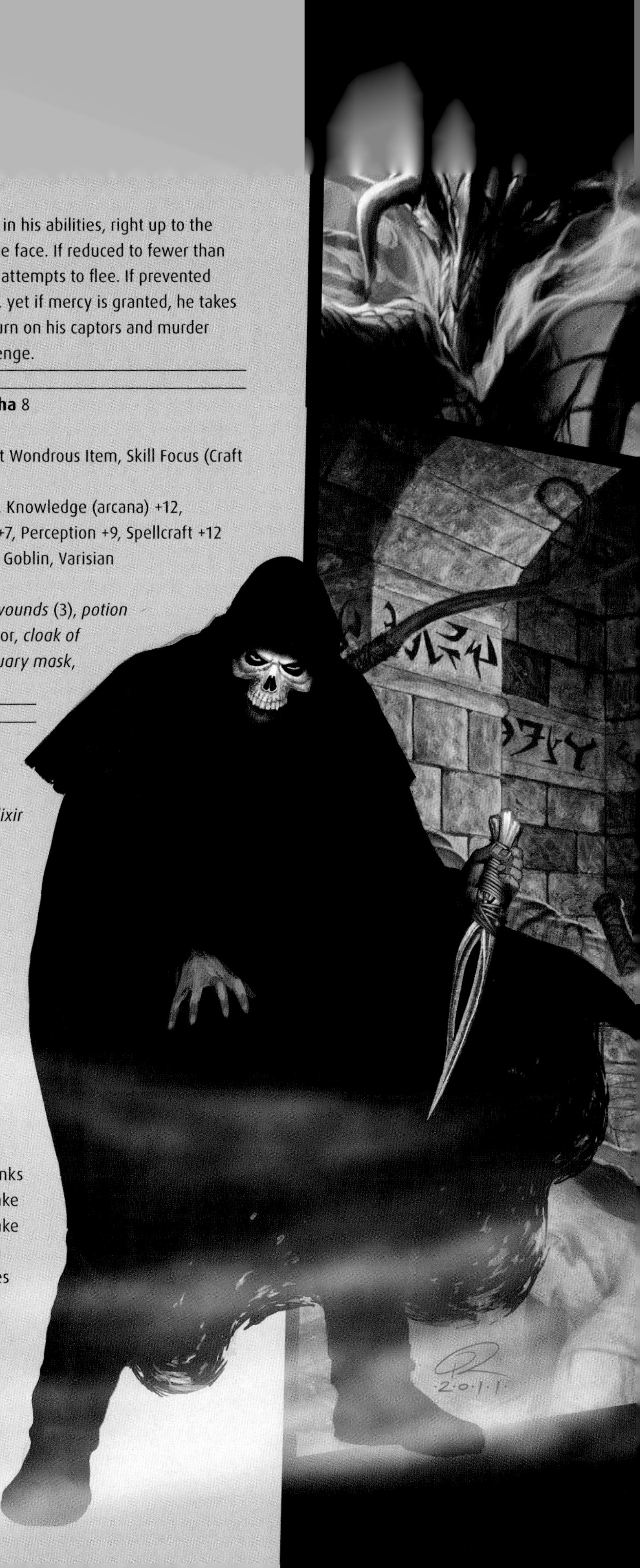

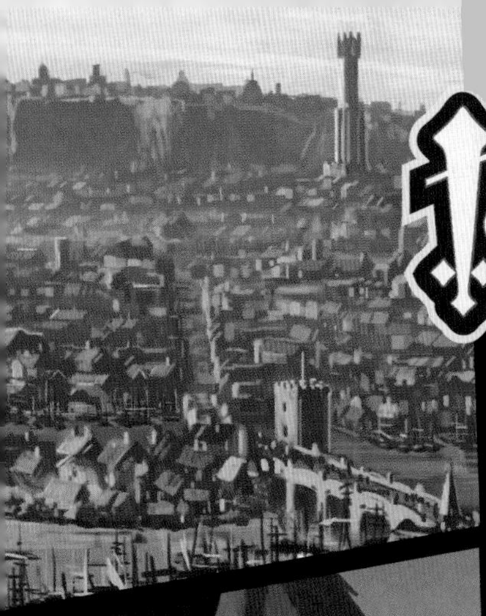

Pathfinder® Chronicles

by James Jacobs

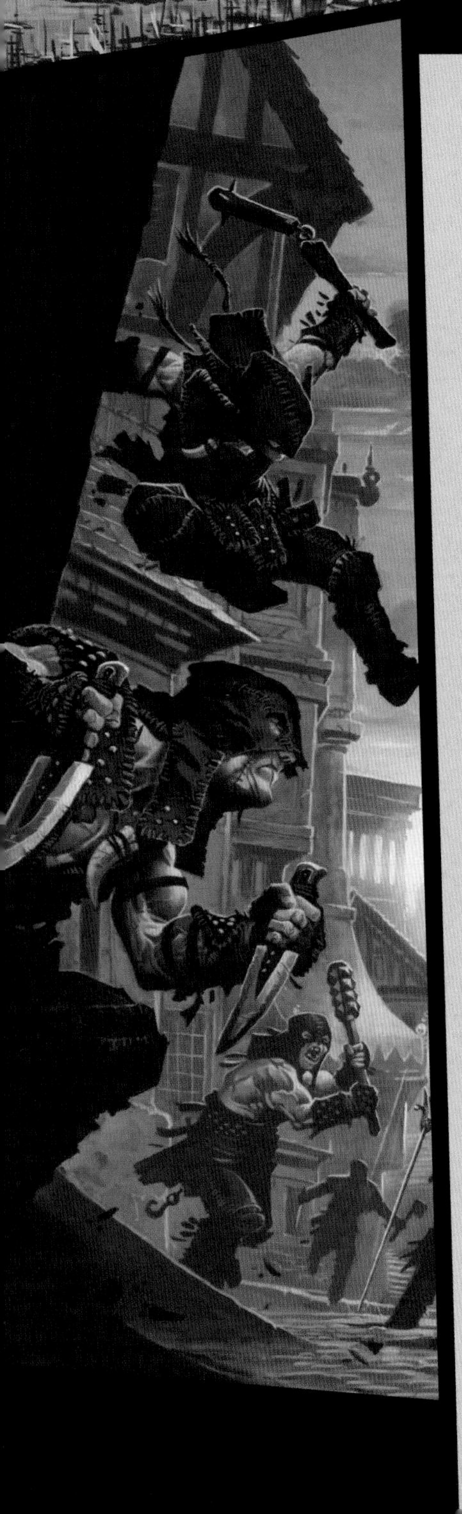

GANGS OF MAGNIMAR

At a mere 105 years, the city of Magnimar is relatively young when compared to many of the larger and more infamous cities of the Inner Sea region, yet the so-called City of Monuments has wasted no time in establishing its own numerous urban traditions. As one might expect in a city with no centralized city guard, Magnimar has more than its share of criminal gangs, one of several areas in which the city has excelled over the last century. Dozens of secret societies and criminal organizations have bloomed, flourished, and wilted in that time, but a few in particular have shown the type of tenacity that could vex even the most organized and diligent law enforcement agency.

Brotherhood of the Seven: Both a cult dedicated to Norgorber as Father Skinsaw and a tightly knit secret society, the Brotherhood of the Seven has interests throughout Magnimar, ranging from the shadowy slums of Underbridge to the heights of the Capital District. The Brotherhood presents a facade to society of a small, eccentric group of aristocrats and businessmen, but those whose interests clash with the Brotherhood have a strange habit of vanishing.

Cult of Norgorber: The god of thieves is nothing if not a master of many passions. Worshiped by spies and politicians, footpads and burglars, alchemists and assassins, and murderers and maniacs, his cult infests both the underworld and high society of Magnimar. The city's largest and oldest thieves' guild, the Night Scales, are open worshipers of the Gray Master. Drug dealers and poisoners alike thrive in the city's back alleys or under the guise of legitimate shops. Corrupt politicians and guild masters vie for the upper hand by playing an often deadly game of reputation and slander. And the mysterious Skinsaw Cult is known to have members scattered throughout the city. All four are, in one way or another, acolytes of Norgorber, their movements and actions seemingly manipulated from on high by the god of thieves—or, as some maintain, by a criminal mastermind who must know the city's inner workings better than any other living soul. See the following pages for a sample cultist of Norgorber.

Gargoyles: Gargoyles are common in the City of Monuments, their stony faces lurking amid most of the larger buildings' eaves and rooflines. The name seemed a natural for a guild of highly trained cat burglars, for their second home is the city's skyline. Their members are fond of saying their "first home" is also the one you live in and that they're burglarizing, yet in truth the guild, led by the same matron who founded them decades ago, is believed to be based somewhere in the Keystone district.

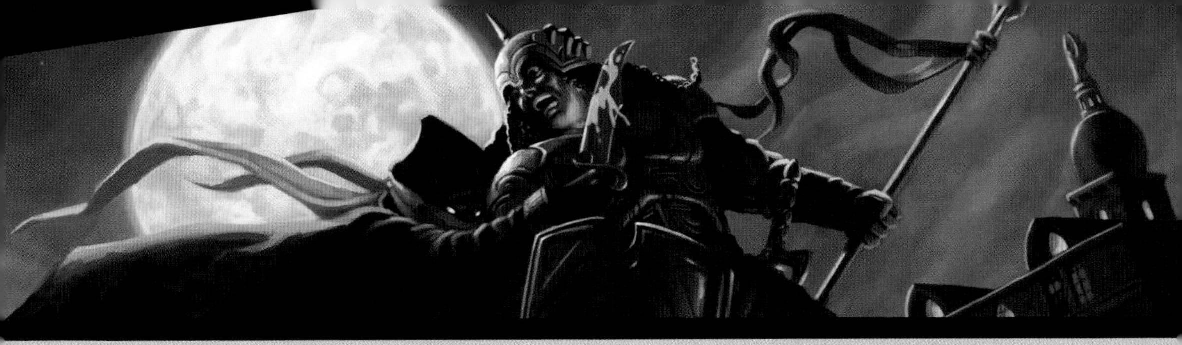

Rushlight Society: Not all of the criminals of Magnimar thrive in or below the city's streets. The group of rogues known as the Rushlight Society operate almost entirely outside the city walls, where they orchestrate highway banditry and other forms of rural robbery along the Lost Coast Road, the Yondabakari, and other pathways and trails that wind their way through the Magnimar hinterlands. (See *Pathfinder Comic* #7 for more details on the Rushlight Society.)

Sczarni: While most would say that the Night Scales represent the oldest guild of criminals active in Magnimar, the Sczarni families would disagree. Unimpressed by pedantry, this (very) loosely organized band of Varisian families has traditions of banditry, robbery, and generalized treachery that dates back as long as the Varisian people can remember. Clashes between various Sczarni families and the Night Scales likely have causes far deeper and more significant than a mere disagreement over which group could legitimately claim the title of "oldest criminal guild of Magnimar," of course. The number of active Sczarni gangs in Magnimar varies, and while the total is never less than a dozen, six of them have become more stabilized and entrenched in their territories over the years: the Creepers, the Tower Girls, the Washside Wringers, the Wreckwash Blades, and the most powerful of them all, the Gallowed.

Shoanti Gangs: The Shoanti, like the Varisians, have lived in this land for thousands of years, yet unlike their more adaptable neighbors, the Shoanti have by and large resisted assimilation into the encroaching society of the southlands. Here in Magnimar, Shoanti are mostly outcasts from their own society, a fact that tends to breed a certain propensity for surliness and short tempers. The city's criminal Shoanti often congregate into small bands of a dozen or fewer thugs—these violent and mostly uncontrolled gangs do little to help the city's citizens abandon the belief that all Shoanti are savage barbarians. Unlike the Sczarni families, Shoanti gangs tend to completely abandon previous tribal and familial ties that they may have had before, and seek instead to build new bonds with new companions found in the city itself. Some of these groups have grown large enough that they have begun to identify as their own new clans, or "quahs" in their tongue. In time, these new quahs may well achieve their own status as legitimate and recognized groups among their people, but for now, Shoanti from elsewhere in Varisia tend to view these urban kin with a fair bit of shame.

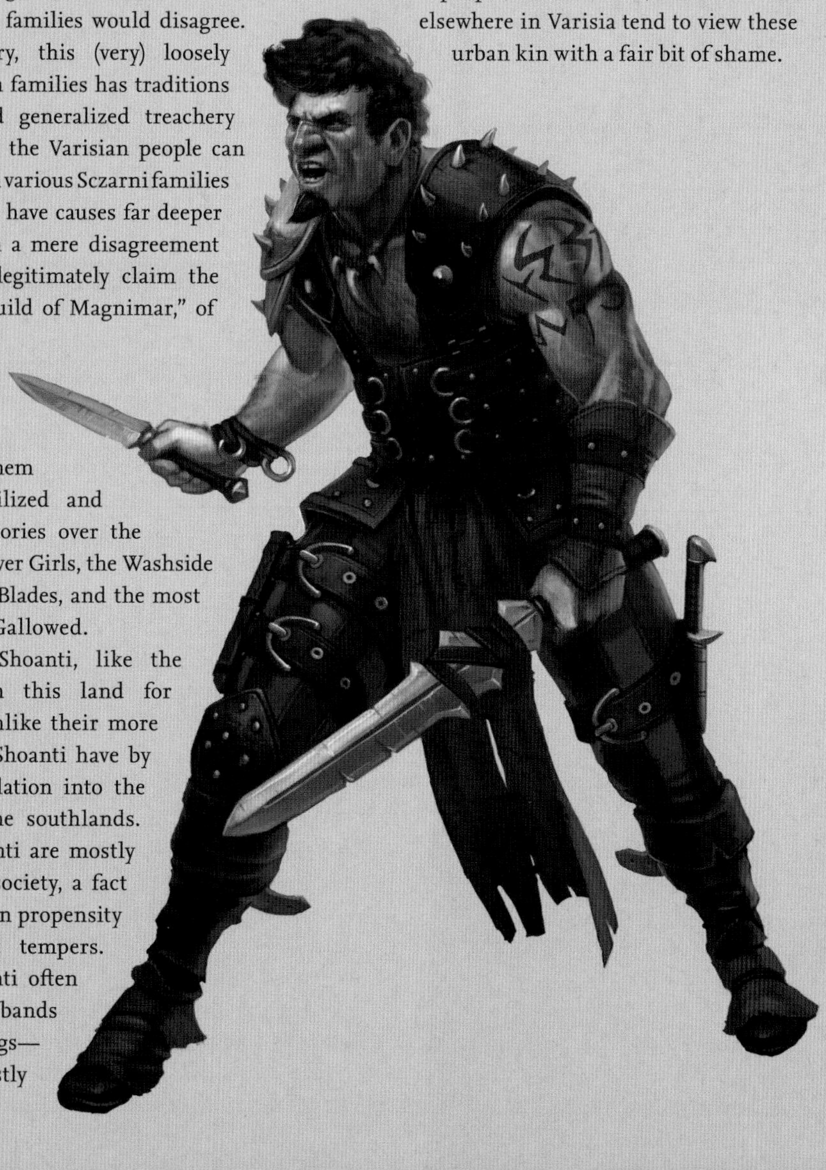

NORGORBER CULTIST

T he cult of Norgorber utilizes many specialized cultists, but in Magnimar, those who are the most valued are those who don't behave as cultists at all. The worshiper presented below is an expert in disguise and slander—a devotee of Norgorber in his incarnation as the Reaper of Reputations. Using his *hat of disguise* and talent for lies, the Norgorber cultist infiltrates high society to corrupt from within. Often such a cultist carries additional magical scrolls of spells like *modify memory* or illusions for use via Use Magic Device to sow discord, but they are just as adept without these tools by spreading slanderous rumors, leaving falsely incriminating messages where they can be found by just the wrong reader, or using mind controlling magic to influence the servants of a manor house to incite discord and scandal. To society, this cultist takes pains to cultivate an appearance of upstanding citizenry. Often, he travels without his weapons or armor, but when he suspects his enemies may be on to him, the cultist makes sure to keep his armaments close at hand—either hidden nearby or concealed on his person with the aid of his *hat of disguise*. Yet combat is a last resort, for to this particular worshiper of the god of thieves, the death of a person's character, honor, and reputation is infinitely more rewarding than a mere assassination. A dead person is merely food for the worms, but a person broken and a life ruined is a lasting triumph that festers and poisons the very structure of society.

NORGORBER CULTIST	CR 7

XP 3,200
Human cleric of Norgorber 5/rogue 3
NE Medium humanoid (human)
Init +7; **Senses** Perception +14

DEFENSE

AC 17, touch 13, flat-footed 14 (+4 armor, +3 Dex)
hp 39 (8 HD; 5d8+3d8)
Fort +5, **Ref** +7 (+1 vs. traps), **Will** +8
Defensive Abilities evasion, trap sense +1

OFFENSE

Speed 30 ft.
Melee *+1 short sword* +9 (1d6/19–20)
Ranged mwk hand crossbow +9 (1d4/19–20)
Special Attacks channel negative energy 5/day (DC 14, 3d6), sneak attack +2d6
Domain Spell-Like Abilities (CL 5th; concentration +8)
　6/day—copycat (5 rounds), dazing touch
Cleric Spells Prepared (CL 5th; concentration +8)
　3rd—*glyph of warding* (DC 16), *speak with dead* (DC 16), *suggestion*[D] (DC 16)
　2nd—*cure moderate wounds*, *enthrall* (DC 15), *invisibility*[D], *undetectable alignment*
　1st—*charm person*[D] (DC 14), *command* (DC 14), *cure light wounds*, *obscuring mist*, *sanctuary* (DC 14)
　0 (at will)—*detect magic*, *light*, *mending*, *stabilize*
　D Domain spell; **Domains** Charm, Trickery

TACTICS

Before Combat This cultist uses *undetectable alignment* every day to blend into society. At least one *glyph of warding* guards the cultist's home. The cultist typically uses the spell glyph option when creating such magical traps rather than blast glyphs, using *suggestion* so that those who trigger the trap become compelled to leave the treasure behind and seek out the spellcaster for punishment.

During Combat The cultist seeks to defeat foes before they know they're under attack, using traps created by *glyphs of warding* or sudden sneak attacks with poison bolts if at all possible—melee is messy and distasteful. The cultist prefers to capture foes alive, but when no other option is available, he takes care to use *speak with dead* on his victims to learn what they know of the cult's activities.

Morale The cultist flees via *invisibility*, *obscuring mist*, and his *dust of tracelessness* if reduced to fewer than 15 hit points, then returns to his hidden shrine or guild to report to his brothers and sisters and organize a surgical strike of vengeance against the one daring enough to resist death the first time around.

STATISTICS

Str 8, **Dex** 16, **Con** 10, **Int** 12, **Wis** 16, **Cha** 14

Base Atk +5; **CMB** +4; **CMD** 17

Feats Combat Casting, Deceitful, Improved Initiative, Skill Focus (Use Magic Device), Skill Focus (Disguise), Weapon Finesse

Skills Bluff +15, Diplomacy +9, Disguise +18, Knowledge (local) +9, Knowledge (religion) +8, Linguistics +6, Perception +14, Stealth +14, Use Magic Device +16

Languages Common, Shoanti, Undercommon, Varisian

SQ rogue talents (finesse rogue), trapfinding +1

Gear *+1 studded leather*, *+1 short sword*, mwk hand crossbow with 10 blue-whinnis-poisoned bolts, *hat of disguise*, *dust of tracelessness*, holy symbol of Norgorber, 600 gp of powdered diamond (for *glyph of warding*), 65 gp

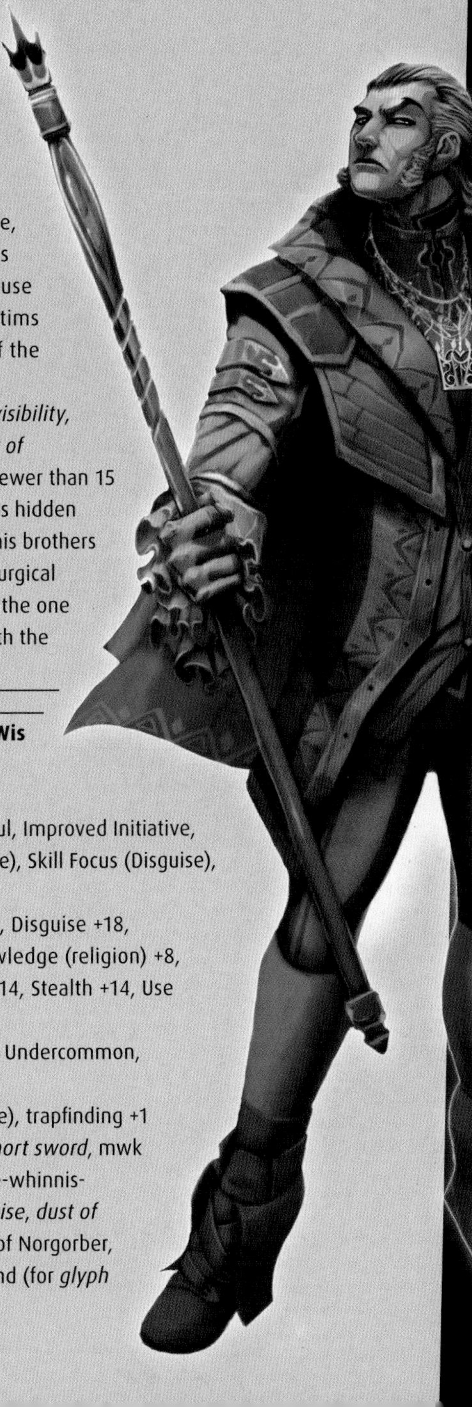

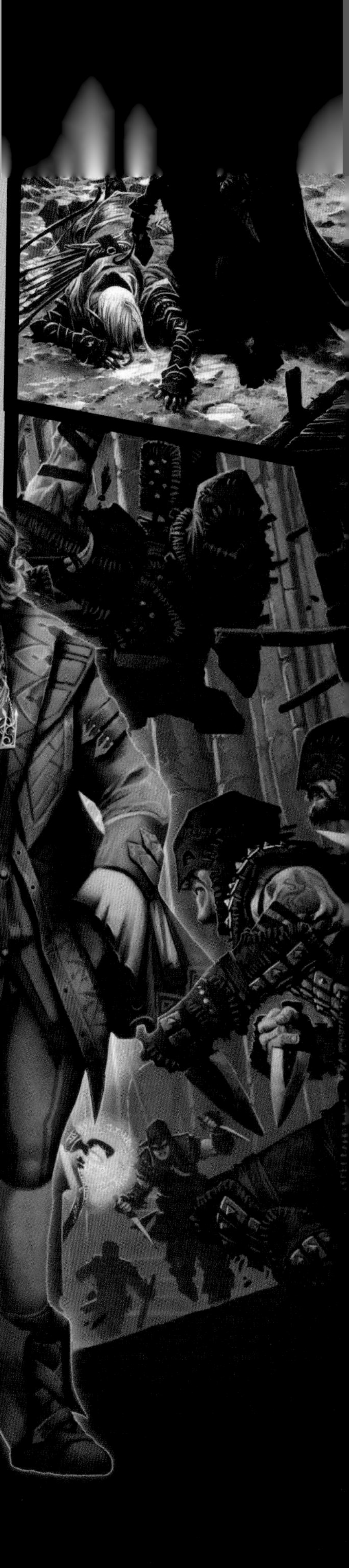

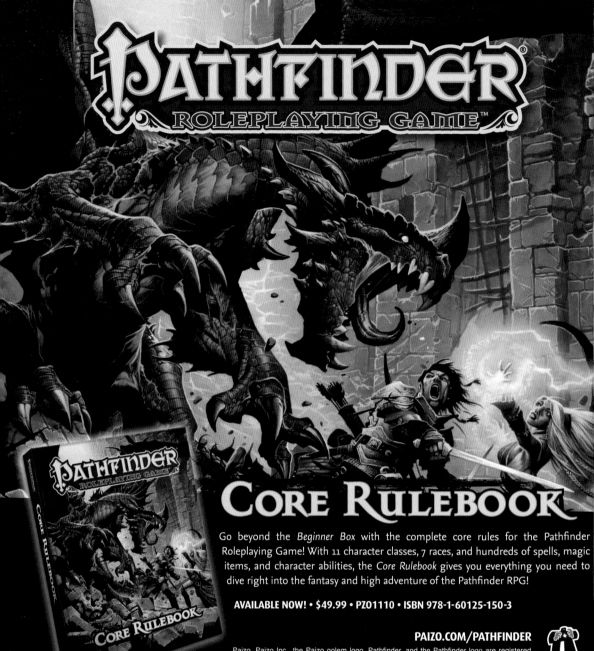

PATHFINDER ROLEPLAYING GAME

CORE RULEBOOK

Go beyond the *Beginner Box* with the complete core rules for the Pathfinder Roleplaying Game! With 11 character classes, 7 races, and hundreds of spells, magic items, and character abilities, the *Core Rulebook* gives you everything you need to dive right into the fantasy and high adventure of the Pathfinder RPG!

AVAILABLE NOW! • $49.99 • PZO1110 • ISBN 978-1-60125-150-3

PAIZO.COM/PATHFINDER